Nationalism and Social Communication

AN INQUIRY INTO THE
FOUNDATIONS OF NATIONALITY

Karl W. Deutsch

Nationalism and Social Communication

AN INQUIRY INTO THE
FOUNDATIONS OF NATIONALITY

Second Edition

THE M.I.T. PRESS

Massachusetts Institute of Technology
Cambridge, Massachusetts, and London, England

Second printing, October 1962
Third printing (first paperback edition), March 1966
Fourth printing, December 1966
Fifth printing, November 1969
Sixth printing, May 1972
Seventh printing, July 1975

Acknowledgment

Permission to quote from *Nineteen eighty-
Four,* by George Orwell, Copyright, 1949,
Harcourt, Brace, & Company, Inc.

ISBN 0 262 04002 6 (hardcover)
ISBN 0 262 54001 0 (paperback)

Library of Congress Catalog Card Number: 53-7949
Printed in the United States of America

Preface

This study aims at filling a gap in the literature of social science. There are outstanding studies of nationalism as a history of nationalistic ideas, as in the writings of Professor Hans Kohn; there are competent descriptions of nationalism as a force in politics, as by the Study Group of the Royal Institute of International Affairs headed by Professor Edward Hallett Carr; and there are important works organizing many of the facts about nationalism in terms of some particular problem, such as Professor Quincy Wright's monumental *Study of War.* But there has seemed to be no answer to the question why nationalist ideas met with wide and strong response at certain times and places, and with almost no response at others.

In certain areas, economic growth has led to national unification; in others to greater national diversity. Why did national sentiments develop in one direction but not in the other? In certain cases, individuals can and do change from membership in one people to membership in another; in other situations they seem almost powerless to do so, and nationality appears as if it were some objective fact beyond the decisions of individuals.

What, then, is ethnic nationality? Under which conditions will a government or a political organization find it an asset? Under which a liability? What is the relation of this nationality to economic life, to incomes, opportunities, and expectations? And how may it become so important to individuals as to override their economic interests, and even their interest in self-preservation?

To make a beginning at answering these questions we need studies about the objective as well as the subjective sides of nationality, and about the long-run trends of national assimilation or differentiation.

The present study represents a very small attempt toward such a theory. Its first chapter surveys some of the outstanding attempts of social scientists to account for nationalism, its structure and development. Its second chapter reviews certain resources from several different disciplines of social science which may be used to build a set

v

of concepts that would correspond to the peculiar structure and development of peoples. The third chapter discusses some implications of these findings for the understanding of political power and the dependence of political power on social communication.

The fourth chapter states the theory of a people as a community of social communication. It tries to distinguish in operational terms an individual's membership in a people from that in a country, a class, or a vocational group, and it discusses the changing importance of nationality in a mobile and competitive industrial society. The fifth chapter discusses various experimental tests that could be arranged to indicate, or even to measure, the extent of complementarity among members of one people in matters of social communication; and some conditions under which national uniformity or diversity will result from social learning.

The sixth chapter offers quantitative concepts which could be applied to social, educational, political, and economic statistics for the prediction of national assimilation or differentiation of mixed populations in a given territory, the probable periods required, and the probability of a future reversal of roles between a predominant and a subordinate nationality, language, or culture. The seventh chapter adds to these quantitative concepts a number of institutional and qualitative factors and considerations, bearing on the quantitative rates of change which are relevant for the development of national unity or differentiation. The eighth chapter adds a discussion of national consciousness and will, as patterns of social communication, and of their accelerating, retarding, or destructive effects on national development. The ninth and last chapter sums up some of the findings and adds a tentative postscript on the prospects of nationalism at the present time.

As should be evident, the theory attempted in this study can at most tell only part of the story. It lacks a discussion of the roles of leading individuals, political organization, and historical decisions. It will require another study of equal or greater length to deal with the historical examples for the growth of peoples and nations, for which only a few bare and abstract patterns have been sketched here. And it will require a third study to work out the implications of this approach for an appraisal of the growth and prospects of nationalism in our present industrial age.

Nevertheless the theory is presented here, as Burke might have said, "in the nakedness of abstraction." Its weaknesses may thus stand forth more glaringly; and it may be easier to judge whether it has to offer any new tools, however modest, to the student of the growth of nations.

A few specific examples have been relegated to the notes; statistics are presented in diagrams and discussed in appendices; and a number of books are listed at the end to indicate the intellectual background of the disciplines from which this approach has been drawn. In order not to discourage the general reader the complete bibliography drawn upon for this study has been reduced to a selected list of about twenty major surveys bearing on nationalism, about fifty recent works on nationalism published for the most part since 1935, and a few books or articles from each related field in social science. For the rest, readers may turn to the literature cited in the notes, and to my forthcoming *Interdisciplinary Bibliography of Nationalism Since 1935,* to be published in 1953–54 by the American Academy of Arts and Sciences and the Institute for the Unity of Science.

Perhaps my greatest debt is to men rather than to books. Professor Rupert Emerson of Harvard University has been a teacher, guide, and friend in this undertaking for many years. If there is anything useful in what I have done, he bears much responsibility for it, but the weaknesses of this study are my own.

There are many others to whose thought, criticism, or questions I am much indebted. None of these people, of course, bears any responsibility for my views or conclusions. They include my teachers, Professors William Yandell Elliott, Michael Karpovich, Hans Kohn, Arthur N. Holcombe, Merle Fainsod, Edwin H. Chamberlin, Gottfried v. Haberler, Seymour E. Harris, Wolfgang Stolper, and Harold Williamson at Harvard University; my colleagues, Norbert Wiener, Walt W. Rostow, Giorgio de Santillana, Walter Pitts, John Bell Rae, and the late Robert K. Lamb at Massachusetts Institute of Technology; Dr. Margaret Mead of the American Museum of Natural History; and Professor Quincy Wright of the University of Chicago. I am further indebted for many stimulating questions, suggestions, or objections to the members of the University Seminar on Organization at Columbia University, particularly to Professors Robert T. Livingston, David B. Hertz, Conrad M. Arensberg, and C. C. Lienau, as well as to Professors Paul F. Lazarsfeld and David Truman of the same university.

Draft versions of the first five chapters were prepared in various years for the meetings of the Conference on Science, Philosophy, and Religion, and were used by the editors of that organization as bases for chapters in the Conference Symposia. I am grateful to the officers of the Conference and to the participants in its meetings for valuable criticisms and suggestions which led to many changes in my text.

Thanks are also due to my students in the Seminar on Nationalism at Massachusetts Institute of Technology; to my former student assistants, William D. Stahlman, Peter B. Neiman, Kerson Huang, Clark C. Abt, Henry G. Lechner, Charles F. Wilcox, Jr., and Herbert D. Bennington, who rendered valuable help with research, statistics, and suggestions; and to two unfailingly helpful research assistants, Mrs. Anne Merrian and Mrs. Hannelore Vanderschmidt.

Professor Howard R. Bartlett and Dean John E. Burchard at Massachusetts Institute of Technology have greatly aided by their understanding and support in the completion of this study at this time. Special thanks are also due to the officers and staffs of the libraries at Massachusetts Institute of Technology, Harvard, Yale University, and the Babson Institute of Business Administration, all of whom have aided me at various times with outstanding helpfulness and patience.

KARL W. DEUTSCH

Cambridge, Massachusetts
August, 1953

Contents

. . . the rapport of the People,
(Full well they know that message in the darkness,
Full well return, respond within their breasts, their brains . . .)
. . . —city to city, joining, sounding, passing,
Those heart-beats of a Nation in the night.

Walt Whitman, *Leaves of Grass*

Some Changes in Nationalism and Its Study, 1953-1965

In the twelve years since the first appearance of this book, major changes have occurred in the reality of nationalism and nationalistic movements in the world, as well as in the study of nationalism with the tools of the different disciplines of social science. Despite these changes, the fundamental characteristics of nationalism have remained. What we see manifest in world politics today are for the most part the implications and consequences of processes already underway twelve years ago. The progress in the social sciences during the same twelve years has made it easier to discern these processes and to chart their course with greater clarity and precision.

Men have not watched the development of nationalism during these twelve years as mere passive spectators. In many countries, particularly in Asia and Africa, but also in such European countries as Poland, Hungary, and France, men have striven hard to increase the degree of autonomy or independence and power of their nation. Elsewhere, as in much of Western Europe, major trends have aimed toward developing supranational visions of political community and toward establishing supranational political institutions and practices to carry these visions into effect. In most of the major countries, finally, these two tendencies, the national and the international or supranational, have remained locked in conflict, either as latent tensions under the surface of public life and within the incongruous thoughts and hopes of individuals, or in open disputes at moments of national or international decision.

We are participants in these decisions, close or remote, by what we do or fail to do; and our fate is at stake in them. A world of nationalist conflicts, or a world of well-policed international political and legal uniformity, or a pluralist world of sovereign nations and diverse social systems striving to avoid fatal collisions and to respect their currently irreducible diversity — these are alternatives among which mankind is deciding during this decade and in the years ahead. Every small gain in our ability to see the world as it is, and as it is changing subtly but cumulatively in our time, may make it easier for us to chart our course for the preservation of human life, human dignity, and human freedom in our own country and in the world.

Some Changes in Nationalist Practices

From 1953 to 1965 the number of sovereign nations has increased considerably, mainly through the emergence of the newly independent states of Africa, many of which have been adding increasingly the political substance of independence to its formal assertion in international law. In 1964, the standard list of countries of the Yale Political Data Program ran to 133, consisting of all members of the United Nations, plus the political entities that had emerged from the post-1945 divisions of Germany, Korea, and Indochina, and a number of territories not yet sovereign. By 1965, the list was still longer: 141 nations and potential nations (for which 1962 data were available) are listed in a new Appendix to the present edition.

During the same period, the scope of the tasks of national governments has continued to grow and so has the number of people in most countries who are in need of some public or governmental services. The enactment in 1965 of broad programs of aids to education and of Medicare in the United States is merely one more example of this world-wide trend. The stakes of politics all over the world have tended to increase, and so have the levels of literacy, of popular education, of mass communications, and of potential participation in politics – and often of actual participation in politics as well.

This has meant that languages and language rights have become more important to more people, and that disputes over language, nationality, and the rights of ethnic, racial, and religious groups have increased.

Oppressed, submerged, or otherwise disadvantaged groups have become less willing to accept their handicaps under the existing political and economic institutions and under the old customs and folkways that operated in their disfavor. Where the hitherto privileged minorities or majorities resisted the claims of the hitherto submerged, tensions and conflicts have increased, and even where substantial improvements were conceded by the majority of the advantaged group – as they were conceded by the majority of white voters in the United States to many of the claims of their Negro fellow citizens – the road to successful adjustment has been long and hard. Where concessions were long delayed on one or both sides, as in Cyprus, or denied outright, as they were denied by the ruling Afrikaner minority in the Union of South Africa, the dangers to political stability have been increasing.

Many countries in the world have become harder to govern, even by locally recruited governments. Almost everywhere, the political and military costs of outright foreign intervention have increased. This trend toward rising costs of foreign intervention is likely to continue.

As a result, the discipline and cohesion of the great Eastern and Western blocs of powers in world politics have declined. Despite the international images in its ideology, Communism has not abolished any major nation-state. The only exceptions, the three small Baltic states of Esthonia, Latvia, and Lithuania, were parts of the Russian Tsarist Empire before 1914. Generally, nation-states have proved remarkably durable even under Communism, and they have given rise, in time, to different varieties of Communist doctrine, as in the cases of Russia, Yugoslavia, and mainland China. Somewhat in this way, centuries ago, the persistent differences between Latins, Greeks, and Armenians were reflected in the rise of different Christian churches, the differences between Arabs and Persians in the rise and taking root of different Muslim sects, and the difference between Mediterranean and Northern Europe in the contrasting triumphs of Roman Catholicism and Protestantism in the different regions of Europe.

The Western world has had milder but not fundamentally dissimilar problems. French opinion has long resisted the idea of having the French nation, the French state, and the French army submerged in any supranational Atlantic or European institutions. President de Gaulle's assertions of French sovereignty and distinctiveness in the early and mid-1960's continued this tradition. Future governments of France may well make some limited gestures and take some limited steps toward greater international or supranational cooperation, but the basic attachment of French elite and mass opinion to French national concerns is likely to remain dominant for at least another decade. This prospect, together with the continuing preoccupation of much of West German political opinion with German national reunification as the "most urgent political task," rather than with European union, puts severe limits upon the possible progress from the European Common Market to any more powerful form of European unification during the next few years.

Even within such peaceful and relatively well-governed constitutional democracies as Belgium and Canada, political collaboration between different language groups has become more difficult, and in some instances precarious. Only the democracy of Switzerland has

withstood well the twin pressures exercised by growing mass mobilization and the increasing scope of governmental tasks upon the capabilities of the government of a modern, multilingual state and upon the
political consensus of its citizens. Even there, however, a sharpening
local conflict in some French-speaking Jura districts of the predominantly German-speaking Canton Bern seem to parallel the world-wide
trend.

In India, the vision of Gandhi and Nehru of a united India in which
neither religious communities nor language differences would have any
major political significance has had to be drastically modified, first in
the separation of India and Pakistan in 1947, and since 1953 in
the shift of the main internal political and administrative divisions of
India to a system of states established chiefly on the basis of language
— a shift which had been substantially completed by 1965.

The nation-state, it seems, is still the chief political instrument for
getting things done. The main basis of its power is, now more than ever,
the consent of the governed; and this consent is easiest to obtain and
to keep among populations with the same language, culture, and traditions of nationality. Nation-preserving, nation-building, and nationalism
or the preference for the real or imagined interests of one's own nation
and its members — these still remain a major and even a still growing
force in politics, which statesmen of good will would ignore at their
peril.

The Paradox of Nuclear Power

In 1949, the United States had 40 per cent of world income and a
practical monopoly of deliverable nuclear weapons. In 1962, the
United States had only 33 per cent of world income, because many
other countries had recovered from the ravages of World War II and
had grown faster during the intervening years; and by 1965 the United
States was one of five nuclear powers in the world, with the U.S.S.R. a
serious rival and with Britain, France, and China possessing limited but
growing nuclear capabilities. At least half a dozen other countries —
including West Germany, Japan, India, Indonesia, Egypt, and Israel
— were widely considered as possible candidates for the acquisition of
some nuclear weapons during the next one or two decades. As for the
Soviet Union, its share of world income rose from 11 per cent in 1949
in the course of recovery from World War II to 15 per cent in 1962;
but the joint share of the United States and the U.S.S.R. in world income still declined from 51 per cent in 1949 to 48 per cent in 1962. By
1965, the period of the singular preponderance of the United States had

passed, and even the period of the bipolar preponderance of the United States and the Soviet Union was gradually but unmistakably passing.

By the mid-1960's, it had become obviously suicidal for the two chief powers, the United States and the U.S.S.R., to engage in all-out nuclear war against each other. Even limited nuclear war, if it should come to include their capitals, might quickly turn into a mutual suicide of the chief decision-making elites of the two countries, most of whose members were concentrated in or near a very few centers. No country could hope to carry out a nuclear "first strike" against either the United States or Russia without incurring a devastating retaliation from the surviving nuclear "second strike" capabilities of the stricken power. Nonetheless, a first strike still promised some limited advantage. If more of the weapons of the adversary could be knocked out by a first surprise attack, a slightly larger fraction of the population of the attacking power might hope to survive the "second strike" retaliation of the survivors in the victim country. This margin of difference was too small to make a "first strike" attack on America or Russia seem attractive to anyone except a madman, but this difference was perhaps still big enough to count if all-out nuclear war should appear to have become inevitable in any case. Then, and then only, would a first-strike or a "preventive" nuclear attack seem to be dictated by strategic rationality.

Since these calculations were well known to the experts on both sides, it became a vital interest of both the United States and the U.S.S.R. never to let all-out nuclear war appear inevitable, and indeed never even to seem very likely to initiate any chain of events that might seem to lead with near certainty to such a war. Both countries found it to their interest to cultivate a reputation for strength and moderation. In each country, the leaders felt that a reputation for irrationality or rashness — or for a readiness to initiate a nuclear exchange — might yield them some marginal bargaining advantages in minor crises, but that such a reputation for unyielding recklessness, if taken seriously, might all too easily invite a preventive nuclear attack.

The result was a paradox. Countries with little or no nuclear power strikingly could afford to continue to act recklessly in international affairs. They could continue to use threats, to mobilize their manpower for conventional warfare, to push limited wars to the point of mass mobilization, and to use their communications media to inflame their domestic public opinion beyond any point of compromise or of return to moderation short of victory, and to use the tools of direct and indirect censorship and persecution to silence all voices among their citizens still advocating a more moderate course.

Recklessness on the path toward conventional war thus became the privilege of those countries – or of those factions in civil wars or revolutions – that had no substantial power. The real nuclear powers, the United States and Russia, by contrast could not afford to use such tactics. They could not mobilize fully their mass armies by means of conscription without inflamming domestic mass opinion; and they could not go all out in inflaming their own mass opinion without giving to the other nuclear power an early warning of the impending escalation of the conflict towards nuclear war, and without thus inviting a preventive nuclear attack upon themselves.

With the chief nuclear powers deadlocked by mutual deterrence, their remaining capabilities for limited warfare and for coping with the age of nationalism – and with its revolutions, civil wars, and pro-vocative acts of non-nuclear powers – became limited indeed. Where a local situation could be controlled by the limited intervention of one of the superpowers, short of the mass mobilization of its conscripts, the superpower still could stay in control. But where military man-power requirements would run into the hundreds of thousands, there even local political and military situations might prove to be beyond outside control by large nuclear powers, unless the active support of the local populations were secured. Thus Russian tanks could intervene in Budapest in 1956, and under less tragic circumstances American marines could land in Lebanon in 1958, without creating an imminent danger of nuclear war. But all-out mobilization of, say 500,000 or a million conscripts and their commitment to sombat mivht prove to be a far more dangerous matter for either of the great nuclear powers unless it were carefully kept from inflaming their domestic opinion.

When and where either of these conditions would obtain, when and where great power influence would stay secure, and when and where outside control would prove untenable – all this was a matter of costly experience, of more or less lucky political guesswork, and of difficult scholarly study and appraisal in crisis after crisis, from Yugoslavia and Hungary to Algeria and Cyprus, and to Cuba and Viet Nam. Under these conditions, the study of nationalism and of the interplay of national and social revolutions became a necessity rather than a luxury or a mere disinterested search for knowledge. Research on nationalism, social communication, and social conflict attracted more social scien-tists, and received more material support, than in earlier periods. The result was a substantial upsurge in relevant research on nationalism between 1953 and 1965.

Another advance in this period was the increase in research on federalism, on international organization, and on national and supra-national integration of existing political units into new and larger ones. This work paralleled to some extent the efforts to promote with some limited success the economic and political integration of Western Europe, and the attempts at political federations in many other parts of the world, including the unsuccessful integrative experiments of the United Arab Republic of Egypt and Syria, the British West Indies Federation, the Central African Federation of the Rhodesias and Nyasaland, or the Mali Federation in West Africa, each of which eventually broke up into two or more separate nation-states. From these cases, too, something was to be learned; and a beginning was made toward developing a theory of the possibilities and limits of the political integration of two or more nation-states into a larger and viable politi-cal unit.

The Development of Research on Nationalism and on Supranational Integration, 1953–1965

An outstanding contribution to the historical and critical understand-ing of nationalism was Rupert Emerson's *From Empire to Nation*.[1] A brief, perceptive, and deep-probing discussion was offered in the chapter on nationalism in Carl J. Friedrich's *Man and His Govern-ment*.[2] A useful general survey of the literature on nationalism was furnished by Louis Snyder's *The Meaning of Nationalism*.[3]

Two pioneers in the historical study of nationalism restated their views concisely and effectively in Carlton H. Hayes' *Nationalism: A Religion*[4] and Hans Kohn's *Nationalism: Its Meaning and History*.[5]

---

[1] Rupert Emerson, *From Empire to Nation: The Rise to Self-Assertion of Asian and African Peoples* (Cambridge, Harvard University Press, 1960; Paperback Ed., Boston, Beacon Press, 1962). See especially Part Two, "The Anatomy of the Nation," pp. 89–209.

[2] Carl J. Friedrich, *Man and His Government: An Empirical Theory of Politics* (New York, McGraw-Hill, 1963), Chap. 30, "State and Nation: Sovereignty and Its Limits," pp. 547–566.

[3] Louis Snyder, *The Meaning of Nationalism* (New Brunswick, N.J., Rutgers University Press, 1954). A useful survey of data from European history was offered by Boyd C. Shafer, *Nationalism: Myth and Reality* (New York, Harcourt Brace, 1955); and an original and extremely interesting approach to the study of new nations derived from the Western tradition was developed by Louis Hartz in his *The Founding of New Societies: Studies in the History of the United States, Latin America, South Africa, Canada, and Australia* (New York, Harcourt, Brace & World, 1964).

[4] Carlton H. Hayes, *Nationalism: A Religion* (New York, Macmillan, 1960).

[5] Hans Kohn, *Nationalism: Its Meaning and History* (Princeton, Van Nostrand, 1955).

Another historical treatment was given by Eugen Lemberg's *Der Nationalismus*.[6] Other aspects or problems of nationalism were illuminated historically and critically in Inis Claude's *National Minorities*,[7] in John Plamenatz *On Alien Rule and Self-Government*,[8] and in Margery Perham's *The Colonial Reckoning*.[9]

Psychological aspects of nationalism were treated by Leonard W. Doob in *Patriotism and Nationalism*,[10] and much of the relevant recent literature from the behavioral sciences was surveyed and summarized in Otto Klineberg's *The Human Dimension in International Relations*.[11]

A rich literature on political development in the newly emerging countries combined the experiences gained from the historical and empirical study of nationalism in Europe with the study of the emerging countries in Asia, Africa, and Latin America. A key work in this field was the collection edited by Gabriel A. Almond and James S. Coleman, *The Politics of Developing Areas*,[12] with important chapters by the editors. The approach developed in this book stressed the importance of interest groups, political socialization, and political culture, and it was carried forward in a series of other significant books, including notably *Communications and Political Development*, edited

---

[6] Eugen Lemberg, *Nationalismus*, Vol. 1, *Psychologie und Geschichte*, Vol. 2, *Soziologie und politische Pädagogik* (Reinbek bei Hamburg, Rowohlt, 1964).

[7] Inis L. Claude, *National Minorities* (Cambridge, Harvard University Press, 1955).

[8] John P. Plamenatz, *On Alien Rule and Self-Government* (London, Longmans, 1960).

[9] Margery Perham, *The Colonial Reckoning* (New York, Knopf, 1962).

[10] Leonard W. Doob, *Patriotism and Nationalism: Their Psychological Foundations* (New Haven, Yale University Press, 1964).

[11] Otto Klineberg, *The Human Dimension in International Relations* (New York, Holt, Rinehart & Winston, 1964). Highly relevant psychological ideas were also developed in Erik H. Erikson, *Young Man Luther: A Study in Psychoanalysis and History* (New York, Norton, 1958); and in the same author's *Childhood and Society*, 2nd Rev. Ed. (New York, Norton, 1964), as well as in Alexander Mitscherlich, *Auf dem Wege zur vaterlosen Gesellschaft: Ideen zur Sozialpsychologie* (Munich, Piper, 1963). Cf. also Lucian W. Pye, "Personal Identity and Political Ideology," *Behavioral Science*, Vol. 6, No. 3, July 1961, pp. 205–221.

[12] Gabriel A. Almond and James Smoot Coleman, Eds., *The Politics of the Developing Areas* (Princeton, Princeton University Press, 1960). For a recent survey of theories of political development, see Robert A. Packenham, "Approaches to the Study of Political Development," *World Politics*, Vol. 17, No. 1, October 1964, pp. 108–120.

by Lucian W. Pye[13]; *Bureaucracy and Political Development*, edited by Joseph La Palombara [14]; *Comparative Political Culture*, edited by Gabriel A. Almond and Lucian W. Pye[15]; and *Turkey and Japan: A Comparative Study of Modernization*, edited by Robert E. Ward and Dankwart A. Rustow.[16] The political socialization of young people into the national bodies politic was further studied with the aid of comparative survey data in Gabriel Almond and Sidney Verba's *The Civic Culture*.[17]

Other comparative treatments of nationalism and national development were offered in the collections edited by this author and William J. Foltz, *Nation-Building*[18]; by John H. Kautsky, *Political Change in Underdeveloped Countries: Nationalism and Communism*[19]; and in the outstanding study by Daniel Lerner, *The Passing of Traditional Society*.[20]

As regards the experience of particular countries, a challenging and illuminating comparison between the early years of the United States and the problems of present-day emerging nations was proposed in

[13] Lucian W. Pye, Ed., *Communications and Political Development* (Princeton, Princeton University Press, 1963); note particularly Pye's Introduction and his Chapters 1, 3, 5, 7, 9, 11, 13, and 15, and Daniel Lerner's "Toward a Communication Theory of Modernization," *ibid.*, Chap. 18, pp. 327–350. Cf. also Wilbur Schramm, *Mass Media and National Development: The Role of Information in the Developing Countries* (Stanford, Calif., Stanford University Press, 1964).

[14] Joseph La Palombara, Ed., *Bureaucracy and Political Development* (Princeton, Princeton University Press, 1964).

[15] Gabriel A. Almond and Lucian W. Pye, Eds., *Comparative Political Culture* (Princeton, Princeton University Press, 1965).

[16] Robert E. Ward and Dankwart A. Rustow, Eds., *Turkey and Japan: A Comparative Study of Modernization* (Princeton, Princeton University Press, 1964).

[17] Gabriel A. Almond and Sidney Verba, *The Civic Culture: Political Attitudes and Democracy in Five Nations* (Princeton, Princeton University Press, 1963). Cf. also Herbert H. Hyman, *Political Socialization: A Study in the Psychology of Political Behavior* (Glencoe, Ill., The Free Press, 1958); William Kornhauser, *The Politics of Mass Society* (Glencoe, Ill., Free Press, 1959); and Morton Grodzins, *The Loyal and the Disloyal* (Chicago, University of Chicago Press, 1956).

[18] Karl W. Deutsch and William J. Foltz, *Nation-Building* (New York, Atherton Press, 1963).

[19] John H. Kautsky, *Political Change in Underdeveloped Countries: Nationalism and Communism* (New York, Wiley, 1962). Cf. also Gino Germani and Kalman H. Silvert, "Politics, Social Structure and Military Intervention in Latin America," *European Journal of Sociology*, Vol. 2, 1961, pp. 62–81; and Kalman H. Silvert, Ed., *Expectant Peoples: Nationalism and Development* (New York, Random House, 1963).

[20] Daniel Lerner, *The Passing of Traditional Society* (Glencoe, Ill., Free Press, 1958).

Seymour Martin Lipset's *The First New Nation*.[21] Another analysis of
the American experience was combined with an insightful discussion of
national character in David M. Potter's *People of Plenty*[22]; and an
appraisal of American nationalism against the background of European
experience was outlined in Hans Kohn's *American Nationalism: An
Interpretative Essay*.[23] Other studies of particular countries or leaders
by Hans Kohn were *Nationalism and Liberty: The Swiss Example*[24];
and *The Mind of Germany: The Education of a Nation*[25]; as well as
Prophets and Peoples: Studies in Nineteenth Century Nationalism.[26]

The understanding of nationalism in the non-Western world was
advanced by such studies as Chalmers A. Johnson's *Chinese Peasant
Nationalism*[27]; Delmer Brown's *Nationalism in Japan*[28]; Ivan Morris'
Nationalism and the Right Wing in Japan[29]; Masao Maruyama,
Thought and Behavior in Modern Japanese Politics[30]; Lucian W. Pye,
Politics, Personality and Nation-Building: Burma's Search for Identity[31];
James Smoot Coleman, *Nigeria: Background to Nationalism*[32]; Leonard

---

[21] Seymour Martin Lipset, *The First New Nation: The United States in Historical and Comparative Perspective* (New York, Basic Books, 1963).

[22] David M. Potter, *People of Plenty: Economic Abundance and the American
Character* (Chicago, University of Chicago Press, 1954).

[23] Hans Kohn, *American Nationalism: An Interpretative Essay* (New York,
Macmillan, 1957).

[24] Hans Kohn, *Nationalism and Liberty: The Swiss Example* (New York, Macmillan, 1956). Cf. also the fundamental study by Herman Weilenmann, *Pax
Helvetica* (Erlenbach-Zürich, Rentsch Verlag, 1951).

[25] Hans Kohn, *The Mind of Germany: The Education of a Nation* (New York,
Scribners, 1960). For a discussion of German nationalism in the 1950's and 1960's,
cf. Karl W. Deutsch and Rupert Breitling, "The German Federal Republic," in
Roy C. Macridis and Robert E. Ward, Eds., *Modern Political Systems: Europe*
(New York, Prentice-Hall, 1963), pp. 269–309.

[26] Hans Kohn, *Prophets and Peoples: Studies in Nineteenth Century Nationalism*
(New York, Macmillan, 1957).

[27] Chalmers A. Johnson, *Chinese Peasant Nationalism* (Stanford, Calif., Stanford
University Press, 1962).

[28] Delmer Brown, *Nationalism in Japan* (Berkeley, Calif., University of California Press, 1955).

[29] Ivan Morris, *Nationalism and the Right Wing in Japan* (New York, Oxford
University Press, 1960).

[30] Masao Maruyama, *Thought and Behaviour in Modern Japanese Politics* (New
York, Oxford University Press, 1963).

[31] Lucian W. Pye, *Politics, Personality and Nation-Building: Burma's Search for
Identity* (New Haven, Yale University Press, 1962).

[32] James Smoot Coleman, *Nigeria: Background to Nationalism* (Berkeley, Calif.,
University of California Press, 1958).

W. Doob, *Communication in Africa*[33]; Thomas Hodgkin, *Nationalism in Colonial Africa*[34]; and David E. Apter, *Ghana in Transition*[35]; and *Political Kingdom in Uganda: A Study in Bureaucratic Nationalism.*[36]

RESEARCH ON SUPRANATIONAL INTEGRATION. Perhaps the most one-sided aspect of my own study, *Nationalism And Social Communication*, was its relative neglect of the problems and prospect of international or supranational integration. Since then, I have tried to restore the balance in my own work by writing *Political Community at the International Level*,[37] and serving as coauthor of such works as *Political Community and the North Atlantic Area*[38] and *The Integration of Political Communities.*[39]

By now, many writers have contributed to the present fairly large literature on political integration. Important contributions include the collections edited by Robert Bowie and Carl J. Friedrich, *Studies in Federalism*,[40] and by W. Arthur Macmahon, *Federalism, Mature and Emergent*[41]; and the general theoretical works by Ernst B. Haas, *Beyond the Nation-State*[42] and Amitai Etzioni, *Political Unification.*[43]

---

[33] Leonard W. Doob, *Communication in Africa* (New Haven, Yale University Press, 1961).

[34] Thomas Hodgkin, *Nationalism in Colonial Africa* (New York, New York University Press, 1956). Cf. also the same author's *African Political Parties* Baltimore, Penguin Books, 1961).

[35] David E. Apter, *Ghana in Transition,* Rev. Ed. (New York, Atheneum, 1963).

[36] David E. Apter, *The Political Kingdom in Uganda: A Study in Bureaucratic Nationalism* (Princeton, Princeton University Press, 1961).

[37] Karl W. Deutsch, *Political Community at the International Level* (New York, Doubleday-Random House, 1954).

[38] Karl W. Deutsch, Sidney A. Burrell, *et al., Political Community and the North Atlantic Area* (Princeton, Princeton University Press, 1957), partly reprinted in *International Political Communities: An Anthology* (New York, Doubleday & Co., Inc., Anchor Books, 1966), pp. 1–91.

[39] Philip E. Jacob and James P. Toscano, Eds., *The Integration of Political Communities* (Philadelphia, Lippincott, 1964).

[40] Robert Bowie and Carl J. Friedrich, Eds., *Studies in Federalism* (Boston, Little, Brown, 1954).

[41] Arthur W. Macmahon, Ed., *Federalism, Mature and Emergent* (Garden City, N.Y., Doubleday, 1953).

[42] Ernst B. Haas, *Beyond the Nation-State: Functionalism and International Organization* (Stanford, Calif., Stanford University Press, 1964).

[43] Amitai Etzioni, *Political Unification: A Comparative Study of Leaders and Forces* (New York, Holt, Rinehart & Winston, 1965). Cf. also Harold Guetzkow, *Multiple Loyalties* (Princeton, Princeton University Press, Center for Research on World Political Institutions, 1955).

Problems of political integration or disintegration in particular areas or countries were notably treated by Ernst B. Haas, *The Uniting of Europe*[44]; Leon Lindberg, *The Political Dynamics of European Economic Integration*[45]; Raymond Lindgren, *Norway-Sweden: Union, Disunion, Reunion*[46]; Robert A. Kann, *The Habsburg Empire: A Study in Integration and Disintegration*[47]; Bruce M. Russett, *Community and Contention: Britain and America in the Twentieth Century*[48]; Richard L. Merritt, *Symbols of American Community, 1735–1775*[49]; Selig S. Harrison, *India: The Most Dangerous Decades*[50]; William J. Foltz, *From French West Africa to the Mali Federation*[51]; and James Smoot Coleman and Carl G. Rosberg, Jr., Eds., *Political Parties and National Integration in Tropical Africa.*[52] Forthcoming studies include *United for Diversity: The Political Integration of Switzerland*[53] by this author and Hermann Weilenmann, and *Backgrounds for Community*[54] by this author and a group of historians.

[44] Ernst B. Haas, *The Uniting of Europe: Political, Social and Economic Forces 1950–1957* (Stanford, Calif., Stanford University Press, 1958).

[45] Leon N. Lindberg, *The Political Dynamics of European Economic Integration* (Stanford, Calif., Stanford University Press, 1964). Cf. also Dusan Sidjanski, *Dimensions européennes de la science politique* (Paris, Pichon et Durand-Auzias, 1963).

[46] Raymond Lindgren, *Norway-Sweden: Union, Disunion, Reunion* (Princeton, Princeton University Press, 1959).

[47] Robert A. Kann, *The Habsburg Empire: A Study in Integration and Disintegration* (New York, Praeger, 1957).

[48] Bruce M. Russett, *Community and Contention: Britain and America in the Twentieth Century* (Cambridge, The M.I.T. Press, 1963).

[49] Richard L. Merritt, *Symbols of American Community, 1735–1777* (New Haven, Yale University Press, 1966).

[50] Selig S. Harrison, *India: The Most Dangerous Decades* (Princeton, Princeton University Press, 1960).

[51] William J. Foltz, *From French West Africa to the Mali Federation* (New Haven, Yale University Press, 1965).

[52] James Smoot Coleman and Carl G. Rosberg, Eds., *Political Parties and National Integration in Africa* (Berkeley, Calif., University of California, 1964). Cf. also the general theoretical essay by Myron Weiner, "Political Integration and Political Development," *The Annals of the American Academy of Political and Social Science,* Vol. 358, March 1965, pp. 52–64.

[53] Karl W. Deutsch and Hermann Weilenmann, *United for Diversity: The Political Integration of Switzerland,* forthcoming. Cf. K. W. Deutsch and H. Weilenmann, "The Swiss City Canton: a Political Invention," *Comparative Studies,* 7:4, July 1956, pp. 393–408.

[54] Karl W. Deutsch, Sidney A. Burrell, *et al., Backgrounds for Community: Historical Cases of Political Integration or Disintegration,* forthcoming. Cf. also K. W. Deutsch, L. J. Edinger, R. C. Macridis and R. L. Merritt, *France, Germany and The Western Alliance* (New York, Scribners, forthcoming).

As even this highly selective list suggests, the various theories of nationalism and of national or supranational integration can be increasingly tested against this growing body of descriptive and historical studies of particular countries and epochs. The theories should also be tested, however, against the growing body of specific propositions and research results produced by the behavioral sciences, and against the rapidly increasing body of relevant quantitative data. Several works have become available to facilitate this task. The results of a great deal of social science research are summarized in Bernard Berelson and Gary A. Steiner, *Human Behavior*.[55] Large bodies of politically relevant quantitative data and their correlations are presented in Arthur S. Banks and Robert Textor, *A Cross-Polity Survey*[56] and with a somewhat greater emphasis on analysis, in Bruce Russett *et al.*, *World Handbook of Political and Social Indicators*.[57] The political theories and statistical methods underlying the latter volume are discussed further in Richard L. Merritt and Stein Rokkan, Eds., *Comparing Nations*.[58] A more specific link of empirical data from opinion surveys and behavioral research to national political perceptions and images is traced in some of the essays in Herbert Kelman, Ed., *International Political Behavior*.[59]

Despite its length, this list of books from the last twelve years, relevant to the study of nationalism, has been highly selective. If any

---

[55] Bernard Berelson and Gary A. Steiner, *Human Behavior: An Inventory of Scientific Findings* (New York, Harcourt, Brace & World, 1964).

[56] Arthur S. Banks and Robert B. Textor, *A Cross-Polity Survey* (Cambridge, The M.I.T. Press, 1963).

[57] Bruce M. Russett, Hayward R. Alker, Jr., Karl W. Deutsch, and Harold D. Lasswell, *World Handbook of Political and Social Indicators* (New Haven, Yale, 1964). Cf. also Bruce M. Russett, *Trends in World Politics* (New York, Macmillan, 1965).

[58] Richard L. Merritt and Stein Rokkan, Eds., *Comparing Nations: The Use of Quantitative Data in Cross-national Research* (New Haven, Yale, 1965). For the relation between theories and data, underlying this approach, see also Harold D. Lasswell, *The Future of Political Science* (New York, Atherton Press, 1963); Karl W. Deutsch, "Toward an Inventory of Basic Trends and Patterns in Comparative and International Politics," *American Political Science Review*, Vol. 54, No. 1, March 1960, pp. 34–57; and "Social Mobilization and Political Development," *ibid.*, Vol. 55, No. 3, September 1961, pp. 493–514.

[59] Herbert Kelman, Ed., *International Behavior: A Social-Psychological Analysis* (New York, Holt, Rinehart & Winston, 1965).

[60] Bruce Lannes Smith and C. M. Smith, *International Communication and Political Opinion* (Princeton, Princeton University Press, 1956).

journal articles had been included, it would have had to be much longer. More extensive bibliographies may be found in B. L. Smith and C. M. Smith, *International Communication and Political Opinion*[60] and in the expanded and revised edition of my own *Interdisciplinary Bibliography on Nationalism*,[61] which is scheduled to be published by the M.I.T. Press in 1966.[62]

Finally, the field of the theory of communication and control has remained relevant to our problem. Here useful surveys were produced by Colin Cherry[63] and by W. Ross Ashby,[64] and significant contributions to social science were made by Herbert A. Simon.[65] The late Norbert Wiener before his untimely death still published a revised and enlarged edition of his classic *Cybernetics,* with important additional ideas.[66] Attempts to apply cybernetic concepts to political theory and to the analysis of national systems of political decision and control were made by the present author in *The Nerves of Government*,[67] and by David Easton in *A Systems Analysis of Political Life*,[68] but much work in this regard remains to be done in the future.

[61] Karl W. Deutsch, *An Interdisciplinary Bibliography on Nationalism, 1935–1953* (Cambridge, The M.I.T. Press, 1956).

[62] Karl W. Deutsch and Richard L. Merritt, *Nationalism: An Interdisciplinary Bibliography, 1935–1965* (Cambridge, The M.I.T. Press, 1966).

[63] Colin Cherry, *On Human Communication: A Review, a Survey, and a Criticism* (Cambridge and New York, The M.I.T. Press and Wiley, 1957).

[64] W. Ross Ashby, *An Introduction to Cybernetics* (New York, Wiley, 1956).

[65] Herbert A. Simon, *Models of Man: Social and Rational* (New York, Wiley, 1957).

[66] Norbert Wiener, *Cybernetics,* 2nd Ed., Rev. and Enlarged (Cambridge and New York, The M.I.T. Press and Wiley, 1962). Cf. also his *God and Golem, Inc.* (Cambridge, The M.I.T. Press, 1964).

[67] Karl W. Deutsch, *The Nerves of Government: Models of Political Communication and Control* (New York, Free Press of Glencoe, 1963).

[68] David Easton, *A Systems Analysis of Political Life* (New York, Wiley, 1965); and *A Framework for Political Analysis* (New York, Prentice-Hall, 1964). Cf. also J. W. Burton, *International Relations: A General Theory,* Cambridge, Eng., Cambridge University Press, 1965.

Chapter 1

Nationalism and
the Social Scientists

The Background of the Problem

Have the events of the last few decades tended to unify the world, or have they split it more deeply than before? Which ideas and attitudes have spread more widely during the last fifty years: internationalism or nationalism, constitutional government or revolution, tolerance or repression, peace or war? Have economic developments during those last fifty years spread the world's wealth more evenly among mankind, or have they tended to enrich the rich and to impoverish the poor? Have the world's peoples become more similar to each other, or more diverse? Has mankind become more nearly one community, or has it become less so?

There is no simple answer to such questions. More people and greater efforts seem mobilized today on both sides of most of these alternatives, and the outcome of their growing conflicts has varied from people to people, from country to country, and from problem to problem. Yet the chances for effective world organization depend in large part on these results, and if we are to understand our opportunities to achieve a stable world order, we shall depend in large part on the ability of the social sciences to suggest answers to these questions.

Our social sciences have not been well equipped to meet this task. They have attacked the problems of nationalism and world community from two broad approaches. One has been the direct approach by specialized students of nationalism, or by writers who at one time or another gave nationalism their special attention. This mode of attack has given us a wealth of empirical data, as well as excellent techniques for the qualitative recognition of characteristic features of nationalism, configurations of its symptoms, or typical sequences of nationalistic behavior. This approach, however, has not yielded quantitative measurements or predictions. Nor has it been able to link nationalism with any accuracy with the results of other social sciences. Not only was there some mutual ignoring of results behind the safe barriers of departmental boundaries, but the many serious attempts to utilize the other social sciences ran all too often into incompatibilities between the structures of the concepts used by each.

This same incompatibility of concepts has hampered progress along the second broad line of attack: the treatment of some limited features of nationalism as particular cases within the broad field of each special science. Good work was done on national languages as a problem in linguistics; on national settlement patterns as a problem in geography; on national governments and international relations as a subject of political science; and on "monetary nationalism" as a problem in monetary theory. Yet the pieces of the puzzle remained unassembled, and, indeed, very often did not fit together.

The dangerous result was that nationalism came to be widely accepted as a mere "state of mind" with few tangible roots. Pessimists might think it ineradicable as part of the supposed fundamental irrationality of human beings. Optimists might feel that this undesirable "state of mind" could be wiped out by force or persuasion, and that then the way toward lasting and harmonious world order would be free. The real sources of nationalistic thought and action—the sources which might reproduce nationalism again after any temporary suppression—these remained largely uncharted.

There was, perhaps, a fundamental reason for this failure. Many important aspects of nationalism are characterized by unevenness, inequality, relative discontinuity toward persons or things outside the national group. They are further characterized by relative immobilities, or slowness of mobility; by preferences or advantages in communication; and by a considerable degree of structure. Yet much of the social sciences of the period emphasized simplicity, uniformity, continuity—gradualness of development and evenness of distribution. Classical economics stressed mobility of men and other factors of production. Mechanical equilibrium furnished the classical model both for economics and for much of political science—a model which had little or no room for irreversible changes in structure, for growth, for self-transforming processes, in short, for history.

To overcome these difficulties, we may have to search the existing social sciences for another set of concepts and methods of investigation. We may have to study particularly those aspects of each social science which deal with the unevenness, the inner structure, and the relative discontinuities of the facts which are its special subject matter. If we can find a set of structural concepts in each specialized social science that has a bearing on nationalism and nationality, then we may consider whether these structural concepts from each special field fit together, in accordance with the structure of the single social reality with which all these disciplines are dealing. If we find that they fit together, we may then ask whether they may suggest a more specific and perhaps more realistic view of the problems of nationalism and world organization.

The rest of this chapter will first convey some of the more important direct approaches to nationality and nationality. Many of these descriptions of nationality will look disparate or contradictory. And yet, they may suggest an underlying unity; certain themes will recur, and many of their very differences may remind us of the complementary pieces of a jigsaw puzzle.

In later chapters we shall survey some of the specialized social sciences which bear on this subject, and the structural concepts developed within each, by which their findings may perhaps be joined with each other, and correlated with the findings of the direct studies of nationality. Finally, we shall try to suggest some inferences from this survey concerning the nature and strength of nationalism in our time.

Some Views of Nationalism and Nationality in the Past

Many writers on political subjects have used the terms people, nationality, and nation. They often state [1] that a *people* is a group of individuals who have some objective characteristics in common. These characteristics usually then are said to include language, territorial residence, traditions, habits, historical memories, and the like. To these are then added by one group of writers certain subjective elements such as mutual affection, consciousness of difference from other peoples, or the will to belong to this particular people.

A *nation* is often said by such writers to be a people living in a state "of its own." By this is meant, it seems, that the ruling personnel of this state consists largely of individuals who share the main characteristics of this people, and that the administration of this state is carried on in this people's language and in line with what are considered to be its characteristic institutions and patterns of custom.

A *nationality* in this widespread usage is, then, a term which may be applied to a people among whom there exists a significant movement toward political, economic, or cultural autonomy, that is to say,

[*] Superior numbers in the text refer to the section entitled "Notes."

toward a political organization, or a market area, or an area of literary or cultural interchange, within which the personnel and the character-istics of this people will predominate.

All these notions involve difficulties. Some of the most frequently cited objective characteristics of a people do not seem to be essential to its unity. As for language, members of the British people may speak English or Welsh; Canadians, English or French; South Africans, English or Afrikaans; Irishmen, English or Gaelic; Belgians, Flemish or French; and the Swiss, German, French, Italian, and Romansch. The same language may include several peoples. The English language area includes at least six sovereign peoples.[2] Spanish is the language of twenty peoples.[3] German is the language of four peoples with traditions of separate identity.[4] Serbo-Croat is the language of the two peoples indicated in its name; and Arabic is the language of a number of peoples from the Persian Gulf to the Atlantic Ocean.[5]

The characteristic of common territory likewise has its pitfalls. The nationalist movement of Zionism which culminated in 1948 in the erection of the sovereign state of Israel had been carried on actively for two generations by members of a people which had not had a common territory for many centuries, and it was most actively opposed precisely by those inhabitants of the original territory whose ancestors had stayed there and adopted Arab speech and culture.

An even more serious difficulty is that the terms "common" or "con-tiguous" territory seem to beg the question. In what sense is there a territorial community or contiguity between a German village on the Swiss border and a German village on the shores of the North Sea? In what sense does this contiguity differ from that with a Swiss village five miles across the political border? In what sense have Corsicans or the people of Nice a "common territory" with France but not with Italy? What contiguity exists between New York and San Francisco which differs from that between New York and Montreal or between Detroit and Toronto? What in the thought of Maurice Barrés made the "common soil" of Alsace and Lorraine common to Frenchmen but not to Germans who are also buried there? In the words of Charles Maurras, "The *patrie* is a natural society, or which comes absolutely to the same thing, a historic one. Its decisive characteristic is birth. We no more choose our *patrie*—the land of our fathers—than we choose our father and mother."[6]

No person can be born at more than one spot on the map. The actual place of his birth has the size of a bed or a room, not the size of a country. If he finds himself in a "country" or within a set of borders, then no numbers of births can have created these borders or any unity of the country within it. Our fathers and mothers are individual persons; their bodies are physically separate from those of everybody else. This physical separateness is precisely what is lacking in most fatherlands; and where physical discontinuity exists, as in the case of islands, nationality has often bridged it, as, for example, in Crete and Greece, Sicily and Italy, or Northern Ireland and Great Britain.

The same difficulty of deciding just what makes a "common" condition or experience effectively common to a people applies to the "community" of history and memories. In the words of John Stuart Mill, "The strongest cause for the feeling of nationality . . . is identity of political antecedents; the possession of a national history, and consequent community of recollections; collective pride and humiliation, pleasure and regret, connected with the same incidents in the past." [7] Ernest Renan saw one of the two essential elements which make up the "soul or spiritual principle" of a nation in the "possession in common of a rich heritage of memories . . . a heritage of glory and of grief to be shared . . . to have suffered, rejoiced and hoped together. . . ." [8]

But *when* is a "common" heritage common? When will glory and grief be shared? A recent investigator emphasizes the obvious fact that Europe is full of different nationalities who for centuries have been settled and intermingled in the same countries, such as Czechs and Germans in Bohemia. Their members have the same land of birth; their ancestors have lived through the same historic events in the same regions; and yet there is no sharing: they continue to look upon these historical events from entirely different points of view, and their very nearness in a single country has merely embittered their conflicts. [9] Instead of being automatically united by a shared history, men at least under some conditions cannot share the historical events through which they live, unless they are already in some sense united. To explain a nation as the result of shared experiences presupposes already this ability to share experience, which is the very thing that cannot be taken for granted.

In this search for a common history as an objectively observable common characteristic of all members of a nation, the Austrian Socialist writer Otto Bauer tried to find it in a "community of fate" which "tied together" the members of a nation into a "community of character." [10]

The question "Doesn't everyone . . . know Germans who nevertheless have nothing of that which otherwise is regarded as the German national character?" he answered by an attempt to distinguish between mere "similarity of character" and a

> deeper conception of a community of character; this no longer means for us that the individuals of the same nation are similar to each other, but that the same force has acted on the character of each individual— no matter how different the other forces may be which are effective beside it. . . . While . . . similarity of character can only be observed in the majority of the members of the nation, the community of character, the fact that they all are the products of one and the same effective force, is common to all of them without exception. This effective force, that which is historical in us, is that which is national in us. It is this which welds us into a nation.[11]

However, this "deeper conception" does not resolve the difficulty. It renounces the hope to test membership in a people by anything observable in living individuals. Instead it falls back on a hypothetical concept reminiscent of eighteenth-century mechanics: "one and the same effective force" from their past history. How is the existence of this force to be observed? Just when or how has "one and the same force" of history been experienced by that majority of the American people whose ancestors immigrated to the United States *after* the American Revolution, or by the smaller but considerable number of first- or second-generation Americans today? Similar questions would arise for most other "nations of immigrants," and for the millions of people who at one time or other have left their own national community and joined another.

Bauer himself recognized the existence of "nations which have no community of descent and are welded into strong unity by a community of culture"; [12] he also recognized the possibility of an individual joining another nation than that of his birth; but in his thought any such "community of culture" remained entirely dependent on the preceding "community of fate." The general question just when historical events are experienced "in common," and when they are experienced or remembered differently, remained as puzzling as ever.[13]

Other writers have looked for some more subtle facts which might be observed in each member of a people. About A.D. 400 St. Augustine saw in a people a *community of values:* "an assemblage of reasonable beings bound together by a common agreement as to the objects of their love." [14] This view was strikingly echoed after World War II by the British writer Professor K. C. Wheare, who wrote of "that sense which people have that they are bound together and marked off from others by common sympathies . . ." [15]

The notion of a people as a community of values has been elaborated by Edmund Burke. It is based in Burke's view on an agreement not of individual decisions but of habits, experiences, and actual existing institutions. "A nation is . . . an idea of continuity in time as well as in numbers and in space. It is a constitution made by the peculiar circumstances, occasions, tempers, dispositions, and *moral, civil, and social habitudes* of the people, which disclose themselves only in a long space of time." [16]

On this view is based Burke's famous pronouncement:

> The idea of a people is the idea of a corporation. It is wholly arti- ficial, and made, like all other fiction, by common agreement. . . . [The] particular nature of that agreement . . . is collected from the form into which the particular society has been cast. . . . When men . . . break up the agreement which gives its corporate form and capacity to a state, they are no longer a people . . . they are a number of vague loose individuals. . . . Many a weary step is to be taken before they can form themselves into a mass, which has a *true, political personality.* . . . To enable men to act with the weight and character of a people, we must suppose them to be in that state of *habitual so- cial discipline,* in which the wiser, the more expert, and the more opu- lent conduct, . . . the weaker, the less knowing, and the less provided with the goods of fortune.[17]

This agreement of habits, disciplines, and institutions is the basis for the "true political personality," for the mental "general bank and capital of nations" on which the individual should rely rather than "trade each on his own private stock of reason"; here is the basis for that state which for Burke is a "partnership in all art; in every virtue; and in all perfection." [18] In this thought of a conservative who insists on welding together the notions of a people, of a state, and of all civilized society, there is a major root of latter-day nationalist thought which will acknowledge no state and no civilization in any other than collective, emotional, national terms.

The concept of a national mind, implicit in Burke, is made explicit by Benjamin Disraeli.

> The phrase "the people" is sheer nonsense. It is not a political term. . . . A people is a species; a civilized community is a nation. Now, a nation is a work of art and a work of time. A nation is grad- ually created by a variety of influences—the influence of original or- ganization, of climate, soil, religion, laws, customs, manners, extra- ordinary accidents and incidents in their history and the individual character of their illustrious citizens. These *influences* create the na- tion—these *form the national mind.* . . . *If you destroy the political institutions which these influences have called into force, and which*

*are the machinery by which they constantly act, you destroy the na-
tion.* The nation in a state of dissolution then becomes a people; and
after experiencing all the consequent misery . . . they . . . again
` . . . establish themselves into a society.[19]

Can we find out more about this "national mind" and its relation to
individuals? Sir Ernest Barker sees in a people a group of "men,
inhabiting a definite territory, who . . . possess a *common stock of
thoughts and feelings* acquired . . . during the course of a common
history. . . ." [20] Otto Bauer, too, considered it

certain that the different nations also have different masses of mental
images (*Vorstellungsmassen*). . . . These differences of knowledge
. . . determine the differences of will . . . thus we arrive at a *narrower concept of national character* which means . . . merely the
difference in the directions of the will, the fact that the same stimulus
releases different motions. . . .[21]

J. V. Stalin, who sharply criticized Bauer, included "psychological
make-up" among his five "characteristic features of a nation," but
insisted that it was only significant in combination with the others:

A nation is a historically evolved, stable community of language,
territory, economic life, and psychological make-up manifested in a
community of culture. . . . It is worthy of note that we never meet
with a demand connected with Bauer's all-embracing "national character." And this is natural; "national character" *in itself* is something
elusive, and, as was correctly remarked by J. Strasser, "what can be
done with it in politics? [22]

These common "masses of mental images," or this "common stock
of thoughts and feelings," have been described more narrowly by
Graham Wallas and Quincy Wright in terms of an observable *attachment to symbols.* Wallas wrote:

The modern state must exist . . . *as an entity of the mind, a symbol.* . . . The possible area of the State will depend, therefore, mainly
on the facts which limit our creation and use of such entities. Fifty
years ago the statesmen who were reconstructing Europe on the basis
of nationality thought that they found the relevant facts in the causes
which limit the *physical and mental homogeneity* of nations. A State,
they thought, if it is to be effectively governed, must be a homogeneous
"nation," because no citizen can imagine his State or make it the object
of his political affection unless he believes in the existence of a national
type to which the individual inhabitants of the State are assimilated;
and he cannot continue to believe in the existence of such a type
*unless in fact his fellow-citizens are like each other and like himself
in certain important respects.* . . . Bismarck deliberately limited the

area of his intended German Empire by a *quantitative calculation as to the possibility of assimilating* other Germans to the Prussian type.[23]

The same view is put still more sharply by Professor Quincy Wright: "Nationalism differs from . . . other opinions supporting the solidarity of groups only in respect to the symbols toward which it is directed. . . . In fact, during the modern period . . . populations have become more intensely, homogeneously, and continuously favorable to the symbols of some nation-state than to other symbols." [24] Carlton Hayes, F. L. Schuman, and other writers have similarly stressed the techniques with which modern governments promote this attachment of individuals to national symbols,[25] but they found it difficult to state the conditions for the success or failure of such efforts.[26]

In less analytical fashion, nations have been defined as "spiritual unities" by Oswald Spengler; [27] as "social souls" by Karl Lamprecht; [28] as "mental communities" (*geistige Gemeinschaften*) by Friedrich Meinecke; [29] and as "collective personalities" by Don Luigi Sturzo and a number of other Catholic writers. Don Sturzo's views are particularly interesting:

> Nation means individuality of a people; and this cannot come about without a stable geographical contiguity, a historical and cultural tradition, an economic interest. When to these preliminary conditions is added an awakened consciousness on the part of the people of one of those sociological syntheses which only great ideas, such as religion, liberty and independence, can bring about, then there develops the collective *personality* which we call nation. For us the *individuality* of a people means only the *de facto* differentiation between one ethnical group and another. On the other hand, the *personality* of a people indicates the active consciousness which springs out of the differentiated group, giving the latter its own cultural and political stamp. Hence the starting point in the formative process of a nation is one of distinction between contiguous and even related ethnical groups. . . .
>
> [The] nation in its essence is not . . . a voluntary society. . . . It is rather the moral binding sense of a people. . . . Like all living moral personalities, the nation will have its increment and development . . . until . . . the national personality will either fade away because its physical subject has . . . nearly perished (as in the case of the Armenians and the Assyrians), or will be transferred to a larger and different personality, reviving in a broader circle of ethnical, cultural and political unity, as Montenegro in Yugoslavia; . . . Provence in France; Bavaria in Germany; . . . or California in the United States.
>
> For us a collective personality . . . is only the simultaneous reflection of the consciousness of the single members who understand the aim for whose attainment they have gotten together, or who understand that aim in a different way and dissent therefrom, so that . . . there

> comes about that maximum and that minimum of consent and of re-
> ciprocal influence which create action . . . [For] such consciousness
> to emerge the social group must have pre-existent within itself those
> values that form the nexus of a national community, such as tradition,
> customs, language, territory, social rights and economic interests. . . .
> The totality of these values, idealized as a reality either to be attained
> or to be defended, forms the collective consciousness of the nation.[30]

These terms seem vague enough. Where is the fire behind all this
smoke? Some recent writers have tried to attack the problem of
nationality in terms "ethnocentrism" or of a community of culture,[31]
and modern anthropologists have endeavored to give this concept of
culture a specific meaning:

> By "culture" we mean those historically created selective processes
> which channel men's reactions both to internal and to external stimuli.
> . . . Culture is . . . the precipitate of history. It includes those as-
> pects of the past which, usually in altered form, live on in the present.
> In more than one sense, "history is a sieve." . . . Not all culture is
> adaptive—in the sense of promoting sheer physical survival. At times
> indeed it does exactly the opposite. We must bring in the concept of
> adjustment (that is, lowering of tension) as well as that of adaptation.
> . . . Aspects of culture . . . may persist . . . after they have ceased
> to have survival value.[32]

This view leads us to the notion of "culture" as a *configuration* of
do's and don'ts, a correlated pattern of mental Stop and Go signs, of
preferences implicit or expressed: "Notice this!" "Ignore that!" "Imitate this action!" "Shun that other!" [33]

As the patterns of Stop and Go signs and the widths of streets and
their connections will do much to determine the flow patterns of
traffic in a city, so, one might infer, the patterns of culture may do
much to determine the distribution of sensitivity and obtuseness, of
remembrance and forgetfulness, of association or dissociation, of
acceptance and rejection in the observable behavior of a community
and in the mental life of an individual.

If culture is such a structure or configuration, what is its relation to
the personality structure of the individual? Culture acts on individuals
perhaps most strongly by its socially standardized patterns of bringing
up children, but it continues to act on individuals of all ages who live
in its context. How strong are these effects of culture, and in particular of national culture, as against the effects of other not culturally
standardized experiences of the individual? *And to what extent can
any national culture* under present day conditions *avoid inner contradictions and incompatibilities* within its own network of channels and

barriers? To what extent, therefore, can any culture today avoid inner conflicts, mental traffic jams, and break-ups of some of its own established patterns, offering to the individuals involved new opportunities for choice and new degrees of freedom? How irrevocably does a people or a nation put its stamp on the individual who was raised within the patterns of its culture?

Answers to these questions may have practical political significance. R. M. MacIver saw in a nationality "a free uniformity, admitting endless difference and dependent on no sanction and no coercion,[34] but both Jewish and German extreme nationalists have insisted on its compelling hold over the innermost personality structure of the individual. "The cultural forces and potentialities which are the true internal bases of a nation . . . cannot be transmitted to any other nation," wrote the Zionist Nachman Syrkin in 1917. "A person . . . lies against his own personal individuality through his separation from his nation." [35]

Prominent German nationalists thought so, too. "We Germans," wrote Heinrich Treitschke, "who know both Germany and France, know better what is for the good of the Alsatians than do those unhappy people themselves. . . . We desire, *even against their will, to restore them to themselves.*" [36]

One reaction against such views has been the attempt to explain nationality entirely in such subjective terms as *consciousness* and *will*.[37] In nationality, according to Hans Kohn, who is summing up a long line of investigators, "the most essential element is a living and active corporate will. Nationality is formed by the decision to form a nationality." [38] A Study Group of Members of the Royal Institute of International Affairs in 1939 similarly included as one of six characteristics of a nation "a certain degree of common feeling or will, associated with a picture of the nation in the minds of the individual members." [39]

In the view of another recent investigator, Dr. Frederick Hertz, "the subjectivist definition of a nation (as a community formed by the will to be a nation) is essentially correct, but it needs careful formulation. . . . *Will . . . in a whole people [is] but a multitude of feelings and vague ideas,* animating a large and influential part of the people, that tend to crystallize in a will in certain conditions." [40]

The difficulty of these subjective terms is in assigning to them any precise meaning. Some modern psychologists are reluctant to use such terms as "consciousness" and "will" precisely because they seem to be so hard to test.[41] They appear to be discarded leftovers of nineteenth-century psychology, concepts detached from the scientific operations of twentieth-century psychologists. So long as this is so, "consciousness" and "will" cannot be used without considerable danger in political science. The danger is that the political scientist will try to describe nationalism and nationality with the help of these words, in the belief that he has then made a meaningful statement. But what is the meaning of such statements, and how and by whom are they to be tested? The political scientist has passed the baby to psychology, but the psychologist does not seem eager to take it.[42]

Some of the difficulties of using the terms *consciousness* and *will*, in political science, have been pointed out by Dr. Hertz:

> In the history of national development . . . *this will was at first only that of a minority* which in the course of time succeeded in gaining more or less the assent of a majority . . . but if a people has not yet reached this stage, or if an old loyalty has been destroyed by historic events, there is no spontaneous national will but merely a welter of conflicting aspirations. . . . *The mere will does not yet make a nation.* A nation . . . is a community of fate, to a large extent brought together and molded by historical events and natural factors, and *the individual has practically little opportunity of choosing his nationality* or changing its fundamental traits. An emigrant may legally . . . acquire [citizenship] of the country where he has founded a new home. But [he or his children] must also assimilate its social outlook and its national traditions, and even if [they] succeed in this task, it is not yet sure whether they will be accepted by the national community as real nationals. . . . Jews have been living in Germany for a very long time . . . and most of them were completely assimilated. Nevertheless, the . . . Nazi regime . . . branded them as aliens. . . .[43]

Is there a way out of this labyrinth? Modern psychologists agree that patterns of culture may actually shape to some extent the personality patterns of individuals,[44] and anthropologists have applied the investigation of child rearing to the study of national character.[45] But there seems as yet no bridge between the anthropologists' investigation of the nursery and the historians' investigation of the state, between the tests of the psychologists and the psychological terms sometimes so confidently used in political science; in short, between all the different disciplines, and even between the various "subjective" and "objective" factors noted in the special investigations of nationality.

Dr. Hertz concluded that

> the subjectivist theory needs to be supplemented by allowance for objective factors. . . . It seems . . . more fruitful . . . to define a nation as a people possessing national consciousness which . . . is also a matter of degree. . . . National consciousness consists in the com-

bined striving for unity, liberty, individuality and prestige. . . . The decisive criterion is whether the idea of a duty to sacrifice particular *interests* to the national has become dominant in the people.[46]

Professor E. H. Carr, the chairman of the Study Group of the Royal Institute of International Affairs, whose 1939 report on *Nationalism* was referred to above, summarized the position in 1945: "*The nation is not a definable and clearly recognizable entity.* . . . Nevertheless the nation is . . . far more than a voluntary association; and it embodies in itself . . . such natural and universal elements as attachments to one's native land and speech and a sense of wider kinship than that of family. The modern nation is a historical group." [47]

Have we come full circle? Does the outcome of the thought of so many men merely leave us where we started? Perhaps not quite. We have found a luxuriant growth of different concepts, and we have found most writers inclined to stress one or a few aspects of nationality over and above all others. But we have also found a good deal of structural correspondence between these isolated pieces of knowledge or insight. Qualitative rather than quantitative, unsuited thus far for measurement, they seem yet to add up to a pattern.

Most serious writers have agreed that nationality is not biological and has little if anything to do with race. They have suggested that nationality somehow involves some common relationships to parts of men's physical environment—their "country"—and to some events in the past, transmitted to the present as "common" history, although they could not tell what made a country or a history "common." It was further suggested that nationality implied some similar elements inside the minds of every individual participating in it, such as common values, thoughts, or feelings, and that some of these might not be similar but rather complementary: interlocking habits and memories in the minds of individuals inducing them to play interlocking roles of helper and helped, or leader and led, as in Burke's state of "habitual social discipline," or in the modern social psychologist's concept of "interlocking roles" as one of the essential characteristics of a social group. These interlocking habits and roles were seen as linked to actual social institutions which formed another element of nationality. The further element of a "common attachment to symbols" likewise implied an interlocking relation between those who manipulate these symbols and those who accept them; but the causes of the origin and the subsequent acceptance or rejection of such habits, roles, and symbols were not made clear.

All these elements—relations to environment, past, leaders, institutions, and symbols—were further shown as making up structures. They formed configurations, it was urged, in which no single trait need be as important as the mutually reinforcing, and in part self-sustaining, pattern of the whole. These high-order configurations of social behavior were called "collective personalities" by some writers, and "cultures" by others, but there seemed to be some agreement about the reality of the structures of behavior described by these different words. These social patterns then in turn were found to be related to the personality structure of individuals. Each individual's personality, and thus to some extent his nationality, were found to involve his "consciousness" or "will," though these latter terms usually remained somewhat vague, and it was not settled to what extent they represented causes, and to what extent. effects. Furthermore, it appeared that each individual retained some chance to change his nationality, or his place or attitudes within it, but that most such changes were laborious, slow, and often even impossible to complete within a single generation. There was wide agreement, finally, that nationalism and nationality, like their elements, were in some sense historical in origin and in development.

In all the works surveyed, these findings were qualitative rather than quantitative. Not merely had measurements not been made, but the very concepts themselves furnished no bases for them. Where predictions were nonetheless attempted, their reliability was small on the average, and sporadic at best.

Many writers have transmitted to us generous visions of a future world-wide community of mankind. How to reach these goals in a world of stubborn facts, and how to develop a social science of nationalism and nationality capable of showing the probable consequences of decisions—these are goals toward which many steps have yet to be taken. It is for stepping-stones along this path that we must now turn to the various special fields of social science.

Chapter 2

Building Blocks
of Nationality
SOME BASIC CONCEPTS FROM
OTHER SOCIAL SCIENCES

Our task in this chapter will be to survey a group of social sciences in order to see whether some of their basic concepts cannot be brought into a pattern which might apply more effectively to the problems of nationality as a whole. We shall ask whether the structure of this group of concepts in each field might not show some similarities to the structure of concepts in another, and whether all of them together might then show some similarity to the structure of the facts which each of these sciences is trying to survey from a different viewpoint.

In each of these fields we shall look not only for some ways of describing even distributions of data, but, on the contrary, for means to take account of discontinuities and uneven developments. A theory built on assumptions of evenness would clash with a world of exceptions. For this reason we shall reverse this procedure. We shall seek working hypotheses which take unevenness and discontinuities as their starting points; and we shall then always be able to treat an occasional even distribution as a limiting case.

Society, Institutions, Caste, and Class

We have begun our discussion of nationality with the concept of *society* as a group of individuals united by the division of labor: "persons who have learned to work together."[1] This division of labor is based on social institutions and technology, that is, on men's learned habits to work with each other in particular patterns of teamwork ("social institutions" or "relationships of production," in the language of the various schools of thought) and to work in particular ways with particular types of physical equipment on particular aspects of physical nature ("science" and "technology").

Key patterns of technology may put a premium on particular social institutions; changes in technology may tend to undermine others;

and these, in turn, may make for differences in social institutions, and thus help to mark off peoples from each other. In this manner the differentiation of the Dutch people from the North Germans was aided by the particular importance of dikes and polders in medieval Holland, which fostered a distinct way of life and indirectly the growth of a feeling of separateness.[2] The rise of Switzerland from the thirteenth century on was related to the changes in the technology of transport and bridge building which made the St. Gotthard Pass crucial in world trade and furnished the economic basis for an independent "pass state" in that region.[3] The particularly ample supply of timber, bog iron, and iron tools in early medieval Norway had something to do with the growth of an advanced technology of shipbuilding which furnished the basic equipment for the Viking way of life.[4] Again, in early medieval North Africa, the Arab language and the Mohammedan religion spread along the oases and caravan trails of the Sahara Desert with a new instrument of transportation, the camel, and a new type of agriculture, the planting of date palms.[5]

But the relationship may also work the other way: certain patterns of social teamwork may facilitate the development of certain patterns of technology; and other types of social institutions, such as, for instance, chattel slavery, may effectively hamper the making of certain technological discoveries, or at least their application. Social institutions are not simply determined by technology. Rather the two interact in a sequence of steps which must be studied by the methods of history, and in which it may be decisive just which step came before which others.

At each stage, society is divided within by the division of labor. All more elaborate societies which have been observed thus far have involved divisions into *occupational groups,* such as the fundamental division between town and country; and into social castes or classes. Differences of caste may coincide with differences in culture or race, or with the remnants of differences in the past. Within a single country, they may greatly hinder the development of a single closely knit people, as in India; [6] or they may go so far as to raise the question whether they are not separating two different peoples, rather than mere subgroups of a single one, as in the case of Southern Whites and Negroes in the United States.[7]

Castes often overlap in part with classes, but they differ from classes perhaps mainly in that they contain a strong cultural element: they usually involve special groups of occupations which have become bounded by cultural barriers to substitution and communication. Thus members of different castes are often expected not to eat with each other, not to intermarry, to form no informal associations with each other, and to restrict all mutual face-to-face meetings and conversations to a few rigidly standardized rituals and situations.

The notion of ~~class implies a~~ lesser degree of social immobility than that of caste. As it is used in political and social literature, class involves at least four different things: (1) An interest group on the analogy of the market, such as industrial wage-earners, a collection of persons with roughly *analogous positions in the process of production* and in the established pattern of social institutions, so that they may all be thought to have an analogous chance to gain or lose from certain kinds of economic or social change. (2) *A community of habits* and manners, usually reinforced by the effects of long association over several generations, by the frequency of intermarriage, commensality and neighborhood contacts (such as "blue-collar workers" or "men in overalls," eating in the "workers' canteen," and living on the "wrong side of the railroad tracks") and by the expectation of their members that both they and their children will continue in this group. (3) A group of supporters for *particular organizations* designed to increase the income and prestige of such an interest group or such a community of habits (such as a labor union or a "Labor Party"). (4) A group of persons believing that they have a particular *mission in history* (such as replacing "feudalism" by "free enterprise," or "capitalism" by "socialism").

There have been groups and situations in history where these four concepts have largely overlapped; these loom large in the thoughts, e.g., of Karl Marx, and in his view that the character of a nation and its role in world politics would be determined in large measure by the particular class which had succeeded in becoming the "national class" or "leading class" within it.[8] But there have been other situations where the coincidence of these four concepts could not be taken for granted. American workers, for instance, have often been less sharply separated in habits and manners from the rest of the community. They did not necessarily expect that they or their children would remain workers forever, or that being a worker would always involve a peculiarly unfavorable status in the community. Many of them have vigorously promoted their economic interests through labor unions, yet without thus far developing a major labor party; and most of them have remained cool to invitations to identify themselves with any peculiar historical mission or ideology. Much confusion has resulted from using the word "class" as if it had one operational meaning instead of four, or as if these four meanings had to coincide everywhere and at all times, instead of only at particular times and places.

It seems true that, for each particular society, certain patterns of technology and certain institutions are in practice more important than others. These we might call its leading or predominant patterns and institutions, such as the hoe or the plow, or freehold tenure or latifundia in an agricultural society. They make it probable that some particular class or classes will function as the "elite" or *leading or ruling class*. It will then stand out from all others in wealth, power, and prestige, and it will impose its stamp on much of social life.[9] Among this ruling class the four characteristics of interest, habits, organization, and view of history may often coincide more closely: they may all reinforce each other in the defense of the existing social arrangements by which this group is favored, and perhaps in efforts to extend these arrangements still further. Yet the actual extent of this coincidence, and the actual influence exercised by a particular elite in a particular society, or a particular nation, may vary a great deal. It cannot be deduced in advance of investigating each specific case, for neither guess nor theory can replace the need for the facts of each concrete situation.

An example of the realistic study of such an elite may be found in the work of the late Robert Keen Lamb on the social, political, and family connections among the leaders of the American Revolution and of the business life of the new Federal Union. Some aspects of the formation of this new national elite, or leading class, are shown in Lamb's diagram (Fig. 1), and the process by which this national class arose has been summarized by Lamb as follows:

> To form a new American nation-state separate from Britain, a new national elite had to come together, and it in turn had to organize the political, economic and social institutions of a new nation. This process was generated by the Revolutionary war, and channeled by the Continental Congress which first brought together in Philadelphia in 1774 representatives of the elites from all thirteen of the original colonies.
> Once these colonies (each actually a little city-state) were represented at an intercolonial congress, the wheels were in motion to carry the American people from the status of colonial subjects of the British Empire to free citizens of a sovereign republic.
> A major part of the new national elite was brought together in about 30 chief steps by which a New York-Philadelphia coalition developed from the Albany Congress in 1754 until the inauguration of Washington in 1789. Its key figures were: for New York, Philip Schuyler, his son-in-law Alexander Hamilton, and their friend William Duer; and for

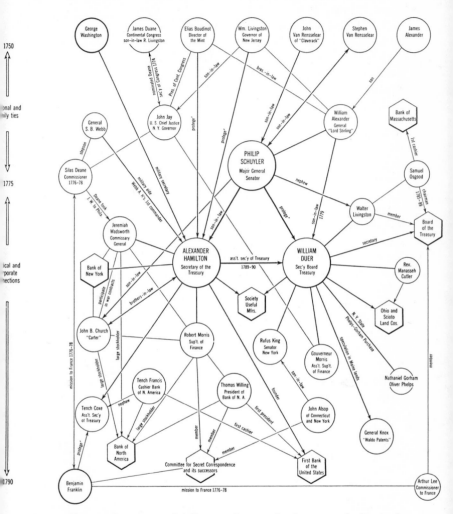

Fig. 1. Clusters of interest and influence; the growth of a national elite in the United States, 1750–1795, according to Robert K. Lamb. Note the personal, family, and business ties between individuals from different colonies such as Virginia, Pennsylvania, New York, and Massachusetts. For details, see pp. 18–20.

Philadelphia, Benjamin Franklin, his associates Robert Morris and Morris' partner Thomas Willing, and their proteges Tench Francis, and his nephew Tench Coxe. These steps culminated in the formation of the United States Treasury and the First Bank of the United States; and they involved the mission to France, of which Franklin, Arthur Lee and Silas Deane were members, as well as the steps leading up to the passage of the Northwest Ordinance and the formation of the Scioto and Ohio Land Companies, which were again tied to the story of the French mission.

The key institutions involved in this process are the Secret Committees, the finance committee of Congress (of which James Duane was chairman), the Congressional Board of War (of which Philip Schuyler was chairman), the committee on foreign affairs (of which John Jay was secretary), the Superintendency of Finance which succeeded the committee on finance (Robert Morris was Superintendent, and Gouverneur Morris was his assistant), The Board of the Treasury which succeeded the Superintendency (where Osgood was chairman, and Walter Livingston, Schuyler's nephew, and Arthur Lee were members, and Duer was secretary), the Bank of North America (of which Thomas Willing was first President, Robert Morris, Jeremiah Wadsworth and John G. Church, Schuyler's son-in-law, were founders, and Tench Francis was cashier, using French war loan specie as a base), the First Bank of the United States (of which Willing was President and Francis, Cashier), and the Treasury of the United States (Hamilton, Secretary; Duer and Tench Coxe, Assistant Secretaries).

The "Diagram," showing the connections of Schuyler, Hamilton and Duer, does not pretend to be a thorough representation of all the interpersonal connections which run through the Continental Congress down to the formation of the first Washington Administration in 1789. Certain key representatives of the two groups of the American Revolutionary elite are represented here, from the states of New York and Pennsylvania, with a scattering of other key individuals with whom they were connected either officially or by mutual interests. The first Continental Congress brought certain of them together in 1774, and they began soon afterwards to form a coalition for control of congressional war finances and foreign affairs.

This chart can best be understood by those interested in the role of elites in the formation of new nation-states if it is read from bottom to top; by those interested in how extended-kinship groups play their role in organizing the aristocratic elites of little city-states it should be read from top to bottom.

In either case it shows the interconnection between the manorial families of New York province (whose members were also active merchants in New York city) and certain key mercantile families of Philadelphia as they came together in the Continental Congress. The Livingstons, and their family connections among the Schuylers and the Van Rensselaers, were prime movers in the Revolutionary movement in New York, but on their own aristocratic terms. Thomas Willing and his partner Robert Morris were equally influential and equally con-

servative (if not more so) in Philadelphia. These men and their intimate friends played an active role in the first three Continental Con-
gresses, and while reluctant to see a declaration of independence pre-
cede the formation of an American confederation, and the negotiation
of a French alliance, they acquiesced when the Lees of Virginia and
the Adamses of Massachusetts led Congress to pass such a Declaration
in July 1776.

Even before that date, the two key secret committees of Congress,
one on foreign affairs and the other on commerce, were largely in their
hands, and the hands of their friends. The ensuing struggle between
the New York-Philadelphia coalition and the Adams-Lee opposition
kept the Congress in turmoil until 1781 when the Confederation was
formed and Robert Morris became Superintendent of Finance. Once
the Confederation had created a formal federation of the American
states, the conservatives began to press for a more permanent and
centralized union of the states. This movement reached its climax at
the Constitutional Convention at Philadelphia in 1787, and after a
struggle for ratification culminated in the inauguration of the Washington Administration in 1789, with Alexander Hamilton as Secretary
of the Treasury.[10]

An investigation of this kind resembles the "sociograms" of J. L.
Moreno and the studies of "interlocking directorates" familiar from
anti-trust investigations. Its results demonstrate that elites or leading
classes are not horizontal slices off the top of some uniform cake, but
that they are the result of connections growing in time and clustering
in space. Wealth, influence, and power come in clusters, it appears,
and so do friendships, cliques, and habits of trust, familiarity and financial and political cooperation. Such clusters are regional or local, and
they are not superseded by some amorphous results of abstract integration, but by larger clusters which again have structure and which again
are effectively marked off from other elites in other societies and countries. And the cluster pattern of elites finds its counterpart in the
cluster pattern of societies.

What are the limits of society? Society involves division of labor
in many respects, not merely in a few. It is, therefore, surrounded by
relative discontinuities. Within the limits of these discontinuities the
division of labor is relatively intensive and involves many kinds of
goods and services; beyond them it is relatively scant and involves
a lesser volume or fewer kinds. We will, therefore, have several societies rather than one single homogeneous world society. Several of
these societies may be linked among each other by a higher degree of
the division of labor than they are with other societies elsewhere. Men
can therefore be at one and the same time members of more than one
society, in the sense that several societies may be separated from each

other by some discontinuities and yet form together one *civilization* or "great society" which in turn may be separated by deeper discontinuities from other civilizations or "great societies." To the extent that these latter discontinuities should become lessened we may be justified in speaking of a *world civilization* or "world society." It will be a question of fact to what extent in any particular period of history there will be any real relationships corresponding to these last concepts.

To sum up, we may see society as based on the division of labor, carried on in each case through specific combinations of social institutions and technology. These in turn have functioned through divisions into occupational groups and into classes or castes. Among the institutions and technological practices, certain ones stand out in each case as particularly important for the reproduction and growth of each particular society. These are that society's leading *institutions* and leading technologies, to which have corresponded a peculiar *ruling class* or *elite*, most closely linked to and favored by these institutions, and more or less united for their preservation by relatively stable cluster patterns formed in terms of family ties, interest, habit, organization, and ideology. Every such society is bounded by relative *discontinuities*, corresponding to drops in the extent of the division of labor; but several societies may preserve a somewhat larger degree of division of labor among each other than with other societies, and so form a "great society." These latter in turn may or may not show enough remaining division of labor to give observable meaning to the term "world society."

Cultural Centers and Civilizations

Corresponding to these terms, we found *culture* based on the community of communication, consisting of socially stereotyped patterns of behavior, including habits of language and thought, and carried on through various forms of social learning, particularly through methods of child rearing standardized in this culture. Patterns of culture have sometimes been described under the name of "national character." The term has been much misused, or used naively, and some writers have tried to deny it all meaning.[11] Anthropologists, however, have come back to speaking of national "subcultures" or "national character,"[12] and we shall have occasion to speak of it further in this chapter, and in Chapter 4. Social learning functions largely through smaller divisions of the culture, such as family or sib; village or neighborhood; tribe, or the "folk" of some region, as in Howard Odum's conception of the "South" in the United States.[13] These divisions have usually implied cultural stratification in terms of the distribution of preferences or values, particularly of prestige. In any culture certain behavior patterns stand out as *leading* or *model* patterns; certain groups of persons as *cultural models* and *bearers of prestige;* certain regions as *cultural centers.* In this sense, Paris, London, and New York are currently centers of fashion for large parts of the world; about 1750, French manners and French taste were the model of refined behavior for large parts of Europe, somewhat as Spanish manners and Spanish taste had been 150 years earlier, and Italian manners 50 years before that; and at a far earlier period Athens had boasted of being the "school of Hellas."

Cultural communities are bounded by relative barriers to communication. These discontinuities may be weaker among certain cultural communities which then may form a *civilization* in the sense of A. J. Toynbee, or of the *Kulturkreise* of some German writers. Thus Toynbee speaks of the "Hellenic" or Graeco-Roman civilization as against the "Syriac" civilization, or as against the civilization of Western Christendom; [14] and the theory of "cultural orbits" or *Kulturkreislehre* has been applied to Africa by Leo Frobenius and to the West by Oswald Spengler.[15] If there were enough communication in a particular historical period, the term "world civilization" might be justified.

All societies and cultures have their *history.* Within that history, there may stand out certain *decisive periods* of particularly large and rapid change in the course of which technologies, social and economic institutions, and the patterns of culture are reshaped, dissolved, or newly recombined. There are periods of "incubation" when elements for a new pattern are assembled; there are decisive periods of formation when this new pattern of action begins to function and becomes relatively fixed for transmission to subsequent generations; there may be a final period when this transmission ends in a relative discontinuity and the pattern is dissolved or changed "beyond recognition," i.e., to the extent where it loses its relative "identity" so that its major patterns can no longer be predicted as near-repetitions of the past.

In this sense it has been said that important aspects of the French national character hardened during the French Revolution, and that the Alsatians became Frenchmen during this period.[16] The Swiss nationality and national character are said by some to have hardened between the thirteenth and sixteenth centuries, during the decisive struggles for Swiss independence.[17] Dutch national consciousness and national character became established largely, according to G. J. Renier, during the Wars of Independence against Spain [18] although other historians believe the process to have started earlier and to have been more continuous.[19] Almost all of these views are controversial, although most of them may contain at least elements of truth. To assess the role of historical changes in the making of a people would require a group of separate studies; here and now we can only note the probable importance of such key periods in history in the growth of nations.

Population Cluster, Country, and Ecumene

Cultures and societies appear to the human geographer as *settlement patterns* on a map, connected by natural or man-made facilities for *transportation*. The effects of the facts of physical geography vary with the technologies and social institutions which are brought to bear on them: whether an ocean functions as a barrier or as a highway may depend on the technology of shipping and of the resources allocated in a given society to its development. In this fashion the barriers of the Swiss Alpine passes were turned into major highways in the thirteenth century by improvements in roads and bridges.

Regions of settlement are held together by facilities for transportation and separated from each other by relative discontinuities in their effectiveness. Settlement patterns are thus found to consist of local and regional clusters (Fig. 2).[20] Such clusters and transportation facilities are not evenly distributed. Within each "country" of the political geographer there stands out a *nuclear area* or *ecumene:* "The ecumene of each state may be thought of as the region or regions which are well peopled and given internal coherence by a network of transportation lines. It is distinguished from sparsely populated or uninhabited parts of the same country, penetrated only here and there by routes." [21] Related to this approach is the human geographer's notion of a *capital city* or principal city, which need not be identical with the administrative center of the area where it in fact predominates.

A variety of this is found in the relationship of *key cities* or key areas or *nodal areas* to the often much larger regions of *hinterland* which they may dominate in terms of transportation, strategy, or economics. Typical examples of key areas are harbors and river mouths which may dominate much larger river valleys in matters of trade and transportation. Control of such key areas by members of one nationality gives them power over the lives of the members of other peoples in the hinterland so that the simpler notions of "national self-determination" become difficult to apply.[22]

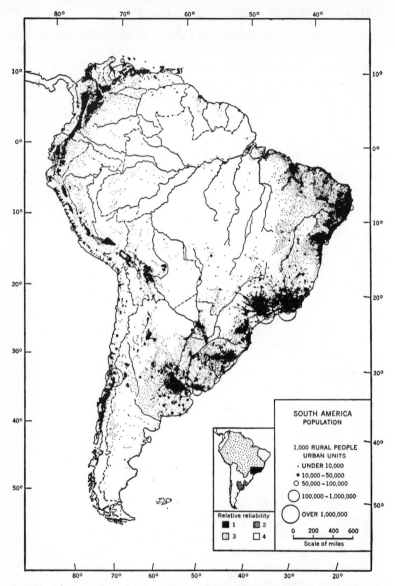

Fig. 2. Clusters of settlement; the population of South America, according to Preston E. James. (From *Latin America*, New York, Odyssey Press, 1942. Reproduced by permission.) Note the clusters or groups of clusters that make up the cores of Argentina, Uruguay, Chile, Bolivia, Peru, Ecuador, Colombia, and Venezuela; and note the difficulties presented to national integration by the five or more distinct major settlement clusters of Brazil, several of which were involved in civil wars against each other as late as the 1920's and 1930's. Compare also the clusters of settlement with the differences in national incomes shown in Fig. 11.

Units of human geography are bounded by relative discontinuities in settlement and transportation; transportation discontinuities involve not necessarily a drop in the quality and number of roads but rather in the density of traffic moving over them, although in practice the two will often be related. Nevertheless, each discontinuity will apply to some particular operation or group of operations; we may expect to find, therefore, not sharp and simple borders but rather bundles of borders; if enough of these are close enough together we may speak of *boundary zones.*

Such zones may bound a *country,* that is, a relatively larger area within which observation shows a markedly greater degree of transportation and economic interdependence than with any other area.[23] Several such countries may show markedly greater interdependence among each other than with the rest. To these sometimes the term "great space" (*Grossraum*) has been applied. There is currently a significant degree of transportation interdependence between the most developed areas all over the world, and the concepts of world transportation and "world ecumene" are therefore meaningful.[24]

Speech Communities, Standard Languages, and Dialects

Where the anthropologist may look for communities of culture, and the human geographer for communities of transportation, the student of *language* deals with communities of speech. A community of language is a community of information vehicles: most words of the language, or at least the words most frequently used, will be recognized and spoken by most members of the group, with identical or closely similar denotations. As regards less frequently used words, or their connotations (i.e., the amount and kind of memories evoked by them), the effects of the community of language may be modified by the effects of the community of culture. Ties of transportation, economic intercourse, social stratification, cultural similarity, and similarity in already existing speech habits, as well as relative barriers and discontinuities in all these respects will all have their effects in determining what the actual speech community will be at any one time. Philologists have imagined maps of such *speech communities,* on which each speech contact would be represented by a single line, so as to show their relative *densities of speech traffic* over a period of time. Such a map could perhaps be accurately constructed for small samples, using such measuring techniques as the concept of message unit from communications research. However, it might be important to distinguish between several major *kinds* of speech communication: the number of

Fig. 3. An example of a language center; the region of the *Francien* dialect, the basis of modern standard French, according to Marcel Cohen. (From *Histoire d'une langue: Le Français*, Paris, Ed. Hier et Aujour d'hui, 1947, p. 81. Reproduced by permission.)

times a newsboy says "five cents" to his customers is not equivalent to the number of times he talks things over with his friends.

Within almost any major language we find regional divisions into *dialects* and social divisions of *linguistic stratification.* We find again *language centers* and *leading groups;* these groups in these centers set the *standard language* both in its colloquial and its written form. Thus Francien, the dialect of the Ile de France and to some extent of the Champagne region, came to set the national standards for both literary and colloquial French, particularly after the influence of the Langue d'Oc dialect had been reduced by relative economic decline and military defeat of these regions in the thirteenth century. (See Fig. 3.)

In the words of Leonard Bloomfield,

> The main types of speech in a complex speech-community can be roughly classed as follows: 1. literary standard . . . 2. colloquial standard, the speech of the privileged class . . . (in England only if spoken with the southern "public school" sounds and intonation); 3. provincial standard . . . spoken by the "middle" class . . . 4. sub-standard, spoken . . . by the "lower middle" class . . . without intense local difference (ex. "I ain't got none"); 5. local dialect, spoken by the least privileged class; . . . the varieties . . . often incomprehensible to each other and to speakers of 2–3–4 (ex. "a hae nane").[25]

Examples of the manner in which the speech habits of the linguistic centers and elites have been imposed on a variety of local dialects, and have thus brought about a sharper delimitation of language areas, have been cited from Romance philology, from the history of Dutch, and from the history of Serbian and Bulgarian.[26]

The history of China offers a striking example of the interplay of the geographic distribution of fertile land, waterways, and settlement patterns on the one hand with early language centers and later patterns of linguistic integration and differentiation on the other. Standard Mandarin Chinese as well as its related spoken dialects seem to have been derived from the language of the populous Northwest, which was settled early and connected by relatively efficient transport facilities with other parts of China. The separate spoken dialect or language of the Canton region developed in an area which was well connected internally, but marked off in just these respects from most of the rest of the country.[27] The maps of Figs. 4 through 8 may help to tell the story by showing a comparison of present dialect areas and river communications with earlier densities of settlement.

Language is preserved by special techniques and institutions: language standards, grammars, dictionaries, schools, printing, and radio.

Yet it continues to change. Where a previous community of intercourse has ceased to exist, a formerly common language will slowly
develop into increasingly different dialects which may in the end

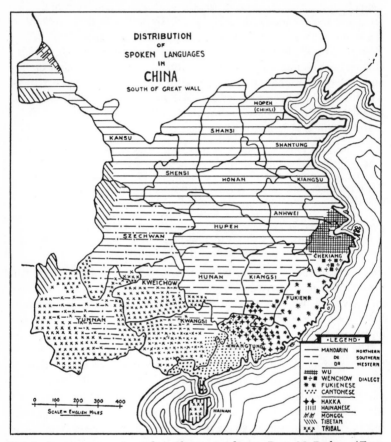

Fig. 4. Language areas in modern China, according to Percy M. Roxby. (From
"China as an Entity," *Geography*, March 1934, pp. 1–20. Reproduced by permission.) Note the concentration of the Cantonese and Wu dialects, and the wide
spread of Mandarin Chinese.

become mutually incomprehensible. Language communities are
therefore bounded by barriers of dialect and language, geographically
between regions, sociologically between strata, and historically in time.
Attempts have been made to grade the effectiveness of language
barriers to communication.[28]

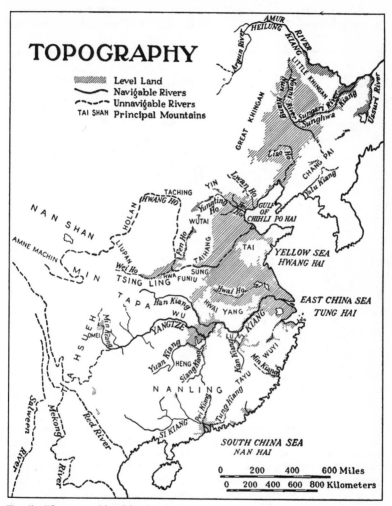

Fig. 5. The areas of level land and navigable rivers in China, according to George B. Cressey. (From *China's Geographic Foundations,* New York, McGraw-Hill, 1934, p. 40. Reproduced by permission.) Note the area of level land linking the lower part of the Hwang Ho and Yangtze River valleys; the separate river system of Southern China; and their partial correspondence, respectively, to the areas of Mandarin and Cantonese speech.

Several different standard languages may belong to a *language family*, although this has little practical effect on communication between the more remote members of such families. A "world language" has

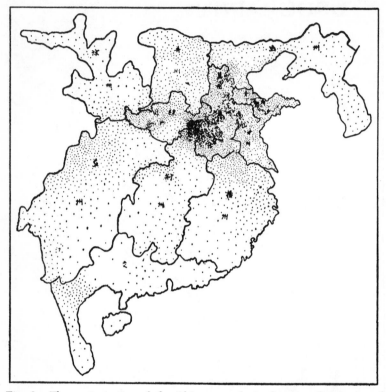

Fig. 6. The concentration of the Chinese people in the past; distribution of population according to the census of A.D. 2 ("Former" or "Western" Han). Each dot represents 10,000 persons. (From Percy M. Roxby, "China as an Entity," *Geography*, March 1934. Reproduced by permission.) Note the population cluster in today's Mandarin-speaking area.

been often proposed, and actual languages for specialized types of communication over entire cultural areas have existed in the past, such as Latin or Church Slavic. In the most successful case of such unification, that of the Arabic-speaking peoples, the original "foreign" language eventually has been adopted by the descendants of a number of "non-Arab" peoples in North Africa and the Near East.

Markets, Mobility, and Monopolistic Competition

Where other specialists look for settlement patterns or social institutions, the analytical economist might look for *markets*. A market

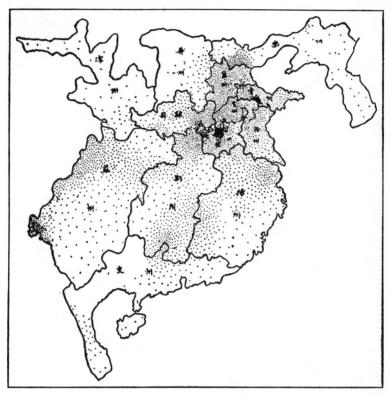

Fig. 7. Five generations later—the spread into Central and Western China; distribution of population according to the census of A.D. 140 ("Latter" or "Eastern" Han). Each dot represents 10,000 persons. (According to Percy M. Roxby, "China as an Entity," *Geography*, March 1934. Reproduced by permission.) Note the scarcity of population in the Cantonese area.

for each individual seller of a commodity is the collection of all buyers whose effective demand is relevant for the sales price and sales volume of that commodity; for each buyer of a commodity, a market is the collection of all sellers whose offers are relevant for the price and volume of his purchases of that commodity.[29] A *commodity* in

this sense is a salable good "bounded on all sides by a marked gap
between itself and its closest substitutes." [30]   To the extent that the

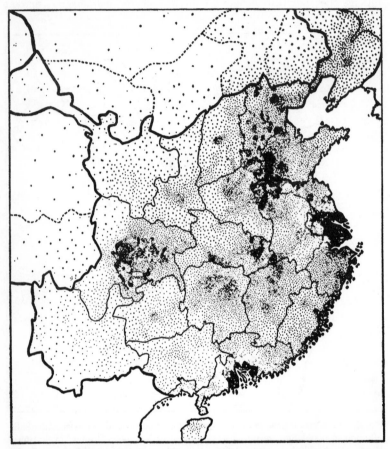

Fig. 8. The distribution of population in modern China. Each dot represents
25,000 persons. (According to Percy M. Roxby, "China as an Entity," *Geography*,
March 1934. Reproduced by permission.) Note the continuing concentration
in the northeast and the new clusters in the South and West. Note also the
connection between the Western and North-Eastern clusters by the Yangtze River
valley (cf. Fig. 5), and their common membership in the Mandarin speech area.

individual markets and commodities of economic theory overlap, they
cluster together to form the *market areas* of the economic geographer
and the economic historian.

Goods, services, and parts of nature such as land all may function as commodities if they are *for sale*. But they can only be for sale in the context of certain kinds of cultural habits and social institutions. Where no such things are for sale, or very few kinds only, as in a precommercial culture, there will be no markets, or only relatively unimportant ones. To create a national market under these conditions may require the destruction of precommercial habits of production and consumption and their replacement by new economic institutions such as new types of property rights, and new culture patterns such as factory-made clothes. Such a process has characteristically occurred in the rise of modern national states in many parts of the world. A decisive step towards later social and national mass conflicts occurred when *land* and *labor* were separated from their precommercial social contexts and turned into commodities.[31]

On this cultural and institutional basis, markets function through *differences in factor equipment* between groups of persons in the same region, or between inhabitants of different regions. By the brief term "factor equipment" is meant the conditions of supply of capital, land, labor, skills, and all other factors of production. Being unevenly supplied with such factors of production, some persons and regions will prove relatively best equipped—having a "comparative advantage"—for making one kind of commodity, and others may find themselves, at worst, relatively least badly equipped to produce another kind. If some of the *factors* of production are *relatively immobile*, because of their nature, such as a mineral deposit, or because of transportation costs at that time and place; and if at the same time their *products* are relatively *mobile*, then that kind of trade should follow which economists have described in terms of their "Law of Comparative Advantage."[32]

Any more extended trade usually will imply a *market center*, as well as a center of *credit* and *currency*. In a large market, this center will attract considerable service industries providing commodities which cannot be transported far, and thus may become surrounded by a *metropolitan region*. If the supply of credit and currency should become increasingly important for the volume and stability of trade, and if this monetary supply should be thought of as subject to management, rather than as being fixed as if by a law of nature, then the population of this market area and metropolitan region are apt to conclude that this monetary supply vital to their area should be managed from within their area, and not from any "world banking center" or automatic gold standard from without. To the extent that they have experienced difficulties with the volume of credit in the course of the business cycle, this trend to "monetary nationalism" is apt to grow stronger.

Markets are bounded by discontinuities in transportation, and more sharply by national currencies, tariffs, quotas, exchange-control measures, and the like. Even within the same currency and customs area, however, barriers to the mobility of customers and goods may be quite effective. Where there are such barriers there usually is a basis for monopolistic competition.[33]

Where markets can be thus separated, sellers or buyers may reap monopolistic gains by deliberate concerted action, or without step-by-step reasoning, by adopting such "traditions," cultural "myths," "emotions" or "prejudices" as will have the same economic effect. In this event, these practices may become "prosperity policies" for the discriminating group, and "irrational" cultural preferences and the "rational" experiences of economic gain will reinforce each other.[34] The separate markets in all these cases may become subject to *price discrimination,* in proportion to the relative urgency and inflexibility ("inelasticity") of the demand in each market. The result is something like a *stratification* of markets: "the sub-markets will be arranged in ascending order of their elasticities, the highest price being charged in the least elastic market," [35] and the buyers there will be relatively worse off. Given enough monopolistic elements, this pattern may well occur in the economic relationships of metropolis to province, or of a key area to its hinterland, or of a group of people acting in greater concert and with greater bargaining power in their trade with their neighbors.

Currency, customs, and related controls are major bounding factors between "domestic" and "foreign" trade. Yet several states with their national currencies may be linked by a markedly larger and steadier volume of trade, or by easier movements of capital, or labor, or easier transfer of currencies, so as to comprise formal or informal *"economic blocs,"* such as the "sterling area" of the 1940's. Finally, there is world trade, and it is possible to some extent to speak of a world economy.

Markets are bounded not merely geographically, by discontinuities in transportation, customs, or currency areas, but also in other dimensions, by discontinuities in the chains of substitutes for any one commodity, and by discontinuities in their conditions of supply, that is, in the ease with which additional supplies can be obtained, in the prices that have to be paid for larger volumes, and in the dependence of supplies on changes in other circumstances.

To the extent that different commodities are often joint products of the same technological process, or confer external economies on each other's production, they form something like *clusters* of commodities produced in some particular area in more or less close association with each other. In these cases, often some *key commodities* will stand out as leading products for domestic or foreign trade; their sales may significantly influence the money supply, factor employment, capital investment, and general prosperity for this particular area.[36]

This situation may involve a stratification of factors of production. To the extent that these key commodities have been produced by the cooperation of other industries and factors in the region, these, too, will be linked more closely to this cluster of economic activities, and the outside demand for the leading product will have the effect of a *joint demand* for the factors of the whole cluster or region. If so, then the *largest part of the benefits* from any increase in this joint demand will go *to those factors of production* which can be *least easily increased in supply* (such as scarce land, or scarce capital, or highly skilled or organized labor) and the least benefits to those factors, like unskilled labor, which are most easily recruited.[37] Similar differential rewards from joint demand can be obtained by nationalistic or racial restrictions of a critical supply of labor. "A notable fact about farm labor in California," Carey McWilliams noted in 1939, "is the practice of employers to . . . establish different wage rates for each racial group, thus . . . keeping wages at the lowest possible point." [38] Some nationalistic restrictions of this kind, such as those on immigration to Australia, have been well known,[39] but it has been less widely realized how great the national differences in the wages of unskilled labor, as shown in Fig. 9, have become throughout the world.

On the demand side, there are *discontinuities in consumers' preferences* even within groups of commodities otherwise closely suited for substitution. We then may find a stratification of commodities; and the sellers of the preferred kinds may try to increase the difference in their favor by product variation or branding, and to manipulate the customers' preference still further by advertising. Again, these preferences may be linked to cultural or nationalistic divisions: colonizing powers may try to instill in peoples under their rule such preferences for their goods and services. Thus the French Government continued to press for a privileged position of the French language in the secondary and higher schools of Syria and Lebanon, after these latter areas had emerged as independent states in 1945, on the grounds of

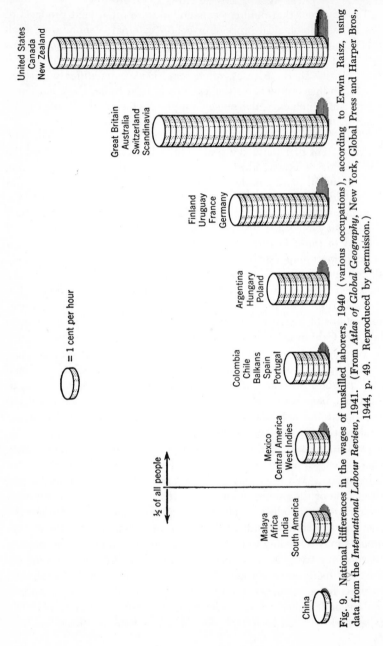

Fig. 9. National differences in the wages of unskilled laborers, 1940 (various occupations), according to Erwin Raisz, using data from the *International Labour Review*, 1941. (From *Atlas of Global Geography*, New York, Global Press and Harper Bros., 1944, p. 49. Reproduced by permission.)

= 1 cent per hour

½ of all people

United States
Canada
New Zealand

Great Britain
Australia
Switzerland
Scandinavia

Finland
Uruguay
France
Germany

Argentina
Hungary
Poland

Colombia
Chile
Balkans
Spain
Portugal

Mexico
Central America
West Indies

Malaya
Africa
India
South America

China

the economic and political disadvantages to France, if French should be replaced by English.

The uneven structure of markets and commodities applies strikingly to the *labor market,* both as to the supply of different kinds of labor and as to the demand for its services. There are barriers to geographical and occupational mobility: rigidity of habits, costs of moving, length and costs of training to gain skills. The strength of some of these occupational barriers has been stressed in the economists' theory of *non-competing groups of workers* who are not even potential substitutes for each other.[40]   Perhaps among these group two *key groups* stand out: the highly skilled workers and the mass of the white-collar workers; they are relatively protected from the entry of competitors by the requirements of training and schooling, but can themselves enter other fields of occupation if they choose, and while in their favored occupations, they furnish models for the aspiration of parents and youngsters in much broader strata to enter their ranks themselves or through their children. These favored groups of labor stand to gain if their own numbers remain small, by keeping off all human or mechanical *substitutes* for their services, and they stand to gain further from any increase of the number of workers or amount of equipment which might function as *complements* for their labor. The more sharply other groups of labor can be kept separated from them, by sex, language, citizenship, race, or color, so as *to be available as complements but not at all as substitutes,* so much the greater their advantage. To be sure, changes in technology may upset the particular pattern of substitution and complementarity of skills on which their advantage rests; but a nationalistic or racial separation, such as between jobs reserved for "white" and "colored" workers, respectively, has in some regions thus far survived a number of technological changes.

The relative gains of the most favored of the "non-competing groups" from the joint demand for their and their less favored fellows' services may be quite compatible with discriminating monopoly on the part of their employers, where these are united by agreement or custom. Where labor is divided into separate groups by effective barriers, each group can be treated as a separate source of labor, with its own elasticity of supply. As discriminating buyers of labor services, employers would then stand to gain by hiring somewhat less labor from the "most elastic" sources, that is, from those groups whose need for employment was most urgent, and to lower their wages below those offered to the other groups to a lower level than would correspond to any dif-

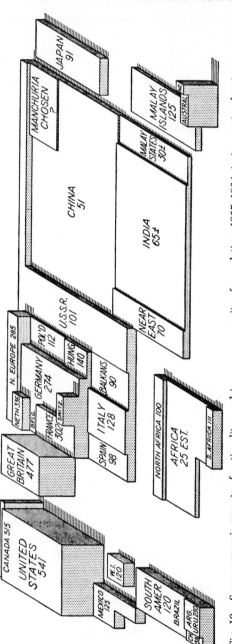

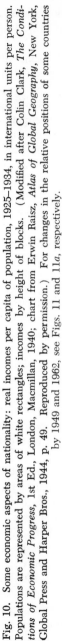

Fig. 10. Some economic aspects of nationality: real incomes per capita of population, 1925–1934, in international units per person. Populations are represented by areas of white rectangles; incomes by height of blocks. (Modified after Colin Clark, *The Conditions of Economic Progress*, 1st Ed, London, Macmillan, 1940; chart from Erwin Raisz, *Atlas of Global Geography*, New York, Global Press and Harper Bros, 1944, p. 49. Reproduced by permission.) For changes in the relative positions of some countries by 1949 and 1962, see Figs. 11 and 11*a*, respectively.

ferences in their relative efficiency. Folkways or mores bringing about such discrimination—such as the treatment of Oriental labor in Californian agriculture in the 1920's and 1930's—might thus "pay off" for significant numbers of employers and members of the most favored labor groups.[41]

Wealth, Capital Formation, and Factor Equipment

The economic analysis in the preceding section has been largely in terms of the theory of monopolistic competition, which emphasizes the fact that most goods and services in the world are not sold under the conditions of "pure competition" envisaged in old-fashioned economics textbooks, and that most buyers and sellers deal with limited markets, with partially differentiated goods and limited possibilities of substitution—in short, with a world in which partial monopoly and partial competition are inextricably blended, and in which buyers and sellers can gain from foreseeing the effects of their own decisions on the market, and from manipulating many of these markets to a limited extent by forming suitable economic or political organizations.

In terms of this monopolistic competition, we found a relative stratification of commodities and services in terms of monopolistic competition. Clusters of commodities are linked together by relatively easier possibilities of mutual substitution. Finally, the aggregate of *all* commodities for sale in an economy forms perhaps a meaningful concept. It corresponds to *wealth,* or generalized purchasing power. By this aggregate we can measure the "wealth" of a man or a country: by the total range of goods and services that are for sale, and by the percentage share of the total which this man or country can command. This applies particularly to modern private enterprise economies and some of the motive patterns found in them.

More generally, *wealth* could be viewed as the aggregate of goods and services *available for reallocation,* whether by buying and selling, by custom, by governmental planning, or by any combination of methods.[42]

The available wealth of an economy may grow or shrink in time. It will depend not so much on putting up existing objects for sale, but mainly by production. This in turn in an industrial age depends on *investment.* Investment functions through capital accumulation, the growth of inventions, and the decisions whether, where, and how to innovate. Investment is not continuous; it occurs in units given by the state of technology in terms of minimum or optimum plant size. It is located in space, unevenly, in patterns studied by the theory of

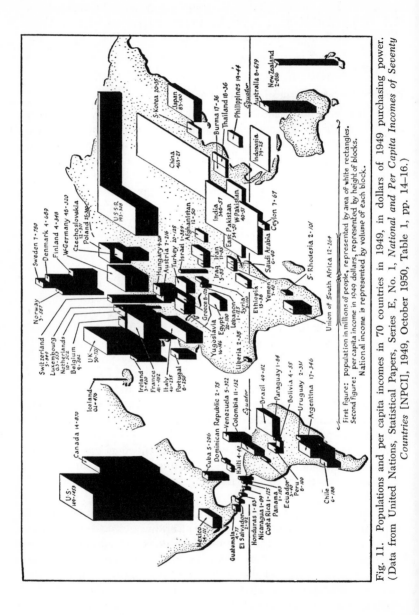

Fig. 11. Populations and per capita incomes in 70 countries in 1949, in dollars of 1949 purchasing power. (Data from United Nations, Statistical Papers, Series E, No. 1, *National and Per Capita Incomes of Seventy Countries* [NPCI], 1949, October 1950, Table 1, pp. 14–16.)

location, and remains to a considerable extent tied to its location by the specificity of some of the factors of production it has to use. In all this, there may stand out *key* industries and key locations, giving rise to conglomerations of industry. Since capital occurs unevenly in regions separated by barriers to the mobility of some of the other factors of production, the invested capital may under certain conditions function as a complement to these factors, increasing their rewards. This may be important for the level of real wages, and for the striking differential in national incomes and living standards between countries poor or rich in invested capital and productive equipment. The extent of these differences in terms of real income is represented somewhat inadequately for the period 1925–1934 in Fig. 10, and more realistically for 1949 and 1962 in Figs. 11 and 11a, respectively.

The present differences between the living standards, or the real incomes per capita of occupied population, in the United States on the one hand, and in much of Asia and Africa on the other, are of the order of one to ten; and the inequality of income distribution for the world as a whole in 1949 is approximately represented by the diagram in Fig. 12. The average differences in mere calories of daily food are of the order of one to two. An approximation to a world map of hunger, as published by the *New York Times* at the end of 1949, is reproduced in Fig. 13. Compared to the United States and less than a dozen similarly well-equipped countries, almost one-half of mankind is about twice as hungry and ten times as poor.[43]

These *differential living standards* have had much to do with the ever-growing barriers to the mobility of labor between different countries since about 1910, as well as with the nationalistic differences which kept them in conflict. There are industrial regions; there are areas of similar living standards; and we may speak of world industry; but there is thus far very little of a "world living standard," merely extreme differences between people.

There is some reason to suspect that the differences between the richest and the poorest populations of the world have been increasing in the years since 1920. The diagram of prewar real incomes between 1925 and 1934 in Fig. 10 shows a difference between the per capita incomes of China and of the United States of the order of one to ten. About twenty years later, after the war-caused devastation of China and the war-borne expansion of American industry, the corresponding United Nations figures for 1949 show a contrast between the two countries of the order of more than one to fifty. This fivefold increase in the spread between American and Chinese real incomes is matched,

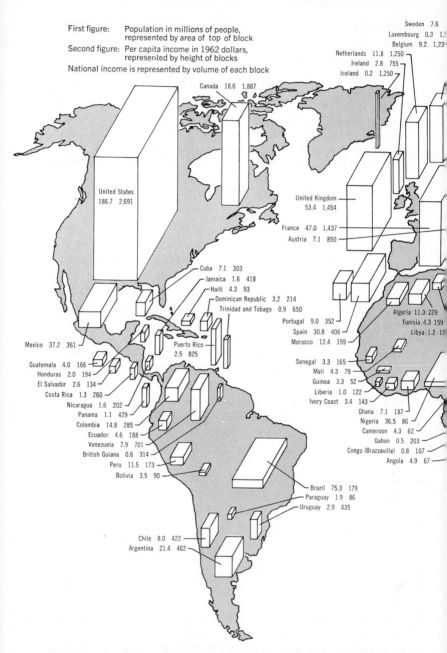

First figure: Population in millions of people, represented by area of top of block
Second figure: Per capita income in 1962 dollars, represented by height of blocks
National income is represented by volume of each block

Sweden 7.6
Luxembourg 0.3 1,
Belgium 9.2 1,23
Netherlands 11.8 1,250
Ireland 2.8 755
Iceland 0.2 1,250

Canada 18.6 1,887

United States 186.7 2,691

United Kingdom 53.4 1,454

France 47.0 1,437
Austria 7.1 850

Cuba 7.1 303
Jamaica 1.6 418
Haiti 4.3 93
Dominican Republic 3.2 214
Trinidad and Tobago 0.9 650
Portugal 9.0 352
Spain 30.8 406
Morocco 12.4 159

Algeria 11.3 229
Tunisia 4.3 159
Libya 1.2 18

Mexico 37.2 361
Puerto Rico 2.5 825

Guatemala 4.0 166
Honduras 2.0 194
El Salvador 2.6 134
Costa Rica 1.3 260
Nicaragua 1.6 202
Panama 1.1 429
Colombia 14.8 285
Ecuador 4.6 188
Venezuela 7.9 701
British Guiana 0.6 314
Peru 11.5 173
Bolivia 3.5 90

Senegal 3.3 165
Mali 4.3 79
Guinea 3.3 52
Liberia 1.0 122
Ivory Coast 3.4 143
Ghana 7.1 187
Nigeria 36.5 86
Cameroon 4.3 62
Gabon 0.5 203
Congo (Brazzaville) 0.8 107
Angola 4.9 67

Brazil 75.3 179
Paraguay 1.9 86
Uruguay 2.9 435

Chile 8.0 422
Argentina 21.4 462

Fig. 11a. Population and per capita income in 110 countries in 1962, in dollars of 1962 purchasing power. (Data principally from *United Nations Demographic Yearbook, 1963* and *United Nations Yearbook of National Accounts Statistics, 1963*.)

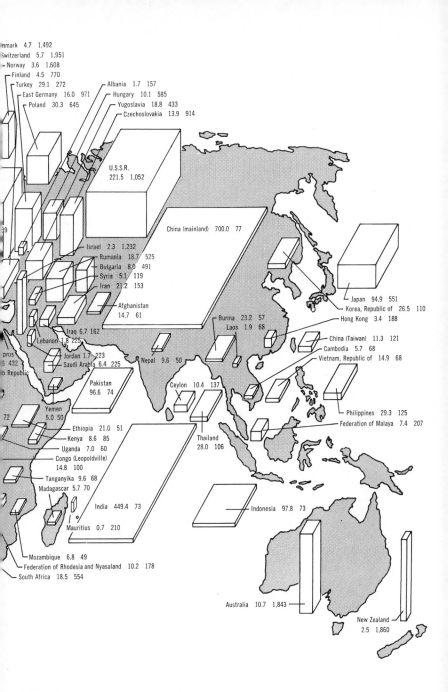

nmark 4.7 1,492
Switzerland 5.7 1,951
Norway 3.6 1,608
Finland 4.5 770
Turkey 29.1 272
East Germany 16.0 971
Poland 30.3 645

Albania 1.7 157
Hungary 10.1 585
Yugoslavia 18.8 433
Czechoslovakia 13.9 914

U.S.S.R.
221.5 1,052

China (mainland) 700.0 77

Israel 2.3 1,232
Rumania 18.7 525
Bulgaria 8.0 491
Syria 5.1 119
Iran 21.2 153

Afghanistan
14.7 61

Burma 23.2 57
Laos 1.9 68

Japan 94.9 551
Korea, Republic of 26.5 110
Hong Kong 3.4 188

China (Taiwan) 11.3 121
Cambodia 5.7 68
Vietnam, Republic of 14.9 68

Iraq 6.7 162
Lebanon 1.8 225
Jordan 1.7 223
Saudi Arabia 6.4 225

Nepal 9.6 50

prus
432
Republic

Pakistan
96.6 74

Ceylon 10.4 137

Philippines 29.3 125
Federation of Malaya 7.4 207

Yemen
5.0 50

Ethiopia 21.0 51
Kenya 8.6 85
Uganda 7.0 60
Congo (Leopoldville)
14.8 100
Tanganyika 9.6 68
Madagascar 5.7 70

Thailand
28.0 106

India 449.4 73

Mauritius 0.7 210

Indonesia 97.8 73

Mozambique 6.8 49
Federation of Rhodesia and Nyasaland 10.2 178
South Africa 18.5 554

Australia 10.7 1,843

New Zealand
2.5 1,860

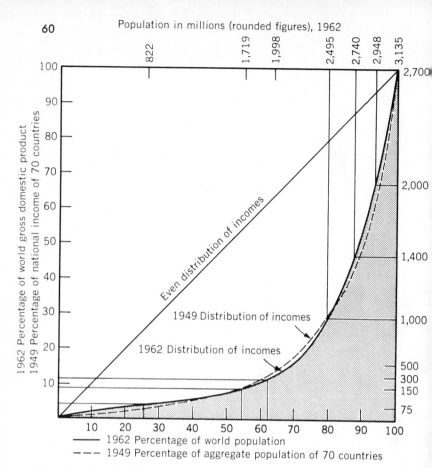

Fig. 12. The distribution of world income in the age of nationalism. Data from 141 countries, comprising 98 per cent of the world's population. (Source, as in Fig. 11, *United Nations Yearbook of National Accounts Statistics, 1963*, and *United Nations Demographic Yearbook, 1963*.)

The poorest 26 per cent of population lives in 36 countries, has 4 per cent of income. The poorest 55 per cent of population lives in 58 countries, has 9 per cent of income. The poorest 64 per cent of population lives in 91 countries, has 12 per cent of income. (See rectangles in lower left corner.)

The richest 6 per cent of population lives in 1 country, has 33 per cent of income. The richest 13 per cent of population lives in 12 countries, has 54 per cent of income. The richest 20 per cent of population lives in 17 countries, has 71 per cent of income. (See rectangles in upper right corner.)

Between these two groupings, 14 per cent of the population forms something like an "upper middle" group with 17 per cent of the total income. Countries in this group include East Germany, Czechoslovakia, Italy, Venezuela, Argentina, South Africa, and Japan.

In 1949 this "upper middle" group included the U.S.S.R., Israel, and West Germany, but by 1962 the U.S.S.R. and Israel had made their way into the richest to some extent, by the threefold increase of the spread between the real per capita incomes of India and the United States, from one to eight in 1925–1934 to more than one to twenty-five in 1949. By 1962, some seventeen years after World War II, the difference between Chinese and U.S. per capita incomes had been reduced from one in fifty in 1949 to one in thirty-five in 1962, largely as a result of the massive economic development programs of the Chinese Communist government. In regard to the gap between United States and mainland Chinese income levels, however, this still represented an increase of three- to fourfold over the pre-World War II figures. In the case of India — a non-Communist country — the one to eight pre-World War II contrast with the U.S. per capita income which had grown to one to twenty-five in 1949, widened still further to one to thirty-seven in 1962, an increase of between four- and fivefold since the prewar period. Although these exact figures should not be taken too seriously, since they are derived from a range of very different statistics, they do suggest a significant increase in the magnitude of international economic contrasts.

---

20 per cent of the world's population, and West Germany had joined the richest 13 per cent.

The Lorenz curve shown above gives an overall picture of the inequality of distribution of incomes in the world. The more curved such a line, the greater is the inequality. Since the curve gives a picture of the total amount of inequality among all countries, it is highly resistant to the effect of error in single countries, even in large ones.

The effects of possible errors of up to 20 per cent in estimates of gross domestic product for various countries are indicated in Fig. 26 of the Appendix.

If we examine the 1962 distribution curve in comparison with the 1949 curve, it becomes evident that in those countries where per capita income ranged between $80 and $1,000 in 1962, inequality in the distribution of incomes has actually increased since 1949. There is greater equality in those countries with per capita income above $1,000, and there has been a very slight increase in equality below the $80 per capita figure. The decrease in inequality above the $1,000 level is a somewhat more reliable statistic, since the countries involved were represented in both the 1949 and the 1962 U.N. figures, and their statistics are somewhat more developed. The apparent increase in equality for those below the $80 per capita figure, which comprise almost half of mankind, is less reliable, since many of these countries were not represented in the 1949 survey, and their statistics are less well developed.

The increased inequality in countries where income is between $80 and $1,000 per capita, which represent a little more than a third of mankind, deserves serious consideration. It should be regarded with caution so far as individual countries are concerned, but it is based on statistics from over 80 countries, and even substantial errors in the income figures for individual countries or group of countries would not appreciably alter the curve. (See Appendix, Fig. 26.)

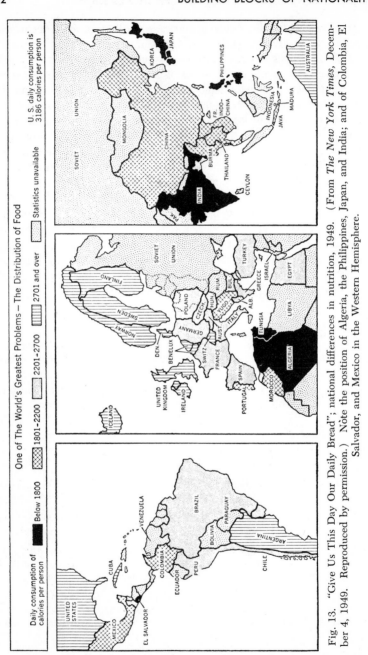

Fig. 13. "Give Us This Day Our Daily Bread"; national differences in nutrition, 1949. (From *The New York Times*, December 4, 1949. Reproduced by permission.) Note the position of Algeria, the Philippines, Japan, and India; and of Colombia, El Salvador, and Mexico in the Western Hemisphere.

If we try to speculate how large these contrasts may have been in 1900, or in 1850, or in 1800, we find that, as far as real per capita incomes are concerned, the peoples of Asia can hardly have been very far below the subsistence levels on which they are today. Even if we were to assume the almost incredible, that their real per capita incomes about 1850 were one-half their levels of today—even then we should have to face the obvious fact that American or West European real per capita incomes in 1850 were far less than one-half what they are today, and that in this respect the gap between the poorest and the richest regions of the world has not narrowed but widened. President Truman's "Point Four" program of economic assistance to under-developed countries, and the similiar aspirations expressed by Presidents Eisenhower, Kennedy, and Johnson, may thus involve the task of reversing the trend of a century.

However much or little reliance we wish to place on these considerations, a comparison between the prewar economic contrasts indicated by Fig. 10 and the postwar contrasts revealed by Fig. 11 should offer food for thought.

The Interdisciplinary Study of Specific Cases

All the concepts and techniques from the different disciplines we have just surveyed could be applied jointly to the study of concrete situations. If we were invited to investigate the prospects for the future national unity, let us say, of an independent Nigeria, we might try to map the basic settlement and traffic patterns, the areas of languages, dialects, and cultures, the effective market areas for major commodities and services, together with the areas of predominance of important social institutions, classes or castes, and the distribution of the major concentrations, if any, of capital goods, skills, and wealth.

The result might well be a map of overlapping clusters, together with indications of the volume of actual communication and traffic between them. The patterns of migration and mobility, the movements of students to school, the numbers of readers of newspapers and listeners to radios, the movements of workers seeking employment and of farmers going to market, as well as the main patterns of informal communication should eventually appear on such a map. The results of all these surveys together would not give us an answer about the future success or failure of political leaders or movements to unify Nigeria, but they would give us a background of conditions and a measure of the difficulties under which such movements would have to labor.

If we could thus survey some of the basic conditions for the future unity of Nigeria, then we could also survey by similar methods some of the conditions for the prospects of the unity of Western Europe, or, for another part of the world, for the unity of the Arab peoples. In all such situations the final decision would come from the realm of politics, but our surveys could help us to start out with a more detailed and realistic picture of the very uneven world in which politics must function.

Three Rank Orders of World Politics in 1962

The following three tables deal with population as a measure of human needs, gross domestic product as a measure of potential political power, and per capita gross domestic product as an indicator of human welfare.

All countries are listed which are among the 15 highest ranking states for at least one of these three variables. This gives a group of 28 countries, each of which leads in at least one of these aspects out of a total of 141 countries for which data were available. Together the 28 countries included in the tables comprised 75 per cent of world population and 89 per cent of world income in 1962.

In order to show changes in world politics from 1949 to 1962, the 1949 data have been added wherever possible. It should be noted that the changes in the percentage figures are more revealing than the changes in the absolute dollar amount of income since the dollar values reflect not only a real growth of world income but also a change in the value of the dollar.

In order to bring 1949 dollars up to the level of 1962 prices, they should be multiplied by a coefficient of 1.31. This figure is a coefficient which represents the average value in 1962 prices of that fraction of the U.S. gross national product which could have been bought for $1.00 in 1949. According to U.N. figures $1.00 bought in 1949 about as much as $1.31 did in 1962.

In studying the second of these tables, the rank order of potential power, the reader should note that the bipolar power system of the U.S. and the U.S.S.R. had held more than half of the world's potential power in 1949 (51 per cent) but in 1962 controlled only 48 per cent or less than half.

TABLE 2.1
A RANK ORDER OF HUMAN NEEDS
POPULATION

Rank No. 1962 Population	Population 1949 (In Thousands)	Per Cent of 1949 World Population[1]	Per Cent of 1949 U.S. Population	Population 1962 (In Thousands)	Per Cent of 1962 World Population[2]	Per Cent of 1962 U.S. Population	Net Change In Per Cent of World Population 1949–1962	Net Change In Per Cent of U.S. Population 1949–1962
1. China (mainland)	463,493[3]	20	311	700,000[4]	22	375	+2	+64
2. India	346,000[5]	15	232	449,381	14	241	−1	+9
3. U.S.S.R.	193,000	8	129	221,465	7	119	−1	−10
4. United States	149,215	6	100	186,656	6	100	0	0
5. Indonesia	79,260[3]	3	53	97,765	3	52	0	−1
6. Pakistan	73,855	3	49	96,558	3	52	0	+3
7. Japan	82,636	4	55	94,930	3	51	−1	−4
8. Brazil	49,340	2	33	75,271	2	40	0	+7
9. West Germany	47,585	2	32	54,061	2	29	0	−3
10. United Kingdom	50,363	2	34	53,441	2	29	0	−5
11. Italy	45,996	2	31	50,170	2	27	0	−4
12. France	41,180	2	28	46,998	2	25	0	−3
13. Mexico	24,448	1	16	37,233	1	20	0	+4
14. Nigeria	—	—	—	36,475	1	20	—	—
15. Spain	—	—	—	30,817	1	17	—	—
16. Poland	24,500	1	16	30,324	1	16	0	0
28. Canada	13,549	0.6	9	18,600	0.6	10	0	+1
30. East Germany	—	—	—	16,044	0.5	9	—	—

TABLE 2.1 (Continued)

	Population 1949 (In Thousands)	World Population[1] Per Cent of 1949	U.S. Population Per Cent of 1949	Population 1962 (In Thousands)	World Population[2] Per Cent of 1962	U.S. Population Per Cent of 1962	Net Change In Per Cent of World Population 1949-1962	Net Change In Per Cent of U.S. Population 1949-1962
38. Netherlands	9,956	0.4	7	11,797	0.4	6	0	− 1
42. Australia	7,912[5]	0.3	5	10,705	0.3	6	0	+ 1
48. Belgium	8,614	0.4	6	9,221	0.3	5	−0.1	− 1
55. Sweden	6,956	0.3	5	7,562	0.2	4	−0.1	− 1
66. Switzerland	4,640	0.2	3	5,660	0.2	3	0	0
70. Denmark	4,230	0.2	3	4,654	0.1	2	−0.1	− 1
79. Norway	3,233	0.1	2	3,639	0.1	2	0	0
93. New Zealand	1,881[6]	0.1	1	2,485	0.08	1	−0.2	0
133. Luxembourg	295	0.01	0.2	322	0.01	0.2	0	0
141. Iceland	139	0.01	0.09	182	0.01	0.1	0	+ 0.01

1. World population, 1949: 2,378 million. Source: U.N. Demographic Yearbook, 1949–1950, p. 10.
2. World population, 1962: 3,135 million. Source: U.N. Demographic Yearbook, 1963, p. 142.
3. Rough estimate.
4. For assistance in arriving at these figures I am indebted to Professor Alexander Eckstein, whose forthcoming book on China will be published in the winter of 1965–1966.
5. 1948–1949.
6. 1949–1950.

Sources: 1962 figures: U.N. Demographic Yearbook, 1963.
1949 figures: Statistical Office of the United Nations, Statistical Papers, Series E, No. 1, "National and Per Capita Incomes, Seventy Countries — 1949" (New York, October 1950).

TABLE 2.2

A RANK ORDER OF POTENTIAL POWER*

THE INCOME OF NATIONS

Rank No. 1962 GNP	1949 National Income[1] (In Million $ U.S.)	Per Cent of World[2] National Income 1949	Per Cent of U.S. National Income 1949	1962 Total GNP[3] (In Million $ U.S.)	1962 Total GDP[1] (In Million $ U.S.)	Per Cent of 1962 World GDP	Per Cent of 1962 GDP of U.S.	Net Change in Per Cent of Income of World, 1949–1962[4]	Net Change in Per Cent of Income of U.S., 1949–1962[4]
1. United States	216,831	40	100	556,190	502,187	33	100	−7	0
2. U.S.S.R.[5]	59,500	11	27	256,300	233,000[6]	15	46	+4	+19
3. West Germany[7]	15,300	3	7	89,425	77,229	5	15	+2	+8
4. United Kingdom	38,922	7	18	89,120	77,724	5	15	−2	−3
5. France	19,857	4	9	79,225	67,552	4	13	0	+4
6. China (mainland)	12,384	2	6	59,500[8]	54,091[6]	4	11	+2	+5
7. Japan	8,260	2	4	56,173	52,315	3	10	+1	+6
8. Italy	10,800	2	5	52,597	45,985	3	9	+1	+4
9. Canada	11,797	2	5	39,414	35,090	2	7	0	+2
10. India	19,572	4	9	—	33,183	2	7	−2	−2
11. Poland	7,344	1	3	21,500	19,545[6]	1	4	0	+1
12. Australia	5,374[9]	1	2	18,979	17,212	1	3	0	+1
13. East Germany	—	—	—	17,135	15,577[6]	1	3	—	—
14. Netherlands	5,000	0.9	2	16,371	14,746	1	3	+0.1	+1
15. Sweden	5,426	1	3	15,664	13,863	0.9	3	−0.1	0
16. Mexico	2,960	0.5	1	—	13,454	0.9	3	+0.4	+2
17. Brazil	5,530	1	3	15,354[10]	13,118[10]	0.9	3	−0.1	0
19. Spain	—	—	—	13,476[11]	12,516[11]	0.8	2	—	—

TABLE 2.2 (Continued)

Rank No. 1962 GNP	National Income 1949[1] (In Million $ U.S.)	Per Cent of World[2] National Income 1949	Per Cent of U.S. National Income 1949	1962 Total GNP[3] (In Million $ U.S.)	1962 Total GDP[1] (In Million $ U.S.)	Per Cent of World GDP 1962	Per Cent of GDP of U.S. 1962	Net Change in Per Cent of Income of World, 1949–1962[4]	Net Change in Per Cent of Income of U.S., 1949–1962[4]
20. Belgium	5,015	0.9	2	12,999	11,428	0.7	2	-0.2	0
21. Switzerland	3,940	0.7	2	11,890	11,043	0.7	2	0	0
27. Pakistan	3,760	0.7	2	—	7,043[10]	0.5	1	-0.2	-1
28. Indonesia	2,000	0.4	0.9	—	7,024[10]	0.5	1	+0.1	+0.1
29. Denmark	2,908	0.5	1	7,902	6,945	0.5	1	0	0
32. Norway	1,898	0.4	0.9	6,462	5,852	0.4	1	0	+0.1
34. New Zealand	1,610[12]	0.3	0.7	4.869	4,623	0.3	0.9	0	+0.2
44. Nigeria		—	—	—	3,078	0.2	0.6	—	—
80. Luxembourg	162	0.03	0.07	522[10]	489[10]	0.03	0.1	0	+0.03
103. Iceland	66	0.01	0.03	262[13]	228[13]	0.01	0.05	0	+0.02

* Power is considered to be potential rather than actual because actual power depends upon the desire of the country to buy guns or butter. The countries at the top of this list do, however, have more choice than others.

1. National income is "the sum of the incomes accruing to factors of production supplied by normal residents of the given country before deduction of direct taxes." It is equal to "the value at factor cost of [the goods and services produced], after deduction of provisions for the consumption of fixed capital, attributable to the factors of production supplied by normal residents of the country."

Gross domestic product at factor cost is defined by the U.N. as follows: "the value at factor cost of the [total value of the goods and services of a country], before deduction of provisions for the consumption of fixed capital, attributable to factor services rendered to resident producers of the given country." It differs from gross national product at market prices by "the exclusion of net factor incomes received from abroad" and by the exclusion of "the excess of indirect taxes over subsidies." (*U.N. Yearbook of National Accounts Statistics, 1963*, p. xi.)

2. 1949 world national income is estimated at $540,298 million,

5.30 per cent above the national income of the 70 countries used in the U.N. study. The calculation is based on the ratio between GDP for these countries and for the rest of the world in 1962.

3. Gross national product at market prices. This is defined by the U.N. as follows: "the market value of the [total goods and services produced] before deduction of provisions for the consumption of fixed capital, attributable to the factors of production supplied by normal residents of the given country. It is identically equal to the sum of consumption expenditure and gross domestic capital formation, private and public, and the net exports of goods and services plus the net factor incomes received from abroad." (*Ibid.*)

4. These figures are based on a comparison between 1949 national income figures and 1962 GDP figures. For most countries the difference between national income and GDP should be slight, but for particular countries deriving a high percentage of their income from abroad this could understate their 1962 national income. The figures, even though inexact, however, do indicate relative orders of magnitude of considerable interest.

5. Source: U.S. Congress, Joint Economic Committee, "Annual Economic Indicators for the USSR," February 1964, Washington, U.S. Government Printing Office, 1964, p. 96.

6. Calculation based on the assumption that the GNP is approximately 10 per cent above the GDP.

7. Includes the Saar, and excludes West Berlin.

8. For assistance in arriving at these figures I am indebted to Professor Alexander Eckstein, whose forthcoming book on China will be published in the winter of 1965–1966.

9. 1948–1949.

10. 1961.

11. GDP figures were obtained by projecting the 1953–1958 growth rate to 1962.

12. 1949–1950.

13. These figures, from the *U.N. Yearbook of National Accounts Statistics, 1963,* were calculated by the U.N. by converting GDP figures in local currencies by the prevailing dollar exchange rates, rather than the parity rates used for the other GDP figures in the table. (See below, under Sources.)

Sources: Except where otherwise noted, all dollar figures for gross domestic product are from the *United Nations Yearbook of National Accounts Statistics, 1963.* These figures are based on official GDP figures in national currencies from the international tables of the Yearbook. They are converted into U.S. dollars by means of calculated parity rates, estimated by adjusting the official or free market exchange rates in 1958 to the year in question, between the U.S. and the country concerned.

TABLE 2.3
A RANK ORDER OF HUMAN WELFARE
PER CAPITA INCOME

Rank No. 1962 GDP	1949 Per Capita National Income (In $ U.S.)	Per Cent of U.S. per Capita National Income, 1949	1962 Per Capita GDP (In $ U.S.)	Per Cent of U.S. Per Capita GDP, 1962	Net Change in Per Cent of U.S. Income, 1949–1962*
1. United States	1,453	100	2,691	100	0
2. Switzerland	849	59	1,951	73	+14
3. Canada	870	60	1,887	70	+10
4. New Zealand	856[1]	59	1,860	69	+10
5. Sweden	780	54	1,833	68	+14
6. Norway	587	40	1,608	60	+20
7. Australia	679[2]	47	1,608	60	+13
8. Luxembourg	553	38	1,543[4]	57	+19
9. Denmark	689	47	1,492	55	+8
10. United Kingdom	773	53	1,454	54	+1
11. West Germany[3]	320	22	1,439	54	+32
12. France	482	33	1,437	53	+20
13. Iceland	476	33	1,250[5]	47	+14
14. Netherlands	502	35	1,250	47	+12
15. Belgium	582	40	1,239	46	+6
17. U.S.S.R.	308	21	1,052[6]	39	+18
18. East Germany	—	—	971[7]	36	—
20. Italy	235	16	917	34	+18

Rank No. 1962 GDP	1949 Per Capita National Income (In $ U.S.)	Per Cent of U.S., per Capita National Income, 1949	1962 Per Capita GDP (In $ U.S.)	Per Cent of U.S. Per Capita GDP, 1962	Net Change in Per Cent of U.S. Income, 1949–1962
25. Poland	300	21	645[7]	24	+ 3
31. Japan	100	7	551	21	+14
40. Spain	—	—	406[8]	15	—
43. Mexico	121	8	361	13	+ 5
73. Brazil	112	8	179[4]	7	– 1
98. Nigeria	—	—	86[4]	3	—
104. China (mainland)	27	2	77[7,9]	3	+ 1
106. Pakistan	51	4	74[4]	3	– 1
107. India	57[2]	4	73	3	– 1
108. Indonesia	25	2	73[4]	3	+ 1

* These figures are based on a comparison between 1949 per capita national income figures and 1962 per capita GDP figures. For most countries the difference between national income and GDP figures should be slight, but for particular countries deriving a high percentage of their income abroad, this comparison could understate their 1962 national income. The figures, even though inexact, however, do indicate an order of magnitude of some interest.

1. 1949–1950.
2. 1948–1949.
3. Includes the Saar; excludes West Berlin.
4. 1961.
5. These figures, from the *U.N. Yearbook of National Accounts Statistics, 1963*, were calculated by the U.N. by converting GDP figures in local currencies by the prevailing dollar exchange rates, rather than the parity rates used for the other GDP figures in the table. (See below, under Sources.)
6. Source: U.S. Congress, Joint Economic Committee, "Annual

Economic Indicators for the USSR," February 1964, Washington, U.S. Government Printing Office, 1964, p. 96.
7. Calculation based on the assumption that the GNP is approximately 10 per cent above the GDP.
8. GDP figures were obtained by projecting the 1953–1958 growth rate to 1962.
9. For assistance in arriving at these figures I am indebted to Professor Alexander Eckstein, whose forthcoming book on China will be published in the winter of 1965–1966.

Sources: Except where otherwise noted all dollar figures for per capita gross domestic product are from the *United Nations Yearbook of National Accounts Statistics, 1963*. These figures are based on official GDP figures in national currencies from the international tables of the Yearbook. They are converted into U.S. dollars by means of calculated parity rates, estimated by adjusting the official or free market exchange rates in 1938 to the year in question, between the U.S. and the country concerned.

Chapter 3
<hr>

Sovereignty and Politics
CENTERS AND AREAS OF POWER

Politics, in the style of a "hardboiled" school of thought, has been viewed as the production, use, and reproduction of power over men, and we shall set out by making provisional use of this notion which we shall later have occasion to revise.

Such power over men is related in some respects to power over nature, since power over nature—economic and technological progress —requires manpower and equipment which power over men can sometimes mobilize. Growing power over nature—increases in productive capacity, land, equipment, scientific and technological knowledge—may then furnish the resources for exercising greater power over men. In fact, these two types of power have fed on each other in Western Civilization since the Middle Ages. Since then, they have given our civilization that unceasing power drive which contrasts so strongly with the trends predominating in many other cultures. Yet it is primarily in so far as it changes the opportunities for exercising power over men that economic, scientific, or technological growth is of political importance.[1]

A Provisional View of Power

Power, in all its forms, has certain characteristics in common. In all cases, it seems, it occurs in situations of interaction between two or more systems of partly different inner structures which are in part incompatible with each other. Individuals, social groups or organizations, or even complex biological or physical processes all have such inner structures, such as the self-reproducing pattern of a flame or a whirlwind, the biological pattern of a living cell, and the psychological or cultural patterns of memories, traditions, and values—acquired preferences—of human beings. Often, when two such structures interact, one or the other cannot be preserved. Thus, wet logs in a fire cool the flames which touch them. Which pattern will endure, that of the fire or that of the logs? We say that wet logs will put out a "weak" fire but will feed a "strong" one. Our estimate of their relative "strength" and "weakness"—their relative power—is derived from the probable outcome of their interaction. We might say, then, that power consists in the probability of preserving the inner structure of one of the systems in a clash, with little or no relevant modification, at the price of bringing about relatively large modifications in the structure of the systems which clash with it.

In other words, power consists in accepting the least amount of non-autonomous change in one system while producing the largest amount of non-autonomous change in another. In human relations, we may speak of some men or groups of men "imposing their will" on others. More generally, we may speak of power as the ability of preserving order in one system by imposing relative disorder on others. In terms of the theory of communications, we might call power the capacity to preserve negative entropy in a limited part of the universe by increasing positive entropy elsewhere.[2]

If this sounds unfamiliar, the point may bear elaboration. In all situations in which we use the word "power" we are referring to the ability or probability of preserving some pattern, structure, or arrangement, or of continuing and bringing out some additional arrangements already implied, at least in part, in its present workings. From an operational point of view, "power" always refers to the preservation, continuation, or elaboration of such limited existing patterns of relative order, and it is by identifying such patterns and observing or predicting the extent of their persistence or continuation that meaningful statements about power can be made.

The concept of power, in short, always involves the concept of order. But there is no operation by which "absolute" order or "absolute" disorder can be tested, and it seems debatable whether these absolute concepts have meaning. All operations by which order can be tested involve the operation of matching; they can only be applied to limited systems; and the order they reveal is limited and relative. Situations of "strength," "hardness," or "power" then arise, where two or more systems of such limited, relative order have come into contact, when they are similar enough to interact yet different enough to be at least partly incompatible with each other. In these situations, then, arise the age-old questions of life and politics: "Who conquers whom?" "Who must give in?" "What must give way?"

If the two clashing systems are dynamic systems, if they are processes in nature or society, then each of them has a probable future in terms of the present disposition of its elements and resources. Each dynamic system is at any moment, at least to some extent, a program of its own potential future.[3]

When such systems clash, their futures clash and are modified more or less in the outcome. The old questions then can be restated: "Which potential future will reach fulfilment?" "Which future will be thwarted?" "Which future must give way?"

Where such systems finally involve patterns of symbols, values, thoughts and dreams, where we find a clash of minds, personalities, or groups of persons, there the questions read: "Which values will be overridden?" "Which dreams will go?" "Which hopes and habits will survive?"

The Need for a Broader Concept of Power

What we have sketched so far has been the narrowest and most general notion of power. In one sense it is true, but it is only partly true. Carried to extremes it will ring hollow, in formulations that border on insanity. "How does one man assert his power over another?" asks a protagonist in a recent novel. ". . . By making him suffer. Obedience is not enough. Unless he is suffering, how can you be sure that he is obeying your will and not his own? Power is in inflicting pain and humiliation. Power is in tearing human minds to pieces and putting them together again in new shapes of your own choosing." [4]

Such statements are expressions of pathology, not analyses of politics.[5] They illustrate a state of mind, a state of disgust, boredom, inner fear, and desperation; they illustrate a danger of our times, without any understanding of its limits or conditions.

No viable political movement could be built and long kept together on such principles. On the contrary, as a recent writer on the subject has remarked, "power . . . wins its title to be legitimate only by conforming to what is in the general view the legitimate form of Power; it wins its title to be beneficent only by making its ends conform to those which men in general esteem; . . . its only strength is, at any rate in most cases, the strength which men think it their duty to lend to it." [6]

Problems of power, it appears, cannot be solved in narrow power terms alone. The "hardboiled" definition of politics which we provisionally used at the outset of this section must now be amended. Politics, we may suggest on second thoughts, consists in such production, use, and distribution of power as will prove compatible with social inclusiveness and growth beyond the narrow power field alone. That social group or structure has most strength, we may now say, which can undergo the widest range of changes without losing its cohesion in a few essentials, so as to be able to include other patterns and structures within itself without losing its identity or its continued capacity for growth.

Why, then, has so much of political power—both narrow persuasion or coercion, and wider change and growth—thus far remained limited to ethnic, regional, or national units?

Memories and Preferences: The Distribution of the Inner Sources of Power

The answer should perhaps be clear. Even the narrowest kind of power over men requires two things: first, the assembly of an effective inner structure, an effective past, within the individual or group; and second, the assembly of means to carry into effect the implications of this inner structure, to impose them on institutions in the outside world. The first of these two requirements we sometimes speak of as the forming of a tradition, or the "forming of a political will." Of the second requirement we sometimes speak as the execution of a set of policies, or the execution of a will.

Both requirements for political power are based on concrete social and physical facilities which are unevenly distributed.

The inner source of political power—the relatively coherent and stable structure of memories, habits, and values—depends on existing facilities for social communication, both from the past to the present and between contemporaries. Such communication requires facilities for storing, recalling, and recombining information, channels for its dissemination and interaction, and facilities for deriving further information, as well as new changes in purposes and values, from these processes. Such facilities are, however, unevenly distributed. Towns, libraries, archives, telephone and railroad networks, school systems, broadcasting stations, language communities, settlement patterns, densities of economic intercourse—all these show the characteristic cluster distribution, with relatively crowded central areas separated by regions of relatively lower density. To be sure, the cluster distribution for almost each set of such channels varies from the others, so that settlement patterns do not correspond completely to language communities or to transportation charts. But these variations do not cancel out.

Many "pluralistic" writers on federalism or world government have suggested, it seems to me, that these clusters and connections would somehow cancel out. If every man could be made a citizen or member of sufficiently many overlapping groups or units of government, such as towns, regions, states, churches, or labor unions, they seem to say, then he would no longer be swayed by any one group of interests or loyalties, and he would thus no longer be tempted either to use the power of a federal or world-wide government for the interests of "his own" group against others, or else to oppose such a government as "alien" to his concerns. Such an abolition of separate loyalties through their dispersion may succeed under very special circumstances, but in the world at large there seems at present very little evidence to promise such an outcome. In the world of stubborn facts, the result of the uneven distribution of many overlapping clusters of communication facilities is not an even distribution, but still one very uneven *distribution of overall social communication,* even though this overall unevenness differs somewhat from the unevenness of every single set of facilities which went into its making.

Thus the moderate extent of unevenness among the American colonies could be bridged by federation, and class and sectional differences served to counterbalance each other, as James Madison had foreseen in the Tenth Federalist letter; but the considerable gaps in communication between the United States and Canada or Mexico have not been bridged by federal institutions to this day, and the bridging of the corresponding gap between the United States and India or China seems a long time away.

Nor could these unevenly distributed communication clusters be incorporated easily into some one pattern of empire. For this unevenness is neither so simple as to be symmetrical, nor is it organized around one single center.

This cluster distribution is made even more discontinuous by differences between different clusters as to their inner social structure. Particular political groups or social classes might exercise great influence in one cluster but have little or no power in another. Large landowners lost most of their power in the North after the American Revolution; but large landowners were still very influential in the South at the beginning of the Civil War. Jacobins were the rulers of France in 1793, but they and their doctrines were abhorred in the leading circles of the contemporary monarchies of Europe. In our own time, the difference between the social groups and political ideologies which predominate in different parts of the world have perhaps become sharper than ever. Yet it seems clear that the character of the ruling social group or ideology can do much, in time, to shape the patterns of the underlying community and the thoughts of its members.

For all these reasons, there is not, and there cannot be, at this time, one single "body politic" for all mankind—to borrow a term recently used again by Jacques Maritain [7]—nor could such a world-wide "body politic" now be created by political means. Nor would it be possible, therefore, to erect a world state—a world-wide instrument of enforcement—without having this machinery of enforcement (these international generals, ministers, and bomber pilots) very soon lose contact with the large masses of mankind. The result would be a superstate "supreme *separately* from, and *above,* the whole" of all the diverse peoples ruled by it—that is, a superstate characterized by what Jacques Maritain has considered the extreme features of absolute sovereignty.[8] The power of such a world state would be rudderless. It would be power without sustenance or direction, like the drifting armies of declining Rome. This would be true even if it could maintain cohesion, for any length of time, among its own soldiers and statesmen, and if it could enforce its decisions everywhere on earth.

The Distribution of Opportunities for Enforcement or Persuasion

Actually, such a state would not be able to enforce its decisions. Just as the sources of every political decision are unevenly distributed, so is the range and effectiveness of the means of executing it. Power is exercised by force or persuasion. Force may be applied directly, as destruction, violence, or their threat; or indirectly, as the withholding of economic necessities, or the withholding of knowledge. None of these forms of force, either singly or in combination, is uniformly effective in the world today, nor is their coercive effectiveness increasing.

Spheres of relatively greater or lesser effectiveness of coercive power are not a mere invention of statesmen. They are an empirical fact. Coercive power is effective in regions near its sources, or against minor centers of social organization. It is ineffective or unpredictable over extreme distances or against major aggregations of mankind. It may, at most, destroy, but it cannot compel, and it cannot govern.

What is true of the limits of power to coerce seems equally true of the power to persuade, as well as of the wider ability of politics to relate, to include, to organize. All these powers or abilities depend on existing social structures and facilities of communication. Persuasion requires not merely facilities to spread information, and to influence its composition—such facilities, such as the media of mass communication are quite unevenly distributed—but it requires most of all a susceptible public.

To be susceptible to persuasion, men must already be inwardly divided in their thought. There must be some incompatibilities in the facts they remember, or in the facts they can be induced to accept. There must be some contradictions, actual or implied, among their habits or values. In short, there must be something for persuasion to get started on, and something substantial for persuasion to maintain its hold for longer periods. What matters, therefore, is the distribution of individuals and groups that can be persuaded—and kept persuaded —within any given time. This distribution is in part a function of the general distribution of social communication, past as well as present, and it is, therefore, necessarily uneven.

The existing distribution of governments is therefore necessary in its essence, though it may well be arbitrary in its accidents. Governments are organizations to enforce patterns of behavior, if necessary, by violence. They must have patterns of behavior which are to be enforced. A sufficiently large part of these patterns must be habitually acceptable to a large part of the population, and they must be sufficiently enforceable among the rest. Governments must be able, therefore, to count on two probabilities: (1) a significant probability of enforcing their commands; together with (2) a significant probability of finding them voluntarily complied with by their subjects. Finally, governments must have effective social channels to receive and accept information about major changes in the needs and habits of their population, or in the other relevant conditions of their power. Governments can only endure at such centers, and maintain their sway over such areas, as fall within the range of these conditions.

This dependence on the limited social bases of power, and on the limits of its sway, was already true for the "night-watchman" states of nineteenth-century *laissez-faire* liberalism. It is even more true of the emerging welfare states and production planning states of our own time. The slow but widespread shifts in emphasis from law to administration, and from local government to regional development authorities, point in the same direction.

Sovereignty and Diplomacy: The Distribution of States and Coalitions

The distribution of sovereign states is an expression of these realities. It expresses them inaccurately, but it does express them. Governments can modify communities, and they can make communities in rare and favorable situations; but on the whole it is the communities which make governments, or rather, it is the distribution of communities at any one time which both offers and limits the opportunities for governments to consolidate or extend their power.

It is this same unevenness of the underlying social structure which makes these governments sovereign, in the sense that they are not subject, in the ordinary run of affairs, to effective coercion by another power. They cannot be coerced by force or threats, either because they are powerful themselves or, in the case of smaller states, because an attack on them would involve their attacker in conflicts with other powers, with undesirable or unpredictable consequences.

Governments which are not so defended, directly or indirectly, may have sovereignty as a matter of legal form, but not of political substance. On the other hand, regions or minority groups, which do not have any formal sovereignty, may derive some real protection from the seriousness of the political repercussions which their unfavorable treatment might have abroad. There are shades and gradations of sovereignty here, on both sides of the legal borderline, and they keep changing with time. Yet, no matter how doubtful and shifting the effective borders of any concentration of sovereign powers, there seems little doubt about its reality at its core.

Similar limits apply to the effectiveness of economic power, that is, the power to offer or withhold facilities; and of the power to withhold information. Both goods and knowledge can often be duplicated, or obtained from elsewhere. Their control will be an uneven, and in the long run probably ever less effective, instrument of coercion.

We may think, therefore, of politics as the mobilization and application of consent and power in the various and partly overlapping clusters and areas of human interaction.

Below the level of the sovereign state, the most important of these areas and units are not merely those of local government, but rather the units of metropolitan area and of region, province, or section. Some of these regional units may have a single set of governmental machinery corresponding to them, such as a state under a federal form of government. Other regions are united only by the underlying social and communications structure which finds expression in the frequent parallel actions taken by the formally separate governments of their smaller parts, as in the case of the South in the United States. With or without unifying political machinery, the distinct political behavior of such regions may be quite persistent, as in the case of our South, or of the Flemings and Walloons in Belgium, or Bavaria in Germany, or Ulster in Ireland.

If the differences between several such regions or communities become too strong, they may lead to the partial or complete dissolution of the central governments which held them together. This happened centuries ago in the destruction of the Burgundian power, and somewhat later of the Spanish power, on the European continent. It happened during our own lifetime in the dissolution of the Ottoman and Habsburg Empires. It has been happening since World War II to Britain and the Netherlands in India, Pakistan, Burma, and Indonesia. What remains from this process, at any one time, is those sovereign governments which have no critical regional or community cleavages in their territories, or which are still able to hold their regions together, or even to weld them slowly into larger units by deep changes in the underlying structure of social organization.

Sovereignty is usually neither complete nor easily eradicable. If most of the world's sovereign governments were wiped out today, many of them, more or less changed, would tend to rise again in the future. Yet no government or region is *completely* self-sufficient, though a few may attain, at a price, relative self-sufficiency in essentials by utilizing the growing science and technology of substitutes.

The incompleteness of national sovereignty in its external relations is also expressed in the persistence of groupings and blocs of states. In one sense, we might call the formation of such blocs an exercise of sovereignty, but the "sovereign" choice here is usually one between severely limited alternatives; such blocs are often joined for reasons of self-preservation. Such blocs may be regional in terms of geography, or transportation, or military strategy, or past association, as in the Scandinavian countries. They may be based on language and culture, such as the Arab League. Or they may be based on currency and trade, such as the sterling bloc; or on subsidies and credits, such as the bloc of the Marshall Plan countries; or on partly similar historical traditions and institutions, such as, to some extent, the community of American Republics. In most cases, several or all of these factors may be involved; and considerations of current interest, or the hopes and fears of governments and peoples, will almost always be essential. Although all these factors will not coincide in all marginal cases, they tend to overlap for the states which form the core of a group. The result is a complex structure of blocs and regions, a discontinuous distribution of sympathies, influences, and power, centering currently around the two remaining "superpowers," the United States and the U.S.S.R., in the bipolar power pattern which has prevailed since 1945.

Does this mean that there will be soon only one supreme government—or two supreme governments—in the world? Neither of these
two "superpowers" can destroy the other without grave risk. Nor
can either of them readily impose complete unity or uniformity of
political or economic structure on the states in its camp. On the contrary, the existing discontinuities and problems in social communications may be multiplied during the third quarter of this century by
the increasing participation of broad masses of people in politics
everywhere, and particularly in Asia and Africa. This growing participation is an intrinsic part of the social and technological changes
of our century, and it is now being accelerated by the social and political appeals of the competing powers and ideologies. The probable
spread of atomic weapons to several additional governments may
endow additional political centers with the sovereign power of destruction. All this suggests that effective sovereignty will not be limited
to one or two powers for many years to come.

There is perhaps a connection between the empirical recognition of
sovereignty [9] and the conduct of diplomacy. Sovereignty, at least in
one of its aspects, is the status of governments which ordinarily
cannot be coerced from the outside. Diplomacy, then, is the art of
conducting negotiations between governments which cannot coerce
each other, or which cannot do so without considerable risk. The
prediplomatic methods of persuasion, majority voting, and enforcement
were already tried out more than four hundred years ago at some of
the great councils of Western Christendom which preceded the Ref-
ormation, and so were the methods of propaganda and of armed
attack, by some of those who found themselves in the minority. Only
after vast bloodshed did Catholics and Protestants accept the fact that
they could neither overrun nor persuade nor coerce each other, and
the tradition of diplomacy became finally established after the Thirty
Years' War.

In the world of the 1950's and 1960's, the world which still can neither
be overrun nor persuaded nor compelled—though it might possibly
be destroyed—our best hope for survival might still rest with what
Walter Lippmann has called "the lost art of diplomatic negotiation."
To be successful, such negotiation must be based on the vigorous culti-
vation of our own material strength, together with a sober awareness
of its limits. As Edmund Burke persistently suggested, in another age
of great unrest, we need a deeper and firmer dedication to the moral
and spiritual resources of our own tradition; but, as he also suggested,

one of the most dangerous delusions for any statesman or people would be the delusion of omnipotence.

Problems of Strength and Integration in an Unevenly Developed World

We have come to a dead end in the pursuit of a narrow concept of power—a power which was essentially manipulative or coercive, whether by outright force or by deception or persuasion. Perhaps there is another aspect of power—or let us call it strength—which has been slighted thus far in our discussion, and which might offer a more promising answer.

Strength may be thought of as the ability of a system to preserve only a few essentials of its structure while being capable of change in a wide variety of other aspects. In this manner, the molecules in a steel bar may flow into new patterns under stress so as to enable the bar to hold, whereas the molecules in a bar of cast iron may hold out at first more rigidly in their original position, until the relatively early collapse of the structure. Steel, we may say, is strong; cast iron is brittle.

In a loose way, this difference is well known: we speak of "rigidity" and "flexibility" in social or political organizations, or in the habits and personalities of individuals. More strictly speaking, what we are dealing with here might be called *learning capacity*: the ability of an individual or an organization to reallocate or recommit a large part of its resources to new uses, without destroying the organization as a whole. "Learning capacity," in this sense, is proportionate to the uncommitted resources of the system. Such resources need not be idle; but it is essential that they can be detached from their present committment so as to meet the exigencies of a new situation. The "operational reserve" in an army, or under certain conditions, the "liquid reserve" in a business enterprise, may serve as examples.

In the long run, the strength or adaptability or "learning capacity" of an organization may be expected to increase with three elements:

1. The total amount and variety of resources available to it;

2. The ease or speed with which these resources can be recommitted from one employment to another, without disrupting the essential minimum complementarity within the organization; and

3. The range of new patterns for recommitment available to the organization.

The first of these three factors is a matter of physical intake or receptivity, or of the ability to establish new channels of communications and control. The second is a matter of internal organization and reorganization. The third is a matter of "invisible intake," of receptivity to new patterns of information, and of the ability not merely to store them, but to allocate on occasion physical resources to act on them.

A really strong organization, then, will treat its surroundings not merely as an area on which to project its own preferences, nor even as a mere source of disintegrated materials to serve as building blocks for its own preconceived ends. Rather, it will treat its surroundings and its neighbors as resources not merely of material but of information; not merely in matters of detail but potentially for larger patterns of behavior; not merely for immediate needs but as something to be understood, respected and accepted as potential resources to meet the unforeseeable variety of conditions in the future.

Cultural anthropologists have spoken of this approach as that of cultural pluralism; psychologists have applied it to individuals under the name of "integrative behavior." Its political implications are obvious, and have been stressed.[10] In international relations it has appeared as the ability to make and hold together broad coalitions, or to unite diverse elements in one wider political community.

In all these cases the building of strength seems to follow a zigzag movement, somewhat like a ship that tacks against the wind. On the first "tack" when power must be organized, or a community must be built, the prime need is for cohesion, for the close complementarity of parts to force them into one dependable whole. Here we meet the builders of states and nations, the princes, the revolutionists, or the nationalistic spokesmen, as the great simplifiers, the destroyers of diversity and localism on the one hand, and at the same time as the great "narrowers," as the eliminators of foreign influences, as the relative isolators of their developing communities from much of the rest of the world. Only the most carefully screened and selected influences from the outside world are henceforth to be admitted to the budding nation, and usually they are to be confined to narrowly technical, economic, or scientific matters, in regard to which the foreigners are to be "overtaken and surpassed," without admitting any broader foreign values, habits, or culture patterns to consideration.

Later, as this first tack gains momentum, the phase of mass technical learning from abroad may come to an end; a little may continue among specialists, and there may be some genuine interchange in those circles;

but the bulk of the population are now expected to live within the patterns of a well-established national culture, complete with its own school system, mass communications, and technology. The national culture has been revived and established: all that remains is to spread it, and perhaps to impose it on others.

At this point our "first tack" of nationalistic and cultural single-mindedness approaches its dead end—the dead end of stereotyped, repetitive, coercive power which we surveyed in the earlier parts of this chapter. The world is still uneven; the means of enforcing power remain limited; and other nations and cultures remain refractory, or increase their opposition. Any frantic attempts to "homogenize" the planet in the image of one's own cherished way of life lead to growing frustration, exhaustion, or destruction.

Here, perhaps, is the point where each nation may have to try the other tack: to increase its own powers of inclusiveness and understanding; to broadcast somewhat less and to listen somewhat more; to lift international discourse from the dreary level of "mutually interrupted monologs"; to learn from one's neighbors, and, without losing one's own identity, to draw on their strength and their values for one's own larger growth.

Specifically, nationalism or patriotism on the "second tack" would require a drastic increase in the skills and facilities of social communication. It would require a community well enough established to transcend lingering feelings of insecurity and fear, and their overcompensation by nationalistic bravado; a set of institutions flexible enough to permit reform and change even on a large scale, and to permit cultural hospitality and tolerance to become more than merely verbal; and finally, but by no means least, an amount of material resources, technical skills, and equipment to permit an effective sharing of economic opportunities without fear of sliding back into poverty.

The combination of these desirable conditions does not seem to exist in the required measure in any major country in the world today. To approach it, we should need a far better understanding of economic growth and political freedom, and perhaps above all a long period of sustained allocation of sufficient resources to produce actual economic growth on a world scale. Until the world's major countries come to grips with this problem, much of international politics will continue to deal with developments on the "first tack," the awakening of submerged peoples, the simple consolidation of national power, the groupings and regroupings of power blocs, and the groping attempts of statesmen and nations to make the turn to the "second tack" of growth, integration, inclusiveness, and creativity. Success in taking this new course may well mean leadership for the nation which accomplishes it first. Here is a rendezvous with destiny which excels any other that the United States has ever faced.

Throughout this period of transition, nationalism and the persistence of sovereign states will remain stumbling blocks to all theories which ascribe omnipotence to any single factor in human affairs. As our brief glance at the social sciences has suggested, nationalism and sovereignty are not isolated phenomena of politics. Rather, they have many deep roots in the multiple social fabric of mankind, which must be traced separately with the aid of each particular discipline. Only by identifying these roots, one by one, can we hope to guide our efforts to overcome them, and to replace them, in due time, by the stronger foundations of a growing world community.

Chapter 4

Peoples, Nations, and Communication

Social scientists have collected a vast number of facts on the changing alignment of individuals in peoples, national cultures, and national political movements. We know that these problems are important, that even experienced statesmen have often seriously misjudged them, and that we need to understand them better. But what is meant by understanding?

To seek understanding means to seek a conceptual model of the processes of nationalism and nationality. We seek a model which will fit the known facts, and facilitate some prediction and control of events. More than that, we want it to suggest new questions and new fact-finding techniques, which in turn may some day lead to further ideas. Altogether, we are looking for a set of concepts which should meet as closely as practicable the following conditions:

1. Each concept should be operational. It should be clearly specified in terms of possible observations or measurements, from which it is derived and by which it can be tested. In this it should go beyond a mere explanation which uses familiar images but which cannot be so tested.

2. Each concept should be fruitful. It should suggest some further observations or experiments.

3. Each concept should be "critical." It should permit statements specific enough to exclude the possibility of certain observational data or results, so that, if these results are found, the concept clearly will have to be revised. The concept must not be so vague and elastic as to fit all conceivable empirical results.

Several concepts will have to be used together in a description of the processes of nationalism and nationality.[1] Such a description should meet as nearly as possible the following conditions:

1. It should apply to the behavior of individuals as well as to groups.

2. It should apply to rational as well as to so-called "irrational" behavior of groups or individuals.[2]

3. It should utilize data observable by strictly external methods, as well as subjective data available from introspection, and indirectly from literature.

4. The description should generally utilize the power of specialized disciplines and fit their findings within each field.

5. It should link the specialties so as to permit the transfer and recombination of their knowledge between different fields; and

6. It should, therefore, permit group attack on data too voluminous for one investigator.

Looking for such concepts, we may perhaps find them in the notion of communication. Processes of communication are the basis of the coherence of societies, cultures, and even of the personalities of individuals;[3] and it may be worth while to see whether concepts of communication may not help us to understand the nature of peoples and of nations.

Society, Culture, and Communication

One set of facts about nationality deals with it in terms of society. By *society* is meant here a group of individuals made interdependent by the division of labor, the production and distribution of goods and services: "A 'society' refers to a group of people who have learned to work together."[4]

To the extent that there are marked differences in the degree of such interdependence, not just in respect to a few particular goods and services, but in regard to many services, we may consider one society as separate from others. A few special commodities may be carried over long distances from one society to another, just as jade in the Stone Age or cotton and rubber in the first half of the twentieth century. But exchange of a few special goods does not make a society; it takes the exchange or combination of many goods and services to accomplish that. A society in this sense is a group of individuals connected by an intense division of labor, and separated from other societies by a marked drop in this intensity.

In the past, any more elaborate division of labor has implied a division of society into *occupational groups* (such as "town" and "country") as well as into *social strata, castes, or classes* (which cut across some of these special occupations). Several societies may be connected with each other by a larger interchange of goods and services than with any other societies. In this case we might say that together they form a sort of *great society,* something parallel in some respects to what is sometimes called a civilization, but not identical with it.

It is essential to distinguish this concept of society sharply from that of *community* or *culture,* as used by anthropologists.[5] Culture at first sight seems to consist of institutions, such as a particular dance, and a marriage ceremony, and of particular things, such as a particular kind of axe or spear, or food, or clothing. On looking more closely, we then find that these things somehow hang together: the same people are used to certain kinds of axes and clothes and food and marriages; they have similar accepted ideas about beauty in ornaments, and of "good" behavior in children and adults. All these things, it appears, somehow hang together in their minds. They form, as the technical term has it, a culture *configuration.*

If we look still more deeply into each configuration of culture, an Indian *pueblo,* a German *Gesangverein,* or the basketball team of Middletown High School, we find in each of these, behind the visible configuration of accepted things and accepted behavior, an invisible *configuration of values,* of do's and don'ts, of rules for discriminating between actions as good or bad, beautiful or ugly, familiar or strange, safe or dangerous, interesting or indifferent. The positive elements in culture, the acts we see, the words we hear, the things we touch, are set, as it were, in the background which consists in each culture in the particular behavior which we do *not* see, because there it is regarded as unseemly, the words we do not hear because they may be *tabu,* the things which are not there because they are not used. Silences are eloquent. Without silences there is no speech, and it is their culture which teaches men when to speak and when to be silent. Culture in this sense is a screen or sieve, a configuration of "historically created selective processes which channel men's reactions both to internal and to external stimuli."[6]

A common culture, then, is a common set of stable, habitual preferences and priorities in men's attention, and behavior, as well as in their thoughts and feelings. Many of these preferences may involve communication; it is usually easier for men to communicate within the same culture than across its boundaries. In so far as a common culture facilitates communication, it forms a *community.*

But this is not always so. A particular culture may form a pattern of *interlocking roles,* such as man and woman, father and child, master and slave. If this is carried far, communication between the inter-locking groups may be throttled down to the narrow range of con-ventionalized words, subjects, and sentiments permitted by established etiquette. Such an etiquette restricts communications between Whites and Negroes in some parts of the South: they may meet for years, always making the customary gestures and phrases, and yet know very little of each other. Despite this wide rift in communications, some writers still speak of one "culture" comprising Whites *and* Ne-groes in such situations; other writers have compromised by speaking of separate "subcultures" of Whites and of Negroes within this frame-work. On any showing, in such extreme situations, the common culture—common, that is, to both groups—is relatively poor. It is a restricted culture, restricted by its own inner barriers, which make it at the same time a restricted community.

No terminology should try to be more accurate than life. "Culture" and "community" can be used interchangeably because they describe a single complex of processes. When we say "culture," we stress the configuration of preferences or values; when we say "community" we stress the aspects of communication; just as, when speaking about traffic flow in a city, we may sometimes speak of the network of streets, and sometimes of the sets of traffic lights. But without the city streets, the "stop" and "go" lights would be meaningless. Similarly, we must never forget that it is the channels of culture which give to the values of culture their meaning.[7]

There is another side to this description. When we say "culture," we stress the habits, preferences and institutions as such, as if they were a configuration of disembodied ghosts. When we say "commu-nity" we stress the collection of living individuals in whose minds and memories the habits and channels of culture are carried.

Both terms, then, have their distinct usefulness. In much of the rest of this book, nationality will be discussed in terms of community, as here defined. But a great deal of valuable literature on peoples and nations has been written in terms of the culture concept. The overlapping relationship between community and culture should be remembered in order to maintain the connection between these dif-ferent approaches, and to prevent any rift in this field of knowledge that could only work to the detriment of both.

The channels of culture, like those of society, consist of material facilities. Like those of society they originated through processes of history, are changed by history, and may be destroyed by it.[8] But they are utterly unlike the channels of society in the kind of thing that passes through them.

The kind of thing that is transmitted through the channels of culture is exceedingly hard to describe. Our everyday language has no single word for it. Some parts of it we call knowledge, others we call values, still others, customs, mores, or traditions. Still other parts of it are mere gossip or just news, and still others are orders or commands. We have a qualitative understanding of these things. We can recognize them when we see or hear them, and we also know that they are interrelated, that they often shade over into each other. Yet, there is no everyday word that expresses their unity or the connections between them, and there is no long-established concept familiar to social scientists that would permit accurate analysis or quantitative measurement of them.

Perhaps the most effective way to overcome this difficulty would be for us to borrow a concept from another group of sciences and adapt it to our purpose. At best, such a concept will yield us only a simplified model of an inexhaustibly rich reality, yet we may hope that it will make at least some significant aspects of that reality stand out more clearly.

The Concept of Information

A concept for that which knowledge, values, traditions, news, gossip, and commands all have in common has been developed by communications engineers. They have called it information. In building a telegraph line or a telephone network, the main problem of communications engineers has not been the content of the messages that were to be transmitted. They might be true or untrue, profane or sacred, facetious or profound. They might contain descriptions of physical matter or of human affairs. They might be messages about other messages; or they might be orders intended to redirect men's attention or to change their behavior. The communications engineer had to care for what was common to all these messages: the need to get them transmitted quickly, with least effort and with least distortion.

Communications engineers therefore developed methods of analyzing messages into small, discrete units—letters in an alphabet, dots and dashes in a Morse code, black and white points on a television screen—and they learned to measure how many of these elements of a message, how many of these units of information, were transmitted through a channel and how many were lost. In so doing they found an accurate way of measuring the loss or distortion of messages, and of measuring the capacities of a system of communication.

In the beginning, this involved ignoring the content of the messages and concentrating on the mere fact of their complexity. A very crude line screen might take the same number of image points to transmit a picture from a comic strip or a crude likeness of Leonardo's "Mona Lisa." A good reproduction of the Mona Lisa however, would require a much richer system of communication, a much larger number and greater variety of image points. Although communications engineers therefore could not predict what kind of messages a communications system would carry, they could predict the potential performance of which it would be capable.

It is these concepts of *information,* of the *capacity* of a communications system, and of the *complementarity* of its parts,[9] which would be helpful in the field of social science. For all cooperation among human beings requires at least some degree of communication. The richer their cooperation in producing tangible goods and services, in developing highly organized societies, and in developing and sharing intangible treasures of knowledge, art, and values, the greater their need for rich, varied, quick, and accurate communication. We cannot measure directly the piety, beauty, courage, or steadfastness of human beings, but we can measure to a significant extent the ranges and kinds of messages which they can transmit to each other, the speed and accuracy with which they can do so, and the price in effort and in lost information which they have to pay.

What we are interested in here is the observable ability of certain groups of men and women to share with each other a wide range of whatever might be in their minds, and their observable inability to share these things nearly as widely with outsiders. We all know that men can share with each other much more easily what is in their hands than what is in their minds, and yet the difference between the community that arises from the one kind of sharing and the community that arises from the other has rarely been seen in its full significance.

In what follows, therefore, I shall accept the view of anthropologists that both society and community are developed by social learning, and that a community consists of people who have learned to communicate with each other and to understand each other well beyond the mere interchange of goods and services.

I cannot use for this analysis the concept of community which a group of eminent social scientists have introduced from the field of biology where a "community" of plants and animals is sometimes described as a collection of plants and animals which happen to exist next to each other in some particular locality.[10] "Society" for this group of scientists is, then, a group of persons who have become conscious of "belonging" together in some sense.[11] The distinction which is proposed here for an analysis of nationality differs from both these poles. Rarely shall we be interested in mere coexistence, and, on the other hand, before analyzing or discussing consciousness, we shall try to understand what are the objective facts of which man can become conscious, even though these facts should exist as habits, mores, or preferences inside our own minds.

For this discussion I shall have to borrow terms from the study of communications, and I must apologize for the barbarous and quasi-mechanical sound which they may have in the ears of readers unfamiliar with them. I have three grounds for my apology: first, that the scientific study of processes of communication does not in fact lead to a mechanistic philosophy, but rather to its opposite; second, that I am using the simplified terms merely in order to make easier the tracing of certain infinitely larger and more complex social processes (much as a simple bell may facilitate the tracing of the movements of a far more complex cat); and third, that this approach in the end might be justified by its results.

Societies produce, select, and channel goods and services. *Cultures produce, select, and channel information.* A railroad or a printing press is a matter of society. A traffic code or an alphabet is a matter of culture. Society can build walls; culture can impose tabus. Society communicates tangible goods or inputs of energy called work; culture communicates patterns. These may be patterns of the arrangement of objects in space, from pottery and ornaments to tools and buildings. They may be patterns of action, such as games, dances, or models of graceful behavior. Or they may be patterns of preference, of do's and don'ts, such as standards of morality or taste. Or, finally, they may be codes and symbols, that is, patterns so arranged as to convey information about other patterns, up to the vast extent of what the biologist J. S. Huxley called "man's unique biological characteristic of tradition," [12] and of what Edmund Burke identified with the state when he called it a "partnership in all art . . . and all perfection." [13]

If we knew how to compare and measure the ability of groups and cultures to transmit information, we might gain a better understanding of their behavior and their capacities. But how can information be measured?

Possible Measurements of Information

The distinction between society and culture, or society and community, corresponds in a sense to the distinction in modern technology between power engineering and communications engineering. Power engineering transfers amounts of electric energy; *communications engineering transfers information.* It does not transfer events; *it transfers a patterned relationship between events.*

When a spoken message is transmitted through a sequence of mechanical vibrations of the air and of a membrane, thence through electric impulses in a wire, thence through electric processes in a broadcasting station and through radio waves, thence through electric and mechanical processes in a receiver and recorder to a set of grooves on the surface of a disk, and is finally played and made audible to a listener—what has been transferred through this chain of processes, or channel of communication, is something that has remained unchanged, invariant, over this whole sequence of processes. It is not matter, nor any one of the particular processes, nor any major amount of energy, since relays and electronic tubes make the qualities of the signal independent from a considerable range of energy inputs.

The same principle applies to the sequence of processes from the distribution of light reflected from a rock to the distribution of chemical changes on a photographic film, and further, to the distribution of black and white dots on a printing surface, or the distribution of electric "yes" or "no" impulses in picture telegraphy or television. What is transmitted here is neither light rays nor shadows, but information, the patterns of relationships between them.

In the second group of examples, we could describe the *state* of the rock in terms of the distribution of light and dark points on its surface. This would be a *state description* of the rock at a particular time. If we then describe the state of the film after exposure in terms of the distribution of the dark grains of silver deposited on it and of the remaining clear spaces, we should get another state description. Each of the two state descriptions would have been taken from a quite different physical object—a rock and a film—but a large part of these two state descriptions would be identical, whether we compared them point by point or in mathematical terms.

There would again be a great deal of identity between these two descriptions and several others, such as the description of the distribution of black and white dots on the printing surface, or of the electric "yes" or "no" impulses in the television circuits, or of the light and dark points on the television screen. The extent of the physical possibility of transferring and reproducing these patterns corresponds to the extent that there is "something" unchanging in all the relevant state descriptions of the physical processes by which this transmission is carried on. That "something" is *information—those aspects of the state descriptions of each physical process which all these processes had in common.*[14]

To the extent that the last state description in such a sequence differs from the first, information has been lost or distorted during its passage through the channel. This amount of lost information can be measured. We can measure it in very refined ways, as in telephone or television engineering, where a message is broken up into very many electric impulses, sound frequencies, or image points. The percentage of the impulses or image points arriving at the other end is measured on a statistical basis, and their significance is evaluated in terms of the change each of them makes in the probability distribution of the picture which is already there. Or, we can measure it in simpler terms, by breaking up a message into a few simple parts, and asking how many of these parts were transmitted within a given minimum standard of accuracy, and how drastically the probability of the picture at the other end was changed by the absence of the pieces which were lost.

Refined or crude, more accurate or less, each of these methods would give us some quantitative measure of the *fidelity* of a communications channel in comparison with other channels. By either technique, we may derive a measure for the *efficiency* of a channel, as well as of the relative efficiency or *complementarity* of any parts or stages of the channel in relation to the others.

Other measures for the performance of a communications system, or for the complementarity of its parts, would be the speed at which information could be transmitted, or the range of different kinds of information that could be carried. Common to all of these approaches would be the fact that patterns of information can be measured in quantitative terms. They can be described in mathematical language, analyzed by science, and transmitted or processed on a practical industrial scale.[15]

Some Implications for Social Science

This development is significant for wide fields of natural and social science. Information is indeed the "stuff as dreams are made on." Yet it can be transmitted, recorded, analyzed, and measured. Whatever we may call it, information, pattern, form, *Gestalt*, state description, distribution function, or negative entropy, it has become accessible to the treatment of science.

Information differs from the "matter" and "energy" of nineteenth-century mechanical materialism in that it cannot be described adequately by their conservation laws. But it also differs, perhaps more so, from the "idea" of "idealistic" or metaphysical philosophies in that it is based on physical processes during every single moment of its existence, and that it can and must be dealt with by physical methods. It has material reality. It exists and interacts with other processes in the world, regardless of the whims of any particular human observer, so that its reception, transmission, reproduction, and in certain cases its recognition, can be mechanized.

As spaced dots of animal footprints, patterns of information were the basis of primitive hunting and tracking. As varied electric impulses, patterns of information are today the basis of modern telegraphy, electronics, and automatic equipment. As patterns of sound, sight, or action, they have always been the basis of signaling, of language, of society, and of culture. There is no communication without physical processes, without work. But the information transmitted is separable from any one process by which it is carried. There is no community nor culture without society. And there can be no society, no division of labor, without a minimum of transfer of information, without communication. Yet the difference between society and community is crucial, for it is the complex interplay between society and community which is at the root of many of the baffling problems of nationality.[16]

Individuals of different cultures often live in one society, such as Czechs and Germans in Bohemia, or Moslems and Hindus in Bengal. For many years they may exchange goods and services but relatively little information. They may have very few complementary channels of communication. Many of their experiences in their common society may be similar, as were those of Czech and German miners in the same mining town, but they are not necessarily shared. On the other hand, within each community of communication many experiences of certain individuals may be quite dissimilar, such as those of German miners and German mine owners, but they can be shared; in particular, information about some of the German mine owners' experiences may be shared vicariously by the German miners. Here are the baffling cases cited by Professor Chadwick: members of different peoples may live through the same events for generations and yet emerge from this supposed "community of fate" quite dissimilar in behavior, or even bitterly opposed.[17]

Communication and the Concept of a People

The community which permits a common history to be experienced as common, is a community of complementary habits and facilities of communication. It requires, so to speak, equipment for a job. This job consists in the storage, recall, transmission, recombination, and reapplication of relatively wide ranges of information; and the "equipment" consists in such learned memories, symbols, habits, operating preferences, and facilities as will in fact be sufficiently complementary to permit the performance of these functions. *A larger group of persons linked by such complementary habits and facilities of communication* we may call a *people.*

The test of *complementarity* of any set of communications equipment is communicative effectiveness. How fast and how accurately do messages get through? How complex and voluminous is the information that can be so transmitted? How effectively are operations on one part of the net transmitted to another? The extent of complementarity for any set of facilities, or any community, will be indicated by the answers to these questions.

Complementarity or communicative efficiency is a function, an overall result. The same or a closely similar result may be reached by several different combinations of elements, or even by the entire replacement of some elements by others. This is obvious in the simple examples from communications engineering which were cited earlier, but it also applies to social communication. The communicative facilities of a society include a socially standardized system of symbols which is a language, and any number of auxiliary codes, such as alphabets, systems of writing, painting, calculating, etc. They include information stored in the living memories, associations, habits, and preferences of its members, and in its material facilities for the storage of information, such as libraries, statues, signposts, and the like; and a good deal more. Some of these facilities, individual and social, also deal with the treatment of information, its recall from storage or memory, its transmission and recombination to new patterns. Taken all together, they include, therefore, in particular the elements of that which anthropologists call culture. If these elements are in fact sufficiently complementary, they will add up to an integrated pattern or configuration of communicating, remembering, and acting, that is, to a culture in the sense of the citations quoted earlier in our discussion; and the individuals who have these complementary habits, vocabularies, and facilities are what we call a people.

It is now clear why all the usual descriptions of a people in terms of a community of languages, or character, or memories, or past history, are open to exception. For what counts is not the presence or absence of any single factor, but merely the presence of sufficient communication facilities with enough complementarity to produce the overall result. The Swiss may speak four different languages and still act as one people, for each of them has enough learned habits, preferences, symbols, memories, patterns of landholding and social stratification, events in history, and personal associations, all of which together permit him to communicate more effectively with other Swiss than with the speakers of his own language who belong to other peoples.[18] "I found that my German was more closely akin to the French of my [French-Swiss] friend than to the likewise German (*Ebenfallsdeutsch*) of the foreigner," says the editor of a prominent German-Swiss paper in his reminiscences. "The French-Swiss and I were using different words for the same concepts, but we understood each other. The man from Vienna and I were using the same words for different concepts, and thus we did not understand each other in the least." [19]

What is proposed here, in short, is a functional definition of nationality. Membership in a people essentially consists in wide complementarity of social communication. It consists in the ability to communicate more effectively, and over a wider range of subjects, with members of one large group than with outsiders.[20] This overall result can be achieved by a variety of functionally equivalent arrangements.

This function of nationality differs from the old attempts to specify nationality in terms of some particular ingredient, somewhat as modern technological trends towards evaluating materials in terms of their performance differ from the older practice of evaluating materials in terms of their composition. In both cases, "composition specifications" are replaced by "performance tests," based on more detailed analysis of the functions carried out.[21]

Peoples are held together "from within" by this communicative efficiency, the complementarity of the communicative facilities acquired by their members. Such "ethnic complementarity" is not merely subjective. At any moment, it exists as an objective fact, measurable by performance tests. Similar to a person's knowledge of a language, it is relatively independent of the whim of individuals. Only slowly can it be learned or forgotten. It is a characteristic of each individual, but it can only be exercised within the context of a group.[22]

Ethnic complementarity, the complementarity that makes a people, can be readily distinguished by its relatively wide range from the narrow vocational complementarity which exists among members of the same profession, such as doctors or mathematicians, or members of the same vocational group, such as farmers or intellectuals. Efficient communication among engineers, artists, or stamp collectors is limited to a relatively narrow segment of their total range of activities. In most other things they do, in their childhood memories, in courtship, marriage, and parenthood, in their standards of beauty, their habits of food and drink, in games and recreation, they are far closer to mutual communication and understanding with their countrymen than with their fellow specialists in other countries.

The facts of social class may change this picture. But if and where they change it, they will do so not because of anything in the theory but because they are facts, and to the extent that they are facts. Where workers in industry are cut off from the rest of the community, from better housing on the "right side" of the railroad tracks, from conviviality and intercourse, from education and careers, from comforts and income, from security and prestige—there Disraeli's word of the "two nations . . . the rich and the poor" may express a real state of affairs.[23] Under such conditions, men may discover more similar experiences and greater mutual understanding with their fellow workers in other countries than with their "own" well-to-do countrymen who will see them only at the servant's entrance.

At certain times and places the barriers of class may thus outweigh the ties of language, culture, and tradition. Wage earners may then deliberately seek to advance their fortunes in a competitive society by seeking international class alignments; or they may choose to press for improvement of their lot along national lines, trying to keep out cheaper foreign labor, and to secure for themselves some share in the national prosperity of their employers.

Where, on the other hand, wage earners have more ample ties with the rest of the community, and fuller opportunities, not merely in words but in substance; if they find not merely factories and slums but schools, parks, hospitals, and better housing; where they have a political and economic "stake in the country" and are accorded security and prestige, there the ties to their own people, to its folkways and living standards, education and tradition, will be strong in fact. There will be a greater stock of common experiences, a greater flow of social communication across class lines, more conviviality and informal social association, more vertical mobility and intermarriage, and, as a result of all these, probably far more effective complementarity of social communication within the people than across its borders. Social reforms, as Bismarck knew, may knit a people more closely; [24] high wages, as Lenin observed, may tend to assimilate the outlook of workers to that of their middle-class compatriots; [25] and periods of democracy and social progress, as Otto Bauer predicted, may leave different peoples more unified internally, but more sharply marked off from each other.[26]

The critical facts of social communication and intercourse can be surveyed, tested, and to some extent measured, before political decisions must be taken. "To the blind, all things are sudden." [27] But for enlightened statesmanship it should be possible to do systematically what some men, like Disraeli himself, did in a rough and ready way: to appraise the many specific channels of communication within a people, and between its different classes, so as to be able to estimate how such a group will respond to a strain. Will India's Hindus and Moslems form in the long run one nation or two, and what are the chances for an eventual reunion between India herself and Pakistan? Will French workers turn right or left in politics? With careful investigation of the elements which go into the making of these social decisions, their outcome could at least be guessed at more intelligently before policy finds itself overtaken by events.

Even where we have one people, the range and effectiveness of social communication within it may tell us how effectively it has become integrated, and how far it has advanced, in this respect, toward becoming a nation. "That universal circulation of intelligence," Arthur Young noted on the eve of the French Revolution, "which in England transmits the least vibration of feeling or alarm, with electric sensibility, from one end of the kingdom to another, and which unites in bands of connection men of similar interests and situations, has no existence in France." [28]

The notion of complementarity might be extended so as to include the actual or probable communicative efficiency of individuals over a range of different social arrangements. In this sense complementarity would be lower if it permitted efficient communication between individuals only in a very few relationships, such as, perhaps, only in the context of their familiar native village, or of their familiar economic institutions. Burke and Disraeli assumed such a limited type of complementarity when they prophesied that Frenchmen or Englishmen would cease to be a people if they should lose their traditional aristocratic social institutions, and that in such an event they would have to take "many a weary step" before they could regain "a true political personality." [29]

Complementarity is greater if it permits individuals to communicate efficiently no matter how often they change their residence or their occupations. In this sense complementarity may be that elusive property of individuals which, in the words of Dr. Hermann Finer, "makes society cohere," [30] or which in our terminology makes it a community, perhaps even despite considerable variations in external circumstances. This, on the whole, has been the experience of the American nation. Men could move from the theocracy of Massachusetts Bay to the freedom of Rhode Island, or from the established institutions of the tidewater regions to the new conditions of the frontier, and yet retain their capacity to cooperate and form a nation. "A nation well regulated," Benjamin Franklin wrote, "is like a polypus: take away a limb, its place is soon supplied, cut it in two, and each deficient part shall speedily grow out of the part remaining. Thus, if you have room and subsistence enough, . . . you may, of one, make ten nations, equally populous and powerful; or, rather, increase the nation tenfold in strength." [31]

Peoples are marked off from each other by communicative barriers, by "marked gaps" in the efficiency of communication. Such gaps are relative. In geography, divides between river basins are effective, not by their absolute heights or steepness, but by the difference between their opposite slopes. Similarly barriers to communication are more or less effective not only according to the difficulty of communication across them but also according to the relative ease and attractiveness of alternative channels of communication available to the individual.

What are the effects of these cultural channels and barriers in a modern society, divided by its peculiar economic institutions and divisions of labor into metropolitan centers and less developed areas, and into different social strata and classes?

Nationalism and the Position of Peoples in a Stratified Society

Here we find that a *people* forms a social, economic, and political alignment of individuals from different social classes and occupations, around a center and a leading group. Its members are united by more intensive social communication, and are linked to these centers and leading groups by an unbroken chain of connections in communications, and often also in economic life, with no sharp break in the possibilities of communication and substitution at any link, and hence with a somewhat better probability of social rise from rank to rank.[32]

The primary basis of this alignment is the complementarity of communication habits. Its secondary basis is the complementarity of acquired social and economic preferences which involve the mobility of goods or persons. These are the widespread preferences for things or persons of "one's own kind" (that is, associated with one's particular communication group) in such matters as buying and selling, work, food and recreation, courtship and marriage. A third factor has made all such alignments more important: the rise of industrialism and the modern market economy which offer economic and psychological rewards for successful group alignments to tense and insecure individuals —to men and women uprooted by social and technological change, exposed to the risks of economic competition, and taught to hunger for success. For almost any limited group within a competitive market, both security and success can be promoted by effective organization, alignment of preferences, and coordination of behavior. Vast numbers have felt a need for such a group and have answered it by putting their trust in their nation.

In the political and social struggles of the modern age, *nationality*, then, means an alignment of large numbers of individuals from the middle and lower classes linked to regional centers and leading social groups by channels of social communication and economic intercourse, both indirectly from link to link and directly with the center.[33]

A "leading social group" in this sense may be, but need not be, the established "upper class" of the moment. The upper class—such as the aristocracy—may function as such a leading group if it promotes nationalism or accepts the leadership thrust upon it by a national or regional movement. If its main interests and ties, however, lie elsewhere, perhaps outside the country, or if it has accepted alien speech, habits, or religion, or if, finally, it has come to care only for its own group interests in a quite narrow manner, then the national and social leadership may devolve upon the next class below it, or still farther down to whichever class is sufficiently strong, respected, and locally accessible to become in fact the "leading group of the national movement." Thus the English Crown and aristocracy were assigned the function of national leadership in Bolingbroke's concept of the "patriot King," and again by the "Tory democracy" of Disraeli. The German aristocrats received a similar mandate from the German middle class in the Bismarckian era. On the other hand, José Ortega y Gasset has said of Spain since the seventeenth century that "beginning with the Monarchy and continuing with the Church, no national power in all that time has thought of anything outside itself. When did the heart —in the last analysis, a foreign heart—of Spanish monarch or Spanish church ever beat for ends that were profoundly Spanish? Never." [34] Similarly, important spokesmen of the French nobility before 1789 refused to accept membership in the French nation; and in 1941 the French socialist ex-Premier Leon Blum drew up a long and specific denial of the ability or willingness of the French middle class henceforth to lead the nation.[35] Just who the "leading social group" is going to be, therefore, may well change from period to period, but there is usually some such group at any given time, and its character will in turn have its influence on the character of the national movement.[36]

At all times, however, it will be necessary for the "leading social group" to be "above" some of the main groups to be led, at least in terms of current prestige, and usually in the long run in terms of economic, political, and social opportunities, skills, wealth, organization, and the like, so that a member of another social group, on joining this "leading group" would have in some sense a real experience of "rising in the world," or, as some sociologists have termed it, of "moving vertically in society." [37]

As an alignment with a center and a leading group, nationality offers to its members the possibility of vertical substitutions unbroken from any one link to the next. In a competitive economy or culture, nationality is an implied claim to privilege. It emphasizes group preference and group peculiarities, and so tends to keep out all outside competitors. It promises opportunity, for it promises to eliminate or lessen linguistic, racial, class, or caste barriers to the social rise of individuals within it. And it promises security, for it promises to reduce the probability of outside competition for all sorts of opportunities, from business deals to marriages and jobs.

To the extent that the division of labor in a particular society is competitive and stratified, nationality can thus be used to hamper "horizontal" substitution from individuals outside the group, and to facilitate "vertical" substitution within it. To the extent of these conditions, the barriers and patterns of communication gain added significance and power from the barriers and patterns of society. Once the pressures of uprooting and insecurity are then added to these horizontal and vertical barriers, the stage is set for the rise of the political movement of modern nationalism—that is, for the vast effort to convert the channels of culture into stormladders for masses of individuals to social advancement and economic privilege.

There are significant variations in this process among different peoples and in different areas. Nationalism may indeed appear simply as a rapid process of Westernization, as it did, at least on the surface, in the Turkey of Kemal Ataturk, in the 1920's, and perhaps in Indonesia in the 1930's and 1940's. Or it may, on the contrary, assert its allegiance to the old ways and the old traditions; it may continue to acknowledge the prestige and leadership of the old social classes, symbols, and institutions, with little drive towards serious modernization, as in the case of much of Arab nationalism between 1917 and 1952.[38] Sometimes, again, the appearance may be conservative, as in the Japanese Meiji "Restoration" of 1868 with its battle cry "Revere the Emperor!" although the substance of the process may be one of drastic and far-reaching change. Thus the Meiji Restoration replaced the power of the Shogun's court by that of the "outer clans"; it offered new opportunities to the impoverished lower nobility, the "Ronin," and to the merchants of the cities; it dispossessed through the pressure of taxation a sizable portion of peasants; and it created a modern Japanese industry, a modern labor market, modern metropolitan centers, and a modern army and navy.[39]

Yet perhaps the common elements prevail. Either the "prenationalistic" ruling class could accept the new movement and promote it for reasons of its own, as did some rulers, nobles, or landowners in Germany, Austria, England, and Japan, all of whom promoted manufactures, or improvements in agriculture, education, or military efficiency, and reaped as a byproduct an increase in nationalistic or patriotic sentiment. Or the rulers may cling to the substance of the social *status quo*. If they fail, they may be swept away, as were the Bourbons of France, the Sultan of Turkey, and the Emperor of China. If they succeed, and if the river of social change is not yet running fast in their territory, their position may remain secure for the time being, and nationalism among their people may be impressive in rhetoric, but feeble in power or performance.

In any case, the strength of the nationalist or patriotic process—the two may not yet be distinguishable at this stage [40]—may then depend on two major elements. First, it may depend on the extent to which the ruling class itself promotes this process, not merely in its outward trappings, but in its social substance; the extent, therefore, also to which the ruling class remains accessible to the members of other classes for communication, entry, alliance, or alignment. Second, it may depend on the extent to which the masses of the people have become mobilized, with or without the cooperation of their rulers, for realignment with the new nationalist movement and the new changes in their old ways of life.

Both of these elements involve the problem of coercion. What are the means of social compulsion in a given area, and in the service of which groups, which policies, and which patterns of behavior will they continue to be used? As nationalism gains ground within a people, it comes to approach this inevitable question of power. In trying to gain and exercise power for its ends, the efforts of nationalists may transform a people into a nationality.

Nationalities and Nation-States

In the age of nationalism, *a nationality* is a people pressing to acquire a measure of effective control over the behavior of its members. It is a people striving to equip itself with power, with some machinery of compulsion strong enough to make the enforcement of its commands sufficiently probable to aid in the spread of habits of voluntary compliance with them. As the interplay of compliance habits with enforcement probabilities, such power can be exercised through informal social arrangements, pressure of group opinion, and the prestige of national symbols. It can be exercised even more strongly through formal social or political organizations, through the administration of educational or economic institutions, or through the machinery of government. Whatever the instruments of power, they are used to strengthen and elaborate those social channels of communication, the preferences of behavior, the political (and sometimes economic) alignments which, all together, make up the social fabric of the nationality.

All group power thus acquired by members of the nationality leads them to ask for more. Formally or informally, dissenters find themselves pressed into line, while a significant part of the members of the nationality begin to demand control of the state or part of it.

Once a nationality has added this power to compel to its earlier cohesiveness and attachment to group symbols, it often considers itself a *nation* and is so considered by others. In this sense, men have spoken of a Polish, Czech, or Irish nation, even after these groups had lost their earlier political states, or before they had yet acquired control of any state at all.

In all these cases, nationalities turn into nations when they acquire power to back up their aspirations. Finally, if their nationalistic members are successful, and a new or old state organization is put into their service, then at last the nation has become sovereign, and a *nation-state* has come into being. At this moment, if not earlier, the successful nation may face a new immediate problem: how to use its new panoply of power against the claims of other nationalities. The more successful it has been in promoting its own members into privileged or controlling positions in society, the more it will now have to fear from the rise of other peoples and other nationalist movements.

At the end of this road a successful career of nationalism might turn a nation into a class. All its members in that event would become members of the privileged strata of society, and none would have to stoop to humbler occupations, for other peoples would be made to furnish the drawers of water and the hewers of wood. The national channels of communication would no longer even in part cut across the barriers of society; on the contrary, the barriers of class would become reinforced by the barriers of nationality, language, and culture. Something of this was implied in the vision of some British empire builders towards the end of the nineteenth century, and it found its extreme expression in the Nazi idea of a German *Herrenvolk*. But every step toward this goal has to be paid for with an increase in danger. Ever more remote from fundamental economic production, ever more cut off morally and politically from the majority of mankind, the would-be "master race" would of necessity become the obvious target for all social and national processes of revolt and of destruction. Nationalism, which set out to make the nation strong, may at this point begin to make it potentially weaker and more vulnerable. Whether men and women will follow nationalist leaders to the end of this path, or whether they will be able to break the fatal cycle may well depend on the availability of alternative leadership, and perhaps even more on the nature of their own experiences and aspirations drawn from their everyday life.

Nationalism and "Cultural Autonomy"

One suggestion may emerge already at this stage from our discussion of nationality, culture, and communication. Culture and complementarity of communication are not things apart from the rest of life, as the Sunday supplements of some newspapers are apart from the serious business of carrying the day's news. At every step we find social communication bound up indissolubly with the ends and means of life, with men's values and the patterns of their teamwork, with employment and promotion, with marriage and inheritance, with the preferences of buyers and sellers, and with economic security or distress—with all the psychological, political, social, and economic relationships that influence the security and happiness of individuals. Nationality, culture, and communication are not the only factors that affect all these, but they are always present to affect them.

It seems therefore utopian to imagine a blissful state of "cultural autonomy" where "culture" will be carried on detached from real life, where schools will be detached from taxes and students from the need for jobs, where families and businessmen need not worry about tariffs or government controls, nor office workers about employment or promotion. All these problems can be dealt with and are being dealt with in many countries; but they cannot be dealt with completely apart from the problems of culture and nationality on the one hand, and of political and economic life on the other.

Culture itself is of interest to men and women only to the extent that it does go into the daily texture of their lives. "Cultural autonomy" cannot be divorced from the personal, local, regional, or occupational autonomy of human beings. Every step in the tragic rise of nationalistic violence during our century has shown us individuals struggling not merely for an abstract "cultural autonomy" but for something that involved the very fabric of their lives and the places and regions where these lives are lived; and every wave of nationalism has reasserted even more stridently this claim to its "integral," "total," ever more inclusive character.

How far these developments can go, how and from whom they exact their heavy price, and how they can turn against the leading groups and social institutions to which they were linked in their beginnings—these questions cannot detain us now. Our immediate question will be: How, in practice, can our basic concept of nationality be tested?

Chapter 5

Nationality and Social Learning
PROBLEMS OF TESTING AND PROBLEMS OF CHANGE

We have called a people a community of complementary habits of communication. All actual acts of communication, as well as all actual channels or equipment, consist of specific physical processes and must be tested by specific operations. All these operations will deal in some way with information, and over a considerable range of applications they should give identical or very similar results.

How Can This Concept of Nationality Be Tested?

It is important that there should be many tests rather than just a few, for operational concepts, so to speak, cannot live alone. If we are to infer some reality behind them, they must be confirmed not merely by the results of one operation (no matter how often repeated) but by at least two different operations independent from each other. They are based on the correspondence between the results of two or more mutually independent sets of tests, and they hold good for that range of situations over which this correspondence continues. Beyond this range of agreement each test may either fail or give results different from those of the others. Less formally put, an operational concept should be sharp in the middle but is apt to get frayed at the edges. Several operational tests should give us fair agreement about the main facts of the existence of a people, but each test may give us its own particular answer in borderline cases.[1]

Tests Based on Transmission or Substitution

One group of such tests for complementarity in communication, and indirectly for nationality, might be based on the operations of *transmitting information*. A simple form of such a test is an old children's game: two chains of players compete by transmitting whispered sentences from ear to ear to the end of the chain; the fun of the game is in the distortions which result. It is clear that the efficiency of any such chain could be greatly reduced by inserting persons ignorant of the language, or merely of the different accents or vocabularies of the other players.   Psychologists have developed veritable batteries of reading tests, comprehension scores, IQ tests, and the like, and the effect of differences in language or nationality on the performance of individuals or teams in these terms could be measured.   If this were done, we might know more accurately in quantitative terms to what extent differences in language, dialect, or nationality impede communication.   We might also compare the barriers to transmitting information between different peoples, or between inhabitants of different regions among a people, to the barriers existing between different classes.   From such a test we might learn whether, and to what extent, a people is a community of more efficient communication.

Some beginnings in this direction have been made.   Professor Gordon W. Allport and his coworkers developed an experimental technique for the study of rumors, in which a detailed, semi-dramatic picture was seen and described by a test person, and this description was then passed on through a chain of other persons who had not seen the picture.   The percentage of details lost at each stage of transmission was measured, and the extent of the distortions recorded. "Negro subjects took part along with white, a fact which . . . had important consequences when the test-pictures depicted scenes with a 'racial angle.'" [2]

Another group of tests might be organized around certain operations of teamwork.   We might call these tests of *organizability*.   Such tests for the speed and effectiveness of team formation have been developed for purposes of personnel selection in a number of countries, both for military purposes and for civilian industry.   Candidates in such tests have to form a team and accomplish some standardized task as quickly and accurately as they can.   Some of these tests are primitive, others somewhat more elaborate.   It would be interesting to note again the effects, if any, of language or nationality on the test scores.   In particular, we might compare the performance of nationally mixed teams against those which are nationally homogeneous.   Here again these comparisons could be made on a quantitative basis.

A group of such tests might measure what we might call *general complementarity*, that is, the reassignability and reorganizability of members of a group into different patterns of teamwork, or for widely different tasks.   Such tests might measure their group adaptability to unfamiliar situations, in contrast to their team performance of familiar tasks.

These tests already involve to some extent processes of *learning*. There are numerous tests of the speed and efficiency of learning. Some of these might be adapted to measure in quantitative terms the advantage conferred by learning in one's "own" language, from one's "own" teachers; they could be used to measure the effect of national homogeneity or national diversity on the learning processes. The significance of this effect has often been asserted by nationalists, particularly by spokesmen of national minorities, but there has been little in the way of quantitative data.[3]

Teamwork and learning involve the problem of *substitution*. What effect on the efficiency of a team has the substitution of a member from another people or culture group? What are the costs of substitution in terms of efficiency units lost, or in terms of adaptive efforts necessary, in industrial production? Are they different for skilled or unskilled labor, or for white-collar occupations? Such substitutions need not be observed merely or mainly in the laboratory. What have been the experiences of industry? What were the experiences in wartime? What have been the experiences in this respect of bringing established industrial processes to foreign countries? Is a people a community of easier substitution?

Related to the problem of substitution is the problem of *intermarriage*. What has been the ratio of in-group to out-group marriages, and how do the ratio of marriages to divorce compare for each of these? Is a people a community of more frequent or more stable intermarriage? And if so, is it also a community of more frequent inheritance of property, and of the other social and economic opportunities which usually accompany family ties?

Similar questions could be asked for *commensality*, the practice of eating together. What adaptive efforts, if any, in providing for different food habits and eating customs does it require for members of different nationalities? How do these burdens compare with those that would apply to the eating together of members of different income groups, occupations, or classes? Is a people a community of easier commensality? When and to whom is commensality refused? To what extent, if any, are these refusals related to the technical difficulties of catering, and to what extent are they due to quite different reasons?

A *neighborhood* functions as an informal but effective team in bringing up children. How serious are here the effects of differences in language or culture? How do they compare with the effect of other differences, or with the habits of class and occupation?

All these tests and situations reveal something about complementarity and ease of substitution. It is not suggested that political scientists should suddenly begin to try to measure all these things. A good many of them have in fact been investigated by sociologists, sometimes with the help of statistics. What would be desirable, however, would be to have these materials brought together and brought in such a form that their results can be connected with those of the other disciplines.

Tests Based on Predictability of Behavior

Another group of operations relevant for the concept of a people are those which might measure the *predictability* of various reactions of an individual. We are told that many of these reactions are culturally conditioned. How predictable are on the average the results of such conditioning, and to what extent are the members of a people connected with each other by a larger number of predictable reactions than they are with anybody else?

One of the things to be measured here might be predictability of *recall*. Do members of one people tend to give more similar answers to word association tests than members of different peoples? Recall of words and images is involved in the perception and recognition of information presented to us,[4] and some practical guess as to the probable recall and association of other persons is involved in all propaganda and all advertising. It is decisive for the *connotation* even more than for the denotation of words, for the denotation can be specified when the word is used. A group of persons having similar characteristics of recall can foretell each other's responses, catch each other's allusions and private jokes; they *understand* each other.

Recall and association influence the recognition of even well-defined information. They assimilate it to the previously acquired habits, stereotypes, and expectations of the group. In Professor Allport's experiments on rumor, described earlier, white persons were shown a picture which contained a white man holding a razor while arguing with a Negro. "In over half the experiments with this picture, the final report indicated that the Negro (instead of the white man) held the razor in his hand. . . ."[5]

Such experiments suggest the ominous possibility of a people united by a community of delusions. The effectiveness of such a community of clichés could then be measured through its statistical effects on the transmission of information.

Predictability might include the predictability of *emotional responses*. Nationalists have mentioned them with reverence; hardboiled psychologists have measured some of their aspects in terms of heartbeat, blood pressure, and adrenalin release in response to certain symbols. The effectiveness of some of these tests, such as the famous "lie detector," still seems controversial; perhaps some of these tests are more effective in separating indifference and responsiveness, rather than identifying more closely the particular kind of reaction. Even so, do the test scores of members of the same people tend to be more similar to each other than to the scores of other persons? If some political scientists have told us that members of a nation are connected by a "unifying myth," are psychologists going to show us nationality in a community of "lie detector" charts?

Limited aspects of predictability can be tested in the laboratory, but a broader and in some ways more important test is applied in practical affairs. We try to predict other people's behavior by "putting ourselves into their place," by comparing it with the results of our own introspection. We try to predict their overall performance by comparing it with our own. To the extent that we succeed, we say we understand them. Here is one of the most important bases for the notion of a people, for that "consciousness of kind," of familiarity and trust, which we have for people whom we understand, and whom we even understand to be like such excellent people as ourselves.

A people by this test is a community of *predictability from introspection*. The predictive efficiency which results from it should be a measurable fact. If so, it is a fact of political and economic significance, for it will be related to such things as reliability, the "we" feeling, and the willingness to accept substitution, or to intermarry. These, in turn, strongly influence men's business and employment opportunities, and the transfer of property through intermarriage and inheritance. In the history of nationalism, the experience of "foreignness" as unpredictability is related to the *Fremdheitserlebnis*, the "experience of strangeness," so often described by historians of nationalism such as Hans Kohn,[6] and epitomized in Kipling's poem "The Stranger within the Gates." From the point of view of the psychologist, this experience is perhaps related in part to the process of *identification;* however, an identification may in part involve efforts to model our own personality on that which other group members have, or are expected to have in terms of their culture; these considerations have led some psychologists to the concept of "basic personality structure."[7] Perhaps what appears as basic personality structure to the outside observer appears at least in part as predictability from introspection to the individuals concerned.

Prediction from introspection is part of the stock in trade of the politician "who always feels as the average man feels and who is familiar with numerous people of political importance and social leadership." [8]   But this professional art of the politician may fail in periods of rapid social change, and it fails quite frequently when the politician is forced to predict the behavior of foreign peoples or statesmen with whom he is not familiar and whose emotional reactions may not resemble his own.   Politicians successful in domestic affairs are therefore often far less successful in foreign relations.   Neville Chamberlain was so successful in British politics that he became Prime Minister, but he failed fatally when he failed to understand Hitler.

Prediction from introspection should not be confused with *prediction from familiarity*.   Prediction from introspection is based on analogy of structured habits, prediction from familiarity on remembered outside observations from the past.   A white Southerner may think that he can predict what another white Southerner will probably think or do in a certain situation, because he is a man of "his own kind."   The same white Southerner may also believe that he can predict what a Negro will think or do in a certain situation, because, he thinks, he "knows Negroes."   Both types of prediction are very much subject to error, but the second type is merely based on outside familiarity with overt behavior, usually only in a very limited range of situations, even if these limited situations, perhaps such as those of master and servant, may have occurred for many years.   In the words of Alexander Leighton, " 'I know just how these people think and feel' should be classed among 'famous last words' of administrators." [9]

Neither the professional diplomat with long residence abroad nor the native informant recruited from among the foreign people can wholly overcome these difficulties.   Even for them, the failures of prediction from familiarity have been frequent and notorious.   For if a people goes through a process of intensive change in politics, economics, and the patterns of its culture; if certain culture traits and social groups and classes previously repressed or submerged in the community gain new predominance and reshape the community in their own image, as in any major revolution, then members of the people more closely identified with the old regime may well lose their past ability to predict by introspection the behavior of their compatriots.   They understand them no longer; they seem to them like aliens or madmen.[10]   Yet they retain the memory of long familiarity with a past which to them still seems permanent and normal.   They continue to predict; and the failures of the predictions of such long-standing experts on their suddenly changed countries have been well known since the days in 1792 when French emigrés advised the Duke of Brunswick on his ill-starred manifesto to the people of Paris.

If "foreignness . . . essentially . . . is . . . unpredictability," [11] then alien rulers in particular are those whose behavior cannot be predicted from introspection. Native rule, or national rule, exists, on the other hand, in such situations as those described by a well-known anthropologist: In many "occidental countries, or even Japan . . . the ruler is, as it were, an aspect of the ruled so that the individual in a dilemma can discover by introspection what the intentions of the ruler would or should be. . . ." [12] If this is true, then even a democratic regime, with ballots and a written constitution, may appear "alien" to a people, and its results may seem unpredictable or undesirable.

Western political theorists have seen the essence of the "rule of law" in its power to make life predictable.[13] Yet time and again, the Western world has been surprised that its "rule of law" seems to be rejected by large numbers of people outside the West, despite the obvious benefits of predictability which it seemed to bring to them. Perhaps now we can resolve this seeming paradox. Populations may have rejected the Western style "rule of law" quite often because it did not predict their future, or because it predicted for them a future of poverty, insecurity, or subordination which they could not accept. Since the seventeenth century the dominant institutions of Western history have included the economy of the market and the rule of law. Both the legal system and the market system were social devices to produce *predictability by contract*. But this search for predictability through the freedom of contract has been abandoned on many occasions and in many lands where it failed to fulfill some basic human need. The causes of such failure may have been too great differences in culture and tradition, or colonial exploitation, or the partial disruption of the system through acute or chronic depressions and mass unemployment.

Yet, where predictability from contract failed or became unpalatable, for whatever reason, men might still choose another road to make life predictable. They might fall back on predictability from identification and from introspection. Instead of contracting freely for prices, wages, or employment conditions on rigid abstract terms, they might prefer to have these terms set and manipulated "arbitrarily" by an authority which to them did *not* seem arbitrary because it seemed to them an authority "of their own kind," run by persons like themselves. "We don't want higher bread prices, we don't want lower bread prices, we don't want unchanged bread prices—we want National Socialist bread prices!" shouted a Nazi speaker to a wildly cheering peasants' meeting before Hitler's rise to power. Peter Drucker recorded the incident in a book appropriately titled, "The End of Economic Man." [14]

Yet it seems clear now why we should differ from the thesis suggested by this title. "Economic man" has no single beginning and no single end. He stands for a pattern of behavior which was adopted in history in the course of human efforts to make life calculable and predictable, and which often was abandoned when they turned to failure. Predictability from contract was abandoned in favor of *predictability from identification,* and even from privilege, the predictability that comes from membership in a tribe or group welded together for more or less effective mutual protection.

How "economic man" survives even this abandonment, how indeed, far from having been cast out, he reappears in a new costume, how the predictability of free contract may be replaced by *predictability from monopoly,* or power—all this must be discussed elsewhere. Suffice it here to say that the shift from market to monopoly, and from contract to identification, is powerfully aided by persistent and widespread facts of unequal complementarity of communication, and of nationality, cultural community, and predictability from introspection.[15]

The predictability of existing behavior patterns of individuals may be supplemented by the predictability of the outside models to which these persons may look for further guidance. In this sense a people is a community of *models for imitation.* Some of these models are regional: where do men and women look for their nuclear region and their capital city, the place which sets the standards of taste and elegance? This was the test by which Greek nationalists classed certain inhabitants of Macedonia as "Bulgarian-speaking Greeks." [16] Other models are linguistic: after what region and after which group of persons will they shape their speech? Both kinds of models overlap, and they may involve a more general, sociological model: which class or social group is the accepted model of behavior? [17]

We have surveyed a fairly long list of operational tests of membership in a people, and probably it could be made much longer. The broad result of many of these tests may be quite obvious, particularly where extreme differences in language delimit the communities of communication. Yet what will count will be the cumulative results. Language or memories, or habits of cooperation, or orientation to geographical cultural centers, or predictability of behavior, or historical indoctrination may weigh most in any particular case. . But it will be the function built up by all of them, the overall result of complementarity, which will be decisive.

A Pitfall: Compatibility and Social Learning

Complementarity, we have argued, can be measured; and from the results of many such measurements we might be tempted to make inferences about the probable complementarity of members of different ethnic groups. Thus we might be tempted to guess at their mutual compatibility. Compatibility might, then, appear to us as something that was somehow independent from their individual histories and present efforts; regardless of what they themselves might do, American citizens or immigrants of certain stocks—say of South European, or African, or Asiatic ancestry—would be incompatible, or less compatible, with the rest of the American people than those of certain other stocks.

Here lies a pitfall. Tests or measurements, as we discussed them, can only register the results of social learning that has occurred in an individual *up to this moment*. They say little about the long-range results of his future learning, and next to nothing about the probable future results of the social learning of his children and grandchildren, *unless* we make a larger number of very specific assumptions about the future social setting in which they will live.

In special situations the desire to assimilate to a group or to imitate a model may not lead to success, if there is a major lack of *compatibility* between the group and the new candidate, or between the model and the would-be imitator. Some minor difficulties of compatibility may be physical. Some money is earned by manufacturers of hair-straightening cosmetics sold to American Negroes who are trying to adopt their white neighbors' hair style. Most problems of compatibility, however, arise in social learning. Are the habits previously learned by the individual compatible with those now expected of him in his new surroundings? Often the claim of incompatibility has been used to deny equality or immigration to members of certain races or peoples— to a point where "compatibility" and "incompatibility" have approached the status of more polite substitutes for racism and discrimination.[18] If desired by the individual, national and cultural assimilation through social learning can go very far within the first generation, and there seems to be no *inherent* obstacle to its being substantially completed in the second, or, at most, the third. It is well known that persons of the most different racial or cultural stocks have made important contributions to American welfare.

If assimilation is unsuccessful, despite the individual's efforts to accept the new culture in place of the old, the reason lies usually with the community which is taken for a model, or in which assimilation is sought. Many American-born children of Japanese immigrants—the Nisei—had become thoroughly Americanized by 1941; and many of them fought in the United States Army during World War II. If many of them had been evacuated from California in 1942, and kept in camps, often for no other reason than their ancestry, and if some of these evacuees then renounced their American citizenship and after 1945 returned to defeated Japan, there is a good deal of evidence that the situation at bottom was not so much one in which assimilation to American culture had failed, but one in which assimilation had been effectively refused to a minority by native pressure groups.[19] A much larger and ultimately far more tragic version of a forced reversal of assimilation culminated during the same World War in Europe in the expulsion and mass extermination of Jewish minorities in Germany and a number of other European countries.

Apart from such tragedies caused by specific denials or reversals of assimilation—denials usually with very specific political and economic reasons behind them—men's habits of mutual understanding and communication are subject to continuous change as they live and learn together, or learn to grow apart. Are there any regularities in the results of this learning?

How Do Communications Habits Change?

Will the experiences of life in a particular society tend to standardize the communications habits of its population? We saw that all habits relevant for communication are learned habits, subject to change. It is to the learning process that we must look for an answer.

Here the crucial process involves memory. Generally, in communication the message that emerges from a communications channel is the result of the message that was put in, as modified by the characteristics of the channel. One way of modifying messages going through a channel is to superimpose on them other messages, perhaps some messages previously stored and now recalled from some device of memory. It is characteristic of communication in society and culture that all messages moving through their channels at any time are apt to be modified by the effects of previously stored information from their past. Current experiences from social life are thus perceived, acted upon, and again stored in memory, with some modification. So modified, however, this stored information may affect the learning process both of the individuals concerned and of their community, for both individuals and communities continue to learn at least to some extent almost as long as they live.

Information about a social experience, therefore, as modified by the channels of language and culture,[20] and as further modified by the stored memories of individual and group, is then acted upon and remembered by the same group which has just transmitted it. Men and groups of men, like certain simpler devices, include the results of their own actions among the new input signals or "experiences" by which they guide their further action. And, as with all learning processes, they need not merely use this new information for the guidance of their behavior in the light of the preferences, memories, and goals which they have had thus far, but they may also use them to *learn*, that is, to modify this very inner structure of their preferences, goals, and patterns of behavior.

To impose the same social experience on members of two different peoples means, therefore, to feed the same kind of information into two different processes of learning. If the members of the two different peoples continue to live in the same society they may, therefore, at most continue to receive an identical stream of outside information. But this is not their only information. Each of them receives not merely its own peculiar information recalled from its own past but also a continued stream of information about its own peculiar responses to the present. Each member of two different peoples in the same society will, therefore, receive at least three streams of information: the standardized stream of experiences (as we assume it to be) from social and economic life; second, the peculiar stream of information from the past within his own community and from such present peculiar messages as may originate within it; and third, the feedback stream of information about the results of his own peculiar responses which he made in the light of the interplay of all three streams.

It seems clear from these considerations that the outcome of these processes of national assimilation or disassimilation within the same society cannot simply be predicted once for all, but that it can perhaps be estimated for each particular situation in quantitative terms.

If the statistical weight of standardized experience is large, and the weight of recalled information within the group is relatively small, and the statistical weight of feedback information about the group's peculiar responses is likewise small, *then* the responses of such a group would differ from the responses of other groups in the same situation by a converging series, until the remaining differences might fall below the threshold of political significance. This is the process of *assimilation*.

It would follow from its structure that this process will at best occur only slowly if the separate learning process of the minority group remains intact; that it may not occur at all if this learning process of the group is highly elaborate; but that it may occur quickly if this separate learning process of the minority should be broken up and its members be deprived of their peculiar group communications and traditions. The known facts about the speed and extent of recorded cases of national assimilation or disassimilation of larger groups seem to bear out these conclusions.

Perhaps this approach may also suggest something about the relative costs of rapid group assimilation as against the costs of group assimilation which is slow. For any given volume of standardized experience from society, group assimilation can only be further accelerated by reducing or destroying the "competing" information recalled from the unassimilated past, and by reducing or repressing the unassimilated responses to which it would give rise in the present. But this repression or destruction of past experience implies some destruction of learning, and, to the degree that a rich structure of information and habits from the past is essential to satisfactory life and efficient performance in the many different situations of modern civilization, the rapidly assimilated ex-members of the minority may find themselves painfully the poorer. In so far as they will find it essential to replace their old and now destroyed habits and patterns of behavior by new ones, this effort will take up much of their time and uncommitted resources for learning a new set of basic linguistic and social habits. It may leave them with correspondingly fewer uncommitted resources, that is, with a smaller learning capacity, for the new learning of scientific or technological skills which industrial society may require. Slower group assimilation, on the other hand, might under these conditions involve less destruction of cultural heritage and more of its gradual transfer, leaving a larger amount of learning capacity available at every stage to cope with the needs of expanding technology in our time.

Changing Speeds of Assimilation with Changes in Experience

What has been said would seem to apply to different rates of assimilation against an unchanged, and perhaps a relatively low, input of assimilatory experiences from society. However, assimilation can be accelerated very greatly by increasing the rate of new experiences from society. This may occur by a total change of environment, such as in group migration, if the experiences in the new country should in fact prove to be new, varied, and numerous. In practice, the radical change in external experiences due to a new country will usually be supplemented by the loss of many ties and channels of communication with the surroundings and culture which the migrant left behind. The relatively rapid and effective assimilation of Gaelic-speaking Highlanders in Glasgow at the end of the eighteenth century, or the assimilation of immigrants to the United States is a case in point. On the other hand, where contacts with the new environment are cut down to a minimum and a newly settled group insists for political or economic reasons on living as much as possible in a new replica of its own older environment, the results may well be the perpetuation of unassimilated islands of privilege for long periods of time.[21]

Immigration is not the only way in which a greatly increased stream of new similar experiences may come to bear upon the members of two different peoples. Instead of packing up and going where the new experiences are, the members of several peoples may stay put and have a flood of new experiences come to them in a period of major social change. What is required then, of course, is more than a change in some minor aspect of society. It would have to be a change affecting profoundly the stream of experiences in their daily life, such as the French Revolution of 1789, which changed the patterns of land holding, taxation, choice of occupation, symbols, education, distribution of prestige, and a host of other things in almost every village, and so welded large numbers of Alsatians, Bretons, and Provençals into Frenchmen.[22] Or it might be a slower but still rapid stream of changes such as the English Industrial Revolution which transformed many aspects of British life in about two generations.

It is only in part the fact of such changes in experience, their mere rate and extent, which has these effects. To an important degree it is the *content* of the changes which influences their results. The new experiences of the Alsatians after 1789 included many important new opportunities for them to follow goals which they had previously held: they gained land, equality before the law, freedom of enterprise, and much besides.[23]

Another factor may be the timing of such changes in the sequence of events. The British sense of unity was deepened by the Industrial Revolution, but it had already grown during the two centuries that went before, so that those who remained to be integrated after 1760 were in one sense only fringe groups, though they were important from the point of view of Wales and Scotland.

Altogether, the kinds of changes most conducive to assimilation may be specified: they are changes promoting more intensive communication among contemporaries, and more opportunities for the pursuit of goals and values already held from the preceding period.

If common experiences lack these qualities, if they even involve, on the contrary, a shrinking of social communication and individual opportunities, if trade shrivels, cities shrink in population, or populations are driven back to villages or fixed to the land—even then assimilation may proceed, but it seems apt to proceed a great deal more slowly. Thus the Slavic settlers in the Peloponnesus were assimilated to the Greek speech of the towns during the "dark ages"; the peasants of Egypt gradually changed their Coptic speech for Arabic between the seventh and the twelfth centuries A.D. (although the process may not have been completed until the sixteenth); and the Wendish peasants of Eastern Germany gradually became Germans between the tenth and the eighteenth centuries. Assimilation in all these cases was slow, but it was not reversed. It may be noted that populations in these three cases remained in their villages; they were not uprooted; their assimilation in the long run tended to increase both their own security and that of the dominant group; and there was no powerful group on the scene which would have stood to gain from forcing them to stay apart.

Some Conditions of National Differentiation

We cannot foretell in general whether similar experiences will unify dissimilar communities, though we have been able to say something about certain conditions under which they may do so. We may be able to answer, however, the opposite question: *Will dissimilar experiences differentiate originally similar communities?*

From our consideration of the learning process the answer should be yes. If different experiences are consistently fed into similar systems of communication and learning, the information stored in each such system, and then the system's output which that stored information helps to shape will become different. The differences may be slight at first. But, since the results of these different responses are also fed back into each system (in other words, because each community remembers what it did and what then happened), these differences should then tend to grow in a diverging series, and perhaps in the shape of an ever steepening curve.

The cumulative effects of dissimilar experiences could perhaps be overbalanced by increased communication from within each group. An isolated minority in a strange new country might increase its efforts to recall its past and to standardize its behavior, so as to erase again and again the eroding effects of the new environment on its traditional culture. If such a group can at the same time find some special niche in the common society, so that even its social and economic experiences will be less similar to those of other groups than they otherwise would be, then this group may retain its separate cohesion for long periods of time. The history of special "trading peoples," such as Parsees, Armenians, and Jews, may offer examples.[24]

Some writers have claimed that modern transportation and technology should similarly tend to resist assimilation. The German immigrant in North or South America, according to this reasoning, can now receive by mail German newspapers and German books; print will stabilize his spelling and grammar (the radio, by this logic, should stabilize his pronunciation); travel by rail and ship (and now by airplane) should keep up his personal contacts; education in the minority school should preserve tradition for his children; and all these effects should be reinforced by letters, telegraph, and telephone, and all the other modern channels of communication. As a result, cultural boundaries between peoples should not become dimmer or weaker, but sharper and more permanent than ever.[25] This prediction was converted by Adolf Hitler into a political program: ". . . We do not surrender a single German who lives beyond the frontiers of the German State and within the frontiers of another civilized State or colony, as regards his national membership with the German Reich." [26]

It is well known that in the Western Hemisphere these predictions proved quite false and that they have proved similarly false in many other cases. The resistance to assimilation by some German minorities in Eastern Europe, which seems to have impressed these authors in the first place, was not due to excellent communications with Germans in Germany; until their expulsion after 1945, these groups had been just as resistant to assimilation since the thirteenth century, long before railroads or telegraphs had ever been heard of. There was probably more letter writing and more travel between Germany and Milwaukee during the last three generations, than between, let us say, Germany and some German village in Rumania. Yet the highly literate German immigrants of Milwaukee became Americans, and the less literate Germans in Rumania stayed German. The effects even of radio and airplanes look quite different from a quantitative point of view: both adults and children still spend most of their hours living and working, and not in ships, trains, or airplanes, nor in minority school classrooms, nor in listening to broadcasts or reading books in the old language of their parents. With whom they live, with whom they work, and with whom as a result of these experiences they will continue to communicate in daily life will be decisive.[27]

The quantitative balance between the effects of a community of communications inherited from the past, and the stream of new experiences from social and economic life in the present, has been discussed above. There seems to be no evidence that improvements in the arts of passenger transport, printing, and telegraphy have as yet made a major difference in this balance.

The whole discussion thus far has been in terms of communication, and therefore quite one-sided. The process of learning can be described as a sequence of four steps: drive, cue, response, and reward. Communication can tell us much about the stages of *cue* and *response*, but only very little about *drive* and *reward*. The facts which are decisive for these latter steps belong to the fields of other social sciences. In general terms they may have to be discussed with the help of the findings of sociology and economics; in specific terms we need the facts of geography and history. This discussion would have to be carried on separately for each particular, and in some respects unique, situation. All we can do here and now is to suggest that the fundamental concepts of the several social sciences could be brought in such a relationship to each other that the methods of these different sciences can be applied in combination to each particular case.

Perhaps we may try to make a small beginning in this direction by looking now at some of the forces that furnish much of the "drive" behind the making and breaking of states: the national effects of social mobilization and their quantitative relationships to the merging and dividing of peoples and nations.

Chapter 6

National Assimilation
or Differentiation
SOME QUANTITATIVE
RELATIONSHIPS

Situations favorable to ethnic assimilation or differentiation often have been produced by the acts of persons who neither foresaw nor desired any such results. Migrations were undertaken for economic, political, or military reasons; employers recruited labor; speculators sought and found buyers for their land; generals sought soldiers; landowners wished to enhance the value of their holdings by promoting industries or mining operations, and by teaching new skills to the serfs or tenants on their estates.

Where towns or industries grew quickly, they created a social "updraft," a veritable "lift-pump effect" on the population of surrounding —or even distant—country districts, attracting thousands and eventually millions into new settlements, occupations, and patterns of intensive social intercourse.

Masses of people were uprooted when landowners replaced tenants by sheep, as in England since the Tudors, or by deer-parks, as in Scotland in the nineteenth century; when famine drove families from the land, as in the Ireland of the 1840's, or in China during much of the eighteenth century; or when slave raiders seized and transplanted populations bodily; or when education and eagerness made people able and willing to emigrate. In all these cases masses of people were set adrift to collect eventually, sometimes after generations, in the rising centers and areas of settlement, within their "own" country or abroad, within the area of their own language and culture or outside it, for national assimilation or for national conflict.[1]

The more people moved from village to town, from farm to factory, from old houses and countries to new ones—and the more new ways of life moved out even to those who had stayed where they had been born—the more drastically was the "cake of custom" broken for ever larger parts of the world's population, and the more critical became for them the question of cultural and national assimilation or differentiation in their new surroundings.

A critical question; yet it was posed unwittingly, by the deeds of men who often knew little and cared less about these consequences; and it was posed to masses of people most often unaware of what was in store for them.

There are cases where unassimilated minorities collect as the result of migrations, changes in settlement, or in the economic division of labor: thus Greeks settled in Asia Minor, Chinese came to Malaya, Germans were scattered over parts of Eastern Europe. Or the unassimilated group, now set in motion and collecting in ever larger numbers in new areas of commerical or industrial development, may turn out to be a majority of the population of the territory—a majority whose members now break through, as it were, the thin veil of foreign speech and culture that had been spread over the country at an earlier time when most of its inhabitants were still quiescent in secluded villages. Thus, already in the Middle Ages, brewers and other guildsmen in fourteenth century London brought the English language into the Norman courts; Flemings recaptured control of Bruges from the French in 1302; and a Czech majority in 1418 seized the government of Prague from her German patricians. Later, Dublin, first built by the Danes, and then long governed by the English, gradually became ever more of an Irish city during the eighteenth and nineteenth centuries. Today Dublin is the center of an Irish State; and the roll of similar cases of "national awakening" in Asia and Africa extends from China to Morocco, and from Hong Kong to Johannesburg.

Some of these developments were foreseen by perceptive observers, others would have come as a surprise to some of the policy makers who took some of the major steps that led to them. Yet, in either case, results often seemed to force their way almost independently from men's foresight or desire.

On the other hand, intense national consciousness and deliberate planning often came to nought. In the United States, immigrants proud of the traditions of their native cultures saw their children grow away from the old-world language and customs of their parents. Foreign language schools, journals, and societies were founded in profusion to keep the immigrants in touch with each other and with the culture of their old country, and yet most of these institutions withered away after a few years or decades. Acute consciousness and deliberate will seemed powerless to halt the objective processes of cultural and national assimilation.

What are the laws that underlie these processes? What are the observable regularities and the quantitative relations which furnish the framework within which men and women make their own decisions and their own history?

Perhaps we may gain by attacking first a simpler aspect of the problem in the case of linguistic assimilation. How do large populations acquire a new language? How is an old language extinguished? The principles which we may discover in cases of this kind may then perhaps prove applicable to the social learning and unlearning of other habits of communication relevant for the waxing or waning of nationalism and nationality.

The Rate of Assimilation

As a first approximation we may say that assimilation to a new language is progressing if the number of persons who are learning it during a given period—i.e., who are added to the *assimilated population*—is larger than the number of persons who are as yet ignorant of it but who are entering into intensive economic, social, or political contact with its speakers, that is to say, who are added to the "mobilized population," as explained below.

If we remember our distinction between society and community, we may say that assimilation is gaining ground if, in a given territory, community is growing faster than society. In other words, assimilation progresses if the ability to communicate over wide ranges of subjects is spreading faster among men than is necessitated by their working together directly and by the limited but direct communication which this entails. The need for communication does not immediately produce the proportionate ability to communicate. Assimilation occurs if this ability grows faster than this need; differentiation is sharply felt if the need outruns the ability.

Assimilation in language or culture involves the learning of many new habits, and the unlearning of many old ones—habits, in both cases, which often interlock and reinforce each other. Such learning as a rule is slow; its changes are counted in decades and generations.

The growth of an economy or a technology, on the other hand, may be much more rapid; transportation systems and markets can grow very quickly; workers or immigrants may be recruited and imported within a few years, or sometimes even months. Much of this economic or technological development may force people into new and inescapable contacts with each other as workers, customers, and neighbors—

contacts far narrower, perhaps, than the range of human relations that can be communicated within one culture; but contacts far wider than the relations which can be communicated in the absence of a common culture to outsiders. Linguistically and culturally, then, members of each group are outsiders for the other. Yet technological and economic processes are forcing them together, into acute recognition of their differences and their common, mutual experience of strangeness, and more conspicuous differentiation and conflict may result.

The Rate of Mobilization

Within any geographical setting and any population, economic, social, and technological developments mobilize individuals for relatively more intensive communication.[2] We may call this the social and political public, or the *mobilized population*, and we may delimit this mobilized population (i.e., population mobilized for mass communication) by various yardsticks of measurement: the set of persons who live in towns; the set of persons engaged in occupations other than agriculture, forestry, and fishing; the set of persons who read a newspaper at least once a week; the set of persons who pay direct taxes to a central government; or who are directly subject to military conscription; the set of persons who have attended public or private schools for at least four years; the set of persons attending markets at least once a month; the set of persons sending or receiving a letter at least once a month; the set of literate adults, of movie-goers, or radio listeners, of registered voters for elections, or of insured persons under social security schemes; or all persons working for money wages in units with five or more employees; and many more.

The fourteen sets just specified should overlap a great deal. Together they might well serve to indicate the public or the mobilized population, perhaps as that part of the population for whom at least two of these fourteen criteria coincide. If this public could then be indicated on a population map, similar to the cluster maps shown in Chapter 2, then the areas of intensive communication could be shown there. If, on the other hand, the mobilized population could be indicated on a sociological profile of the population, showing the numbers of persons on different levels of income or occupation, then the distribution of the public could be shown in this "vertical" dimension of society. Finally, if both the "horizontal" geographic and the "vertical" sociological pictures of intensive intercourse could be drawn for the same country or region at different periods, then the rate of growth of the mobilized population, the shifts of its centers in space, and the changes in its sociological level could all be calculated.

Why, you will object, should we furnish frameworks for statistics which do not exist? For if they existed, would we not all have read them? The answer to this objection is, first of all, that many of these statistics do exist for a number of countries, such as Austria-Hungary and her successor states. Far more statistics of this kind exist, moreover, in the files of census bureaus and statistical offices of many countries. Many countries have statistics of literacy, of town and country population; they have income statistics, occupational statistics, and statistics of the nationalities and language groups among their population. All the data we need could be obtained from the correlation of these data which exist.

Sometimes it seems that such correlations have been made but that governments were loath to publish them: why reveal complete data about a delicate situation at the risk of furnishing ammunition to political opponents? Why not rather select for publication only those "sound" data which would support one's own righteous case? The omitted correlations between the social and the national statistics of some Central European countries speak an eloquent language.

In other cases, the figures are available. Of the 49 countries listed in a recent United Nations survey as publishing census data on their rural and urban population, 12 are also listed as publishing at least some cross tabulations of their rural-urban figures with some data on languages or ethnic nationality.[3]

As regards developments within the United States, a good many data are available. We know, e.g., the number of American Negroes in town and country, in the North and in the South, their birth rates in the different areas; we know a good deal about their occupations, their migration patterns, their far-reaching cultural assimilation, and their small rate of racial assimilation or "passing," and the various calculations suggested here and in the rest of this chapter might provide useful background material for a prognosis on some of the problems of the Negro people in the United States.[4]

It is not our purpose here to collect all these statistics, but rather to show that they can be collected and that they are worth collecting. If we succeed in showing this, then the means and manpower for the processing of the available statistics may well be found some day.

With this objection out of the way, let us proceed to the groups of people we need to investigate.

The Crucial Population Groups

Altogether, we shall need to know the numbers for nine groups of the population and for six rates of change in order to be able to calculate, at least approximately, the probable developments towards either national assimilation or national conflict in a given area. Examples of such groups from the case of Swedes and Finns in Finland are given in Fig. 14, and are discussed in a later section of this chapter. The rates of change are discussed in the last section of this chapter.

The first quantity is the number of *total population* in an area, which we shall call P. The second is the public, or the socially *mobilized population* of an area, which we shall call M. To find the third group, let us assume for the time being that every person can either be considered mobilized for intensive communication, or not so mobilized. Let us neglect for the time being the persons who may be exactly halfway in transition between these two states. If we make this assumption, then that part of the total population which is not mobilized for intensive communication forms the inactive or *underlying population* and we shall represent their number by the letter U (and obviously, $U = P - M$).

The fourth group we are interested in is the *assimilated population,* those who have already become speakers of the predominant language, and we shall designate this group by the letter A. If we assume again that all persons either are or are not assimilated to this language or culture, and thus neglect for the time being those who have progressed just about halfway on the point toward assimilation, we arrive at the *differentiated population,* the fifth group, whom we shall designate by the letter D (and, of course, $D = P - A$).

In actual fact, every individual in the population is at one and the same time a member of three of these groups: he is always a member of the total population P; he must be, on our assumption, either a member of the mobilized population M or the underlying population U; and he must also, on our assumption, be either a member of the assimilated population A or of the differentiated population D.

The actual combination of memberships in certain of these first five groups gives the remaining four of our nine groups. The sixth of these is the set of persons who are both *mobilized and assimilated;* they have been mobilized for intensive communication and assimilated to the predominant language or culture. They will be the most active carriers of this nationality and the national language; in conflicts they will form the national spearhead, and we shall designate them by the letter *N*.

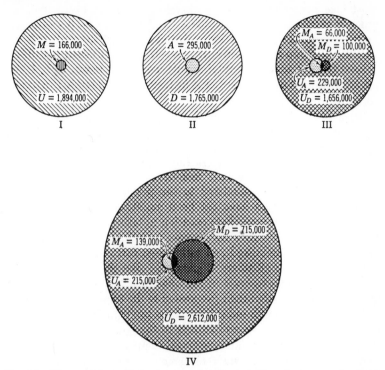

Fig. 14. The crucial population groups; Swedes and Finns in town and country in Finland, 1880 and 1940. I: Mobilized population *M* vs. underlying population *U*, approximated by town vs. country population, 1880. II: Assimilated population *A* (Swedish speakers) vs. differentiated population *D* (Finnish speakers), 1880. III: Sets I and II combined; the nationality situation in town and country, 1880. IV: The changed nationality situation in town and country, 1940. *U*, underlying population; *M*, mobilized population; *A*, assimilated population; *D*, differentiated population; M_A, Swedish speakers in towns; M_D, Finnish speakers in towns; U_A, Swedish speakers in country; U_D, Finnish speakers in country. M_A, M_D, U_A and U_D correspond, respectively, to the general groups *N*, *H*, *Q* and *R* listed in the text. For statistical sources, see Appendix I. Diameters of circles are proportional to the number of persons in each group. (Areas of circles and segments are therefore *not* representative. A more accurate graphic representation is given in Fig. 15.)

Seventh, there are those persons who are *mobilized but differentiated;* they have been mobilized for intensive communication but have not been assimilated to the predominant language and culture. These persons have remained culturally or linguistically different from the members of group N, and they are frequently and acutely reminded of this difference by the intensity of social communications in which they must take part. These persons therefore are more likely than any others to experience national conflict, and they are the persons who first take part in it. We shall designate this nationally heterodox (if not "heretical") group by the letter H. The share of mobilized but differentiated persons among the total population, in our terms, H/P, is the first crude indicator of the probable incidence and strength of national conflict.

When there is national conflict within the mobilized population between those mobilized individuals who are culturally assimilated and those who are not, two additional groups may be significant. The first of these—or the eighth of our nine—is the *underlying assimilated* population. It consists of those members of the underlying population who are already assimilated to the predominant language and culture. These persons have not been mobilized for social communication and have no immediate occasion to take part in national conflict, but if and when they do become mobilized, they will enter it on the side of the mobilized and assimilated carriers of the dominant culture and become members of group N. We shall designate these quiescent population reserves of the dominant language by the letter Q; and we may note that their proportion to the total population, Q/P, may give us some rough indication of the probable long-run strength of the dominant language and culture in the area, as more and more people are mobilized for intensive social communication.

As our ninth group, finally, those among the underlying population who are culturally or linguistically unassimilated may be designated by the letter R. This *underlying differentiated* group R forms a potential reserve for a national irredenta, and may join eventually the ranks of the mobilized differentiated group H, provided that their mobilization will proceed faster than their assimilation.

Four Examples

FINLAND. The processes of mobilization and assimilation may be illustrated rather strikingly in the case of Finland where statistical records reach back for over 200 years, and fairly detailed records for almost a century. The most important of these data are summarized in Fig. 15, with further details given in Appendix I.

Finland in 1749 had a little over 420,000 inhabitants, and only about 5 per cent of these—about 21,000—lived in towns. The country was then a Swedish colony; the Swedish element in the population num-

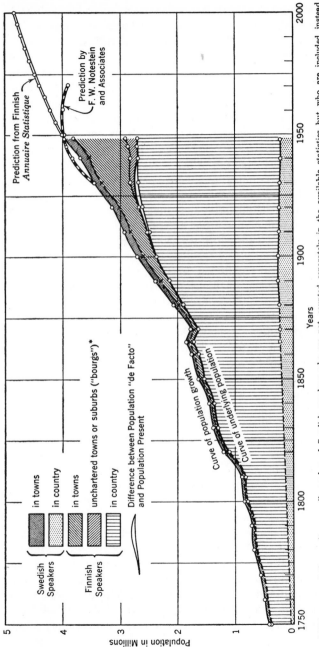

* This representation omits a small number of Swedish speakers who are not counted separately in the available statistics but who are included instead among the total number of Swedish speakers in rural areas.

Fig. 15. Social mobilization, population growth, and national assimilation in Finland, 1750–1948. Early in the period, Swedish language and culture were predominant in letters, business, politics, and urban life, and Finns in these occupations were assimilated to it. Later, assimilation was outstripped by social mobilization and population growth; Finnish replaced Swedish as the predominant language and culture, and the direction of assimilation was reversed. The trends of this process appear to have been continuous, despite several major changes in political regime. For statistical sources and methods used, see Appendix I.

bered 16.3 per cent or about 68,000, which included, in all likelihood, most of the inhabitants of the towns. The dominant language and culture of the country were Swedish; Finnish had little or no status in politics, business life, literature or society.

Half a century later, by 1800, the total population had grown to almost 833,000 and the population in the towns to about 47,000; and in the towns there were more Finns than before. The process continued: the total population grew, but the urban population grew faster, and the numbers of Finns moving into the cities were greater than the numbers of Swedes (which we shall use here as a shorter word for "Swedish-speaking citizens of Finland"), which were added in the cities by birth, migration and assimilation put together. There is some reason to think that Finns came to outnumber Swedes in the towns before 1830, although mere numbers at that time could not outweigh the advantages of Swedish class position and prestige.

By 1865, the first year for which we have separate figures of Swedes and Finns for the country as a whole, Finns were clearly in the majority among the urban population; by 1880, when separate language counts began to be taken for towns and country, they outnumbered in the towns the Swedes almost five to three; by 1900 their lead was almost three to one, and it has continued to grow until the present and may well continue to do so in the future.[5]

In the course of this process Finland changed from a Swedish-speaking to a Finnish-speaking country, although Swedish has retained a respected status as second official language. The steps in this process parallel strikingly the curve of mobilization and entry of Finns into the towns. The first edition of the later-to-be-famous Finnish folk epic *Kalevala* appeared in 1835. A generation of "Fennomanes" began to exchange their Swedish-style family names for Finnish ones between the 1840's and 1860's. Finnish became the official language of the country in a series of steps between 1863 and 1902; and a national system of primary schools, as well as a rapid expansion of secondary schools, came into being after 1868.[6]

Some of this process was accelerated by the political separation of Finland from Sweden after 1811 and her connection with Russia as a Duchy with a significant degree of autonomy. The Swedes in Finland hoped for support from Finnish popular feeling in their desire not to be submerged by Russia; and the Imperial Russian Government, true to the time-honored logic of "divide and rule," preferred the Finns to feel like Finns rather than to have them feel and act like Swedes. Yet the course of Finnish social mobilization and national awakening swept on over the decades in a manner which seems to dwarf the political manoeuvres of each day. When Finland became an independent country after 1918, the Finnish and not Swedish character of her culture had become fully, and it seems irrevocably, established.

BOHEMIA, 1800–1900. A second example, from an area of even greater national conflicts, can be found in the case of Czechs and Germans in Bohemia.[7] (A later section of this chapter considers this area in greater detail, but an outline may be sketched in at this point.)

Early in the nineteenth century, probably less than a third of the total population of Bohemia was mobilized for intensive communication by any of our tests. (A rough measure of the number of persons who were mobilized about the years 1815 or 1820 would be the inhabitants of towns.) At the same time, somewhat more than one-half of this mobilized population was assimilated to German language and culture, being either of predominantly German descent or else of a predominantly mixed or Czech extraction, having become assimilated to German language and culture during preceding generations. At the same time, more than two-thirds of the inhabitants of the country belonged to the underlying population that took little or no part in intensive social communication; and, since about two-thirds of the total population was Czech, the Czech share in the underlying population was even higher.

There was considerable population increase among both Germans and Czechs during the hundred years that followed, but the increase in industrialization and social mobilization among both peoples was still considerably higher. By 1900 the share of unassimilated Czechs among the mobilized population corresponded much more closely to their share in the total population than it had a hundred years before. A clear majority of the mobilized population M was by now Czech, and the national conflict was intense. At the same time, the reserves of the underlying Czech population were not yet exhausted, and, so far as the population within the country of Bohemia was concerned, there seemed to be no chance to keep the German language and culture from losing their dominant position and being replaced in that role by the language and culture of the Czechs, with all the political and economic consequences that this might entail.

If their privileged position was to be preserved, the only way out for the members of the old group N, the mobilized Germans, was to change the entire political and economic unit within which the process of mobilization would continue. They had to try to make Bohemia a part of Greater Germany and to make the old Austro-Hungarian Empire a part of a German-ruled *Mittel-Europa,* so as to be able to draw upon whatever reserves might be available among the underlying German rural population as well as among the poorer German urban strata in other areas. They had to rely in the meantime on accelerated assimilation of the Czechs, and on political, economic, and military compulsion, to maintain the national *status quo.*

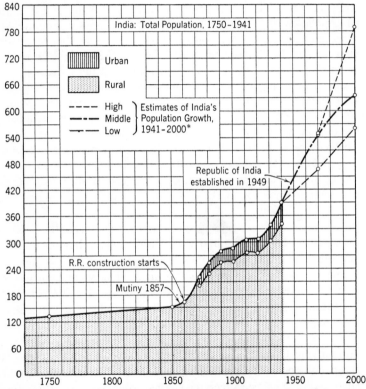

Fig. 16. The case of a very large underlying population: total population growth and urbanization in India and Pakistan, 1750–1941, and three projections of population growth to A.D. 2000. (Based on data from Kingsley Davis, *The Population of India and Pakistan,* Princeton, Princeton University Press, 1951, pp. 89–90. For full references, see Appendix III.)

INDIA. A rough quantitative analysis of this sort can be applied to the problem of "international" languages such as English in British India, or Latin in medieval Western Europe. (Some of the data for

India are summarized in Figs. 16 through 18, and further details are discussed in Appendix III.) In both these cases the group N was very small, since very few people were mobilized for communication and assimilated to these international languages; and further, the group Q, the quiescent but assimilated people who ordinarily form the first reserve for N, was relatively very small, approaching zero. Thus in India in 1931 the number of persons who were considered literate in

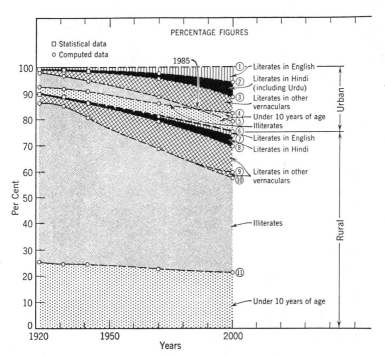

Fig. 17. Possible effects of growing urbanization and literacy on nationality and language; a schematic projection, in per cent of population, for India and Pakistan, 1920–2000. For statistics and methods used, see Appendix III. The percentage of total population under 10 years of age, both rural and urban, adds up to a constant 28.5 per cent.

English was about 1 per cent of the total population, and the number of those who listed English as their first or second language in that year was less than $\frac{1}{4}$ of 1 per cent.[7] On the other hand, in both India and medieval Europe, the quiescent but unassimilated population R was vast in numbers, and any process of social and industrial mobilization operating among these vast numbers of group R was almost certain to mobilize numbers of people of a magnitude quite out of proportion to the small number of persons who could be assimilated to the international languages and cultures of English or Latin during any one generation.[8]

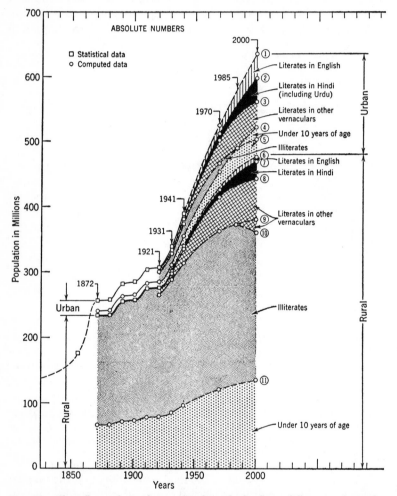

Fig. 18. The effects of population growth, and of a large differentiated population, combined with growing literacy and urbanization; a schematic projection, in millions of population, for India and Pakistan, 1850–2000, assuming a moderate estimate of population growth. Note the growing numbers of literates in languages other than Hindi and Urdu. For details and statistics, see Appendix III.

The result of this, of course, was that the mobilized but unassimilated population H was likely to grow until the use of its own language —or its one or two dozen major languages—became unavoidable in mass communication and in the conduct of political and economic business, literature, public education, the administration of justice, and all the rest, so that the erstwhile "international language" was replaced in one field after another by the vernaculars, with the speakers of the latter increasingly succeeding to positions of power and prestige.

SCOTLAND. A fourth type of situation occurred in the case of those Scottish Highlanders who were mobilized and assimilated—from Gaelic to English speech—between 1760 and 1860 during the British Industrial Revolution. Some of the Scottish figures are presented in Fig. 19, and a discussion of Scottish data is given in Appendix IV.

In this case, the mobilized and English-speaking group, N in our terminology, was already strong by 1760, comprising almost the entire population of all Scottish cities; and its reserves Q were very strong in the underlying but assimilated (i.e., here, English-speaking) population of the Lowlands and Midlothian. The underlying differentiated group R, i.e., here, the Gaelic-speaking Highlanders themselves, were only moderately strong. Rapidly mobilized and thrust into big cities by the pull of industrial employment and the push of evictions by their landlords, they formed there for a time a relatively large mobilized and differentiated group H, such that in Glasgow a number of new churches had to be provided for services in the Gaelic language.[9] In the absence of any large continuous reinforcements from the Highlands, however, the "bottom of the barrel" was soon reached, and assimilation made English the sole language of the industrial areas well before the end of the nineteenth century. Finally, in the 1880's and 1890's, when the further expansion of communication and schooling reached even the remote parts of the Highlands themselves, most of the remainder of the underlying population there were mobilized, willy-nilly, for communication, since, in fact, schools and communications came to them, and the Gaelic speech of this remaining group became once again an issue. This time, however, it really was the bottom of the barrel: the numbers concerned were small, with only the empty sea behind them, the pull of employment opportunities in the English-language area was strong, and the substantial victory of English never was in doubt.

Further Possibilities of Graphic Representation

Perhaps a rough picture of each of the situations discussed so far could be expressed by a diagram showing the peculiar variations of

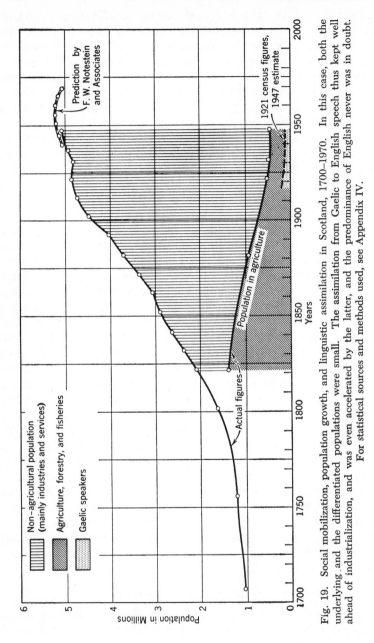

Fig. 19. Social mobilization, population growth, and linguistic assimilation in Scotland, 1700–1970. In this case, both the underlying and the differentiated populations were small. The assimilation from Gaelic to English speech thus kept well ahead of industrialization, and was even accelerated by the latter, and the predominance of English never was in doubt. For statistical sources and methods used, see Appendix IV.

each case from a common pattern. In one respect, the diagrams can be made more realistic than the verbal descriptions used thus far; we may now drop the assumption of rigid thresholds separating the assimilated from the differentiated, and the mobilized from the underlying, population. Instead, we may represent on our diagrams the ranges of adjustment as continuous, bearing only in mind that at some point along the scale a change in degree may turn into a change in kind, and that, therefore, threshold effects, although no longer postulated by the theory, may yet quite easily turn up in practice.

With these cautions, let us assume a cross of coordinates of the usual type, and let an individual's divergence from the predominant language or culture be measured along the abscissa, or x axis.[10] Let, furthermore, the individual's extent of mobilization for communications purposes be measured along the ordinate, or y axis, perhaps by the tests suggested earlier in this chapter, and assigning greater weight to those tests which indicate participation in the making of political, economic, or cultural decisions, and lesser weight to mere participation in communication. (A politician, officer, property owner, and editor of a large newspaper would rank higher on this scale than a voter, sergeant, employee, and subscriber to a paper; and both would rank above a person who was merely literate and paid taxes.)

Given this cross of coordinates, any individual's position at a given time could be indicated by a dot in the field which they define. Individuals highly assimilated to the dominant language or culture—i.e., with a low index of differentiation—would be represented by dots close to the ordinate; and individuals with a high index of mobilization would be represented by dots high above the abscissa.

The set of persons both mobilized and assimilated who are therefore the active carriers of nationality, and whom we designated by the letter N, will now appear in the upper left-hand corner of the field between the two axes; their counterparts, the mobilized but differentiated population H, will appear in the upper right-hand corner; the underlying assimilated population Q, which supplies the quiescent reserves of the predominant culture, will appear in the bottom left-hand corner; and in the lower right-hand corner the underlying differentiated population R, which, if mobilized, may furnish under certain conditions the potential rebels or resisters reinforcing D, will round out the picture. Now, however, individuals may be represented anywhere between these locations, and concentrations of dots may be found wherever in the field their placement has been warranted by the facts.

Linguistic or cultural differences between individuals or groups will be indicated on such a diagram by the horizontal distances between the symbols representing them; and differences in their mobilization for communication will be indicated by vertical distances.[11]   The numbers of individuals involved will be indicated by the number of dots, or by the number and size of symbols chosen to represent tens, hundreds, thousands, or millions of individuals.   Finally, if three nationalities are involved, and if communicative differences between them can be represented roughly on a straight line with nationality II somewhere between I and III,[12] then the intermediate language or culture may be represented at the ordinate, with one of the differing languages or cultures represented to the left, and the other to the right, of the y axis.[13]   At the moment, we may not have all the information which such a diagram could represent.   Its eventual collection might be speeded, however, by the consideration that it is now possible to organize so many specific data and to present them in a single meaningful pattern that could be recognized at a glance.

In a more schematic diagram—such as Fig. 20—we could use one symbol for each million inhabitants, and arrange our symbols in two horizontal rows, and in three vertical columns cutting across them. Symbols in the top row would represent the numbers of mobilized population for each nationality; symbols in the bottom row would represent the underlying populations.   The mobilized and underlying populations for each nationality or language group would form one vertical "national" column.

In our schematic example, let the total population be 30,000,000.   Of these, let 9,000,000 speak language X, 3,000,000 language Y, and 18,000,000 language Z.   Let, furthermore, 1,000,000 of the 9,000,000 speakers of language X speak a dialect X' which is intermediate between X and Y, so that in time they could be assimilated to either one of these two languages, and let most of them be in the early stages of mobilization so that their choice of a standard language is becoming increasingly acute.

As to the horizontal rows, altogether 6,000,000 people make up the mobilized population, and 4,000,000 of these speak language X.   At this time, therefore, these speakers of X made up two-thirds of the mobilized population, and most of town life, politics, and culture will probably be carried on in this language.

If there is economic growth, social communication probably will spread and social mobilization will progress.   In this process, another 2,000,000 speakers of language Y may join the mobilized population,

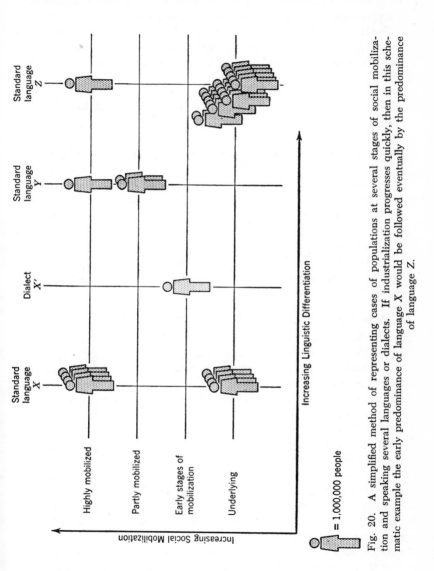

Fig. 20. A simplified method of representing cases of populations at several stages of social mobilization and speaking several languages or dialects. If industrialization progresses quickly, then in this schematic example the early predominance of language X would be followed eventually by the predominance of language Z.

and political, economic, and cultural life during this period may appear dominated by languages X and Y in competition, with Y a seemingly strong minority which is rapidly gaining ground.

Finally, if nearly the entire population should become mobilized for intensive communication, the 17,000,000 speakers of language Z will make their weight felt and may well make theirs the effective majority language.

It should be noted that this particular technique tends to neglect changes due to assimilation in the numbers of speakers of the different languages. If important, these would have to be represented by other means.

In any actual example, of course, there would be far more overlapping, more intermediate positions, and far fewer symbols neatly fitting into columns, but the main clusters would still stand out. However, even actual examples may have to be represented by a few schematic categories, depending on the categories under which the available statistical data have been lumped together by the agencies that publish them. The more refined presentation of the data, as outlined above, would be quite practicable, however, as soon as any agency should care to apply it to the data which often are already in its files.

A More Detailed Example: Bohemia 1900–1947

Thus far we have taken mostly cross sections of the process of change in the distribution of nationalities and occupational groups, and we have glanced at diagrams of the development of some of these changes in the course of industrialization or urbanization in such different countries as Finland, India, and Scotland. What happens if we follow one more such process in greater detail, and extrapolate its trends into the future?

For a concrete example of the rough work possible with the current type of published statistics, let us take the German and Czech inhabitants of Bohemia in the year 1921; and let us assume, as a first and very loose approximation, that we may count all persons occupied in agriculture and forestry as members of the underlying population U (putting aside, for the time being, the fact that many peasants by that time had entered into a great deal of social communication and political activity). Let us further count among the mobilized population M_1 all persons active in industries and crafts (although some small craftsmen among them might in fact lead a rather retired existence); and let us count all persons active in commerce, banking, transport,

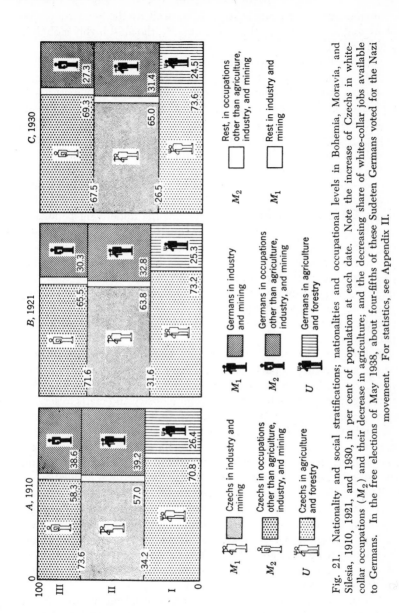

Fig. 21. Nationality and social stratifications; nationalities and occupational levels in Bohemia, Moravia, and Silesia, 1910, 1921, and 1930, in per cent of population at each date. Note the increase of Czechs in white-collar occupations (M_2) and their decrease in agriculture; and the decreasing share of white-collar jobs available to Germans. In the free elections of May 1938, about four-fifths of these Sudeten Germans voted for the Nazi movement. For statistics, see Appendix II.

communications, and administration, as well as the rentiers, professions, and miscellaneous others, as group M_2, the most highly mobilized among all three.

We then find that, on these assumptions, the underlying population, in 1910, comprised more than 34 per cent of the total; the more highly mobilized industrial group comprised 39 per cent; and the most highly mobilized group accounted for the remaining 26 per cent. (Twenty years later, in 1930, the bottom group had shrunk to 24 per cent; the middle group had grown slightly, to 42 per cent; and the most highly mobilized group had grown to about 36 per cent of the total.)

We have the nationality figures for each of these categories for 1921 for Bohemia (together, this time, with the smaller territories of Moravia and Silesia which do not change the picture materially).[14] We find, then, that in 1921 almost three-quarters of the underlying population were Czechs, and only just above one-quarter were Germans; among the industrial group, almost two-thirds were Czechs and just above one-third Germans; and among the most high mobilized group less than three-quarters were Czechs (73 per cent) and more than one-quarter (27 per cent) were Germans. These relationships are clearly shown in our diagram, Fig. 21B, in which population numbers are proportional to the respective areas shaded or left blank at each occupational level.

This diagram for 1921 shows, at once, that any further mobilization of the underlying population would have tended to reduce further the German share on the upper levels; but at the same time it shows that any substantial shift of persons from industry and crafts to services and administration—in the language of Colin Clark, any shift from "secondary" to "tertiary" occupations [15]—was bound to increase significantly German-Czech competition in these most highly mobilized occupations, well beyond what might have been inferred from the overall proportions of Czechs and Germans in the total population.

These shifts did in fact occur. Democracy, prosperity, and competitive private enterprise were accompanied by increasing social communication, easier access to higher education, and widespread shifts from factory to white-collar occupations. The very grave troubles in Bohemia that were to follow after 1921 are already foreshadowed on our simple diagram for 1921, and on the corresponding diagrams 21A and C for 1910 and 1930.

A study of the trends of nationalities and social mobilization in the three western provinces of Czechoslovakia between 1900 and 1950, represented in Fig 22, shows a remarkable continuity in the mobiliza-

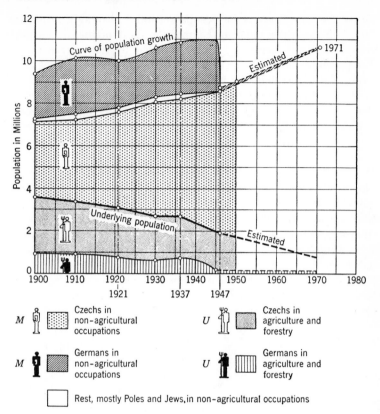

Fig. 22. Social mobilization in a nationally mixed area, where both the assimilated and the differentiated groups were large; Czechs and Germans in agricultural and non-agricultural occupations in Bohemia, Moravia, and Silesia, 1900–1971. Note the steady expansion of the Czech population in towns, industries, and services, despite two world wars and several major changes in political regime. (Sources: Austro-Hungarian Government statistics, 1900–1910; Czechoslovak Government statistics, 1920–1947; 1971 population calculated from estimate in *Statistical Bulletin of Czechoslovakia*, 1948, No. 1. For details and statistics, see Appendix II.)

tion of the Czech people for occupations other than agriculture, with
the result that the number of Germans in these urban and industrial
occupations was increasingly overshadowed by that of the Czechs.
The possibility of such a development had been foreseen by a German
writer, Professor Heinrich Rauchberg, shortly after 1900,[16] and the
process continued under the Austrian monarchy and the Czechoslovak
Republic during years of prosperity and of depression, during years of
peace and during two world wars.

Of the major discontinuities in the process, one, the German occupation of 1939–1945 with the attempted Germanization of the parts of
the area, has left no trace in the picture of the overall trend. The other
discontinuity is all the more conspicuous: the forcible expulsion of
approximately 3,000,000 Sudeten Germans and their deportation to
Germany in 1947 (with the active support of all Czech political parties
from the right to the left) show up as the sudden dwindling of the
strips representing Germans on the diagram. This change was radical,
indeed; and yet the fundamental trend toward a Czech character of
trade and industry seems to have become established long before that
time, and to have persisted with little change in direction for almost
fifty years, and perhaps even from a still earlier period in the nineteenth century. The diagram of the nationality changes in the course
of the urbanization and industrialization of Finland (Fig. 15) goes
back over a period of more than a century, and suggests a similar
constancy of trend. Trends of this kind seem to give every indication
of continuing in the future, and, if they should do so, their stability
in the past may perhaps be an indication of the size of the forces that
would be required for any attempt to change or stop them.

A further breakdown of the mobilized population into one group
occupied in industry and mining, and a second group occupied in the
white-collar occupations of commerce, transport, services, and administration (Colin Clark's "tertiary industries"), as shown in Fig. 23, re-
inforces the picture of the trends already found. White-collar occupations involve the use of language, and their members are a well-known
source of supporters for nationalist movements. The diagram shows
how much faster these white-collar strata grow than the mobilized
population as a whole, and how thus the manpower pool of potential
nationalists may tend to grow at an accelerated rate.

If we can obtain a still more detailed breakdown of statistical data,
we might dispense with the kind of simplified diagram just used and
go on to the less schematic "density-map" type of static diagram de-

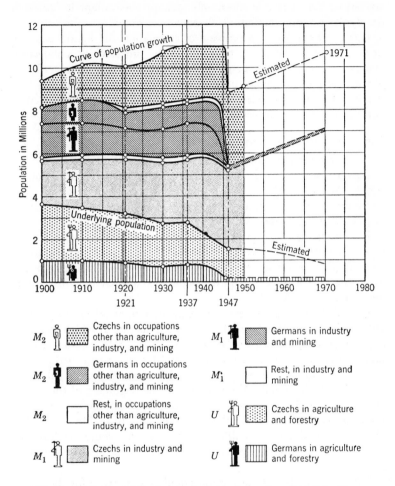

M_2 — Czechs in occupations other than agriculture, industry, and mining

M_2 — Germans in occupations other than agriculture, industry, and mining

M_2 — Rest, in occupations other than agriculture, industry, and mining

M_1 — Czechs in industry and mining

M_1 — Germans in industry and mining

M_1' — Rest, in industry and mining

U — Czechs in agriculture and forestry

U — Germans in agriculture and forestry

M — The mobilized population, is approximated by the numbers of persons with dependents, active in occupations other than agriculture and forestry.

U — The underlying population, is approximated by the numbers of persons with dependents, active in agriculture and forestry.

Fig. 23. Social mobilization in Bohemia, Moravia, and Silesia, 1900–1971, by occupations in agriculture, industry, and services. Note the shift from agriculture to industry, and to administrative and service occupations, as a factor influencing the national conflict. M and U, same as in Fig. 22. (Sources: same as Fig. 22. For statistics, see Appendix II.)

scribed earlier in this chapter, and perhaps even adapt it further to the dynamic representation of changes over time.[17]

This point leads to the problem of calculation. If figures can give us a series of snapshots, so to speak, of the processes of mobilization and assimilation at some given moment in time, we will naturally ask about their rates of change in order to be able to guess what may happen in the future, or to see what trends in the past were changed by particular events or decisions.

The Major Rates of Change

To do this, we shall need at least six such rates of change.

The first of these is the natural rate of growth of the total population P. We shall call this rate p, and define it as the average excess of births over deaths, computed per capita of the total population at the beginning of the period.

The second is the rate of natural increase (that is, again the net excess of births over deaths) of the mobilized part of the population M (e.g., the net birth rate in the towns). We shall call this b, and again compute it per capita of the population already mobilized at the beginning of the period.

The third is the rate of entry, that is, the rate at which people born outside the group M enter that group (e.g., the rate at which towns are entered by people born in the country). This rate we shall call m, and we shall compute it as the average of the net excess of those who enter the mobilized population over those who leave it, calculated per capita of the mobilized population at the beginning of the period. If during some period people should stop reading newspapers, leave their towns, and return to the seclusion of village life, or if their children should grow up illiterate, the rate m would be less than zero, since the mobilized population then would be shrinking and not growing.

The fourth is the rate of natural population increase for the assimilated population A, and we shall designate it by the small letter a. It will be computed for the population A in the same way as the natural rate of increase b was computed for the mobilized population M. In practice, rates a and b may be close together in many cases, but there may be important exceptions (e.g., the net birth rate among Latin-using intellectuals in the Middle Ages was perhaps lower than it was for the population of the towns in general). On the other hand, both a and b may frequently differ quite considerably from p, the rate of increase of the total population, in the many cases where an urbanized population assimilated to some industrial culture may have a considerably lower birth rate than is found among the population as a whole.

The fifth is the rate of assimilation, which we shall call c. This is the rate at which persons born outside the assimilated group are entering it at a later time. It will again be computed as the average net excess of those who enter the assimilated group (for instance, Poles who become Germans in East Prussia) over those who leave it (e.g., Germans in the same area who become Poles), and it will be calculated per capita of the assimilated population at the beginning of the period.[18]

Sixth, there is d, the rate of natural increase of the differentiated population D, which will be computed for that population in the same way in which the rate of increase p was to be computed for the total population P.

We can compute these six rates from data in the past wherever suitable published statistics are available, and we can then project them into the future, not as accurate predictions of what is to come, but rather as lines of guidance suggesting what might happen if the past situation were to continue without change, and to suggest the kinds and magnitude of changes to look for if a different outcome were to be expected. Some formulas for such calculations will be given in Appendix V, but we can already say that they should permit us to make predictions for the number of persons likely to be assimilated at any future date *if* a particular trend of assimilation should continue. Similarly, we could predict the number of people likely to be mobilized *if* a trend of mobilization should continue.

We could even calculate the length of the mobilization period $z(U)$, which is the number of years from the base period until the date when the underlying population will approximate zero, that is, in other words, when the entire total population of the area will have been made literate or otherwise mobilized for intensive social communication. Another such period would be the total assimilation period $z(D)$, that is, the number of years until the date when the linguistically or culturally differentiated population will approximate zero, in other words, when the entire population will have become assimilated to the predominant language or culture.[19]

By means of these quantities and rates we could also try to predict whether the number of the most likely bearers of national conflict, the mobilized but differentiated population H, would tend to shrink or grow in some particular country. The underlying population might never become exhausted (i.e., $z(U)$ might approach infinity) if the birth rate among the underlying population should remain as high as, or higher than, the rate of mobilization, so that at least as many persons are born each year in the villages as are moving to the towns. This may well still be the case in India and China at this time, and it may continue there until the birth rate in the villages falls—which under the conditions of village life does not seem likely—or until the rate of mobilization is drastically speeded up.[20]

Similarly, the time required for complete assimilation, $z(D)$, might turn out to be quite long, or even infinite, if the birth rate among the nationally or linguistically differentiated population D (which, as we know, equals $H + R$) remained as high as, or higher than, the number of persons assimilated during the same time.

We might also try to predict with the help of these methods whether, and when, national predominance in a particular country might be reversed. This would happen if the mobilized but differentiated group H should continue to grow faster than the mobilized assimilated group N, so that the active and indigestible minority would come to outgrow the present leading group at some future date which could be roughly calculated.

It could also be calculated whether, and when, even this higher rate of growth for the active unassimilated group H might be automatically stopped or reversed in its turn. This might happen if the reserve for H, the underlying differentiated population R, were small in numbers, so that at any high rate of mobilization its ranks would soon become exhausted. In such a case the national challengers, the mobilized differentiated population H, would grow rapidly for a period, but later its growth would be stopped by the lack of new influx, and still later its numbers might begin to fall, if the rate of assimilation c happened to exceed its rate of natural increase. This may have been the case in Scotland (see Fig. 19, above).

The important thing in each calculation will be this relationship of the rates of increase or the rates of social shifts (such as mobilization or assimilation) to the absolute numbers involved. Even a moderate rate of natural increase operating among a large, underlying, and nationally or culturally differentiated population might add larger numbers to the population than the rates of mobilization m, and of assimilation a, could cope with. Some such situation may have existed for several centuries in China. The cities there may have undergone a moderate growth, and a part of the population may have been taught, or otherwise assimilated to, the predominant speech and culture by the educational and social institutions of the country. Yet, if population growth as a whole was larger than the number of people who could be brought into contact with Mandarin Chinese, assimilation to that standard language might consequently have lagged behind total population growth, with the result that an increasing number of Chinese would grow up speaking only the local dialects.[21]   See Figs. 4–8 on China, and 16–18 on India, above.

This approach might suggest a quantitative mechanism for separating even well-established languages into a standardized language for an educated minority and a group of diversified popular dialects below it.   It requires in all such cases that both the rate of assimilation c and the rate of mobilization m should be small, and that the underlying population U should be large in relation to the total numbers of the population involved.   A large rate of natural increase of this underlying population would further accelerate the process.   The split between High German and Low German, and between Russian and Ukrainian, might be examples of such situations.   Other cases in point might be the separation of the "pure language" of modern spoken Greek (*katharevusa*) from the popular language; or the distinction of nineteenth-century Dano-Norwegian from the speech of the Norwegian country population; or the difference between the "Czechoslovak" language of Czech and Slovak Protestants at the beginning of the nineteenth century and the actual speech of Slovak peasants of the period; or again, the difference between the elegant Castilian Spanish and the Spanish spoken in most parts of Latin America.

Once such a split has grown, a later increase in the rate of mobilization may no longer be sufficient to heal it completely.   If the population has once drifted away from the old standard, and people with the two standards are then rapidly brought into intensive communication with each other, the result may be assimilation no longer to the old standard but to a new "sub-standard" speech, such as the *demotike* of Greece or the *seseo* and *yeismo* pronunciations of Latin American Spanish.[22]

In all such cases, our suggestion is not that everything could or should be explained by the sheer weight of numbers, but rather that the factors of attraction, habit patterns, opportunities, institutions, and prestige cannot be evaluated fairly so long as the background of numbers is not known.   With this limitation in mind, some of these qualitative factors will be discussed in Chapter 7.

Another important group of situations could be treated by this method: the cases where social communication does not grow in a particular area because there has been economic retrogression or a throttling down of social communication due to a hardening of class or caste barriers. Trade routes may shift, cities may shrink instead of grow, natural resources may become exhausted, populations may be forced to return to the land or to more primitive ways of living, or colonial administrators may decide that the native populations under their charge should be deliberately kept in their old tribal groups or secluded in reservations under the rule of their territorial chieftains rather than be mobilized for intensive communication amid the uncertainties of modern life. In all such cases, assimilation may continue even though mobilization has stopped or is running in reverse, and assimilation may in turn be successful.

Thus far, we have treated all the rates of change as completely independent from each other, and we may do this for rates calculated from the statistics of the past since any independent changes are likely to be already reflected in the data. However, we already know empirically that the rate of assimilation among a population that has been uprooted and mobilized—such as immigrants coming to America—is usually considerably higher than the rate of assimilation among the secluded populations of villages close to the soil. If we want to take account of this and if we can find or collect the necessary statistics, we may refine our rates of change. In addition to the rate of natural increase of the total population p we might try to calculate rates n, h, q, r, as the respective rates of natural increase of the population groups N, H, Q, R, respectively, and we might further try to calculate the rates of n', h', q', and r' for the net number of people who enter each of the respective groups N, H, Q, and R, for reasons other than birth.[23]

Probably the theoretical investigation of these quantitative aspects of the merging or splitting of nations could be carried still further. One reason to stop here might be that we know now what statistical information is worth looking for, but that there seems little point in going further until more of the relevant statistics have been collected, processed, and published by the organizations who at present have access to the data.

The other reason for stopping now is perhaps the more commanding: we have been discussing the quantitative aspects of nation building, but we have put to one side the qualitative aspects of the processes which in their own way may be equally significant for its outcome. It is to some of these qualitative elements in the process of national assimilation or differentiation that we must now direct our attention.

Chapter 7

Unity or Diversity
THE BALANCE OF QUANTITATIVE
AND QUALITATIVE FACTORS

Most of our discussion thus far has dealt with those aspects of the social process that lend themselves readily to quantitative measurement. There are a number of other factors, however, which have a bearing on these quantitative rates of change and on their interplay, and which therefore may be worth discussing, although they can be stated for the time being only in qualitative terms. Even though many of these factors will be qualitative or institutional, they have the advantage that they can be known in advance and that they can be used therefore to estimate, at least roughly, some of the changes which the rates of growth observed in the past are likely to undergo in the future.

Social Mobilization in Terms of Supply and Demand

The first group of such elements or factors are those which have a bearing on the *rate of mobilization*. We may think of any actual rate of mobilization, that is, any increase of the mobilized population M observed from statistics,[1] as the outcome of the push and the pull of a demand and supply balance involving several distinct processes. Statistics may tell us, for instance, that a certain number of newcomers from the country has arrived in towns. We may then think of the number of these new arrivals as largely dependent upon the number of persons uprooted from the villages, either through a gradual excess of the natural population there over the available opportunities to make a living, or uprooted by more sudden events such as famines, wars, evictions, enclosure movements, the breakup of tribal landholdings, critical crop or market failures, agricultural depressions, and unusual increases in unemployment; plus the number of potential immigrants available from rural areas outside the territory. Together all these will make up the *gross supply of new entrants* from the underlying population U to the mobilized population M.

The task of assimilating these persons to the predominant language and culture of the already assimilated population N will depend first and most obviously on the proportion among them of newcomers from an already largely assimilated rural population Q (such as Irish immigrants to the United States, or German-Austrian peasant girls to Vienna) as against the *net supply* of newcomers *from the differentiated underlying population* R (such as Polish immigrants to the United States, Czech peasant girls to Vienna, or Peruvian Indians to Lima).

The usual methods of social or economic statistics should be adequate to measure these processes, except perhaps for one peculiar effect of social structure on ethnic learning: the more highly educated or socially privileged the members of a group, the less willing they will ordinarily be to migrate, and if they do migrate, the less willing they may be to assimilate to a new nationality, language, or culture, if this should imply for them even a temporary reduction in status or prestige. The skilled, the educated, and the well-to-do then may tend to resist the pressures toward mobilization and assimilation, unless either the road is paved for them with facilities for high horizontal social mobility, permitting them to take over intact into their new environment much of the habits, privileges, and prestige claims of the past, or unless the pressure to leave their old communities has come to appear to them overwhelming.

So much for the forces behind the newcomers which are pushing them forward. On the demand side are some of the forces that pull individuals toward the city, or generally into the mobilized population M. Together, these forces make up the *gross demand for new entrants* into urban or secondary and tertiary occupations at the prevailing rates of remuneration.[2] This gross demand can be measured or estimated by the standard methods of labor statistics or manpower statistics, as they have been developed during and after World War II, both as to the collection of data and of the drawing of inferences from them. We can further check on these data, and go a step behind them, by noting that manpower needs in an economy at any given time depend on general economic growth which can be measured in some of its aspects by a number of well-known methods.[3] More specifically, manpower needs depend to a significant degree on the supplies of capital, land, and purchasing power organized in markets, and thus on previous patterns of land settlement, agricultural and industrial technology, capital formation, and investment.

To this gross demand for entrants into M we should add the possibly competing demand for new entrants into the underlying population U.

If new agricultural settlers are sought for remote rural areas, some or all of the potential migrants to cities in a particular area may prefer to live again in secluded villages, though now in another region and under more promising auspices. The settlement of German peasants in Russia by Empress Catherine II, the settlement of French peasants in the Province of Quebec, and domestic resettlement schemes in Germany or Ireland all had the immediate effect of withdrawing for the time being the individuals attracted from any potential urban population.

If new problems of national diversity are created by this process, they remain dormant for a time until at some later stage intensive social communication is extended to these villages, or until larger numbers of their inhabitants go forth to seek new occupations among the mobilized population. When either of these processes finally takes place, however, the latent national diversity, created by the settlements of long ago, may suddenly emerge into the actuality of latter-day political conflict. Striking instances of such idylls turned into dramas were furnished by the Boers in South Africa,[4] and by the Volga Germans in Russia after the Nazi invasion of 1941.

Large-scale rural resettlement processes of this kind are relatively rare—although a number of overseas countries are currently expressing a strong preference for "bona fide agriculturalists" as immigrants, together with a marked aversion against candidates for tertiary occupations, such as clerical workers or businessmen. Where such situations of agricultural resettlement occur on a scale large enough to be important, the effects on the manpower balance can be measured and dealt with by conventional statistical methods.

The gross demand for new entrants into the mobilized population M can be further subdivided into two parts. The first of these consists of the demand for new entrants who have already mastered the predominant language, and perhaps have also otherwise become assimilated to the predominant culture. Such a demand is often found when there is a need for more lawyers, salesmen, administrators, and the like, that is, for new candidates for occupations where the use of language and personal contacts with clients or customers is particularly important. In effect, these requirements may constitute a specific demand for new entrants into group N, the mobilized and assimilated population, to be met by a supply of new entrants from the assimilated underlying population Q and newly assimilated entrants from the differentiated population groups H and R.

The second part of the gross demand for entrants into M is that which is left over, once the specific demand for assimilated entrants into N has been allowed for. It is *the net demand for unassimilated entrants* from the underlying differentiated population R. More accurately, the net demand for entrants from R would consist of that part of the indiscriminate demand for entrants from either R or Q—the underlying assimilated population—which was not in fact being filled by newcomers from Q.[5]

It is the interplay between these various elements of demand and supply which determines the general rate of mobilization m, and the sometimes perhaps even more suggestive rate $m(R)$, the rate of mobilization of the underlying differentiated population R.[6]

Thus far, we have pretended that the elements that influence the rate of mobilization are independent of each other. Actually, of course, they are not. The fact that a large mobilized assimilated "national" group N has accumulated will mean automatically an increased demand for certain services, such as those of teachers, writers, innkeepers, etc., for which members of N are preferred. There will be a certain "multiplier effect" observable in the growth of N, and a similar "multiplier effect" in the growth of the mobilized but differentiated group H.[7] That is to say, for the case of N, there will be a series of increases in N which sometimes may be summarized in terms of a single number which they approach as a limit. Unlike the case of the multiplier familiar to economists, however, we cannot be sure that the increases in the assimilated or differentiated populations will always form a converging series; rather, in some cases of national assimilation or differentiation, more complex or unstable patterns may result.

National Assimilation in Terms of Six Balances of Factors

The *rate of assimilation* measures the second great process which, together with the process of mobilization, determines largely the outcome of national development. The rate of assimilation in its turn depends on a considerable number of elements. We may perhaps best visualize these as acting on each other in six overall balances. The first two of these balances are largely technical and linguistic; the third and fourth balances are largely economic. The fifth and the sixth are largely cultural and political in nature. Together, in the interplay, they determine the nature and the speed of the process of assimilation.

SIMILARITY OF COMMUNICATIONS HABITS. The first of our balances I should call the *similarity balance*. Assimilation in general becomes easier the greater the similarity and compatibility of the mental, social, and communications equipment of the persons in both language groups; assimilation is more difficult the more different or incompatible are their linguistic or cultural habits. The similarity or dissimilarity in their vocabulary, their alphabets, and their grammatical structure can be measured. Many such measuring techniques have been developed by philologists, and some additional techniques for measurement from the viewpoint of communications are forthcoming.

The opposite traits, elements of differences or incompatibility, will of course weigh on the other side of this balance. It may also happen that the linguistic similarity is very strongly in favor of assimilation, but the cultural balance is weighted toward the other side by considerable differences or partial incompatibilities in matters of value and culture. This, according to George Bernard Shaw, has long been the situation of the English and the English-speaking Irish people whom he considered "separated from each other by the same language." [8]

FACILITIES FOR LEARNING AND TEACHING. The second balance I should like to call the *learning-teaching balance*. Assimilation proceeds more rapidly the greater the learning capacities of the newcomers. These learning capacities are largely determined by the newcomers' previous culture, and by the learning capacity of the particular group in the old culture from which the newcomers have been recruited. Despite occasional fears of lowered status and notions of their own cultural superiority, most refugees or immigrants from the intellectual strata in Germany during the 1930's—and their children even more—assimilated much more rapidly to the languages, and in part to the cultures, of their new homelands than had those early immigrants to overseas countries who had been recruited from the villages of southeastern Europe.

Another factor in this balance is the availability and quality of teaching facilities and teaching techniques by means of which newcomers can be taught the new language and ways of behavior.

Taken together, these first two balances, the similarity balance and the learning-teaching balance, determine the average cost of acquiring the new language to any specified standard of proficiency. There are languages and alphabets which the average newcomer may hardly need to learn at all. Others may require on the average a year's sustained study, and still others may not be mastered with anything less than several years of application. Such average costs can be measured or estimated in terms of time, effort, and perhaps money, and may then become the data for the economic facts which are to be taken into account by the next two balances in our collection.

FREQUENCY OF CONTACTS. The third balance in our series we might call the *contact balance*. It is the balance of the frequency and the range of communications of the average individual across linguistic or cultural barriers, as against the frequency and the range of the same person's communications within the confines of his own group. Perhaps we might find it necessary to distinguish between the cross-cultural communications that actually occur, and the number of situations in which they should occur, that is, of situations of contact between the newcomer and some members of the assimilated group, where he is expected or required to use the predominant language of the country. To the extent that such situations multiply, the newcomer will experience the need to assimilate to the new language and new ways of behavior. To the extent that his time and energy are taken up by communications in his old language, and with members of his own cultural group, assimilation may be retarded.

The contact balance can be measured quantitatively, at least in part, by the standard methods of social communications research. These may be supplemented by some qualitative investigations which would reach behind the actual number of contacts or contact situations recorded. Such qualitative studies would take into account the economic and social patterns of behavior, and the prevailing institutions in the society at large, which may extend certain kinds of contacts, as is done by markets, and exclude others, as is done by castes.[9]

MATERIAL REWARDS AND PENALTIES. The fourth balance on our list and second of the economic balances is the *balance of material rewards*, which measures the material rewards for assimilation in terms of employment, promotion, higher income, freedom of choice, security, and prestige. Such rewards would tend to speed up assimilation, whereas penalties would have the opposite effect. Penalties for assimilation may be loss of previous employment or loss of social status where the newcomers are required to start at the bottom of the social or economic scale and may have to spend laborious years to work themselves up again to the level of income or prestige which they already enjoyed in their old culture.[10]

The other side of this balance consists, of course, of the material rewards for non-assimilation. What does a newcomer to a country stand to gain in terms of employment, income, security, or prestige if he clings to his old culture? This may be very little if the newcomer should be a Belgian in New York. It might be somewhat more if he should be a German in nineteenth century Milwaukee, and it might be a great deal if he should be an Englishman in nineteenth century Buenos Aires.

Of course, remaining in one's old culture group may also have peculiar penalizations. Some of these may be economic: the inability to avail oneself of particular economic or educational opportunities existing in the new country. Others may be social and psychological. The old culture of the newcomers may have a traditional pattern of authority under which women, children, and adolescents are harshly subordinated to the power of the head of the family. Adolescents of the next generation may then promptly discover that by rejecting the old language and culture of their parents they may escape from their father's domination.

The elements which can take up the balance of material rewards can be measured in part by economic surveys and investigations such as statistics on wages or employment opportunities; other elements, such as those of security, can be measured by the methods which are used for the computation of risks in the field of insurance; finally, considerations of status and prestige can be investigated by the methods of group psychology and sociology.

Altogether, the importance of the balance of material rewards is very great. It is empirically known, for instance, that members of many peoples often assimilate very slowly, or not at all, in new countries of residence where the average standard of living is much lower than it was in their country of origin, and that they often assimilate far more readily in countries where the living standard is considerably higher than it was in the regions where the newcomers came from. The persistent non-assimilation of the Germans in most of Southeastern Europe, their easier assimilation in France, and their ready assimilation in the United States are cases in point.

VALUES AND DESIRES. The last two of our balances are cultural and political in character. Most of the general cultural elements are collected in the fifth of our balances, *the balance of values and desires.* Every group of people teaches inevitably some values and desires to the children it rears. By overt statement or implication from behavior, children are taught preferences of action and images of goals.

Many of these goals and preferences may contradict each other. Many an immigrant to the United States has recorded what his own civilization has taught him to admire or desire, things which it could not provide for him but which he would acquire later on in the different civilization of America. "But here I was now with a poppy red fez," remembers Stoyan Christowe, "my feet in the gondola-shaped *tsaruhia* with their toes turned up like sprouts from which bloomed the pom-poms, like bouquets. I thought to myself how many plates of beans I'd have to eat before I could grow up and be half so grand as Gurkin." (Gurkin was the Balkan villager who had become wealthy in America, and who had now returned for a visit to the village.) Later, young Stoyan himself left his Balkan village for America and remembers, "The men gave me coins, *metaliks, piasters,* tiny symbols of the big money I would earn in America. Before they gave the coins to me they rubbed them against their beards. That meant I should earn as many coins in America as there were hairs in their beards." [11]

Stoyan's village culture had taught him to wear a fez and upturned shoes, and later, as a grown-up, a huge mustache. But it also taught him and all his fellow villagers to desire money, and if the desire to earn money came in conflict with the enjoyment of wearing the shoes, the fez, and the mustache, then, at least in Stoyan's case, the shoes, the fez, and the mustache would go.[12]

This sort of outcome is not inevitable. There are culture patterns where traditional standards of birth and behavior are considered more important than the acquisition of money or tangible goods. In such cases, the balance of values and desires may tilt the other way. The populations concerned may refuse to migrate or to engage in wage labor, or even if they have to do so they may refuse assimilation despite what may seem to be its obvious material advantages. The important point is that the material rewards (which we counted in our fourth balance above) are only rewards *if they are valued as rewards* by the individual in terms of the values and desires which he has at the time. Any statement about material rewards automatically contains, there-fore, certain cultural assumptions.

To be sure, material rewards are still means of power and of sur-vival, even if they are not valued by a particular culture. In this respect their significance is in large part cross-cultural, and thus inde-pendent from the values or prejudices of a particular culture. But men must have already accepted a certain kind of culture pattern in order to be interested in such things as survival and power, and in the objective resources that may be used to support them. There are culture patterns or value systems which are not particularly interested in survival, and the fact that they may succeed in accomplishing the social suicide which they prefer to a fundamental change of behavior does not permit the social scientists to neglect them during their some-times quite considerable periods of existence. The death-glorifying value pattern of the German Nazis and the long frozen culture of ancient Sparta would be cases in point.[13]

Generally, the rate of assimilation will be influenced not only by the balance of conflicting values within the old culture pattern of the as yet unassimilated population but also by the balance between the common and conflicting values in the old culture pattern on the one hand and in the new and predominant culture pattern on the other. Germans may have been taught in childhood to be proud of being Germans, to be thorough, and to esteem the soldier more highly than the business-man. Yet, they have also been taught to value wealth, cleanliness, speed, power, and the conspicuous consumption of certain valued goods such as private motor cars. Now, if such Germans have settled among a non-German population, there must now be added to the conflict between the divergent values of their own culture, the conflict between this entire old culture and the new values taught to their children by the children of their non-German neighbors. Where this cross-cultural pull to assimilation is reinforced by the intracultural balance among conflicting values, assimilation may be rapid and may bridge even apparently large differences.

As regards measurement, the balance of values and desires may be approached by the methods of social science and cultural anthropology, with the aid of such techniques as preference ratings, inventories of values, rank-order tests, and similar devices.

SYMBOLS AND BARRIERS. The last of our six balances is specifically social and political. It is the *balance of national symbols and barriers*. One part of it consists of the pull of unifying symbols, that is, symbols promoting assimilation, as against the effectiveness of social and symbolic barriers against the actual joining of the predominant national group. A tragic example of the conflicting forces in this balance has been the fate of many persons in Germany who had come to think of themselves as "Germans of Jewish descent" or as "Germans of Jewish religious denomination," and who therefore not merely registered at all censuses their German nationality but volunteered in considerable numbers in World War I for the German armies. These persons, however, were frequently rejected as Germans by German nationalists. Some German theorists of nationalism and nationality were careful to specify "acceptance by the national group" as an indispensable condition of membership in a people,[14] and Dr. Goebbels carried the rejection to its climax by ordering the names of twelve thousand dead German soldiers of Jewish extraction erased from the German war memorials of World War I.

A second balance of national symbols and barriers applies, of course, within the unassimilated group. What are the symbols and political ties urging newcomers to remain within their minority culture? What are the barriers or obstacles which separate them from the predominant language and culture? The outcome of the balances of all these forces, the symbols and sentiments urging the people to leave the differentiated population D and to join the assimilated population A, as against the symbols and sentiments working in the opposite direction, will determine the overall push or pull that results.

The balance of symbols and barriers must largely be investigated by qualitative methods. Symbols and institutions can be studied by the methods of history, political science, and perhaps cultural anthropology, but the significance of these qualitative findings can be checked to some extent against the residue of the quantitative data, that is, against the rest of the observed changes which remains after all the quantitative factors have been allowed for. This is an unsatisfactory approach at present, but it might become more effective as the quantitative data for the rate of mobilization and for the first five balances behind the rate of assimilation become more accurately known.

National Assimilation and the Underlying Population

It should be noted that assimilation may proceed even if there is no mobilization at all or if its gains are negative. When cities shrink instead of growing and people are kept on the land or returned to their villages instead of being enticed away from them, assimilation may still proceed. In the nature of the case it will then be mainly assimilation between two groups of the underlying population U: the underlying assimilated population Q and the underlying differentiated population R. Assimilation among people firmly rooted in their own communities and their native setting usually proceeds far more slowly than it would among the mobilized population, but it does proceed even though it may take many generations. The Coptic-speaking peasants of Egypt completed during the thirteenth to sixteenth centuries A.D. their acceptance of the Arab speech of their conquerors, 600 to 900 years after the Arab conquest of their country.[15] Similarly, Cornish speech died out in Cornwall, and the Slavic "Wendish" speech died out in Saxony during the eighteenth century, in both cases more than 700 years after the original English and German conquests.

The direction of assimilation among the underlying population depends on the balance of factors within the underlying population and not necessarily on the balance of factors visible among the mobilized part of the population. Thus, during the eighteenth century Bohemia was dominated and administered by Germans, and, among the small mobilized population of the period, German language and culture were predominant. Yet, during the same period, villages of German peasants settled in the midst of Czech country people in central Bohemia were turned into Czechs and their descendants have remained Czechs to this day. In the same manner, Magyar villagers settled in the midst of Slavic peasants in the Slovak mountain valleys became assimilated to the Slavs in a period during which the whole country was under the Hungarian crown and Magyar was the dominant language of the country.[16]

Any more general quantitative comparison between the relatively high assimilation speeds among mobilized persons and the considerably lower assimilation speeds among the underlying population remains to be worked out. Likewise to be worked out would have to be the *mutual interaction* of the different rates of change which thus far have been discussed as if they were wholly independent of each other. Actually, an increase in the mobilized and assimilated population N amplifies under certain conditions the demand for new recruits for N, just as growth in the mobilized but differentiated population H may create under certain conditions a secondary demand for more recruits for H. In mathematical terms this could perhaps be expressed by a multiplier, or by models based on "feedback" patterns rather than on simple equilibrium.[17] But such refinements will have to wait until a good deal more data are accumulated.

Some Limits and Opportunities for Policy

We have surveyed a broad approach to quantitative analysis of a historical process. What can any analysis of this kind accomplish?

First of all, it can separate the factors which men cannot change, or can change but little, and it can thus show the limitations which they pose to what men can do in the future; and second, by contrast, it can single out the most promising areas for action.

The existing numbers and locations of different language groups and nationalities are factors of history which cannot be changed quickly. Although minorities up to about 3,000,000 people have been forcibly transferred from one country to another, the political, economic, and human costs of such an enterprise are vast.[18] The even larger German attempt to exterminate the Jews and the earlier Turkish attempt to exterminate the Armenians both ended in failure, despite the vast numbers of their unhappy victims. The forced migration of perhaps

6,000,000 Muslims into Pakistan and 5,000,000–6,000,000 Hindus and Sikhs into India after the separation of the two countries in 1947 cost about 1,000,000 lives, but left substantial minorities in both countries.[19]

Somewhat more amenable to change is the degree of mobilization of the members of the different national language groups, since it depends on the growth or shrinking of capital investments, markets, industries, towns, and white-collar occupations, and on the development of a press, mails, and educational facilities. All these are still largely subjects of economic history, and are processes whose effects may work themselves out blindly and automatically *unless major efforts are made to foresee and control them.* Together with the given distribution of nationality or language groups, this semi-automatic process goes far to determine the balance of contacts, as well as the balance of material rewards and penalizations for either mobilization or assimilation.[20] So far as these revolutions are economic in nature, they may work themselves out automatically unless there is a great deal of deliberate and effective interference.

If these two balances were largely economic and only to be changed at the price of major efforts, then the two linguistic balances, the balance of similarity and the learning-teaching balance, are even less amenable to political control. Both of these balances can be changed slowly at best.

There remains the balance of values and the balance of national symbols and barriers, which are most amenable to the political and social process. Here we are confronted with things about which something can be done, particularly if social, political, and economic changes are initiated in coordination; and the historical, material, and technical balances which we surveyed before may tell us something about the limits and costs of any such action. But within those real limits action is possible. We can do much to change economic and social conditions, and we can find the strength to change our habits. We may venture to believe that man's mind is greater than the collection of habits and preferences which it has accumulated at any one time, no matter how deeply ingrained they may seem at the moment. Too often men have viewed language and nationality superficially as an accident, or accepted them submissively as fate. In fact, they are neither accident nor fate, but the outcome of a discoverable process; and as soon as we begin to make this process visible, we are beginning to change it.

Chapter 8

National Consciousness and Will

Without consciousness, the philosopher Heraclitus told the Greeks, men act like men asleep; with it, they act like men awake.[1] From his day to ours there has stayed in our tradition this image of awakening. "Methinks I see in my mind a noble and puissant nation rousing herself like a strong man after sleep . . ." John Milton wrote two thousand years later about Cromwell's England, "Methinks I see her as an eagle mewing her mighty youth, and kindling her undazzled eyes at the full midday beam. . . ."[2] In the ages of social, national, and political "awakening" that followed the world over, "awakening" has meant just this: that men became aware of their own situation in a process of social and political change, and began to act in the light of this awareness.

Consciousness is a political fact. Its rise is marked by changes in observable political behavior and eventually in the course of history. But what is it to be aware? What is this consciousness? In an earlier chapter we noted the reluctance of many psychologists and social scientists even to use these terms.[3] We all know awareness from introspection; we can describe it in vague terms; we can state some of its apparent consequences; but can we analyze it? Can we say anything specific about the inner structure of its processes?

In our survey of studies of nationalism in our first chapter, we found that consciousness and will have been stressed as crucial by many twentieth century writers, even though these concepts seemed to lack both structural and quantitative definition. Thus far, these factors have been slighted in our own discussion. We cannot attempt to here treat them thoroughly, but we can try to do three things in this chapter.

Our first task will be to arrive at some agreement as to the importance of the areas indicated by the words "consciousness" and "will," and to inquire to what extent empirical, intuitive, and qualitative insights into national consciousness and will are compatible with the quantitative and structural approach of our present analysis.

Our second task will be to restate the operational content of these notions in the analyzable, verifiable, and in principle measurable terms of a theory of communication and organization. This will involve showing that the processes of consciousness and will may themselves be studied in terms of structural patterns of channels of social communication, and of flow patterns of messages in them.

Finally, we shall ask whether this approach might permit us to identify pathological or self-destructive developments in nationalism where they occur, and perhaps to predict them in their early stages, as well as to suggest approaches to policies that might tend to prevent nationalistic conflicts from leading to national and social destruction. This will involve a glance at the prospects of nationalism in the future, and at some of the things that social scientists could do about them.

For all these tasks, a look at the nature of communication and control processes may prove helpful.

Communications, Memory, and Self-Determination

In every system which shows a significant degree of self-control, external action is guided by the interplay of circulating streams of information. When we pick up a pencil, we receive a stream of information through our eyes, which keep us informed where the pencil is, and hence where to put our hand to pick it up. At the same time we receive a stream of information through certain nerves in our arm and hand—the proprioceptors or kinesthetic receptors—which keep us informed where our hand is at any instant, and hence how far away it still is from its goal. The stream of information resulting from all these data is fed back into the stream of impulses to the muscles moving our hand nearer to the goal, so that the subsequent movement of the hand is directed by data about its remaining distance from its goal. In short, our hand is guided by data which include its own position. The control system, by which our hand is guided, observes its own position, feeds back this information into the making of decisions about its own behavior, again observes the results of its own actions and feeds them back into its own behavior until the goal is reached. The whole process, in picking up the pencil, usually is nonconscious, and complete in less than a second.

This loop pattern of circulating information has been called the *feedback* by communications engineers. Neurophysiologists have found it in the patterns of nerve impulses and hormones which carry processes of control in the bodies of animals and men. Independently from them, engineers developed similar feedback circuits in many kinds of automatic control machines which guide their own behavior to some limited extent by means of electric or mechanical feedback processes. Finally, fundamental patterns of feedback can be found in the flow patterns of information and action in teams of men in organizations, peoples, cultures, and societies.[4]

Even the simplest self-steering systems must have receptors and effectors, and some feedback channels to connect them. For any more complex self-steering process there are required some facilities fulfilling some of the functions of *memory,* that is, at least, the storage and recall of information.

Such extended self-steering—or autonomy—requires then essentially the interplay of two streams of information in a more complex feedback pattern: there must be a stream of "intake," i.e., of incoming information from the outside world, including the system's own position in it; and there must be a stream of recalled information from memory, to act upon the selection and treatment of the intake data from the outside world, and on the feeding back of orders to the effectors for action.

Autonomy, then, requires both intake from the present and recall from memory, and selfhood can be seen in just this continuous balancing of a limited present and a limited past within a limited system making its own decisions affecting its future.

In organisms or automata, these limits are given by the physical limits of the body or the machine, and the limited extent of the receptors, effectors, and memory facilities within it. But what of the separateness and self-hood of an organization or a group of people?

Its limits will be the limits of its effectiveness in transmitting and circulating information. They will be the limits of its effective complementarity, in the sense in which this concept was discussed in an earlier chapter.[5] And since one of the most effective complementary information networks is a people, the question about the identity and autonomy of a people will be meaningful.

The selfhood of any social organization will be based on the limits of its "proprioceptors," that is, the receptors—men or institutions—which receive and circulate information about parts of this complementary information system itself. It will at the same time be based on the effectiveness of memory, and of the feedback of data from memory into intake and action. And it will depend, finally, on the system's continued openness to intake of information from the outside world.

No further self-determination is possible if either openness or memory is lost. A person blind and deaf, or insensible to further impressions; an organization or people effectively isolated to all messages or experiences from its larger physical or social environment; a guided missile with its receptors gone dead—all these tend to lose more or less of their power of self-steering. To the extent that they do so, they approach the behavior of a bullet or torpedo: their future action becomes almost completely determined by their past. On the other hand, a person without memory, an organization without values or policy, a people without effective tradition, a ship or missile without set goal or course—all these no longer steer, but drift: their behavior depends little on their past and almost wholly on their present. Driftwood and the bullet are thus each the epitome of another kind of loss of self-control, and a ship may serve as a symbol of the far more difficult process of steering that lies between those primitive extremes.

The preceding paragraphs contain operationally verifiable assertions of a qualitative kind. They assert that certain operations and elements of communications equipment are essential for certain kinds of observable behavior. These assertions can be confirmed or refuted by observations or experiment, or they could be proved by the same methods to be in need of modification.

Beyond these broad problems, however, a great many of these processes are measurable in quantitative terms, particularly where they occur in aggregations of machinery, and to a lesser extent in the case of biological organisms and of social organizations.

In a machine such as a homing torpedo, we can measure the rate at which incoming information is received and the rate at which information about the machine's own position and output is added to the data guiding its subsequent behavior. We can measure the speed of its responses—or its opposite, the extent of their *lag*—as well as their effectiveness, or *gain*, in reducing the effects of preceding steering errors. From the data for lag and gain, the rates of change in the position of the target and the torpedo, and the rate of input of information into the latter, we can calculate the effectiveness of the steering system in question, and the probability of its breaking down under certain conditions of load.

Similarly, we can calculate the capacities for information storage and recall in a mechanical or electronic memory device. As we can measure memory, so we can also measure self-steering or autonomy by two classes of tests: by inner structural capacity, and by externally observable performances. The question to what extent measured performance lags behind inferred structural capacity should likewise be operationally meaningful for organizations of all kinds, including nations, just as it has long been meaningful in studies of industrial capacity.

If we accept the relevance of such topics for research, we shall become interested in factual data which may have been known or accessible before, but the significance of which has largely been neglected. Such data are the records and measures of national responses and readjustments to new tasks, as expressed in the facts and figures of the acceptance of technological, social, or economic innovations. Other relevant data are the speed and efficiency of mobilization of economic resources and manpower to meet foreseen and unforeseen emergencies in war or economic depressions in peacetime. How large a proportion of resources or efforts were reallocated? How quickly? At what costs? With what results on the overall performance of the organization, industry, economy, or country? From the speed with which a number of fundamental innovations are accepted in a country or among a people, we might inquire whether there is a *national learning rate,* that is, whether the average speed at which, let us say, ten basic innovations become generally accepted in a particular country (e.g., in each case for 80 per cent of the output of the industry concerned) will indicate, at least within limits, the speed at which the eleventh or twelfth innovations will be so adopted.[6] To the extent that such processes of innovation or social learning are found to depend on national governments or cultures, they would furnish measures or at least indicants of the learning or steering performance of the national community of communication, or of the relevant communication patterns within it.

Another class of tests can be suggested to supplement the tests of large-scale performance just discussed, and the relatively simple test of communicative complementarity discussed earlier in the fourth chapter of this book. This present group of tests could be called "cohesion tests," to distinguish them from the "complementarity tests" just mentioned, and they would be derived from the concept of a quantitative *signal-to-noise ratio,* familiar to communications engineers, who measure by it the strength of the relevant messages relative to all others. What is the frequency of national messages or signals, relative to that of personal or local ones? What is the operating priority—as distinct from the theoretical or honorific—given to such national messages, symbols, or orders? Frequency counts and rank order tests could indicate answers. There is a large amount of factual information available on political participation in particular countries or peoples, which could be ordered and utilized in this context.

From all such information, we might gain starting points for inquiring further into specific patterns of consciousness in the development of nations.

National Consciousness

A person, an organization, or a social group—such as a people—can do more than merely steer some of its behavior by balancing its current experiences with its recalled traditions. It can achieve *consciousness* by attaching secondary symbols—that is, symbols about symbols—to certain items in its current intake of outside information, and to certain items recalled from memory.

I can watch the man opposite me automatically; or I can become aware of the fact that I am watching him. In the latter case, that of awareness, it seems that I have added a second item of information about my watching to the data about the watched man which were moving through my nervous system. In like manner, a cat may be belled to warn the birds; or certain goods may be tagged for special treatment as they move down an assembly line; or intelligence reports may be saddled with summaries, routing slips, or document control notations as they are moving through the appropriate offices in the State Department or some other agency. In the last of these cases, information about information has been added to the primary data moving through the channels of the agency; and the higher-level policy committees or department heads may only be aware of the primary items through the brief summaries or control slips which alone reach them.

Consciousness, in this view, is the interplay and feedback of secondary symbols in an information-processing system. By interplay is meant here their interaction with each other; by feedback, their feedback into the sequence of decisions about the behavior of the system. Among the obvious results of consciousness is the chance of much greater speed and comprehensiveness with which many classes of items of information can be represented, recalled, subjected to simultaneous inspection, and brought to bear on each other. Among its obvious dangers is the misrepresentation of the primary information in the system. The consciousness may be false consciousness; the distribution of the primary items may be very different from that of the secondary ones; men and peoples may have quite misleading ideas of some of their own traits, or of themselves as a whole. Among its obvious costs should be included the physical facilities required to carry its processes, in terms of energy, matter, or more complex resources, and perhaps some delay imposed on completing a reflex or similar simple cycle of information carrying signals between the system and the outside world.

Such costs of "consciousness" in terms of resources, efforts, and delays should be measurable in all communications systems that use feedbacks of data from internal monitoring. They could be contrasted with the possible gains in performance from the additon of such feedback channels of "awareness." Such gains might be twofold: from a more efficient performance of already existing functions, and from the addition of new functions which had not been performed before. In either case, in principle, changes in structure could be mapped, and changes in performance measured.

No description of the kind we have just given can exhaust consciousness, either in an individual or in a people. In a human being, consciousness as a process may well be inexhaustible as long as life permits.

Rather, our very incomplete analogy may be helpful in two ways: it gives an extremely oversimplified picture of consciousness in an individual, and a somewhat less oversimplified picture of consciousness in a group or nation. This second picture of consciousness is less oversimplified because consciousness in a group or nation is a far more primitive process, and one more accessible to observation and analysis. In both individuals and groups our recognition of the simplest basic pattern of self-monitoring or consciousness may help us to single out some critical facts for observation, and perhaps make them in time amenable to measurement. The more we find out in this process, not merely about the crude consciousness of groups but about the vastly more complex consciousness of individuals, the more glaringly the inadequacies of our simple communications model will become apparent. Until then, however, we had perhaps best use it and see how far it will take us.

Even at this early stage of the study of national consciousness from the viewpoint of social communications, however, we may pause to glance at the vast difference between the autonomy and consciousness which are possible for a group, and the vastly greater potentialities of the individual. There are more cells in the brain of every single individual than there are people in the world. Any sane individual has vastly greater speed, range of recall from memory, and power of recombination than any organization or group. Groups have longer memories and greater facilities for storage, through writing, tradition, institutions, and the like. But although groups can gather and store vastly more information than individuals, they are far more clumsy in handling the more ample data they possess. Compared to the lightning thoughts or feelings of an individual, any group, such as a nation, has in this respect far less than the mental powers of a cat. Where these groups progress beyond the cat, they do so by shifting the mental work to individuals.

The group, on the other hand, can maintain data and channels beyond the lifetime of an individual; it can bring the thoughts of individuals together for teamwork between the living and the dead. It is this alternation between the thought of individuals in the vastly complex, sensitive, and accurate inner communication channels of their nerves, brains, and bodies, and the slower, far more primitive channels of society, or of a "national mind" or "national culture," which permits the two types of mind to develop more power together than either could accomplish singly.

National consciousness, from this viewpoint, is the attachment of secondary symbols of nationality to primary items of information moving through channels of social communication, or through the mind of an individual. Not wit, but "French wit"; not thoroughness, but "German thoroughness"; not ingenuity, but "American ingenuity"; not meadows on mountainsides, but—as Petrarca was among the first to discover—Italian meadows on Italian mountainsides: [7] these are symptoms of the change. Not plain language, but "plain English"; not just people, but "our people" and "the American people": these are some of the substance of the change.

To have effect, the secondary symbols of nationality must not merely be attached to selected items of information about individual or social life, or the physical environment. They must be fed back into the making of decisions. On a simple level, they may secure for the items to which they are attached quicker or preferred attention, more frequent or speedier recall, greater weight in the process of decision. On another level they may change some of the decision-making system's operating rules for whole classes of items—and thus, in a sense, its operating "values"—with effects on the general behavior of the system, and even on the pursuit of its goals or on their change for new ones.

National consciousness can be studied and, in principle, measured in terms of the proportions of secondary to primary symbols, and of the resources and facilities, physical and social, devoted to each of these kinds of symbols as against the other. How wide is the range of interests and the volume of communications and experiences among the members of a people? To what share of these have national symbols become attached? How often are those national symbols then found in circulation? What persons, things, and institutions are devoted to producing these secondary symbols, and *how important is that portion of the primary communications to which they have become attached?*

This point is crucial. The symbols of nationality are all in the last analysis adverbs or adjectives: they are not things or acts, but labels added to objects or actions. The words "German" or "Argentine" or "English" mean nothing in themselves; they mean something only if they are understood as being added to the words "persons," or "language," or "country," or "habits and customs," or "state." Even where such words are omitted in a kind of verbal shorthand, examination will reveal them as implied. The importance of the things or acts so labeled, and of the actual difference between those labeled and those not so labeled, may well have a bearing on the rise and persistence of national consciousness, and on its power to modify the behavior of individuals and groups.[8]

National consciousness, like all consciousness, can only be consciousness of something which exists. It may—and often does—misrepresent and distort existing facts, by leaving out some and overrepresenting others—or by producing combined symbols on the conscious level—such as Hitler's "master race"—which have no direct counterpart in fact. Yet behind the distortions and weird combinations there must be materials on which they could be based, or from which their elements could be derived. If Ruritanians do not communicate more easily with each other than with outsiders, if they cannot understand more readily each other's behavior, and if they do not experience more quickly or drastically the effects of one another's political or economic actions, then all attempts to cultivate among them a sense of "Ruritanity" (on the model of the *Cubanidad, Argentinidad,* and *Peruanidad* cultivated in all earnest by some governments in Cuba, Argentina, and Peru) will retain an artificial flavor. National consciousness will be the more effective, on the other hand, the more it is based on the existing separateness and cohesion of a country or a people. "To him who hath is given"; and to the people with some cohesion and distinctiveness the reinforcing gift of national consciousness may come with little difficulty.

To permit the rise of national consciousness, then, there must be a minimum, at least, of cohesion and distinctiveness of a people; and these must have acquired at least a minimum of importance in the lives of individuals. Language similarities or differences may be unimportant in the lives of two peasant villages isolated from each other; they may become more important when the sons of their peasants go to compete for jobs in the same industrial or mining area; and very important when their grandsons begin to compete with each other as shopkeepers or as candidates for white-collar jobs.[9]

The effects of cultural or language differences on communication can be measured by methods such as those discussed in Chapter 4, and the frequency and importance of competitive economic and social situations should likewise prove measurable, well beyond their first rough approximation in the rate of mobilization discussed in Chapter 6. All such data could be correlated with the results of surveys of clusters of settlement, communication, and interdependence at different times, as indicated in Chapter 2; with the assimilation and differentiation data obtainable by methods suggested in Chapters 6 and 7, and with the data about the structure and performance of the channels and institutions disseminating the symbols of national consciousness, which thus far have been the subject of our present discussion. From the combination of all these data, we might eventually get a solid structural and quantitative basis to put under the descriptive, intuitive, qualitative and only partly analytical histories of nationalism which today are still in many respects the main source of our knowledge.

In such histories we can trace the gradual assembling of the conditions for national consciousness in one population after another. At an early stage, we find a population with at least a minimum of compatibility in the culture patterns, if not in the speech, of the smaller groups—tribes, villages, or families—of which it may consist. Its area of habitation is delimited largely by gaps in settlement—that is to say, by uninhabited areas—and by natural obstacles to its primitive techniques of providing food, shelter, and transport; but since many of these limits are not conspicuous, there may be little awareness of them. Common experience of gaining a living in the area may strengthen that compatibility which in turn had made it possible for that experience to be made and remembered as common. Experience and complementarity may then continue to reproduce each other, like the proverbial chicken and the egg, in a syndrome of ethnic learning, that is, a historical process of social learning in which individuals, usually over several generations, learn to become a people.

At the same time, their seemingly undelimited area of habitation will turn out to be in fact delimited by its own physical characteristics in conjunction with the economic, technological, and cultural limitations on the population's ability or willingness to move, or to extend communications and contacts. There are always such limitations; and within the region they circumscribe there may be areas of more intensive contacts or traffic, serving as potential centers of further integration within each region, and its further separation from other regions with other limits and centers.

The early stages of this process may be as automatic as talking prose, which is the way we ordinarily talk without being aware of it. They produce not merely gradual assimilation within an emerging country, language, and people (and these three may overlap rather than coincide), but also necessarily their separation or differentiation from other countries, languages, and peoples.

This separation is often deliberate, and it is to some extent fundamental in the nature of communication. Every telephone wire must be insulated, and so must any other channel of communication. Every channel, if it is effective, transmits information better than a random arrangement; information used by the system must be kept within its channels, and unwanted information kept out lest it drown the wanted messages in noise. The more effective a social communication system gets, the more sharply separate does it become from all those groups or languages which it cannot incorporate: unable to bear promiscuity, it must choose marriage or divorce.[10]

The alternative would be social learning leading to a universal communications system, uniting all mankind. Yet such uniform social learning is impossible in a world which is not uniform, so long as the power of the physical environment looms large in the life of every individual. The lower the level of equipment and technology, the greater is the power of the different soils and countries over their populations.

The building up of peoples means, therefore, the development of more closely knit groups, more sharply differentiated from each other, and gradually becoming more dependent in the long run on their social heritage than on their physical environment. For a long time, however, the dependence on this heritage will grow faster, whereas the dependence on the physical environment will diminish but slowly. So long as fixed capital goods grow in demand but remain relatively scarce, the difference between developed and undeveloped areas may even increase in importance, as it seems to have done during the first half of this century.

During a long period, therefore, the distinctions among peoples may be growing; and the emergence of some sort of self-consciousness becomes more likely. The transition from local and agricultural modes of life to commercial and early industrial economies, mobilizing and uprooting ever larger portions of the populations, will then continue to produce a rise of national consciousness in country after country.

Even after extreme economic contrasts will have become mitigated by the eventual world-wide diffusion of technology, the problem of the "signal-to-noise ratio" will continue to plague would-be architects of world government or world community. How can we assure the necessary priority in our own attention for messages from distant regions and peoples over the more numerous and urgent competing messages—the "noise" originating closer to our own environment? How can we do the same for the messages coming to us from some distant federal government, and, in turn, for its adequate reception of the messages we send to it?

This is not primarily a problem of fidelity in long-distance channels, and it is not entirely solved by telegraph, telephone, radio, and television. Decisively, it is a switchboard problem; and all improvements in transmitting gadgets may merely increase the "noise" or traffic jam of competing messages in the minds of the rulers and the ruled. To insure predominance for the two-way signals of world community over the noise of local interests, we must make sure that these world-wide messages and signals correspond closely to the immediately felt local needs and interests of individuals; that institutions of federal or international government remain closely tied and responsive to the population of all regions: and that traffic patterns of messages are created which combine a capacity of handling quickly and adequately a vastly greater load of messages with the continued capacity for unified decision.

Any world government would have to comprise a population sixteen times as numerous as that of the United States, with vastly greater contrasts of language, income, and culture patterns, and with a tradition of interstate migration rates (i.e., migration rates across state borders) of about one-tenth that of the United States since 1850, or perhaps even earlier. To maintain any unified government under such conditions may require ultimately the invention of a range of new techniques, and of new designs for the human networks and switchboards of government, a task which may well prove a challenge to social scientists and men of practical affairs.

There seems little chance of avoiding this difficult task by the use of military power. In the long run, the problem of the signal-to-noise ratio applies to the human networks of armies and military communications systems as much as to all others. Conquering armies in time acquire local interests. Isolating them from local interests and ambitions can at best postpone the day of reckoning. The history of military empires and police dictatorships is replete with the wars of proconsuls and the conspiracies of police chiefs and palace guards. There is no reason to assume that any international army, in and by itself, would remain immune to such disintegration.

For the more modest scale of the territorial or national state, the double task of openness to messages and of speed and unity of decision has given rise to the problem of the national will.

The National Will

We noted in our survey in Chapter 1 that the concept of will has been approached by modern psychologists with misgivings very similar to those felt about consciousness. Yet the notion of will is important in politics, and at least some of its patterns can be stated more explicitly from the viewpoint of communications.

Will, in a self-steering system of the kind described earlier in this chapter, may be described as the set of constraints acquired from the memories and past experiences of the system, and applied to the selection and treatment of items in its later intake, recall, or decisions. Any self-steering system, as we saw, requires some operating preferences. If it is a learning system, it can change some of these, and it may be able to change some of its goals. Will, then, is the ability to inhibit, partially or wholly, any further learning. It is the ability to freeze the setting of the goal, and even the course chosen toward it, once the decision has hardened. No further data, in extreme instances, can then produce any change of course; the person, group, or organization cannot be deflected from its "fell purpose" until it breaks down, or until the goal is reached.

In a social group, this effect can be produced by imposing suitable drastic restrictions on the further intake or circulation of certain kinds of information, or on their recall from memory, or from the institutions, records, or traditions of the group. Thus governments in wartime may ban all items suggesting the wisdom of making peace; or leaders of a nation may ban from its schools all references to the virtues or achievements of its chief foreign rival. Similar results may be obtained by an opposite kind of constraint through the forced intake or recall or forced circulation of selected items supporting the course chosen, in amounts far beyond the usual, so as to drown out all contradictory items.

It is well known that such patterns of constraint or flooding of communication channels can be mapped, and their effects measured by the usual methods of social communication research and public opinion analysis. The data thus obtained, however, could now be correlated in a broader and perhaps more meaningful context.

Ethnic learning may thus develop a people; national consciousness, under suitable historical, social, and economic conditions, may carry it towards nationality; and national will may impose temporary constraints on its further learning, in an attempt to force it into a permanent pattern. The conditions under which this may occur, and the prospects for success may now perhaps be examined somewhat further.

The Spread of National Consciousness and the Change in Values

National consciousness adds a name, perhaps a flag, usually a selective history and a set of related symbols to the existing relative complementarity and distinctness of a people. By material signals, symbols, devices, and institutions, it makes many members of that people explicitly aware of their membership at a time when other, nonnational changes in society, economics, and culture make such linguistic or cultural complementarity, distinctness, and group membership increasingly important to individuals.

Yet this new awareness may hasten denationalization instead of nationalistic development, unless this spotlighted nationality happens to be valued. If it is not valued, its discovery may simply be embarrassing, as Zionism was felt to be embarrassing by some Jewish groups in Western Europe. It drew attention to a cultural distinction which these groups felt to be disadvantageous. Since they desired assimilation, the new emphasis on their separateness merely spurred their desire to assimilate more quickly.

Only if nationality is valued; if it is seen as a winning card in the social game for prestige, wealth, or whatever else may be the things culturally valued at that time and place; or if it fulfills a need in the personality structure which individuals have developed in that particular culture—or if it is at least valued for lack of any more promising opportunities—only then does it seem probable that consciousness of nationality will strengthen its development.

The world-wide rise in national consciousness since about 1700 suggests, therefore, a possible change in the context of other values in

Western civilization, spreading then with it over much of the rest of the world. Behind the spreading of national consciousness there was at work perhaps a deeper change—a new *value* assigned to people *as they are*, or as they can become, with as much diversity of interlocking roles as will not destroy or stifle any of their personalities. After 1750 we find new and higher values assigned in certain advanced countries to children and women; to the poor and the sick; to slaves and peasants; to colored races and submerged nationalities. This change was contemporary with the rise of the mass market and the social and economic mass mobilization for it.[11] This mobilization was continued and enhanced by the Industrial Revolution. The Industrial Revolution, in turn, produced repeated changes in the importance of different crafts and skills. It forced men to learn and change their habits; and since, on the whole, this was done successfully it became rather clear that people were more important than habits, skills, or positions. In a sense successful mobility bred confidence and put a new value on men.

National consciousness thus arises in the age that asserts birthrights for everybody, inborn, unalienable rights, first in the language of religion, then in the language of politics, and finally in terms involving economics and all society. It arises in the course of long development in the world of social and economic fact, at the point where it meets with the results of a broad change of spirit.

Assimilability and intercourse grew in Greece and Rome, but neither Greeks, Romans, nor Barbarians were ever valued in themselves for what they were. They were valued for the excellence with which they copied a pattern. The pattern might be that of Pericles, or of Epicurus, or of Sparta, or of Caesar. But it was the pattern that counted, and not the individual. They were proud to be not Romans, but citizens of Rome. Like the Greeks, they were *politai* and not *patriotai*, in the old distinction which the Greeks had drawn between themselves and the Barbarians.[12]

The fundamental change from this traditional outlook was precipitated by the Commercial and Industrial Revolutions. These slow and silent revolutions taught men to realize their own immense learning capacities, their vast abilities for adaptation to physical and social change, their powers of discovery, creation, and initiative. When the age of geographical discoveries turned into the age of conquest, men were taught a new appreciation of their power; and the consciousness of human power—and thus of the potential power of every human being however lowly he might seem—was deepened and accelerated by the progress of the Industrial Revolution.[13]

What has been stated here is a surmise, but there are facts available to check it. We have a good deal of data about attitudes and values of people, both from past history and literature, and from the attitude surveys and inventories of psychological and anthropological research. If nationalism is correlated, as I suspect, with an increase in the value placed on individuals *as they are,* and with a decrease in the deference paid to internationally standardized culture patterns, and with the general decrease in the willingness to accept one's station in life as given, then all these correlations should be capable of being tested by well-known methods.

In the same way, we could test our second surmise: that this shift in underlying basic attitudes is in turn correlated with an increase in the familiarity of individuals with items of modern technology, the use of money, and participation in markets. One form such tests could take would be to rank various populations in the present-day world in order of the strength of various indicators of nationalism; second, to rank them in order of the value placed on the "unreconstructed" individual—the man who is "a man for all that"—and of the unwillingness to accept previous limitations of status; and finally to rank the same populations in terms of the intensity of their participation in market processes and the diffusion of items of modern technology. If the three rank orders should show a good deal of correlation, our surmise would gain confirmation. If the correlations are poor, they might indicate a need for revising our picture.

Much would depend, however, in either case, on the appropriateness and subtlety with which indicators for the original rank orders would be selected and on the discrimination with which they would be applied to the raw data. Mahatma Gandhi's spinning by hand at the wheel would appear at first glance as a representative of a continuation of an old tradition; on closer inspection it might turn out that it represented rather a deliberate gesture of non-acceptance of the previous inferior status of the Indian textile industries vis-à-vis those of England, as well as of the previously inferior status of Indian village industries. Far from affirming a continuation of the status quo, Gandhi's gesture would turn out to be both a symbol and an instrument of social change, and in its consequence, of the ultimate diffusion of industrial or semi-industrial practices and technologies. Although indicators of social mobilization and of shift in basic attitudes and values would have to be constructed, therefore, with great care, there is every reason to believe that they could be so constructed and applied, and that we could get a verifiable picture of the underlying social changes on the basis of which national consciousness can rise and spread.

Once men formed a people, once they acquired many objective characteristics of nationality, they would become aware of what had happened. If this new awareness should come to them in the midst of a cultural and spiritual change, a change in the fundamental strategy of values, teaching them a new pride and a new confidence in what they were and in their own kind—or teaching them a hunger for this kind of pride and confidence not yet attained—then this new consciousness of nationality would become a potential center for new patterns of individual and social behavior, and of political action. If all this should happen in ages of widening social mobilization and sharpening social conflicts, nationalism would easily turn into a political weapon, a powerful pattern to organize men in the course of their social conflicts, bidding them to abate or defer some of these conflicts in order to concentrate all their strength on winning victories in others. And if these trends to nationalism should become reinforced by the deliberate actions of governments, public education systems, newspapers and other media of mass communication, economic interest groups, and hosts of other private or public agencies—then, indeed, nationalism might appear on the stage as a dominant political force in the nineteenth and twentieth centuries.

Nationalism has in fact appeared as such a dominant power, a power not so much in its own right but, like a whirlpool, the visible expression of the meeting of other forces which created it.

Extreme Nationalism and Self-Destruction: The Inner Problem of the Will

In the course of such events, consciousness of nationality might harden into will. This would mean the refusal to accept communications conflicting with, or even merely different from, the national separateness, or the national unity, or the image of a national character adopted as a goal. The hardening of the "national will" would mean the closing of the "national mind." In practice this meant the closing of inconvenient channels of communication in society, and the attempted closing of the mind of individuals. It was as a harbinger of things to come that Edmund Burke spoke so eloquently of the social and political advantages of prejudice, although he had the wisdom to warn against rigidity. One and a half centuries later, the National

Socialist Government of Germany, with less wisdom, called the official propaganda film of its Party meeting at Nuremberg *The Triumph of the Will.*

The symbols of extreme will are hardness, imperviousness, inaccessibility to any information or consideration that might interfere with the relentless pursuit of the once chosen goal or of a course of action once embarked upon. Shakespeare intuitively saw the implications:

> Come, you spirits
> That tend on mortal thoughts,

cries out Lady Macbeth when she plans the murder of King Duncan,

> unsex me here,
> And fill me, from the crown to the toe, top-full
> Of direst cruelty! Make thick my blood,
> Stop up the access and passage to remorse,
> That no compunctious visitings of nature
> Shake my fell purpose. . . .

Her summons to the will turns into a prayer for blindness:

> . . . come, thick night,
> And pall thee in the dunnest smoke of hell,
> That my keen knife see not the wound it makes. . . .[14]

Toward the beginning of the twentieth century, the nationalism of thousands began to echo Lady Macbeth's prayer. "What we need is hardness, hardness and again hardness," Oswald Spengler adjured the defeated Germans in 1919,[15] and, in the years that followed, hardness and *der blanke Wille* were outstanding topics in German National Socialist poetry, and "Will and Power" (*Wille und Macht*) was the title of the official organ of the Hitler Youth Movement.[16]

The ultimate symbol of will power is the dead man returned from the grave to complete a mission left unfinished. Since he is dead, nothing can deter or stop him. From the beginning of the nineteenth century, such dead men have walked in the political poetry of German nationalism. In France there echoes the integral nationalism of Maurice Barres: *La terre et les morts!* In the Ireland of 1915 Patrick Pearse saw in the "Fenian dead" the guarantee of the invincibility of Irish nationalism,[17] and when Patrick Pearse himself died with his friends a year later in the Easter Rebellion of 1916, another Irishman, William Butler Yeats, felt that all was

> . . . changed, changed utterly.
> A terrible beauty is born.[18]

The Japanese *Kamikaze* flyer in World War II would don his death shirt and go through a burial rite before taking up his airplane on a suicidal mission. But it was in Germany that the wave of this sentiment rose to its crest. No other people thus far has succumbed so deeply to the symbol of the dead man and the magic of the frozen will. In the imagery of National Socialism such dead men marched in serried ranks. Death or the dead were topics in 54 out of 102 songs in the official songbook of the German National Socialist Party in the 1930's.[19]

Often the extreme nationalistic cult of the dead went hand in hand with hate, fear, or despair of the living. "Spain must belong to us or to nobody," was a slogan of General Francisco Franco's "Nationalists" in the Spanish Civil War. "Let Europe crash in flames if Germany falls!" echoed a widespread Nazi song:

> Brach Etzel's Saal in Glut zusammen,
> Da er die Nibelungen zwang,
> So soll Europa stehn in Flammen
> Ob der Germanen Untergang!

The sentiment was acted out, with gruesome thoroughness, in the last-ditch slaughter in Berlin, and the suicides of the Nazi leaders Hitler and Goebbels in the ruins of the *Reichskanzlei* in April 1945.

At this stage nationalism had become will, and this will had become a worship of death and a creed of suicide. But the elements of this worship and this creed are present wherever nationalism waxes strong and wherever it is permitted to harden into will.

What has happened in all those cases where the "national will" has run away with the fate of a nation? Let us not argue about the large or small number of persons who held this "will" at some earlier stage in the process. The trouble lies deeper than in the stock situation of the crafty, small minority persuading the great, gullible majority of some wicked perversion of the truth. Rather, what perversion of the truth there is, what suicidal thought patterns we find are all being reproduced over and over again, in large degree, in the minds of millions of individuals.

What has happened has been the unbalancing of the very sources of decision, the cutting off of whole streams of information—or, what comes to the same thing, their drowning out by the deafening volume of coordinated mass propaganda—the manipulation of mass communication, and of the present intake of new facts as well as of the recall from the community's own real past, from its own actual traditions.

The extreme attempt to preserve unchanged a people with its institutions and its policies leads first to the perversion, and in the extreme case ultimately to the loss of these traditions and institutions. It leads to the loss of self-determination; nationalism at the end of its tether becomes a force for the destruction of the nation.

Such a development could be accurately mapped by research on social communication. It has not been brought about with mirrors, but with channels of communication. Every one of these channels can be mapped out, and so can the steps in its closing; or the steps in its flooding by stepped-up propaganda. Many of these steps have been described: the closing of certain newspapers; the ousting of broadcasters; the restrictions on organizations, parties, speech, and social contacts; the closing of channels from the past—the banned writers, the purged libraries and schools, the books in flames.

What has been less often described—but what could be identified by social scientists—is the gradual manipulation of the decision system of the community: the tacit premises established by endlessly repeated statements, or, more effectively, by endlessly repeated indirect suggestion; the stereotyped images of other peoples or ideas; the frozen policies and policy objectives, the provinces, territories, or borders made too sacred for reexamination—the building up of whole systems of goals, fears, and beliefs, and finally of actions, beyond the point of no return.

Social scientists could point out or predict what has perhaps been least often described: the cumulative impact of all these changes in social communication over time, up to the loss of the ability to assimilate experience, that is, up to collective insanity careening to national destruction.

Germany in the 1930's and 1940's followed this path farther, and with more bitter consequences than any other nation has done thus far, and so in their own way did most of the German minorities in Eastern Europe. But neither the path nor the results were peculiarly German. The closing of channels of communication, and the loss of the ability to understand other peoples and cultures may occur quickly or slowly, by governmental fiat or by the slow accretion of custom, much as channels of water may be closed by dams or choked by silting. The danger of such closing of the avenues of understanding and of the loss of both outside information and internal self-control—these are major and perhaps increasing risks in any of the systems of social communication which we call nations.

It used to be customary to look upon the nineteenth and early twentieth centuries as an age of international amelioration in which the "old prejudices" of nations and peoples gave way to a new tolerance. There are important cases on record where such improvements have in fact occurred. But it will not do to ignore the other side of the record: the increasing *inability* of many nations and peoples to live and work together. The story of the independence of Ireland is the story of the failures of the successive compromises from the attempts at Home Rule in 1914 to the agreements of 1921 and down the years to the independent Irish Republic of the 1940's.[20] The story of the failure of the compromises between North and South in the United States from the Missouri Compromise to the Dred Scott decision and the War between the States has found its latter-day counterparts in many lands.

A generation ago British observers prided themselves on the reconciliation between Boer and Briton in the new Union of South Africa; today they find that "in more recent times the Nationalists have . . . striven for an exclusively Africaner government, disdaining even to make the effort to convert non-Africaners to the Republican way of thinking."[21] The channels, we learn, have been closing in South Africa: the Nationalist leaders since the 1920's have "turned altogether negative—anti-Capitalist, anti-Semitic, anti-Communist, perhaps it may be said also anti-Black, anti-Coloured, anti-Indian, and anti-British. A few allowed their wartime feelings to carry them to a near or altogether Nazi point of view. But the great majority honestly, and narrowly, put 'South Africa First.' It is Sinn Fein over again, ourselves alone, in a more complex society than Ireland."[22]

The collapse of the attempts at compromise between India's Hindus and Muslims is now a matter of tragic history. The bullet of a Hindu nationalist that killed Mahatma Gandhi added one more symbolic victim to the million deaths that came in 1947 with the separation of India and Pakistan. In Palestine, during the same years, the failure of all compromises between Jews and Arabs led to war and ended in the emigration or expulsion of hundreds of thousands of Arab refugees—a number of displaced persons larger than that driven out from that area by the original conquests of Islam in the days of the Prophet Mohammed and the Khalif Omar. The expulsion of the Armenians and Greeks from Turkey during and after World War I, the repatriation of the German South Tyroleans from Mussolini's Italy, the expulsion of the Sudeten Germans from Dr. Edvard Beneš's Czechoslovak Republic in 1947, the more humane but far-reaching "relocation" of

Japanese-Americans from California in 1942, the present difficulties of the Chinese population in Malaya—are not all these indications of the very serious difficulties of different peoples to live together in a common state under the conditions of enforced closeness of contacts so characteristic of modern social and economic life?

The cases we have just surveyed range over four continents and a number of different races and political systems. Yet they have in common this one fatal tendency toward the breakdown of national compromise and reconciliation. They are indications of the power of extreme nationalism in many countries—the kind of nationalism that in the end led to the ruins of Berlin.

Not all nations and peoples need travel this road toward loss of sensitivity and loss of self-control—not even if they have, at one time or another, taken some step in that direction. But the road is here in the middle of the twentieth century, and it is broad, smooth, and paved with nationalists' good intentions.

Chapter 9

A Prospect for Nationalism

A Summary of Findings

Let us sum up what this book has tried to say.

We found an underlying unity and structural correspondence in the seemingly very diversified accounts of nationalism by dozens of observers, which we surveyed in Chapter 1. Nationalism emerged as a challenge to the understanding and the resources not of any one discipline but of a whole array of social sciences working together.

A survey of these social sciences in Chapter 2 showed a structural correspondence between certain key concepts in each field. The picture revealed by all these together is a world not of flat uniformity but of highly uneven cluster distributions. It is a world in which clusters of settlement, nodes of transport, centers of culture, areas and centers of language, divisions of caste and class, barriers between markets, sharp regional differences in wealth and interdependence, and the uneven impact of critical historical events and social institutions all act together to produce a highly differentiated and clustered world of regions, peoples, and nations. Techniques of mapping in each concrete case the areas of these overlapping influences, and the density or scarcity of social communications that result from them promise to shed light on some of the conditions and prospects of national or supranational integration.

An inquiry into the nature of political power in Chapter 3 showed all such power as dependent on the highly uneven distribution of social communication facilities and of economic, cultural, and geographic interdependence. The present distribution of sovereign states and blocks of states was found to be necessary in its essential features, though not in its accidents. To consider problems of federation or international government apart from this fundamental fact of the uneven distribution of interdependence and power would invite the delusion of omnipotence.

A crucial unit within each cluster of intensive social communication is a people. The essential aspect of the unity of a people, Chapter 4 suggested, is the complementarity or relative efficiency of communication among individuals—something that is in some ways similar to mutual rapport, but on a larger scale.

Chapter 5 suggested a number of ways in which this complementarity could be tested and measured in the case of individuals. From these methods there could be derived a number of tests for the membership of individuals in a people, as well as of the extent to which their assimilation to a people may have succeeded, or to which their differentiation from it may have progressed. National assimilation and differentiation were shown to be related to social learning, and some broad inferences from the general theory of learning were found applicable to these processes. Together, Chapters 4 and 5 suggested a number of ways in which some of the specific findings and methods of social psychology, sociology, and anthropology could be related more closely with those of history, economics, and political science.

The quantitative study of large-scale processes of national assimilation and differentiation was discussed in Chapter 6. It was found that the data and methods of economic history, and population theory and statistics permit the identification of crucial population groups, the charting of long-run trends of national assimilation and differentiation, and their tentative projection into the future. A decisive factor in national assimilation or differentiation was found to be the fundamental process of social mobilization which accompanies the growth of markets, industries, and towns, and eventually of literacy and mass communication. The trends in this underlying process of social mobilization could do much to decide whether existing national trends in particular countries would be continued or reversed.

The gross quantitative processes of national assimilation or differentiation, as measured by statistics, were found to depend in turn on a number of qualitative and quantitative factors, and a number of such balances were discussed in Chapter 7. Some of these balances could be measured in principle in terms of supply and demand, of frequency of contacts of different kinds, and of economic rewards and penalties. Other balances were found to be technical and linguistic in nature, and still others appeared to be determined by cultural and political institutions. From the methods outlined in Chapters 6 and 7 mathematical techniques could be developed for calculating probable national assimilation or differentiation periods. A crude beginning towards such mathematical techniques is presented in Appendix V.

The process of national consciousness and will were found in Chapter 8 to be accessible in principle to the same structural and quantitative approach as those employed in the preceding chapters. These concepts had been heavily stressed by twentieth-century writers on nationalism but had been avoided by many psychologists to whom they had appeared vague. It was found in Chapter 8 that crude models for the processes of consciousness and will could be derived from the theory of communication and control, and that with their help consciousness and will in organizations, states, or nations could be mapped or measured in some aspects. Finally, it was found that processes of will form an essential part of the process of autonomous control and are subject to its pathology. Nationalism and national development were found to involve processes of social learning and control which are particularly subject to risks of pathological developments and trends to self-destruction. The experience of German National Socialism was found to be an extreme example for a number of similar, though weaker, trends in other countries. The growing failures of different nationalities since the 1890's to live together peacefully in a common country, and the growing number of secessions, expulsions, population transfers, and barriers to immigration all appear to be related to these potentially destructive tendencies of national development. The destructive as well as the constructive aspects of national development, consciousness, and will were found to be accessible to charting and measurement by social scientists. Development and application of such methods by social scientists could do much to indicate potential danger spots, and application of their findings by policy makers could serve to forestall or minimize destruction and to guide the fundamental processes of social mobilization and national development into constructive channels.

As the summary shows, this is largely a book on research and methods of research. There is in it a good deal of substantive data about nationalism, and of intuitive descriptions of nationalistic situations and behavior patterns by various observers, but the center of interest is in the research that has not yet been done and that could be done by the methods here suggested. At the end of a book of such length which summarizes the results of a number of years of work, the reader may feel entitled to ask: What are your conclusions about nationalism? Stripped of technicalities, what do you think as to where we are and where we are going?

It is a legitimate question, and I shall try to answer it with one essential qualification. What I have to say will be far more tentative and far less substantial than anything I have said thus far. What I think about the prospects of nationalism at this time is based only on empirical study, on first-hand acquaintance with a number of nationalist movements, on abstract inferences from theory, and on intuitive judgments of trends. If I believed that this were a sufficient basis for an adequate understanding of nationalism, I should have written a very different book from the one before you. I have written this book about the need for more research, and for different kinds of research, precisely because I do not believe that our present knowledge is sufficient for our needs.

Whether the unification of Western Europe will be a success or not, whether there will be peace between Hindus and Muslims in India, between Jews and Arabs in the Near East, and between British, Chinese and Malayans in Malaya—these are questions which could be answered, I believe, with the help of research methods outlined in this book, but they cannot be measured by much more than empirical guesswork without it. My own guesses about the prospects of nationalism are thus in the nature of a postscript. They are only in very small part based on the application of the research methods it suggests. They may easily be shown to be in need of revision by the application of these research methods, or by the testimony of events.

A Postscript on Perspectives

Subject to these qualifications, there seems to be considerable prospects for the increasing importance of nationalism in the years ahead. Despite the recent examples of nationalistic self-destruction at the extreme end of the political spectrum, nationalistic movements and practices still seem to be growing in the world.

Yet the same processes which made nationalism probable may soon come to turn against it.

Nationalism was associated with the mass mobilization of precommercial, preindustrial peasant peoples. Their mobilization and their transition to an industrial economy should be substantially completed within the next two generations. Barring a general atomic war, capital equipment by then should become far more widely distributed over the world's more backward regions.

Tying the mobilized populations into national communities and social classes has tended to separate peoples from each other for a time; but it made them fundamentally more alike, and taught many of them to adjust to new and changing patterns of communication.

The unfinished part of the task should not be underestimated. The economic inequality between different groups or classes within each country has been matched, and in some instances in part replaced, by the inequality between different countries and peoples. Since the Industrial Revolution, nationalism has drawn much of its strength from the successively lower levels of material civilization—the *Kulturgefaelle,* as the Germans called it—met in each country by many travelers journeying eastward from America to China, or going southward from the temperate zone to the equator. Everywhere on this ladder of economic inequality, nationalists found richer neighbors to resent and envy; poorer neighbors to despise and fear; but few, if any, equals to respect.

The fact of inequality was perhaps not decisive, but its vast extent, and its tendency to shrink so slowly, or sometimes even to increase was decisive. Economic growth has been so much faster in some countries than in others that today the living standards of Australian and Hindu farmers may well be even farther apart than they were a hundred years ago. That the difference in poverty is so great, and that the world's poorest peoples are so numerous—comprising, as they do, more than one-half of mankind—these are perhaps the fundamental facts behind much of today's nationalistic insistence on national separateness and economic and political barriers. Not before the bottom of the barrel of the world's large peoples has been reached, not before inequality and insecurity will have become less extreme, *not before the vast poverty of Asia and Africa will have been reduced substantially by industrialization, and by gains in living standards and in education—not before then will the age of nationalism and national diversity see the beginning of its end.*

Thus far, the age of nationalism has grouped people apart from each other, and may for a time continue to do so. But at the same time it is preparing them, and perhaps in part has already prepared them, for a more thoroughgoing world-wide unity than has ever been seen in human history.

Even the growth of national consciousness may under certain circumstances contribute to this end. It can become a blinding curse to those who have accepted it uncritically. Like all consciousness, however, it draws much of its strength from being an awareness of something which exists. To reveal what is, to show the true state of affairs for part of the political problems of a part of mankind may serve as a preparation for teaching men to be aware of the whole pattern of their affairs, and of the single problem of mankind on its painful way to unity. As men attain this insight into the essential unity of their fate on this planet, the age of nationalism and of the growth of nations may recede into its proper historical perspective.

Nationalistic parties and leaders have characteristically led their peoples along part of this way. They seem unlikely to lead them to its end. They have tended to be more successful in the stages of national protest than in the tasks of national construction. In underdeveloped countries, nationalists often have been more successful in building parties rather than armies; armies rather than schools; schools rather than factories; and factories rather than fundamental changes in village life. Often they have been political beneficiaries of a process of social mobilization which they had not created and over which they had little influence. They were riding a wave, not chaneling a river, and they would drift as far as they were carried by the current. In general they did not come to grips with the fundamental productive forces of their countries, and they left their peoples often not much less poor and not much better organized than the large and largely anonymous processes of economic growth would make them.

There are very notable exceptions to this pattern. Nationalist statesmen like Alexander Hamilton and Thomas Jefferson in the United States, Cromwell and later Disraeli in England, perhaps leaders like Sarmiento in Argentina, Grundtvig in Denmark, and the architects of the *Zollverein* in nineteenth-century Germany all added the results of conscious effort to the great opportunities offered by the peculiar economic development in their respective countries, and the processes of growth which they started or accelerated continued well beyond their lifetime. But in most parts of the world the pattern has more characteristically been the disunity of Latin America after Símon Bolívar, and of China after Sun Yat Sen; the relative stagnation of Egypt after Mohamed Ali; and of Turkey after Ataturk; and of the nationalistic regimes in the Balkan states between the two world wars. It may take national leaders and movements of deeper realism and greater stature than the nationalists of the years between 1900 and 1950, if the majority of the peoples and nations of mankind are to outgrow the present age of national separation and conflict.

The same considerations apply to the growth of regional blocks, or of blocks cemented by ties of economics, ideology, or power. Such blocks exist already, and for the near future their growth seems more probable than that of any major institutions of world government. All such blocks will be characterized by uneven internal structures based on underlying cluster patterns of settlement, capital, natural resources, and facilities for social communication. The expansion of all such blocks will be subject, therefore, to very real geographic and social limitations, although there might be a lesser limitation on their ability to inflict military damage on each other.

In the long run, the decisive question for any such block will be the same as that for any state or nation of today: Will it prove an instrumentality of inner development and growth or an engine of stagnation and destruction? What may matter most in the end will be not so much the size of the bite as the quality of the chewing. How much of a living unity, how much actual and mutual communication, how much cultural and economic growth will there be among the masses of the populations throughout the territories of each block? From the viewpoint of democracy, genuine freedom and development within a limited block of countries should be preferable to stagnation within a larger area or under an inadequate or premature world government. The larger the area, however, in which *genuine* integration and development can be carried on successfully, the greater will become the probability that eventually the challenge of world order and world government will be mastered.

To hasten this development, we shall have to add much to our present scant understanding of the growth of nations. How the growth of national diversity occurred, how the age of industrialization accelerated it, and how the same age perhaps has been laying the groundwork for eventual world unity will have to be investigated in separate studies. If the present discussion has shown that such studies are worth undertaking, it will have fulfilled its purpose.

Appendices

The graphs shown in the text are not accurate representations of events in the past, nor are they predictions of probable developments in the future. They have been constructed from such incomplete statistical data as were found in the time available. The sources for these data are listed in the four appendices that follow. These data were then extended into the past or into the future by means of certain techniques of calculation and extrapolation, and by making certain assumptions as to matters of fact, past, present, or future. These assumptions of fact, as well as the calculating techniques used, are again set forth in the appropriate appendices.

It is clear, therefore, that the trends pictured on these graphs need not necessarily correspond to any trends in the social reality in the countries to which they refer. At best, they may resemble this reality only to the extent that the assumptions made in their construction should turn out to correspond to matters of fact; that the historical data, statistics, and calculating methods used should have involved no significant inaccuracies or distortions; and furthermore, that no significant elements or factors should have been omitted from the calculations for any of the periods covered. This last caution includes, of course, the assumption that no major changes or discontinuities not provided for in the calculations have occurred in the past covered by these graphs, or will occur in the future into which these trends have been projected.

A projection, in short, is not a prediction; and the graphs given in the text are primarily schematic diagrams designed to exhibit certain fundamental quantitative relationships in the development of nationalities and nations. Beyond this, they may perhaps serve to demonstrate the possibility of gaining a better understanding of such processes in particular countries with the aid of better tools, such as longer series of more complete and more accurate data, more realistic assumptions, and more refined mathematical techniques.

None of these tools, it was felt, should prove impossible to obtain. The first step toward the quantitative treatment of those aspects of nationality that lend themselves to this attack consists in their "conceptual quantification": they must be brought into a symbolic form in which further and more accurate quantitative treatment becomes possible. It is this which the diagrams presented in the text attempt to do; for it was believed that once the possibility was shown there would be a better chance that in time the next steps would be taken.

APPENDIX I

FINLAND, 1749–2000: DATA AND CALCULATIONS USED FOR THE DIAGRAM OF SWEDES AND FINNS AND OF THE URBAN AND RURAL POPULATIONS

Sources Used

Annuaire Statistique de Finlandie 1949, Publication du Bureau Central de Statistique. Helsinki, 1950.

Toivola, Urho, Ed., *The Finland Yearbook 1947*. Helsinki, Mercatorin Kirjapaino Ja Kustannus Oy, 1947.

Thomas, Dorothy Swaine, *Social and Economic Aspects of Swedish Population Movements 1750–1933*. New York, Macmillan, 1941.

United Nations Department of Social Affairs: Population Studies: No. 8: *Data on Urban and Rural Population in Recent Censuses*. Lake Success, N. Y., Statistical Office of the United Nations, Department of Economic Affairs, 1950.

Notestein, F. W., and Others, *The Future Populations of Europe and the Soviet Union*. Geneva, League of Nations, 1944.

Some Categories Used

This section deals with the graphs (Figs. 14, 15, 24, and 25) constructed for Finland, which intend to show the degree of economic mobilization in a nationally mixed area throughout the years 1749–1948.

It was not possible to divide the people of Finland into occupational groups, and so determine with exactness their degree of mobilization, because there are no suitable occupational statistics available for Finland. There are, however, figures giving the number of Finnish speakers and Swedish speakers, called in this discussion briefly "Finns" and "Swedes" (the only national groups of importance) in the towns and in the country. The people in the towns were assumed to approximate the mobilized population, whereas the underlying population was considered to be approximated by the people living in the country. Actually, of course, education and industry have spread well beyond the towns, and the curve of urbanization represents only a minimum measure of the mobilization that has occurred.

According to the definition used by the Finnish statistics, urban areas include all such "places which are *legally established* as urban." [1] The application of this definition under-represents the urban population (used in the sense of mobilized population). People living in a number of listed suburbs or "burghs" are urban for practical purposes, and must be considered socially mobilized for this study; they are therefore included in the urban population in a special section. Only from 1930 on, however, does this segment of population become large enough to warrant its inclusion on the graph in Fig. 15. It was subtracted from the Finnish rural population and added to the Finnish urban section on the assumption that the Swedes in the burghs amounted to a number negligible for present purposes. These few Swedes in the burghs do appear, however, among the rural Swedish speakers, so that the total number of Swedes remains unchanged.

For the years 1910, 1920, and 1930 the Finnish source [2] gives two different total population figures which correspond respectively to the population "de facto" and the population "present" (at the time of the census). The "de facto" figure is clearly larger by the number of people absent at the time the census was taken. In the present graphs the total population at all times equals the "de facto" population. In 1910, 1920, and 1930 the difference between the "de facto" and the present population is given in a separate area on the graph in Fig. 15.

All figures, either calculated or taken from sources, were rounded off to the nearest thousand. An effort was made to keep the graphical errors below 10,000 (people).

The Population in Towns and Country in Finland, 1750–1948

The following paragraph from the *Finland Yearbook 1947* makes it possible to obtain the desired figures for as early as 1750:

> At the time of the first census in Sweden-Finland in 1749, the present Finnish area had a population of slightly over ½ million. In 1811, the population amounted to 1 million, in 1880 to 2 million, and in 1910 to 3 million. The increase in population was partly due to colonization by settlers in the east and north, partly due to the quick growth of towns and industrial districts specially since 1880. In 1749 only 5% of Finland's population lived in towns, in 1880 the inhabitants of urban areas amounted to 9% and in 1936 to 21% of the total population. [3]

[1] United Nations Department of Social Affairs: *Data on Urban and Rural Population in Recent Censuses*, p. 25. (Italics added.)

[2] *Annuaire Statistique de Finlandie 1949.*

[3] Urho Toivola, Ed., *The Finland Yearbook 1947*, p. 17.

Five per cent of 421,000 is roughly 21,000, which was taken as the urban population in 1749. From 1750 to 1800 the urbanization curve was drawn parallel to the curve of total population because there are no urban population figures available for this period. The error thus introduced is negligible because of the small size of the urban segment of the population during this period, and any deviation from this estimate would hardly be visible on Fig. 15.

The figures giving the population in the towns and country from 1800 to 1948 are found in the *Annuaire Statistique de Finlandie 1949*, p. 6.

Finns and Swedes in Towns and Country in Finland, 1750–1948

The number of people in towns and country divided according to language is found in the *Annuaire Statistique de Finlandie 1949*, p. 29, for the period from 1880 to 1940. For 1865 the total Finns and the total Swedes are given. With the help of this pair of numbers and the figures for 1880 and 1890, the corresponding values for 1869, 1865, and 1870 were computed as a relatively crude approximation by the following method:

Let Fc = Finns in the country; Ft = Finns in the towns; Sc = Swedes in the country; St = Swedes in the towns.

The following relation was assumed to hold within the allowed error:

$$\frac{St\ 1890}{St\ 1880} = \frac{St\ 1880}{St\ 1870} \qquad \text{hence} \qquad St\ 1870 = \frac{(St\ 1880)^2}{St\ 1890}$$

Substituting values, one gets

$$St\ 1870 = \frac{(66,000)^2}{78,000} = 55,800 \text{ or, rounded off, } 56,000$$

Applying the same relation to obtain $St\ 1860$,

$$\frac{St\ 1860}{St\ 1870} = \frac{St\ 1870}{St\ 1860}$$

hence $\qquad St\ 1860 = \dfrac{(St\ 1870)^2}{St\ 1880} = \dfrac{(56,000)^2}{66,000} = 47,500$

Finding the arithmetic mean between $St\ 1870$ and $St\ 1860$ one obtains $St\ 1865$.

$$\frac{56,000 - 47,500}{2} = 51,750, \text{ or } 52,000$$

The same set of operations was then applied to the Swedes in the country (Sc):

$$\frac{Sc\ 1890}{Sc\ 1880} = \frac{Sc\ 1880}{Sc\ 1870} \qquad Sc\ 1870 = \frac{(229,000)^2}{244,000} = 215,000$$

$$\frac{Sc\ 1880}{Sc\ 1870} = \frac{Sc\ 1870}{Sc\ 1860} \qquad Sc\ 1860 = \frac{(215,000)^2}{229,000} = 202,000$$

Applying the arithmetic mean to obtain $Sc\ 1865$,

$$Sc\ 1865 = 202,000 + \frac{215,000 - 202,000}{2}, \text{ or } 208,000$$

One may now check the validity of assuming that the simple proportion used above is an adequate approximation. The total Swedish population for 1865 is known and should clearly be equal to $Sc\ 1865 + St\ 1865$ as found above.

Total known Swedish population in $1865 = 256,000$ [4]

and $\qquad Sc\ 1865 + St\ 1865 = 208,000 + 52,000 = 260,000$

which seems a rather close approximation. To make the figure consistent, $Sc\ 1865$ is made equal to

$$S \text{ total } 1865 - St\ 1865 = 256,000 - 52,000 = 204,000$$

To extend the breakdown into national groups from 1930 and 1940 until 1948, the same method was used.

Using the same nomenclature as above for Swedes in the towns:

$$\frac{St\ 1930}{St\ 1940} = \frac{St\ 1940}{St\ 1950}$$

$$St\ 1950 = \frac{(139,000)^2}{121,000} = 160,000$$

To go back roughly to 1948 one multiplies by $\frac{4}{5}$ the population increase from 1940 to 1950 and adds this result to the 1940 population.

$$St\ 1948 = 156,000$$

For Finns in the towns:

$Ft\ 1948 =$ Total town population $1948 - St\ 1948$

$$= 1,062,000 - 156,000 = 906,000$$

[4] *Annuaire Statistique de Finlandie 1949*, p. 29.

For Swedes in the country:

$$\frac{Sc\ 1930}{Sc\ 1940} = \frac{Sc\ 1940}{Sc\ 1950}$$

$$Sc\ 1950 = \frac{(215,000)^2}{222,000} = 208,000$$

$$Sc\ 1948 = Sc\ 1940 + \tfrac{4}{5}(Sc\ 1950 - Sc\ 1940) = 206,000$$

For Finns in the country:

Fc = Total country population $- Sc\ 1948$

$$= 2,927,000 - 206,000 = 2,721,000$$

To construct Fig. 15, a crude graphical method was used to extend the values from 1860 backward. The number of Swedes in towns [5] was plotted from 1860 to 1940. A growth curve was fitted to these points, and, as shown in part in Fig. 24, this curve was extrapolated back to the point where the population reaches a constant value after a period of asymptotic decline. This occurs roughly in 1780, with 30,000 Swedes. The total town population 1800–1880 was then plotted on the same diagram to the same scale. A growth curve was also fitted to this set of points and extrapolated back until it intersected the curve of Swedes in towns. This occurs at the dateline for 1775 and marks the theoretical appearance of Finns in towns whose population up to that time had been assumed to be exclusively Swedish. (All persons who were not Swedes were assumed to be Finns.) It can also be observed from the plot that on these assumptions by 1820 the Finns amounted to 50 per cent of the town population. The seemingly arbitrary range over which points were used to plot the curves of this diagram was determined by the number of points necessary to obtain a growth curve.

Hypothetical population figures for Swedes and Finns in towns from 1860 back to 1775 can now be read off the plot of Fig. 24. The figures beyond 1820 do not appear in Fig. 15, because the urban population segment is too small to make a further subdivision meaningful. The assumption that there appear to have been significant numbers of Finns in towns since 1775 (according to the plot, that is), and before that date almost only Swedes, is indicated in a qualitative manner by the appropriate shading on Fig. 15.

[5] *Annuaire Statistique de Finlandie 1949*, p. 29.

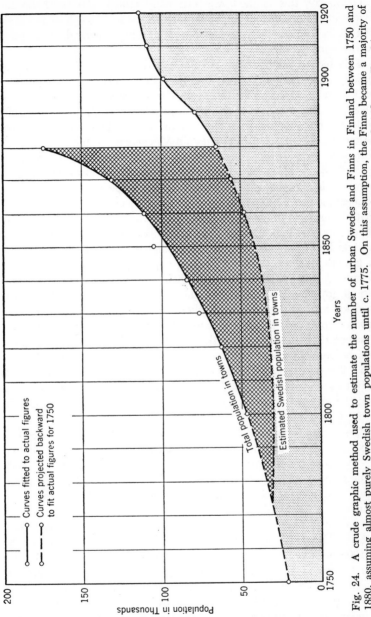

Fig. 24. A crude graphic method used to estimate the number of urban Swedes and Finns in Finland between 1750 and 1880, assuming almost purely Swedish town populations until c. 1775. On this assumption, the Finns became a majority of the urban population about 1820. This was the method used in computing the corresponding data in Fig. 14.

Obviously, this method was extremely crude. To check on the extent of distortion that might be introduced in a graph of the scale of that used in our text, a somewhat more refined method was applied to the same problem.

This second method leads to the construction of Fig. 25. It was based on the assumption that the Swedish-speaking urban population of Finland had grown at the same rate as the urban population of Sweden. The numbers of the urban population of Sweden from 1800 to 1900 were obtained from Dorothy Swaine Thomas, *Social and Economic Aspects of Swedish Population Movements*, Table 7, p. 42, with references to Swedish sources. These numbers were plotted on semilogarithmic graph paper, where the rate of growth between any two numbers is automatically expressed by the slope of the straight line connecting them. On plotting (not reproduced here) it was found that all numbers of Sweden's urban population from 1810 to 1900 lay on or close to two straight lines intersecting at 1850. The steeper straight line from 1850 to 1900 corresponded fairly closely to the rate of growth shown by Sweden's urban population figures during every decade of that period and over the half century as a whole. A lower rate of growth was suggested for the period from 1810 to 1850. From 1800 to 1810, on the other hand, there had been a slight decline in the urban population, possibly in connection with the Napoleonic Wars. It seemed fair to assume that the rate of growth of the urban population before 1800 could not have been greater than that from 1810 to 1850, if indeed it had not been smaller. The straight line of growth 1810 to 1850 was thus extended back to 1749, and was taken to represent the rate of growth of the urban population in Sweden during the entire period 1749 to 1850.

The known numbers of Finland's urban population from 1800 to 1900, and of her urban Swedes from 1880 to 1900 were then plotted on the same semi-logarithmic graph (not reproduced here). The turning point in the rates of growth of Finland's total urban population (comprising both Finns and Swedes) comes somewhat later than that in Sweden. The numbers for all years from 1800 to 1880 except for the war year of 1810 lie on or close to a straight line, but after 1880 the slope of any line fitted to the numbers from 1880 to 1900 becomes considerably steeper. As to Finland's urban Swedes alone, their number was still growing at a relatively low rate between 1880 and 1890, with only a slight acceleration from 1890 to 1900. In the assumption of a parallelism of trends in Finland and Sweden, the growth rate of Finland's urban Swedes was extended back

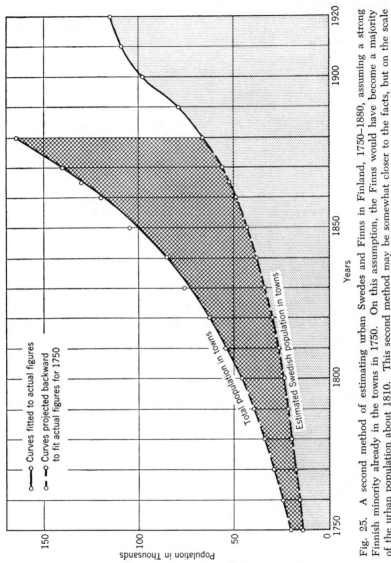

Fig. 25. A second method of estimating urban Swedes and Finns in Finland, 1750–1880, assuming a strong Finnish minority already in the towns in 1750. On this assumption, the Finns would have become a majority of the urban population about 1810. This second method may be somewhat closer to the facts, but on the scale of Fig. 14 the differences were not significant.

to 1850, and from 1850 to 1750 a flatter line of growth was projected, parallel to the projected line of urban growth in Sweden for that period. The intersections of this line with the date lines gave the hypothetical number of urban Swedes in Finland at the start of each decade, and the difference between these numbers and the total numbers of urban population gave the hypothetical numbers for the urban Finns. See the accompanying table.

	Total Towns	$Swedes_t$ (St)	$Finns_t$ $(Total - Ft)$
1750	21,000	14,000	7,000
1760	25,000	16,000	9,000
1770	29,000	18,000	11,000
1780	35,000	20,000	15,000
1790	40,000	23,000	17,000
1800	46,000	25,000	21,000
1810	55,000	27,000	28,000
1820	63,000	30,000	33,000
1830	76,000	34,000	42,000
1840	85,000	38,000	47,000
1850	105,000	42,000	63,000
1860	120,000	48,000	72,000
1865	130,000	52,000	78,000
1870	140,000	56,000	84,000
1880	170,000	66,000	100,000

These are, of course, smoothed-out figures derived from the projected trend, and vary somewhat therefore from the actual figures recorded at certain decades.

If one now plots the approximate figures of urban Swedes on an ordinary graph, as has been done in Fig. 25, one can compare it with the graph of Fig. 24 obtained by our first rough method of estimating Swedes in towns. It appears immediately that the previous method made the curve slope too brusquely, thus giving a constant Swedish urban population from 1770 to 1810. Also, this method assumed that there were no Finns in the towns in 1750. Considering these massive inaccuracies it is remarkable that the more refined method shifts the time when the Finns acquired a majority in the towns by only 10 years, namely, from 1820 to 1810.

A third method would be to allow for the probability of a somewhat slower rate of growth of the urban Swedes during the second half of the eighteenth century, as against the first half of the nineteenth. A simple way of doing this would be to take as a model for our projection back to 1750 the somewhat lesser rate of growth of the urban population of Sweden from 1800 to 1850 (instead of the steeper rate from 1810 to 1850). On this assumption, i.e., that Finland's urban Swedes did not grow faster than the urban population of Sweden from 1800 to 1850, we obtain for 1749 the numbers of 18,000 Swedes and 3000 Finns in the total urban population of 21,000, and the Swedes retain their majority in the cities until 1820, with 33,000 urban Swedes *vs.* 30,000 urban Finns, but become outnumbered during the following decade, with 35,000 Swedes and 41,000 Finns making up the known urban population of 76,000 in 1830.

The conclusion from all three methods would seem to be that on the assumptions of any one of them the majority of Finland's urban population should have passed from Swedish speakers to Finnish speakers at some time between 1810 and 1830, and that the numbers of population involved were too small to make a significant difference in the overall trend shown on the diagram used in Fig. 15.

A word should be added about the estimates of Finland's rural Swedish speakers before 1880. It is possible to divide the country population in 1750 into Finns and Swedes. "In 1749 Finland's Swedes numbered 16.3%. . . ."[6] The town population in 1750 was assumed to have been almost entirely Swedish (see preceding paragraph); and subtracting it from the total number of Swedes given in the above quotation we obtained the Swedish country residents. Subtraction of these from the total country population yielded number of the Finns in the country in 1750.

Because of the lack of suitable statistics for rural Finns and Swedes for the period from 1750 to 1860 a straight line was drawn between these two points in Fig. 15.

Predictions for the Future Growth of Finland's Population, 1950–2000 (Fig. 15)

One set of population estimates for future years was found in the *Annuaire Statistique de Finlandie 1949*, p. 46. It extends until the year 2000, and is represented by a double line on Fig. 15.

The other set of predictions was taken from *The Future Populations of Europe and the Soviet Union*, by F. W. Notestein, p. 278. It covers the period 1940 to 1970. The black-and-white line from 1931 to 1940 on Fig. 15 represents Dr. Notestein's curve extrapolated back from 1940 to 1931, so as to make its trend more obvious.

[6] Urho Toivola, *op. cit.*, p. 18.

POPULATION OF FINLAND 1750–2000

(In Thousands)

Year	Country	Towns	Total
1750	400	21	421
1760	....	....	491
1770	....	....	561
1780	....	....	664
1790	....	....	706
1800	786	47	833
1810	822	41	863
1820	1114	63	1177
1830	1296	76	1372
1840	1361	85	1446
1850	1531	105	1636
1860	1636	110	1746
1865	1720	123	1843
1870	1637	131	1768
1880	1887	173	2060
1890	2145	235	2380
1900	2373	340	2712
1910	2494	427	2943
1920	2612	493	3147
1930	2753	628	3463
1940	2833	863	3696
1945	2866	938	3804
1948	2927	1062	3989
1950			4028
1955			4135
1960			4230
1965			4316
1970			4406
1975			4501
1980			4591
1985			4670
1990			4735
1995			4795
2000			4863

F. W. NOTESTEIN'S FORECAST

Year	Total
1940	3850
1945	3950
1950	4000
1955	4020
1960	4010
1965	3980
1970	3920

POPULATION OF FINLAND ACCORDING TO LANGUAGE SPOKEN
1750–1940

(In Thousands)

Year	Country		Towns		Total
	Finns	Swedes	Finns	Swedes	
1749	350	50	. . .	21	421
1820	914 *	150 †	31 †	32 †	1177
1830	1095 *	165 †	42 †	34 †	1372
1840	1161 *	180 †	49 †	36 †	1446
1850	1331 *	190 †	65 †	40 †	1636
1860	1436 *	200 †	63 †	47 †	1746
1865	1516 ‡	204 ‡	64 ‡	52 ‡	1843 #
1870	1422 ‡	215 ‡	75 ‡	56 ‡	1768 #
1880	1656	229	100	66	2060 #
1890	1898	244	151	78	2380 #
1900	2117	252	236	97	2712 #
1910	2256	231	315	108	2943 # §
1920	2381	227	373	114	3147 # §
1930	2525	222	497	121	3463 # §
1940	2612	215	715	139	3696 #
1948	2721	206	906	156	3989

* Estimated by subtraction of the rural Swedes from the total rural population.

† Estimated by extrapolation of the curve in Fig. 24.

‡ Estimated by calculations shown on pp. 198–200.

§ Population de facto (see p. 197).

The numerical difference between the sum of the country and town population in the first four columns and the total population in the fifth column is equal to the number of people speaking languages other than Finnish and Swedish. Their numbers are listed on p. 208. The additional differences in 1910, 1920, and 1930, due to the discrepancies between "present" and "de facto" population are shown in Fig. 15.

POPULATION OF FINLAND LIVING IN BURGHS *

1930	73,000
1940	126,000
1948	216,000

* "Köping" or rural market towns, *Annuaire Statistique de Finlandie 1949*, p. 10. Cf. the discussion of Swedish classifications, which appear to be analogous, in Thomas, *Swedish Population Movements*, pp. 379–380.

POPULATION OF FINLAND SPEAKING LANGUAGES OTHER THAN FINNISH AND SWEDISH, 1865–1940

1865	7,000	1910	11,000
1880	9,000 *	1920	10,000
1890	9,000	1930	18,000
1900	10,000	1940	15,000

* The actual breakdown in the source (p. 29) of *Annuaire Statistique*) adds up to only 8000 people speaking other languages, which is inconsistent with the total town population figure for 1880 given on the same page.

APPENDIX II

BOHEMIA-MORAVIA-SILESIA, 1900–1971: STATISTICAL SOURCES AND DATA USED FOR "AN EXAMPLE OF ECONOMIC MOBILIZATION IN A NATIONALLY MIXED AREA," FIGS. 21–23

Sources Used

K. K. Statistische Zentralkommission, *Oesterreichische Statistik.* Wien, Vol. e, New Series, 1912.

K. K. Statistisches Zentralamt, *Oesterreichische Statistik,* Wien, Vol. 3, New Series, 1916.

Manuel Statistique de la République Tchécoslovaque, Édition de l'office statistique d'état. Prague, 1920, 1928.

Statistisches Jahrbuch der Tschechoslowakischen Republic, Prague, 1935.

Statistický Zpravodaj. Statní úřad statistický Republiky Československé, Praha, 1948, 1949.

Statistical Bulletin of Czechoslovakia. Statistical Office, Prague, 1948.

Rauchberg, H., *Der Nationale Bestizstand in Boehmen.* Leipzig, Duncker & Humblot, 1905.

Witt, K., *Wirtschaftskraefte und Wirtschaftspolitik der Tschechoslowakei.* Leipzig, Felix Meiner, 1938.

Mehnert, Klaus, and H. Schulte, Eds., *Deutschland-Jahrbuch, 1949.* West Verlag, Essen.

Notestein, F. W., and Others, *The Future Population of Europe and the Soviet Union.* Geneva, League of Nations, 1944.

The Choice of Area

Between 1918 and 1939 the Republic of Czechoslovakia consisted of five main territories. Three of these were industrialized provinces: Bohemia, Moravia, and Silesia. These three made up the western part of the Republic and contained more than two-thirds of the total population. These three areas were relatively homogeneous, had long been parts of a common political unit in the Empire of Austria, and were inhabited largely by Czechs and Germans. The other two areas were Slovakia and "Subcarpathian Russia," which were largely agricultural in character, had long been a part of the Kingdom of Hungary, and were largely inhabited by Slovaks, Magyars, and Ruthenians.

Official statistics of languages and occupations tended to use different areas of reference for the data published after each census. Sometimes certain tabulations were given for Bohemia alone, sometimes for Bohemia-Moravia-Silesia, sometimes for the Republic as a whole. Our attempts to derive from all these figures a single set of comparable data for one area, that of Bohemia, Moravia, and Silesia together—henceforth abbreviated as BMS—are set forth in the rest of this appendix.

Other Characteristics of the Data

The data used were those that gave the distribution of Czechs, Germans, and other nationalities among the different occupations in BMS. The data for the time prior to 1919 were found in the Austro-Hungarian government statistics; after 1919 the material was largely taken from the Czechoslovak government statistics. In some cases adequate data were not available. In such instances assumptions were made and the required numbers were calculated on the basis of these assumptions.

One inconsistency in the data has to be accounted for here. The Austro-Hungarian government statistics divide the people into national groups according to the language they speak, whereas the Czech government statistics classify them according to their "ethnic nationality." At first glance this discrepancy would seem to make the data incomparable, but the actual differences involved are not large. There may have been a tendency in the census of 1920 to increase the number of persons reported as Czechs (at the expense of those reported as Germans), but this might well have occurred under any system of counting, at a time when the influence and prestige of Czechs had greatly risen and that of Germans had declined, as a result of World War I, the Czechoslovak Revolution of 1918, and the emergence of a Czechoslovak state. In any case, the figures of the 1930 census appear to give substantially an unbiased picture of the situation, and the figures of 1921 make no significant difference to the trend from 1910 to 1930.

The nomenclature used in this appendix is as follows: Class I includes all people occupied in agriculture and forestry, and their dependents. Class II comprises people in industry and mining with their dependents, and Class III lists all people and dependents not included in the two aforementioned categories, that is, mainly people in commerce, transports, public service, other professions, and those without profession. (Unemployed persons and their dependents, however, are counted in their respective occupational groups.)

BMS stands for the geographical area to which this study is confined, namely, Bohemia, Moravia, and Silesia; R stands for the Republic of Czechoslovakia as a whole.

An effort has been made to keep the error in all the numbers and also in the drawing of the curves of Figs. 22 and 23 below 0.5 per cent.

The Data for Particular Years

1900. There are no statistics of occupational classes combined with nationality available for BMS in 1900. However, the following three sets of data are obtainable: Bohemia 1900, Bohemia 1910, and BMS 1910. By assuming that during the period 1900–1910 the occupational and linguistic picture in BMS changed in the same direction and to the same degree as in Bohemia alone one can establish the proportion

$$\frac{\text{BMS 1900}}{\text{Bohemia 1900}} = \frac{\text{BMS 1910}}{\text{Bohemia 1910}}$$

and calculate the figures for BMS 1900. BMS and Bohemia are alike enough economically to make this assumption plausible.

The data for Bohemia in 1900 were taken from H. Rauchberg, *Der Nationale Besitzstand in Boehmen,* Table 70, pp. 257–260, columns 5, 6, 9, 10, 13, and 14. These figures include domestic servants among the dependents of each group, but columns 5, 9, and 13 also give separate figures for persons in domestic service among Czechs, Germans, and the total, respectively. For each occupation (sections A, B, C, and D), therefore, those in domestic service were subtracted from the total of each national group, and all those in domestic service were then added to their corresponding national groups in Class III (sections C and D). The figures thus obtained follow (in per cent of total population):

Bohemia 1900	Czechs	Germans	Rest	Total
I	25.3	10.2	*	35.5
II	23.1	18.2	*	41.3
III	14.3	8.7	*	23.0
Total	62.7	37.1	0.2	99.8
				0.2
				100.0%

* Negligible (smaller than 0.5 per cent).

The figures for Bohemia in 1910 were taken from K. K. Statistisches Zentralamt: *Oesterreichische Statistik,* Wien, 1916, Band III, Neue

Folge, Heft (Section) 8, p. 338. Precisely the same adjustments were made as with the data for Bohemia 1900 and BMS 1910. The results in per cent of total population are as follows:

Bohemia 1910	Czechs	Germans	Rest	Total
I	23.0	9.1	*	32.1
II	23.0	17.2	0.5	40.7
III	16.7	10.1	*	26.8
Total	62.7	36.4	0.5	99.6

* Negligible (smaller than 0.5 per cent).

The figures for BMS 1910 were obtained from the *Manuel Statistique* of 1920 and are as follows (in per cent of total population):

BMS 1910	Czechs	Germans	Rest	Total
I	24.2	9.0	1.0	34.2
II	22.2	15.5	1.6	39.3
III	15.3	10.1	0.8	26.2
Total	61.7	34.6	3.4	99.7

Performing the operation

BMS 1900

$$= \frac{\text{BMS 1910} \times \text{Bohemia 1900}}{\text{Bohemia 1910}} \text{ (in per cent of total population)}$$

one gets in per cent of total population:

BMS 1900	Czechs	Germans	Rest	Total
I	26.6	10.1	0.6	37.3
II	22.5	16.4	1.4	40.3
III	13.1	8.7	0.5	22.3
Total	62.2	35.2	2.5	99.9

As the sum is within the allowable error of 100 per cent there is no need to deflate these numbers. Multiplying each percentage figure by the total population one gets the final data given on the graphs for BMS 1900, Figs. 22 and 23.

1910. The figures for this set of data were taken from *Manuel Statistique de la République Tchécoslovaque*, 1920, pp. 19–22 (henceforth referred to as *Manuel Statistique*, 1920). The figures corresponding to Class I are on p. 19, Class II on p. 20, and Class III on pp. 20 to 21. The totals of each class include domestic servants, but its amount is given under a separate column. Domestic servants were therefore subtracted from each total and included in Class III.

Nationality was determined by language spoken. The group named *Rest* includes Poles, foreigners, and all people of other language than those detailed in the statistics which is the sum of columns 4, 5, and 6.[1] Czechs are listed in column 2 and Germans in column 3.

1921. The figures were taken from *Manuel Statistique*, 1928, p. 315. Class I is in section *A*, Class II in Section *B*, and Class III in sections *C*, *D*, and *E*. Czechs are given in column 16, Germans in column 17, and others in column 18. In this set of data domestic service is directly included in Class III, so that no adjustment had to be made in this case.

Foreigners are not included in these figures but were taken into account in the following way: the total population as given in the above statistics was computed by adding the totals of columns 16, 17, and 18, and this number was subtracted from the true total population figure for 1921.[2] The difference gives the number of foreigners and is equal to 190,000. To assign these to their respective occupational classes it was assumed that their occupational distribution in BMS was the same as for Czechoslovakia as a whole for 1921. The distribution for Czechoslovakia (R) is readily found from the numbers in *Manuel Statistique*, 1928, on p. 314, column 9. Within each occupational class, the foreigners were added to the group called *Rest,* i.e., those other than Czechs or Germans. (Since those foreigners who were citizens of Austria or Germany considered themselves usually as members of the *ethnic* German nationality, this procedure makes the "German" group appear very slightly smaller than it would have appeared to Pan-German spokesmen.)

1930. There are no statistics of occupational classes combined with nationality available for BMS 1930. However, as was the case in BMS 1900, three sets of data are obtainable and the unknown set can be calculated from them. The available sets are BMS 1921, the whole republic 1921, and the whole republic 1930. The figures for BMS 1921 were obtained from *Manuel Statistique* of 1928 and are given below in per cent of total population:

[1] *Manuel Statistique*, 1920, pp. 19–22.

[2] From *Statistisches Jahrbuch der Tschechoslowakischen Republik*, Prague, 1935, p. 5.

BMS 1921	*Czechs*	*Germans*	*Rest*	*Total*
I	23.1	8.0	0.5	31.6
II	25.5	13.1	1.4	40.0
III	18.6	8.6	1.2	28.4
Total	67.2	29.7	3.1	100.0

The data for the entire republic *R* 1921, were obtained from the same source as BMS 1921, namely, *Manuel Statistique*, 1928, p. 314. Foreigners are included among the *Rest*. The figures (in per cent of total population) are as follows:

R 1921	*Czecho-slovaks*	*Germans*	*Rest*	*Total*
I	26.4	6.2	6.9	39.5
II	21.5	10.0	2.5	34.0
III	16.6	6.7	3.3	26.6
Total	64.5	22.9	12.7	100.1

The corresponding data for *R* 1930 were calculated from data given in K. Witt, *Wirtschaftskraefte und Wirtschaftspolitik der Tschechoslowakei*, Leipzig, 1938. Multiplying the percentage on Witt's p. 18 by the corresponding population on Witt's p. 15 for each national group and making the adjustments listed below gives the following figures in per cent of total population:

R 1930	*Czecho-slovaks*	*Germans*	*Rest*	*Total*
I	22.7	5.1	6.6	34.4
II	22.8	10.0	2.4	35.2
III	20.4	7.0	3.0	30.4
Total	65.9	22.1	12.0	100.0

Czechoslovaks include Czechs and Slovaks. *Rest* includes Hungarians, Ruthenians, Poles, Jews, all others, and foreigners.

The occupational distribution of 250,000 foreigners and 80,000 Poles was not given in the reference.[3] Hence in each case it was assumed to be the same as in 1921. The total population on which the above percentages are based is 14,660,000, whereas the true population in the Republic in 1930 was 14,730,000; 70,000 people therefore remain unaccounted for above; 50,000 of these are Rumanians whose occupational distribution is not given, and the remaining 20,000 are appar-

[3] K. Witt, reference in text.

ently Russians and Jews, for the figures giving the occupational distribution of these two nationalities do not quite add to 100 per cent in the original source,[4] thus causing a "deficit" of 20,000. Both errors are negligible for the purpose of the present study.

In order to obtain a set of figures for BMS, one now applies the following operation to the three sets of data given above:

$$\text{BMS } 1930 = \frac{\text{R } 1930 \times \text{BMS } 1921}{\text{R } 1921} \text{ (in per cent of total population)}$$

which yields the following results:

BMS 1930	Czechs	Germans	Rest	Total
I	19.8	6.6	0.5	26.9
II	27.0	13.1	1.4	41.5
III	22.9	9.0	1.1	33.0
Total	69.7	28.7	3.0	101.4

The sum of these percentages yields 101.4. Deflating these numbers by the ratio 101.4/100.0, one gets the following numbers:

BMS 1930	Czechs	Germans	Rest	Total
I	19.5	6.5	0.5	26.5
II	26.7	12.9	1.4	41.0
III	22.6	8.9	1.1	32.6
Total	68.8	28.3	3.0	100.1

Multiplying these percentages by the total population (10,670,000) one gets the final data for BMS 1930 given on the graphs, Figs. 21–23.

The assumption implied in the above calculations is the same as the one with whose aid the data for BMS 1900 were obtained: BMS 1921: R 1921 = BMS 1930:R 1930; that is, there was the same trend towards industrial development in Czechoslovakia as a whole as there was in the more industrialized provinces of BMS, and that therefore the differences in the distribution of occupational groups in the two areas of R and BMS, respectively, were roughly the same in 1930 as they had been in 1921. Although this assumption would introduce distortions for particular industries, it was assumed to be tolerably accurate for the overall development in the two areas. Similarly, it was assumed that the data for the Czechoslovaks from the entire republic would be comparable with those for the Czechs from BMS where there was no significant Slovak population before 1947.

[4] *Ibid.*, p. 18.

1937. There are no suitable statistics for 1937. It is known, however, that due to the effects of the world-wide economic depression there was a halt in the industrialization process in Czechoslovakia during the period 1930–1937, with a slight reflux of people to the land. It is therefore acceptable to assume that the fraction of each national group in each occupation and of each occupation in the total picture remained constant. (The higher incidence of unemployment among Germans did not change significantly the occupational affiliation of the unemployed: jobless glass blowers would still have to be counted among the industrial population in Class II.) The percentage figures obtained for 1930 [5] were therefore used to compute a set of data for 1937 by multiplying each percentage figure by the total population of BMS in 1937 (10,895,000).[6]

1947. The data are from the *Statistical Bulletin of Czechoslovakia,* 1948, Vol. 3, No. 6, p. 1. This source gives only the distribution of the population into the three occupational classes without specification of nationality. It is an acceptable assumption, however, to consider all people as Czechs, since by 1947 the Germans had been expelled almost in their entirety from Czech territory.[7]

The data presented in the aforementioned source include the population of Slovakia, which has to be subtracted from the figures given. As the occupational distribution of the Slovaks for 1947 is not available the distribution for 1930 had to be used. The error thus introduced should be slight, as the rate of social mobilization in Slovakia was relatively small from 1930 to 1947. Industrialization in Slovakia in 1930 was relatively slight. During World War II some of the existing industry was probably destroyed. After 1945 a plan for the industrialization of Slovakia was drawn up, but by 1947 its effects could not have gone significantly beyond repairing the war damage. Considering a balance of all these factors the 1930 distribution was adopted, but 100,000 people were shifted from Class I to Class III.

The occupational distribution for 1930 was readily obtained from the 1930 statistics.[8] The total population of Slovakia in 1947 was found in the article by V. Sekera, *Naše populační bilance* [9] (3,400,000 people). The results are as follows:

[5] See the preceding section of this appendix.

[6] *Statistický Zpravodaj*, 1948, No. 1, p. 5.

[7] See the discussion on p. 217, below.

[8] *Statistisches Jahrbuch der Tschechoslowakischen Republik*, Prague, 1935, p. 5.

[9] *Statistický Zpravodaj*, 1948, No. 1, p. 5.

Distribution of Slovaks, 1930

Class I	56.8%
Class II	19.0%
Class III	24.2%
	100.0%

Multiplying each by 3,400,000 and shifting 100,000 from Class I to Class III, we obtain the following figures:

Class I	1,830,000
Class II	645,000
Class III	925,000
Total	3,400,000

Subtracting these figures from the data for the whole republic in 1947 (without Ruthenia) yields the final numbers for BMS:

Class I	1,565,000
Class II	3,740,000
Class III	3,450,000

It was assumed that 200,000 Germans were left in Czech territory in 1947. Unverified estimates state that there were 100,000 Germans scattered among the rural population at that time. The remaining 100,000 were assigned to Class II.

The assumption of only 200,000 Germans remaining in 1947 may be exaggerated, since transports with German expellees and voluntary emigrees were leaving the country in 1948 and, according to an unverified report, as late as 1949. There is little doubt, however, that a drastic reduction in the number of Germans was accomplished by 1947 even if their removal had not been completed by the end of that year.

It will be noticed that the sum of the numbers of persons in Classes I, II, and III yields a total population of 8,755,000, which is 15,000 less than the official figure.[10] This error, however, is well within the allowable range of 0.5 per cent adopted for our diagram.

Results

BMS 1947	Czechs	Germans
Class I	1,465,000	100,000
Class II	3,640,000	100,000
Class III	3,450,000	—

[10] *Statistický Zpravodaj*, 1948, No. 1, p. 5. (The "official" population for BMS in 1947 was obtained by subtracting the population of Slovakia from the population of the whole republic, both of which are given there.)

1950. The same source gives a population estimate for October 1949 and places the population of BMS at 9,208,000 persons at that time.[11]

1971. V. Sekera in his article [12] gives the rate of population growth for Czechoslovakia during the year 1947 as 1.5 per cent and contends that if the population of the republic would continue to grow at half this rate in the future, Czechoslovakia would attain its past population peak of 14,600,000 (of the end of 1938) [13] in 24 years.[14]

To calculate the expected population for BMS in 1971 it is necessary to subtract the expected population of Slovakia in 1971 from 14,600,000. In order to compute the population of Slovakia in 1971 the same rate of growth as has been used for Czechoslovakia as a whole is assumed, namely, 0.75 per cent (one-half of 1.5 per cent).

$$\frac{(dx/x)}{dt} = 0.0075 \qquad \int_{x_1}^{72} \frac{dx}{x} = 0.0075 \int_{t_1}^{t_2} dt$$

$$\text{limit} \begin{cases} x_2 = \text{population Slovakia 1971} & t_2 = 1971 \\ x_1 = 3,402,000 \text{ in } 1947 & t_1 = 1947 \end{cases}$$

$$\ln \frac{x_2}{x_1} \bigg]_{3.4^{02} \times 10^6}^{x_2} = 0.0075 \left[(t_2 - t_1) \right]_{1947}^{1971}$$

$$2.3 \log x_2 - 2.3 \log 3.4 \times 10^6 = 0.0075(24)$$

$$\log x_2 = \frac{0.0075(24) + 2.3 \log 3.402 \times 10^6}{2.3}$$

$$\log x_2 = \frac{0.18 + 6.531(2.3)}{2.3} = \frac{15.0223 + 0.18}{2.3} = \frac{15.2033}{2.3} = 6.609$$

antilog $6.609 = 4,070,000$ Slovaks in 1971

$$\begin{array}{r} 14,600,000 \\ - \quad 4,070,000 \\ \hline 10,530,000 \end{array}$$ people in BMS in 1971 [15]

[11] *Statistický Zpravodaj, loc. cit.*

[12] *Naše populační bilance, Statistický Zpravodaj,* 1948, No. 1, p. 5.

[13] *Ibid.*

[14] *Ibid.,* p. 6.

[15] To check this calculation, we applied to the Slovak population of 1937 the compound interest formula $P_0(1 + r)^n = P$, where $P_0 = 3,402,000$, $r = 0.0075$, $n = 24$, and obtained $P_{1971} = 4,063,000$, which is in fairly close accord with the values found in the text.

It is interesting to note that the estimate of 14,600,000 people for the republic in 1971 is only 300,000 less than the 14,900,000 which Frank W. Notestein and his associates estimated would be the population of the country in 1970 on the assumption that the Germans would remain in the country.[16] Professor Notestein expected no expulsions or transfer of population but counted on a declining birth rate. He expected that the population of Czechoslovakia would go up to 15,700,000 and decrease from then on.

The paragraph relevant to the above calculation from the article of V. Sekera is given in translation below:

> At the end of 1946 when the deportation of the Germans ended, the population of the Czech Republic reached its lowest point with approximately 12,076,000 persons. From this new base the population of the republic is now increasing once more. The first step on the new road was extraordinarily favorable, for both the natural and the migration balances were highly active. From January 1 to May 22 (1947) the increase was almost 100,000 persons, and for the rest of the year a further increase of 80,000 may be assumed. If in the future the population growth would maintain itself even at half this rate, and would therefore be 0.75 per cent, the republic would attain its past population of 14,600,000 persons in 24 years. This would be much faster than when this maximum was attained at the time when the republic had just as many inhabitants as today, namely, 1901 to 1938. It then took a full 37 years before the population increased by these 2,500,000.[17]

Explanations Concerning the Curves on the Graphs, Figs. 22 and 23

1. The curve dividing the German from the Czech peasants was kept flat during the years 1938–1946 because the German agricultural population was assumed to have remained the same in that period. It was assumed that German agricultural policy was the same in the Reich as in the Sudetenland. German figures show that the agricultural population in the "Bizone" of Western Germany increased from 4,405,000 in 1939 to 4,875,000 in 1946, dropping to 4,750,000 in 1947, and thus remaining well above the 1939 level.[18] Although the increase in the agricultural labor force may be due in part to the increased employment of women, as well as the very young and the very old, it seems fair to assume that the proportion of the population engaged in agriculture remained relatively constant.

[16] F. W. Notestein and Others, *The Future Population of Europe and the Soviet Union*, p. 260.

[17] *Statistický Zpravodaj*, 1948, No. 1, p. 6.

[18] Klaus Mehnert and H. Schulte (Eds.), *Deutschland-Jahrbuch*, 1949, p. 146.

In extrapolating the BMS curve to 1970 the number of German peasants was assumed to stay at the 1947 value = 100,000. For a discussion of this assumption, see point 3, below.

2. The mobilization curve was extrapolated to 1970, using the slope of the same curve during the years 1921–1930. Since the avowed policy of the present regime is to accelerate industrialization and hence the urbanization of the country, it was assumed that this regime could do as well as the private enterprise economy during the 1920's, which were by no means wholly taken up by booms, and that they could do better than the country did during the depression (1930's). (The substitution of either American or Russian urbanization rates would, of course, have made the slopes much steeper. [19] The slope of the urbanization curve over the period 1930–1947 was almost exactly the same as in 1921–1930 despite the frequent changes of regime.

Lest the projected industrialization figures for BMS should appear exaggerated it would be well to recall that under the projected curve these three countries would reach about 1965 the degree of industrialization and urbanization that Scotland had in the 1930's, and that by 1970 they would be less urbanized than Great Britain is today.

3. From Figs. 22 and 23 it is apparent that we have assumed that the Germans in Class II would stay at their 1947 number until 1970. Present Czech policy assumes that these will assimilate at a greater rate to the Czech majority than their rate of birth, thus eventually leading to a purely Czech national state. On the other hand, if Germany should return to a position of prominence in either the Eastern or Western camp, some of the motives to assimilate, which the Germans at present may have, would vanish. To balance these factors, their number has been kept constant on the graph.

4. In Fig. 23, the extrapolation to 1970 of the curve dividing Class II from Class III has been drawn parallel to the extrapolation of the population curve. This implies the assumption that the number of people engaged in tertiary occupations, such as clerking and services, will remain the same in the future. Since it is the declared intention of the Czechoslovak Government to avoid an increase in services and trade, and concentrate future growth in the industrial sector, it has been assumed that the government will have enough political power

[19] Cf., e.g., P. M. Hauser and H. T. Eldridge, "Projection of Urban Growth and Migration to Cities in the United States," *The Milbank Memorial Fund Quarterly*, Vol. 25, No. 3, July 1947, pp. 293–307, especially pp. 296 and 300; and F. Lorimer, *The Population of the Soviet Union*, League of Nations, Geneva, 1946, p. 147.

to carry out its aim. A change in this assumption might easily involve a considerable change in this projection.

5. The population curve in Figs. 22 and 23 was kept flat until 1946, where it was made to fall abruptly to the 1947 figure. The expulsion of the Sudeten Germans occurred largely during 1946–1947. According to one unverified report, at the end of 1946 there were still about 3,000,000 Germans in Czechoslovakia.

FIGURES USED FOR BOHEMIA, MORAVIA, AND SILESIA

(In Thousands)

	Group I, Underlying Population Agriculture and Forestry			Group II, Mobilized Population Industry and Mining			Group III, Mobilized Population All Other Occupations			Total Population
	Czecho-slovaks	*Ger-mans*	*Rest*	*Czecho-slovaks*	*Ger-mans*	*Rest*	*Czecho-slovaks*	*Ger-mans*	*Rest*	
1900	2,500	945	55	2,110	1,540	130	1,230	815	45	9,370
1910	2,460	917	100	2,280	1,567	160	1,555	1,030	80	10,148
1921	2,315	800	45	2,550	1,312	140	1,860	860	120	10,006
1930	2,085	695	40	2,845	1,380	145	2,410	950	120	10,670
1937	2,130	710	40	2,910	1,410	150	2,460	970	120	10,900
1947	1,465	100	—	3,640	100	—	3,450	—	—	8,770
1950										9,008
1971										10,530

Data Used for Figs. 21 A–C

BOHEMIA, MORAVIA, AND SILESIA 1910

	Group I 34.2%	Group II 39.4%	Group III 26.3%
Czechs	70.8	57.0	58.3
Germans	26.4	39.2	38.6
Rest	2.6	3.8	3.1

Group I, Agriculture.
Group II, Industry.
Group III, Commerce, transportation, public and military service, liberal professions, and people without profession, domestic help, servants.

The *nationality* was determined according to the *language spoken*. Figures are made up of all people *belonging to the professional group* under consideration.

Foreigners are included under *Rest* of the population. They form less than 1 per cent of the total population and therefore their influence on percentage relations is negligible.

Source: Manuel Statistique, Vol. 1, 1920, pp. 19–22.

BOHEMIA, MORAVIA, AND SILESIA 1921

| | Group I | Group II | Group III |
	31.6%	40.0%	28.4%
Czechoslovaks	73.2	63.8	65.5
Germans	25.3	32.8	30.3
Rest	1.5	3.4	4.2

Total Population, 10,006,000

Group I, Agriculture, Forestry, etc.

Group II, Industry.

Group III, Commerce, banks, transportation, public and military service, domestic service, other professions, professions not specified.

Figures are made up of all people *belonging to the professional group* under consideration.

The *nationality* was determined by *"Nationalité Ethnique."* No adjustment was made to make it comparable to BMS 1910.

To make these data comparable *foreigners* were *included* under *Rest* of the population by means of an adjustment which assumed that the professional distribution of the foreigners in BMS 1921 is the same as in the whole republic for the same year. This is a justified assumption in the range of allowable error.

Source: Manuel Statistique, Vol. 3, 1928, pp. 314–315.

BOHEMIA, MORAVIA, AND SILESIA 1930

| | Group I | Group II | Group III |
	26.5%	41.0%	32.5%
Czechs	73.6	65.0	69.3
Germans	24.5	31.4	27.3
Rest	1.9	3.6	3.4

Total Population, 10,674,386

Definitions of Groups I, II, and III are the same as in BMS 1921.

Figures include all persons *belonging to professional group* under consideration. *Foreigners* are included.

Source: Statistisches Jahrbuch der Cechoslovakischen Republik, Prag, Statistisches Staatsamt, 1935, p. 12–13.

INDIA AND PAKISTAN, 1850–2000: STATISTICAL DATA AND METHODS USED IN CONSTRUCTING THE THREE SCHEMATIC DIAGRAMS OF POPULATION GROWTH, URBANIZATION, LITERARY AND LINGUISTIC CHANGES, FIGS. 16–18

A Note on the Two Diagrams, Figs. 17 and 18

The first projection of urbanization, literacy and languages in India, Fig. 17, is in terms of *percentages* of the total population at various dates between 1920 and 2000. It has been included in order to show graphically certain moderate assumptions about the growth of towns and of literacy during that period.

The second projection, Fig. 18, is in terms of *absolute numbers*. It shows what happens when moderate assumptions of urbanization and literacy are combined with a moderate assumption of population growth (in this case, the medium projection of the three sets offered by Professor Kingsley Davis and shown in Fig. 16).

In one sense Fig. 18 with its absolute numbers of millions of people is closer to the true political and social situation which would result, if events should conform to its assumptions. Yet some aspects of the facts would remain hidden in it, and are brought to prominence by the percentage chart in Fig. 17. For example, there would be more millions of rural illiterates in A.D. 2000 than in 1941, according to the projection, but they would form a much smaller part of the total population.

Both charts, in short, are complementary versions of the same picture. They are designed, as it were, to shed light on each other, each to bring out the other's implications. Since they are constructed from the same data and by means of the same assumptions, the following pages will be devoted to explaining only one of them: the somewhat more extensive diagram, Fig. 18, drawn in terms of absolute numbers. From it, every relevant curve or point on the percentage diagram can be derived by simple arithmetical operations.

The Diagram in Absolute Numbers, Fig. 18

In the absence of complete data, this schematic diagram was constructed by calculating a series of 19 steps, each based on some available data and designated by a letter from A to S. Each step consisted in tracing the changes in the numbers of some population group, and each such group was then used to calculate the next, or to check for various dates the numbers for other groups, which had been obtained by other methods.

The resulting diagram is not in any sense a prediction of the probable future of India and Pakistan, but rather an illustration of the magnitude of the social processes involved in the development of that area, and an illustration, likewise, of the possibility of making more meaningful forecasts from more complete data.

The groups as calculated are:

A. Total population.
B. Rural population.
C. Urban population, as the intervals between A and B.
D. Total population under 10 years of age. This was divided between town and country so as to get:
    E. Rural population under 10. This was plotted upward from the bottom line.
    F. Urban population under 10. These numbers were plotted upward from the curve of total rural population.
G. Total literate population; this was divided between town and country so as to get:
    H. Literate urban population; these numbers were plotted downward from A;
    I. Literate rural population, plotted downward from B.
J. Persons literate in English; their number again was divided between towns and country, so as to get:
    K. English literates in town; the numbers for this group were plotted downward from the total population curve A;
    L. English literates in among the rural population; these numbers were plotted downward from the total rural population curve B.
M. Total of persons literate in Hindi; these were divided so as to get:
    N. Hindi literates in towns; these numbers were plotted downward from the lower edge of the urban English literates;
    O. Hindi literates in the country; these numbers were plotted downward from the lower edge of the rural English literates;
    P. Urban literates in other vernaculars; these were expressed graphically as the area left over between the previously plotted urban literates in Hindi and the previously plotted total literate urban population;
    Q. Rural literates in other vernaculars; these were expressed graphically as the area between the previously plotted rural Hindi literates and the previously plotted total rural literate population;
    R. Urban illiterates, expressed graphically as the area between the total urban literates and the urban population under 10;

S. Rural illiterates, expressed graphically as the area between the total rural literates and the rural population under 10.

The foregoing has been an outline of the intellectual steps taken in arriving at the diagram shown in Fig. 18.

The following is a more detailed analysis of each plotted value. Unless otherwise indicated all the statistics have been taken from Kingsley Davis, *The Population of India and Pakistan* (Princeton, Princeton University Press, 1951), henceforth cited as *Davis*.

i. TOTAL POPULATION (ADJUSTED TO TERRITORY OF INDIA, 1931–1941)

Year	Millions	Year	Millions
1855	175	1911	303
(1867)	(194)	1921	306
1871	255	1931	338
		1941	389
1881	257 *	1970	525 †
1891	282	2000	635 †
1901	285		

The plotted points are from *Davis*, p. 25, Table 6, with the curve adjusted in accordance with Davis' comments, p. 26, column X, Parts 1–3. For the reasons given there the low estimate for 1867 has not been used.

* Davis' estimates of population, based on adjustments of census returns, *Davis*, p. 27, Table 7.

† Projected numbers from *Davis*, p. 89 and p. 90, Fig. 27, using middle projection (logistic curve).

Some of Davis' comments are instructive:

[From] 1871 to 1941 the average rate of increase of India's population was approximately 0.60 per cent per year. This was slightly less than the estimated rate for the whole world (0.69) from 1850 to 1940. India's modern growth, therefore, is . . . close to average. . . . [It] has not been rapid when compared with that of countries farther along in the industrial revolution. The popular notion that it has been farther than in most modern countries . . . is obviously unwarranted . . . During the last three centuries the population of the whole world has been growing at a phenomenally fast rate, the fastest ever known. India's increase is simply part of this world movement. (p. 27.)

This is also true, in Davis' view, of the growth since 1921:

[The] rate of growth since 1921 (1.2 per cent per year) has not been phenomenal for modern times. The United States population increased 16 per cent, during the decade 1920–1930, a rate never yet equalled in India. But because of the massiveness of India's existing population, even a moderate percentage increase means a huge absolute increment. The modest 1.2 per cent annual increase . . . from 1921–1941 added no less than 83 million inhabitants to India's . . . masses, more people than all of Germany contains and nearly two-thirds of the population of the United States . . . What is important about India's recently accelerated growth is not simply the rate, but the huge absolute increments to which it gives rise and the promise of even greater increments in the future. (p. 28.)

ii. RURAL POPULATION. The rural population was calculated for 1881–1941 by subtracting from the total population for each census year the percentages of urban population listed by *Davis,* p. 127:

Year	Per Cent	Year	Per Cent
1881	9.3	1911	9.4
1891	9.4	1921	10.2
1901	10.0	1931	11.1
		1941	12.8

The rural population for 1970 and 2000 was obtained by extrapolating this percentage curve, at a constant rate of growth, using Davis' estimate of 15 per cent urban population for the India-Pakistan area in 1951 (p. 128, par. 4). Under these assumptions, India's urban population would reach about 25 per cent of the total by 2000. This is a relatively moderate proportion, if it is recalled, e.g., that Egypt's urban population is about 20 per cent of the total population of that country at the present time.

iii. URBAN POPULATION. This was calculated by subtracting the rural population (ii) from the total population (i), and was checked against the direct figures from the percentages in *Davis,* p. 127.

iv. TOWN POPULATION ABOVE AGE 10. The town population above 10 was calculated by applying the age structure of 1941 (*Davis,* p. 85, Fig. 23) to the urban population.

v. RURAL POPULATIONS ABOVE AGE 10. The rural population above 10 was calculated in the same manner as the urban population above 10.

vi. TOTAL LITERATE POPULATION. The total literate population for all the years 1891–1941 was calculated by applying for each corresponding year the percentage of literacy of age 10-plus as given by *Davis,* p. 151, Table 70, to the previously calculated numbers of total population above 10. The 1941 figure is based on a sample and correction factor (*Ibid.*):

Year	Per Cent Literate	Year	Per Cent Literate
1891	6.1	1921	8.3
1901	6.2	1931	9.2
1911	7.0	1941	15.1

The total literate population for the years 1970 and 2000 was calculated by first extrapolating the growth of Davis' percentage figures of literacy for 1891–1941; and second, by applying these extrapolated percentage values to the estimated total population above 10 in the years 1970 and 2000.

vii. URBAN AND RURAL LITERATE POPULATION. The total number of literates for any one year was divided between town and country in the ratio of 4:1. This ratio was chosen on the basis of the comparisons of statistics of urban and rural literacy "compiled from seventeen volumes of the *Census of India,* 1931." (*Davis,* p. 143, Table 61 and note 6.)

Sample calculation for 1931 (in millions) (u = urban population above 10; r = rural population above 10; x = number of literates in town; y = number of literates in country):

(A) $x + y = 22.5$, Total number of literates

$$\frac{x/u}{y/r} = \frac{4}{1}$$

(B) $x = \frac{4u}{r} y$

Solving the simultaneous equations *A* and *B* the following values for x and y are found:

$$x = 10.8$$
$$y = \underline{11.7}$$
$$22.5$$

The curve of the urban literate population crosses the curve of the urban population under 10 in the year 1985. This is equivalent to saying that, in that year, under the assumptions of this model, all of the urban populace above 10 would be literate, since the institutions and processes making for literacy were assumed to continue. The

extra-urban literates after 1985 were added to the rural literates—
which is equivalent to assuming that the teaching resources no longer
needed for teaching illiterates in cities would be diverted to the
country.

viii. TOTAL ENGLISH LITERATES. The total number of English literates for the years 1901–1941 was calculated from the total number
of literates and the percentage of English literates among the total
number of literates in any language.

Year	Per Cent
1901	8.5
1911	10.1
1921	12.9
1931	14.9
1941	(18.9)

(*Davis*, p. 159, column I. The 1941 figure is "based on a sample of only six
political divisions" and "is probably too high to represent all of India." *Ibid.*,
note 39.)

For the years 1970 and 2000, in order to make the most favorable
assumptions for the further growth of English literacy after independence, an exponential rate of growth was assumed equal to that
of the 1901–1931 portion of the curve. This assumption yields, between 1941 and 2000, approximately a tenfold increase in the number
of persons literate in English.

ix. URBAN ENGLISH LITERATES. Six out of every seven of the English
literates were placed in the towns. The 6:1 ratio was arrived at by
combining the 4:1 advantage of general literacy in the towns over
that in the country (see references in item vii, above) with the assumption, suggested by data for a number of cities and provinces, that the
share of English literates among total literates may be at least twice
as high in the towns as it is in the country (*Davis*, p. 159, column I,
par. 5). These figures for the urban English literates were then plotted
downward from the curve of the total population, so as to appear as
the top layer of the population in the towns.

x. RURAL ENGLISH LITERATES. The rural English literates were calculated by taking one-seventh of the total English literates, in a manner similar to calculating the urban English literates. The numbers of
the rural English literates were then plotted downward from the curve
of the rural population.

xi. TOTAL HINDI LITERATES. The total number of Hindi literates
was estimated by first calculating the number of Hindi *speakers* at

different dates. This was done by using the number of speakers of Western Hindi in 1931, i.e., 71.4 millions (*Davis*, p. 157), and assuming that the number of Hindi *speakers* grew, and will continue to grow, at a rate equal to that of the population as a whole.

It was then assumed that in 1931, among the population aged 10 and over, the percentage of persons *literate* in Western Hindi was the şame as that of persons literate in any language, but that the number of Hindi literates would have a higher rate of growth, both past and future, equal to that of the English literates, i.e., 0.22 per cent per year.

The number of Hindi literates for 1931 was calculated from the proportion:

$$\frac{\text{Total Hindi population}}{\text{Total population}} = \frac{\text{Hindi literates}}{\text{Total literates}}$$

Then the number of Hindi literates was calculated for each year by letting the theoretical number of Hindi literates in 1931 grow at the same rate as the smaller actual number of English literates in that year.

This could be done graphically by plotting the actual numbers of English literates from 1901 to 1931, on semi-logarithmic paper. These points turn out to lie very nearly on a straight line. On a semi-logarithmic graph a straight line indicates a constant rate of growth; the slope of such a line indicates the rate of growth; and any line parallel to the first represents an equal rate of growth. To let the theoretical number of Hindi literates in 1931 grow at the same rate as the English literates, their number was plotted on the same semi-logarithmic graph, and a second line was drawn through this point parallel to the first line representing the growth of the numbers of persons literate in English. The points of intersection of this second line with the date lines for 1970 and 2000 then gave the projected numbers of Hindi literates for those years.

The growth of the number of Hindi literates, 1941 to 2000, thus was assumed to be as rapid, but not more rapid, than that of the numbers of English literates for the same period, and it was assumed that the number of Hindi *speakers* would only increase through the natural increase of populations and not at all through the assimilation of speakers of other languages. If this latter assumption were to be dropped, and an additional growth of the number of Hindi *speakers* expected through assimilation, then the projected growth rate of Hindi *literates* in the graph might well be too low.

xii. RURAL AND URBAN HINDI LITERATES. Speakers of Hindi were assumed to correspond to the general population in the distribution of literacy and of urbanization. The total number of Hindi literates was, therefore, divided between town and country, in the general ratio of urban literates to rural literates. The number of town or country Hindi literates was then plotted downward from the curves for English literates in town and country, respectively.

Some Inferences from this Schematic Model

I. Under the assumptions of this model—which were chosen to be moderate as to growth and urbanization, and extremely favorable to the spread of English—it appears that any large-scale participation of the population in economic and political life would have to be carried on in languages other than English. Even in the year 2000, and under highly favorable assumptions, persons literate in English would comprise only one-third of the urban population older than 10 years, one-twenty-third of all rural literates, and only one-fifteenth of the total population.

II. Under the assumptions of the same model, literacy in Hindi, despite a rate of growth faster than the rate of growth of literacy in general, would not succeed much better in unifying the nation. Persons literate in Hindi would comprise by A.D. 2000 only about one-third of the urban population older than 10 years, and thus be not more numerous there than persons literate in English. In the country, they would comprise only about one-quarter of all rural literates. Although they would outnumber the rural English literates by about 5:1, they would in turn be outnumbered more than 3:1 by the persons literate in any other of India's vernacular languages.

III. These vernacular languages other than Hindi, of which at least eleven are of major importance, would seem to be the real victors in the contest under the assumptions of our model. Persons literate in these vernaculars would form one-third of the urban population above ten, more than two-thirds of all rural literates, and more than one-half of all the literates in the country. If this should be so for the area as a whole, the geographical distribution of these languages would probably leave Hindi solidly dominant in number of regions, but by the same token would leave one or another of the other vernacular languages firmly entrenched in others.

APPENDIX IV

SCOTLAND, 1707–1970: DATA AND CALCULATIONS USED FOR FIG. 19, THE DIAGRAM OF POPULATIONS IN AGRICULTURAL AND NON-AGRICULTURAL OCCUPATIONS, AND OF THE ENGLISH-SPEAKING AND THE GAELIC-SPEAKING POPULATIONS

Sources Used

Aucamp, A. J., *Bilingual Education and Nationalism*. Pretoria, J. L. Van Schaik, 1926.

Grant, I. F., *The Economic History of Scotland*. London, Longmans, Green, 1934.

MacDonald, D. F., *Scotland's Shifting Population 1770–1850*. Glasgow, Jackson, 1937.

Statistical Abstract for the United Kingdom, Cmd. 5903, No. 82. London, His Majesty's Stationery Office, 1939.

Economic Survey for 1949, Cmd. London, His Majesty's Stationery Office, 1949.

United Nations' Demographic Yearbook, 1948. Lake Success, N. Y., 1949.

Notestein, F. W., *et al.*, *The Future Populations of Europe and the Soviet Union*. Geneva, League of Nations, 1944.

Pei, M. A., *The Story of Language*. Philadelphia, Lippincott, 1949.

Total Population

1707–1801. The figures for this period were either found or calculated from data in MacDonald.[1] The total population figures for 1707 and 1801 are given, and a similar figure for 1755 can be calculated because the annual percentage increase for the period is given as 0.3 per cent for 1707–1755.

The approximate population in 1755 was found by applying to the figures the compound interest formula $P = P_0(1 + r)^n$, where P = population to be found (after n years); P_0 = initial population; r = rate of increase.

1707–1755. Substituting actual figures, we obtain

$$P_0 = 1,048,000$$

$$r = 0.003$$

$$n = 48$$

$$\log P = \log P_0 + n \log (1 + r)$$

$$\log P_{1755} = 6.02 + 48(0.0013009) = 6.02 + 0.0624 = 6.0824$$

$$P = 1,210,000 \text{ (within slide-rule accuracy)}$$

[1] D. F. MacDonald, *Scotland's Shifting Population*, p. 5.

According to this calculation, Scotland's population in 1755 is assumed to have been 1,210,000 inhabitants.

The same source [2] gives rates of growth for the periods 1755–1795 and 1795–1801. These rates, however, are inconsistent with the population figure for 1801, as calculations will show. The calculation of a 1795 population figure has therefore not been included in the present graph.

In other calculations aiming at the same objective a method of integral calculus was used. It assumed that the rate of population growth at any time was the same as the annual average which is usually measured. It is interesting to see how this method and the "compound interest formula" method given above arrive at the same result for practical purposes.

The integrated formula is $[\log p/p_0 = rn]$, where the same nomenclature as above holds. This can be written as $p = P_0\, e^{rn}$, in which e stands for the base of the natural logarithm. This then leads to the expression:

$$P = P_0 \left(1 + rn + \frac{r^2 n^2}{2!} + \frac{r^3 n^3}{3!} \cdots \right)$$

The compound interest formula $P = P_0(1 + r)^n$ gives by binomial expansion:

$$P = P_0 \left[1 + rn + \frac{r^2 n(n-1)}{2!} + \frac{r^3 n(n-1)(n-2)}{3!} \cdots \right]$$

It can be seen that for values of n large with respect to 1 the two formulas give almost identical results.

1821–1937. Figures for the total population for this period were taken from the *Statistical Abstract for the United Kingdom,* Cmd. 5903, p. 5.

1947. This total population figure was found in the *United Nations' Demographic Yearbook,* 1948, p. 105.

1940–1970. F. W. Notestein *et al.,* in *Future Populations of Europe and the Soviet Union,* p. 252, gives total population estimates for this period.

Agricultural Population

1821, 1881. ". . . in 1821 . . . 700,000 were . . . engaged in agriculture, and it employed twice as many persons as all other industries

[2] *Ibid.*

put together." [3]   "[In] 1881 (with a somewhat different classification), the numbers employed in agriculture were 229,000 . . . about one-quarter of those engaged in Scotland in productive industries." [4]

Assuming that the ratio of people occupied in agriculture to total occupied population is the same as that of people "pertaining" to agriculture (dependents included) to the total population, one can compute the agricultural population for the two specified dates with the aid of the above quotation.

1921, 1931. The *Statistical Abstract* [5] gives figures that permit the calculation of the agricultural populations for 1921 and 1931 by the same method as that used for 1821 and 1881. We added males and females in agriculture and fishing, then the total men and women occupied. Dividing the first sum by the second, we obtained the proportion of the persons occupied in agriculture, forestry, and fishing to the total occupied population. Multiplying the total population by this proportion then yielded a figure representing at least an approximate figure for the population in agriculture and related occupations.

1947. This figure was calculated by assuming that the shift of the occupied population from agriculture into non-agricultural pursuits occurred at the same rate in England as in Scotland during the period 1931–1948. Then, $a/b = c/d$, where

a = per cent occupied population in agriculture and fishing in England in 1931;

b = per cent occupied population in agriculture and fishing in Scotland in 1931;

c = per cent occupied population in agriculture and fishing in England in 1948;

d = per cent occupied population in agriculture and fishing in Scotland in 1948.

$$a = 6.0\,[6] \qquad b = 9.5\,[7] \qquad c = 5.3\,[8] \qquad \text{Hence } d = \frac{9.5 \times 5.3}{6.0} = 8.4$$

Total population, Scotland, 1947 = 5,139,000

Agricultural population, Scotland, 1947 = 5,139,000 × 8.4 = 432,000

[3] I. F. Grant, *The Economic History of Scotland,* p. 215.

[4] *Ibid.*

[5] *Statistical Abstract for the United Kingdom,* pp. 125–127.

[6] *Statistical Abstract,* p. 129.

[7] *Ibid.,* calculated from figures on pp. 125–127.

[8] *Economic Survey for 1949,* p. 31.

POPULATION OF SCOTLAND, 1707–1970
(Calculated figures are in italics.)

Year	Total	Agricultural	Year	Total	Agricultural
1707	1048		1871	3360	
1755	*1210*		1881	3736	*933*
1801	1608		1891	4026	
1821	2092	*1395*	1901	4472	
1831	2364		1911	4761	
1841	2620		1921	4882	*513*
1851	2889		1931	4843	*460*
1861	3062		1937	4977	
			1947	5139	*432*

Gaelic Speakers, 1921 and 1947

The approximate number of Gaelic speakers is given in the *Census of Scotland for 1921* as 158,779, or 3.47 per cent of the population of 3 years of age and over. This number is cited in A. J. Aucamp, *Bilingual Education and Nationalism,* p. 36. If we apply this percentage of 3.47 to the entire Scottish population of that year, we obtain a theoretical Gaelic-"speaking" population of 169,000 in 1921.

The estimate of about 100,000 Gaelic speakers for the period following World War II was found in Mario A. Pei, *The Story of Language,* p. 350. No source is given for this figure, which seems to be a rough approximation. A release of the official British Information Service stated in 1950: "The Highlander . . . is a speaker of Gaelic, though nowadays, where he has not lost the tongue altogether, he is nearly always bilingual. There are still some 130,000 Gaelic speakers in Scotland, including some old folk who know no English at all." British Information Service, Reference Division, *Scotland Today: The Development of Modern Scotland,* ID 636/Revised (New York, January 1950, multigraphed), p. 2.

A CRUDE MATHEMATICAL MODEL OF ASSIMILATION AND MOBILIZATION PROCESSES
(With the Aid of Prof. Robert M. Solow)

In Chapter 6, in the section on "Major Rates of Change," the following notations were adopted:

P = total population

P_0 = P at the beginning of the period investigated

P_t = P at T years after t_0

M = mobilized population

A = assimilated population

D = differentiated population

U = underlying population

p = natural rate of increase of P, per capita of P_0

t_0 = year of the beginning of the period investigated

t = any subsequent year

$T = t - t_0$ = number of years since the beginning of the period

b = natural rate of increase of M, per capita of M_0

m = rate of entry of outsiders into M, per capita of M_0

a = natural rate of increase of A, per capita of A_0

c = rate of assimilation of net entry of outsiders into A, per capita of A_0

d = rate of natural increase of D, per capita of D_0

(*Note:* d times D will be written $(d)D$ in order to distinguish it from the differential of D, which is written dD).

In terms of these notations, mathematical models can be constructed so as to approximate the quantitative results of the process of social mobilization and national assimilation under various assumptions.

1. The simplest possible case occurs when each of the rates of increase p, b, m, etc., is constant through time. The following equations then hold:

$$\frac{dP}{dt} = pP$$

$$\frac{dA}{dt} = (a + c)A$$

$$\therefore \frac{dD}{dt} = (d)D - cA$$

if we assume that all the entrants into A come from D.

The solutions of these equations are

$$p(t) = P_0 e^{p(t-t_0)}$$

$$A(t) = A_0 e^{(a+c)(t-t_0)}$$

$$D(t) = \left(D_0 + \frac{A_0 c}{a + c - d}\right) e^{d(t-t_0)} - \frac{A_0 c}{a + c - d} e^{(a+c)(t-t_0)}$$

where P_0, A_0, D_0, are the initial values at $t = t_0$.

There remains the definitional restriction that $A(t) + D(t) = P(t)$, which now implies that

$$P_0 e^{p(t-t_0)} = A(t) + D(t) = D_0 e^{d(t-t_0)} + \frac{A_0 c}{a + c - d} e^{d(t-t_0)}$$
$$+ A_0 \left(\frac{a - d}{a + c - d}\right) e^{(a+c)(t-t_0)}$$

It is easy to see that this, in general, cannot be true; it would require very special values for p, d, a, c. The obvious thing is to abandon the fixed rate of increase of $P(t)$, since the fact is that $P = A + D$ will give a growth pattern for P once the solutions for A and D are determined.

A more realistic solution might be to abandon the assumption of constant values for a and c, since these may change more easily in the course of industrial development. This might be the case, particularly in situations where a large part of the differentiated population D were at the same time members of the underlying population U, and a large part of the assimilated population A were at the same time members of the mobilized population M. An approximate rate $(a + c)$ often can be calculated from the series of absolute figures for A, which are often given in published statistics; and the limits between which the rate a can vary could be calculated from a comparison of the natural rates of increase p and d. Different rates for c could then be calculated for shorter periods, and checked against other information.

However, should either A_0 or D_0 be very large relative to P_0; that is, should either the differentiated or assimilated groups form a large fraction of the total population at the starting point of the development, then the rate of growth of the total population will be approximately constant and approximately equal to the rate of growth of the larger section of the population.

Further, should either A or D fall to zero, the previous pattern of growth would be suspended, and the population would become all A or all D.

2. At what time is assimilation completed; that is, when does $D(t) = 0$?

$D(t) = 0$ when the right-hand side is zero; that is, when

$$\left(D_0 + \frac{A_0 c}{a + c - d}\right) e^{d(t - t_0)} = \frac{A_0 c}{a + c - d} e^{(a+c)(t - t_0)}$$

or, taking the natural logarithm of both sides of the equation,

$$\ln\left(D_0 + \frac{A_0 c}{a + c - d}\right) + d(t - t_0) = \ln\left(\frac{A_0 c}{a + c - d}\right) + (a + c)(t - t_0)$$

It is assumed, transferring the logarithms to the right-hand side of the equation, here, that $a + c - d > 0$.

$$(a + c - d)(t - t_0) = \log\left(D_0 + \frac{A_0 c}{a + c - d}\right) - \log\left(\frac{A_0 c}{a + c - d}\right)$$

and combining the terms

$$= \log \frac{D_0(a + c - d) + A_0 c}{A_0 c}$$

So that
$$t = t_0 + \frac{1}{a + c - d} \log\left[1 + \frac{D_0(a + c - d)}{A_0 c}\right]$$

which is approximately $t = t_0 + \dfrac{D_0}{A_0 c}$, if the term $\dfrac{D_0(a + c - d)}{A_0 c}$ is small. This may be a bad approximation in the early stages of the assimilation process, since at the start it is likely that D is large relative to A_0, as it was in our Finnish case, but it may be more nearly applicable when we start with a later stage of the process, as in our example from Scotland in the text.

If $a + c - d$ is negative, it is possible that $D(t)$ never may become zero.

3. A similar treatment applies to the relation among M, U, and P, only it is necessary here to remember that the definition $M(t) + U(t) = P(t)$ must give a $P(t)$ which matches the $P(t) = A(t) + D(t)$.

The assumptions of the text are that

$$\frac{dM}{dt} = (b + m)M$$

These imply Malthusian growth, so that $M(t) = M_0 e^{(b+m)(t-t_0)}$.

Since $A + D$ and $M + U$ both add up to P, it follows that the underlying population is $A + D - M$, or

$$U(t) = A_0 e^{(a+c)(t-t_0)} + \left(D_0 + \frac{A_0 c}{a + c - d} \right) e^{d(t-t_0)}$$

$$- \frac{A_0 c}{a + c - d} e^{(a+c)(t-t_0)} - M_0 e^{(b+m)(t-t_0)}$$

and it also follows that if the time path of P is approximated by a curve with constant percentage rate of growth p, then

$$P(t) = P_0 e^{p(t-t_0)} \qquad \text{and} \qquad U(t) = P_0 e^{p(t-t_0)} - M_0 e^{(b+m)(t-t_0)}$$

$U(t)$ will become zero, when

$$\log P_0 + p(t - t_0) = \log M_0 + (b + m)(t - t_0)$$

i.e., when

$$t = t_0 + \frac{1}{b + m - p} \log e \frac{P_0}{M_0}.$$

4. One difficulty here is that in the case where $a + c - d < 0$, $D(t)$ will decrease at an ever-increasing rate, instead of declining asymptotically towards zero. This could be altered by relaxing the "Malthusian" (constant proportional rate of increase) assumption used so far, and introducing the kind of assumption which gives rise to the logistic curve. Suppose the proportionate rate of increase of A declines as A increases, i.e.,

$$\frac{1}{A} \frac{dA}{dt} = k(M - A)$$

where k is a constant, and M is the maximum possible population, an upper limit approached asymptotically by A. The solution gives A the shape of a logistic curve:

$$A(t) = \frac{M}{1 + e - ht}$$

where h depends on k and M. If now $dD/dt = (d)D - cA$, where c has now lost its original meaning, we find as solution for D,

$$D(t) = D_0 e^{d(t-t_0)} - cMe^{(d)t} \int_{t_0}^{t} \frac{e^{-dz}}{1 + e - bz} \, dz$$

$D(t)$ may either grow, or decline to zero, first sharply, then more gently than before

It will be seen that this model is crude indeed. Refinements would have to include changes in the rate of assimilation a as a function of changes in the mobilization rate, and particularly as functions of the rise of the mobilized but unassimilated group H. Generally, if H is large, and its rate of growth h is also large, a may tend to decline, at least for considerable periods.

More complex models involving changing rates of growth, and particularly changes in a, d, p, h, etc., could be constructed. There seems to be no reason why the lengthy calculations required by such models could not be handled by existing types of computers, electronic or mechanical, but any calculations and models of this kind would go clearly beyond the limits of this study.

APPENDIX VI

THE DISTRIBUTION OF INCOME IN THE AGE OF NATIONALISM: THE SLIGHT EFFECT OF STATISTICAL ERRORS

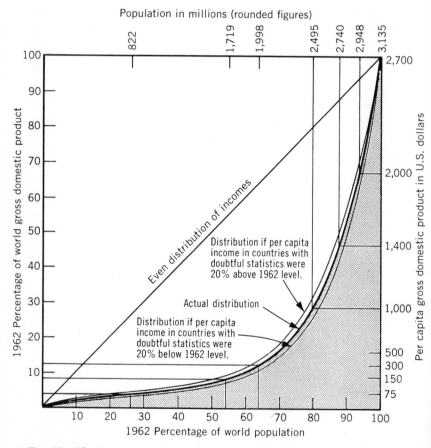

Fig. 26. The Lorenz curve shown above gives an overall picture of the inequality of distribution of incomes in the world, together with the effect upon the curve of errors of up to 20 per cent in countries where our statistics for gross domestic product per capita may be that inaccurate. Since the Lorenz curve gives a picture of the total amount of inequality among all countries, it is highly resistant to the effect of error in single countries, even in large ones.

In drawing the two curves indicating the results of possible errors, the countries of the world were divided into two groups: those which seemed to have reliable statistics, which together comprised about 60 per cent of the world's gross domestic product and 17 per cent of its population, and those whose statistics for one reason or another did not seem reliable. For this latter group it was first assumed that their per capita gross domestic product might be 20 per cent higher than the figures given in Table A VII.1, most of which were reported by the U.N.; it was then assumed that these figures might be 20 per cent lower than the figures in the table. The results of so large and so simultaneous a change were then represented by the thin lines in Fig. 26, which show that even then the changes in the Lorenz curve would not be large.

In fact it is extremely unlikely that all countries with unreliable statistics, countries which are also the poorer countries, would all deviate from the true value in the same direction. If they did not, however, then some of the errors would cancel each other out, and the net deviation from the original curve would be even smaller than has been indicated.

It should be noted that the effect of these hypothetical errors is too small to invalidate the conclusion that world income is far more unevenly distributed than is income within a stable, modern, national state. The effects of such hypothetical errors would be large enough, however, to cast serious doubt on the proposition that any very significant change in international income inequality for the world as a whole has occurred between 1949 and 1962.

APPENDIX VII

RANK ORDERS OF HUMAN NEEDS (POPULATION), POTENTIAL POWER (INCOME OF NATIONS), AND HUMAN WELFARE (PER CAPITA INCOME) FOR 141 COUNTRIES

The following three tables give an overall impression of the standing in the world of 141 countries as regards their human needs, their potential power, and the welfare of their peoples.

Such tables must be introduced with a caveat. As every economist would agree, these figures are open to discussion and may well be subject to considerable error. We have used the best figures available from the United Nations, the Yale Economic Growth Center, and the Yale Political Data Program. These figures are given here primarily as indications of political changes and as aids for policy appraisal. What counts for these purposes are the orders of magnitude which they reveal rather than the certainty of every last digit. We do feel that the orders of magnitude revealed in these tables can be relied upon.

Each table presents statistics for 1949 and 1962, and, with the qualifications indicated in the footnotes, these statistics measure the change over a thirteen-year period. In each case we have attempted to relate the figures for individual countries to the world as a whole and to the United States. Of particular interest in the population table, for example, is the relatively minor effect upon the world of the population growth in mainland China in contrast with the major effect of this growth upon China's proportional relationship to the United States.

In the second table, that measuring gross domestic product of nations, or their income, of particular interest is the change from the 1949 situation, where the United States and the Soviet Union together controlled more than half the world's wealth, to the situation of 1962, where the two countries between them can command less than half the wealth of the world.

The per capita income tables are of interest in their reflection of the major strides made in the Western European countries following World

War II as compared with U.S. growth. In contrast, per capita income in many of the underdeveloped countries, particularly in Latin America, has lagged behind the U.S. pace of growth.

Readers desiring further information should turn to the United Nations publications as well as the *World Handbook of Political and Social Indicators* by Russett, Alker, Deutsch, and Lasswell (New Haven and London, Yale University Press, 1964) and *A Cross-Polity Survey* by Banks and Textor (Cambridge, Mass., The M.I.T. Press, 1963).

TABLE A VII.1
AN INDICATOR OF HUMAN NEEDS:
A RANK ORDER OF 141 COUNTRIES ACCORDING TO 1962 POPULATION

Rank No. 1962 Population	Population 1949 (In Thousands)	Per Cent of 1949 World Population	Per Cent of 1949 U.S. Population	Population 1962 (In Thousands)	Per Cent of 1962 World Population	Per Cent of 1962 U.S. Population	Net Change In Per Cent of World Population 1949–1962	Net Change In Per Cent of U.S. Population 1949–1962
1. China (mainland)	463,493*	19.5	310.6	700,000[1]	22.3	375.0	+2.8	+64.4
2. India	346,000[2]	14.6	231.9	449,381	14.3	240.8	−0.3	+8.9
3. U.S.S.R.	193,000*	8.1	129.3	221,465	7.1	118.6	−1.0	−10.7
4. United States	149,215	6.3	100.0	186,656	6.0	100.0	−0.3	0
5. Indonesia	79,260*	3.3	53.1	97,765	3.1	52.4	−0.2	−0.7
6. Pakistan	73,855*	3.1	49.5	96,558	3.1	51.7	0	+2.2
7. Japan	82,636	3.5	55.4	94,930	3.0	50.9	−0.5	−4.5
8. Brazil	49,340	2.1	33.1	75,271	2.4	40.3	+0.3	+7.2
9. West Germany	49,187	2.1	33.0	56,241[3]	1.8	30.1	−0.3	−2.9
10. United Kingdom	50,363	2.1	33.8	53,441	1.7	28.6	−0.4	−5.2
11. Italy	45,996	1.9	30.8	50,170	1.6	26.9	−0.3	−3.9
12. France	41,180	1.7	27.6	46,998	1.5	25.2	−0.2	−2.4
13. Mexico	24,448	1.0	16.4	37,233	1.2	19.9	+0.2	+3.5
14. Nigeria	24,000[4]	1.0	16.1	36,475	1.2	19.5	+0.2	+3.4
15. Spain	28,023[4]	1.2	18.8	30,817	1.0	16.5	−0.2	−2.3
16. Poland	24,500	1.0	16.4	30,324	1.0	16.2	0	−0.2
17. Philippines	19,356	0.8	13.0	29,257	0.9	15.7	+0.1	+2.7
18. Turkey	19,623	0.8	13.2	29,059	0.9	15.6	+0.1	+2.4

TABLE A VII.1 (Continued)

Rank No. 1962 Population	Population 1949 (In Thousands)	Per Cent of 1949 World Population	Per Cent of 1949 U.S. Population	Population 1962 (In Thousands)	Per Cent of 1962 World Population	Per Cent of 1962 U.S. Population	Net Change In Per Cent of World Population 1949-1962	Net Change In Per Cent of U.S. Population 1949-1962
19. Thailand	17,987	0.8	12.1	27,995	0.9	15.0	+0.1	+2.9
20. United Arab Republic	20,045	0.8	13.4	27,285	0.9	14.6	+0.1	+1.2
21. Republic of Korea	20,189	0.9	13.5	26,520	0.9	14.2	0	+0.7
22. Burma	17,180[2]	0.7	11.5	23,183	0.7	12.4	0	+0.9
23. Argentina	16,555	0.7	11.1	21,418	0.7	11.5	0	+0.4
24. Iran	17,073	0.7	11.4	21,227	0.7	11.4	0	0
25. Ethiopia	15,000	0.6	10.1	21,000	0.7	11.3	+0.1	+1.2
26. Yugoslavia	16,040	0.7	10.7	18,837	0.6	10.1	−0.1	−0.6
27. Rumania	16,007	0.7	10.7	18,681	0.6	10.0	−0.1	−0.7
28. Canada	13,549	0.6	9.1	18,600	0.6	10.0	0	+0.9
29. South Africa	12,112[2]	0.5	8.1	18,508[5]	0.6	9.9	+0.1	+1.8
30. East Germany[6]	18,892[7]	0.8	12.7	17,102	0.6	9.2	−0.2	−3.5
31. South Vietnam	9,766[7,8]	0.4	6.5	14,929	0.5	8.0	+0.1	+1.5
32. Congo (Leopoldville)	11,046[4]	0.5	7.4	14,797	0.5	7.9	0	+0.5
33. Colombia	11,015	0.5	7.4	14,769	0.5	7.9	0	+0.5
34. Afghanistan	12,000*	0.5	8.0	14,684	0.5	7.9	0	−0.1
35. Czechoslovakia	12,463	0.5	8.4	13,856	0.4	7.4	−0.1	−1.0

TABLE A VII.1 (Continued)

Rank No. 1962 Population	Population 1949 (In Thousands)	Per Cent of 1949 World Population	Per Cent of 1949 U.S. Population	Population 1962 (In Thousands)	Per Cent of 1962 World Population	Per Cent of 1962 U.S. Population	Net Change In Per Cent of World Population 1949–1962	Net Change In Per Cent of U.S. Population 1949–1962
36. Sudan	7,558[4]	0.3	5.1	12,470	0.4	6.7	+0.1	+ 1.6
37. Morocco	8,594[4]	0.4	5.8	12,360	0.4	6.6	0	+ 0.8
38. Netherlands	9,956	0.4	6.7	11,797	0.4	6.3	0	− 0.4
39. Peru	8,240	0.4	5.5	11,511	0.4	6.2	0	+ 0.7
40. China (Taiwan)	[9]	—	—	11,327	0.4	6.1	—	—
41. Algeria	8,764	0.4	5.9	11,300	0.4	6.1	0	+ 0.2
42. Australia	7,912[2]	0.3	5.3	10,705	0.3	5.7	0	+ 0.4
43. Ceylon	7,297	0.3	4.9	10,442	0.3	5.6	0	+ 0.7
44. Federation of Rhodesia and Nyasaland	5,976[4,10]	0.3	4.0	10,230	0.3	5.5	0	+ 1.5
45. Hungary	9,165	0.4	6.1	10,061	0.3	5.4	−0.1	− 0.7
46. Tanganyika	7,514[4]	0.3	5.0	9,607	0.3	5.1	0	+ 0.1
47. Nepal	6,910[4]	0.3	4.6	9,550	0.3	5.1	0	+ 0.5
48. Belgium	8,614	0.4	5.8	9,221	0.3	4.9	−0.1	− 0.9
49. Portugal	8,491	0.4	5.7	8,971	0.3	4.8	−0.1	− 0.9
50. Kenya	5,454[4]	0.2	3.7	8,595	0.3	4.6	+0.1	+ 0.9
51. Greece	7,852	0.3	5.3	8,451	0.3	4.5	0	− 0.8
52. Chile	5,709[4]	0.2	3.8	8,029	0.3	4.3	+0.1	+ 0.5
53. Bulgaria	7,160[4]	0.3	4.8	8,013	0.3	4.3	0	− 0.5

TABLE A VII.1 (Continued)

Rank No. 1962 Population	Population 1949 (In Thousands)	World Per Cent of 1949 Population	U.S. Per Cent of 1949 Population	Population 1962 (In Thousands)	World Per Cent of 1962 Population	U.S. Per Cent of 1962 Population	Net Change In Per Cent of World Population 1949-1962	Net Change In Per Cent of U.S. Population 1949-1962
54. Venezuela	4,595	0.2	3.1	7,872	0.3	4.2	+0.1	+1.1
55. Sweden	6,956	0.3	4.7	7,562	0.2	4.1	−0.1	−0.6
56. Federation of Malaya	5,082[4]	0.2	3.4	7,376	0.2	4.0	0	+0.6
57. Ghana	4,209[7]	0.2	2.8	7,148	0.2	3.8	0	+1.0
58. Austria	7,000	0.3	4.7	7,128	0.2	3.8	−0.1	−0.9
59. Cuba	5,199	0.2	3.5	7,068	0.2	3.8	0	+0.3
60. Uganda	5,050[4]	0.2	3.4	7,016	0.2	3.8	0	+0.4
61. Mozambique	6,251	0.3	4.2	6,750	0.2	3.6	−0.1	−0.6
62. Iraq	4,990	0.2	3.3	6,732	0.2	3.6	0	+0.3
63. Saudi Arabia	6,000*	0.3	4.0	6,400	0.2	3.4	−0.1	−0.6
64. Cambodia	3,279[4]	0.1	2.2	5,740	0.2	3.1	+0.1	+0.9
65. Madagascar	4,396[4]	0.2	2.9	5,730	0.2	3.1	0	+0.2
66. Switzerland	4,640	0.2	3.1	5,660	0.2	3.1	0	0
67. Syria	3,407*	0.1	2.3	5,067	0.2	2.7	+0.1	+0.4
68. Yemen	4,500[4]	0.2	3.0	5,000	0.2	2.7	0	−0.3
69. Angola	4,597[4]	0.2	3.1	4,936	0.2	2.6	0	−0.5
70. Denmark	4,230	0.2	2.8	4,654	0.2	2.5	0	−0.3
71. Ecuador	3,378*	0.1	2.3	4,596	0.2	2.5	+0.1	+0.2

TABLE A VII.1 (Continued)

Rank No. 1962 Population	Population 1949 (In Thousands)	Per Cent of 1949 World Population	Per Cent of 1949 U.S. Population	Population 1962 (In Thousands)	Per Cent of 1962 World Population	Per Cent of 1962 U.S. Population	Net Change In Per Cent of World Population 1949–1962	Net Change In Per Cent of U.S. Population 1949–1962
72. Finland	4,015	0.2	2.7	4,505	0.1	2.4	−0.1	− 0.3
73. Upper Volta	3,128[7,11]	0.1	2.1	4,500	0.1	2.4	0	+ 0.3
74. Haiti	3,750*	0.2	2.5	4,346	0.1	2.3	−0.1	− 0.2
75. Cameroon	3,000[4]	0.1	2.0	4,326	0.1	2.3	0	+ 0.3
76. Mali	3,445[7]	0.1	2.3	4,305	0.1	2.3	0	0
77. Tunisia	3,416[4]	0.1	2.3	4,290	0.1	2.3	0	0
78. Guatemala	3,784	0.2	2.5	4,017	0.1	2.2	−0.1	− 0.3
79. Norway	3,233	0.1	2.2	3,639	0.1	1.9	0	− 0.3
80. Bolivia	3,990*	0.2	2.7	3,549	0.1	1.9	−0.1	− 0.8
81. Hong Kong	1,857[4]	0.08	1.2	3,410	0.1	1.8	+0.02	+ 0.6
82. Ivory Coast	2,170[7,11]	0.09	1.5	3,375	0.1	1.8	+0.01	+ 0.3
83. Senegal	2,093[7,11]	0.09	1.4	3,280	0.1	1.8	+0.01	+ 0.4
84. Guinea	2,250[7,11]	0.09	1.5	3,259	0.1	1.7	+0.01	+ 0.2
85. Dominican Republic	2,277	0.1	1.5	3,220	0.1	1.7	0	+ 0.2
86. Niger	2,165[7,12]	0.09	1.5	2,995	0.1	1.6	+0.01	+ 0.1
87. Uruguay	2,353	0.1	1.6	2,914	0.09	1.6	−0.01	0
88. Ireland	2,991	0.1	2.0	2,824	0.09	1.5	−0.04	− 0.5
89. Rwanda	2,128[7,8]	0.09	1.4	2,780	0.09	1.5	0	+ 0.1

TABLE A VII.1 (Continued)

Rank No. 1962 Population	Population 1949 (In Thousands)	Per Cent of World Population 1949	Per Cent of U.S. Population 1949	Population 1962 (In Thousands)	Per Cent of World Population 1962	Per Cent of U.S. Population 1962	Net Change In Per Cent of World Population 1949–1962	Net Change In Per Cent of U.S. Population 1949–1962
90. Chad	2,244[7]	0.09	1.5	2,720	0.09	1.5	0	0
91. El Salvador	2,150	0.09	1.4	2,627	0.08	1.4	−0.01	0
92. Burundi	1,902[7,13]	0.08	1.3	2,600	0.08	1.4	0	+ 0.1
93. New Zealand	1,881[14]	0.08	1.3	2,485	0.08	1.3	0	0
94. Puerto Rico	2,197[7]	0.09	1.5	2,460	0.08	1.3	−0.01	− 0.2
95. Israel	1,016	0.04	0.7	2,292	0.07	1.2	+0.03	+ 0.5
96. Somalia	972[4]	0.04	0.7	2,250	0.07	1.2	+0.03	+ 0.5
97. Dahomey	1,570[7,11]	0.07	1.1	2,200	0.07	1.2	0	+ 0.1
98. Sierra Leone	2,079[4]	0.09	1.4	2,170	0.07	1.2	−0.02	− 0.2
99. Honduras	1,326	0.06	0.9	1,950	0.06	1.0	0	+ 0.1
100. Laos	1,208[4]	0.05	0.8	1,882	0.06	1.0	+0.01	+ 0.2
101. Paraguay	1,304*	0.05	0.9	1,857	0.06	1.0	+0.01	+ 0.1
102. Lebanon	1,240	0.05	0.8	1,760	0.06	0.9	+0.01	+ 0.1
103. Singapore	984[4]	0.04	0.7	1,733	0.06	0.9	+0.02	+ 0.2
104. Jordan	400[4]	0.02	0.3	1,727	0.06	0.9	+0.04	+ 0.6
105. Albania	1,186[4]	0.05	0.8	1,711	0.05	0.9	0	+ 0.1
106. Jamaica	1,374[4]	0.06	0.9	1,641	0.05	0.9	−0.01	0
107. Nicaragua	1,184	0.05	0.8	1,578	0.05	0.9	0	+ 0.1

TABLE A VII.1 (Continued)

Rank No. 1962 Population	Population 1949 (In Thousands)	World Per Cent of 1949 Population	U.S. Per Cent of 1949 Population	Population 1962 (In Thousands)	World Per Cent of 1962 Population	U.S. Per Cent of 1962 Population	Net Change In Per Cent of World Population 1949–1962	Net Change In Per Cent of U.S. Population 1949–1962
108. Togo	977[7]	0.04	0.7	1,523	0.05	0.8	+0.01	+ 0.1
109. New Guinea (Australian)	1,008[4]	0.04	0.7	1,485	0.05	0.8	+0.01	+ 0.1
110. Borneo Territories	948[4]	0.04	0.6	1,345	0.04	0.7	0	+ 0.1
111. Costa Rica	837	0.04	0.6	1,274	0.04	0.7	0	+ 0.1
112. Central African Republic	1,072[7,11]	0.05	0.7	1,250	0.04	0.7	−0.01	0
113. Libya	1,174[4]	0.05	0.8	1,244	0.04	0.7	−0.01	− 0.1
114. Aden[15]	732[4]	0.03	0.5	1,220	0.04	0.7	+0.01	+ 0.2
115. Panama	764	0.03	0.5	1,146	0.04	0.6	+0.01	+ 0.1
116. Liberia	1,648	0.07	1.1	1,010	0.03	0.5	−0.04	− 0.6
117. Ryukyu Islands	909[4]	0.04	0.6	900	0.03	0.5	−0.01	− 0.1
118. Trinidad and Tobago	611[4]	0.03	0.4	894	0.03	0.5	0	+ 0.1
119. Congo (Brazzaville)	684[7,11]	0.03	0.5	820	0.03	0.4	0	− 0.1
120. Mauritania	546[7,11]	0.02	0.4	780	0.03	0.4	+0.01	0
121. Western New Guinea	1,000[4]	0.04	0.7	750	0.02	0.4	−0.02	− 0.3
122. Bhutan	300[4]	0.01	0.2	700	0.02	0.4	+0.01	+ 0.2
123. Mauritius	475[4]	0.02	0.3	682	0.02	0.4	0	+ 0.1
124. British Guiana	408[4]	0.02	0.3	598	0.02	0.3	0	0
125. Cyprus	476[4]	0.02	0.3	580	0.02	0.3	0	0

Rank No. 1962 Population	Population 1949 (In Thousands)	Per Cent of World Population 1949	Per Cent of U.S. Population 1949	Population 1962 (In Thousands)	Per Cent of World Population 1962	Per Cent of U.S. Population 1962	Net Change In Per Cent of World Population 1949–1962	Net Change In Per Cent of U.S. Population 1949–1962
126. Muscat and Oman	830[4]	0.03	0.6	565	0.02	0.3	−0.01	− 0.3
127. Portuguese Guinea	431[4]	0.02	0.3	549	0.02	0.3	0	0
128. Papua	304[4]	0.01	0.2	540	0.02	0.3	+0.01	+ 0.1
129. Portuguese Timor	420[4]	0.02	0.3	528	0.02	0.3	0	0
130. Gabon	416[7]	0.02	0.3	453	0.01	0.2	−0.01	− 0.1
131. Fiji Islands	281[4]	0.01	0.2	421	0.01	0.2	0	0
132. Reunion	252[4]	0.01	0.2	356	0.01	0.2	0	0
133. Malta and Gozo	311[4]	0.01	0.2	329	0.01	0.2	0	0
134. Luxembourg	295	0.01	0.2	322	0.01	0.2	0	0
135. Zanzibar	268[4]	0.01	0.2	320	0.01	0.2	0	0
136. Surinam	214[4]	0.01	0.1	307	0.01	0.2	0	+ 0.1
137. Martinique	270[4]	0.01	0.2	297	0.01	0.2	0	0
138. Guadeloupe	286[4]	0.01	0.2	289	0.01	0.2	0	0
139. Gambia	270[4]	0.01	0.2	269	0.01	0.1	0	− 0.1
140. Barbados	204[4]	0.01	0.1	232	0.01	0.1	0	0
141. Iceland	139	0.01	0.1	182	0.01	0.1	0	0

* Rough estimate.

1. For assistance in arriving at these figures I am indebted to Professor Alexander Eckstein, whose forthcoming book on China will be published in the winter of 1965–1966.

2. 1948–1949.

3. Includes the Saar and West Berlin. *U.N.. Demographic Yearbook, 1963*, p. 158.

4. *U.N. Demographic Yearbook, 1949–1950*, pp. 71–88.

5. Includes Basutoland, Bechuanaland, Swaziland, and South West Africa.

6. Includes East Berlin.

7. *U.N. Demographic Yearbook, 1963*, pp. 148–160.

8. 1953.

9. Presumably included in figure for China (mainland).

10. Southern Rhodesia, 2,022; Northern Rhodesia, 1,640; Nyasaland, 2,314.

11. 1950.

12. 1951.

13. 1952.

14. 1949–1950.

15. Includes the Protectorate of South Arabia.

Sources for all other figures are: 1949 figures: U.N. Statistical Office, Statistical Papers, Series E, No. 1, "National and Per Capita Incomes, Seventy Countries–1949," New York, October 1950. 1962 figures: *U.N. Demographic Yearbook, 1963.*

TABLE A VII.2
AN INDICATOR OF POTENTIAL POWER:
A RANK ORDER OF 141 COUNTRIES ACCORDING TO 1962 GROSS DOMESTIC PRODUCT

Rank No. 1962 GDP	1949 National Income[1] (In Million $ U.S.)	National Income[2] Per Cent of World 1949	National Income Per Cent of U.S. 1949	1962 Total GDP[1] (In Million $ U.S.)	GDP of World Per Cent of 1962	GDP of U.S. Per Cent of 1962	Net Change In Per Cent of World GDP 1949-1962[1]	Net Change In Per Cent of U.S. GDP 1949-1962[1]
1. United States	216,831	40.1	100.0	502,187	32.8	100.0	-7.3	0
2. U.S.S.R.[3]	59,500	11.0	27.4	233,000[4]	15.2	46.4	+4.2	+19.0
3. United Kingdom	38,922	7.2	18.0	77,724	5.1	15.5	-2.1	- 2.5
4. West Germany[5]	15,300	2.8	7.1	77,229	5.1	15.4	+2.3	+ 8.3
5. France	19,857	3.7	9.2	67,552	4.4	13.5	+0.7	+ 4.3
6. China (mainland)	12,384	2.3	5.7	54,091[4,6]	3.5	10.8	+1.2	+ 5.1
7. Japan	8,260	1.5	3.8	52,315	3.4	10.4	+1.9	+ 6.6
8. Italy	10,800	2.0	5.0	45,985	3.0	9.2	+1.0	+ 4.2
9. Canada	11,797	2.2	5.4	35,090	2.3	7.0	+0.1	+ 1.6
10. India	19,572[7]	3.6	9.0	33,183	2.2	6.6	-1.4	- 2.4
11. Poland	7,344	1.4	3.4	19,545[4]	1.3	3.9	-0.1	+ 0.5
12. Australia	5,374[7]	1.0	2.5	17,212	1.1	3.4	+0.1	+ 0.9
13. East Germany	—	—	—	15,577[4]	1.0	3.1	—	—
14. Netherlands	5,000	0.9	2.3	14,746	0.9	2.9	0	+ 0.6
15. Sweden	5,426	1.0	2.5	13,863	0.9	2.8	-0.1	+ 0.3
16. Mexico	2,960	0.5	1.4	13,454	0.9	2.7	-0.1	+ 1.3
17. Brazil	5,530	1.0	2.6	13,118	0.9	2.6	-0.1	0
18. Czechoslovakia	4,625	0.9	2.1	12,659[4]	0.8	2.5	-0.1	+ 0.4

TABLE A VII.2 (Continued)

Rank No. 1962 GDP	1949 National Income[1] (In Million $ U.S.)	Per Cent of 1949 National Income[2] of World	Per Cent of 1949 National Income of U.S.	1962 Total GDP[1] (In Million $ U.S.)	GDP of World Per Cent of 1962	GDP of U.S. Per Cent of 1962	Net Change In Per Cent of World GDP 1949–1962	Net Change In Per Cent of U.S. GDP 1949–1962
19. Spain	—	—	—	12,516[8]	0.8	2.5	—	—
20. Belgium	5,015	0.9	2.3	11,428	0.7	2.3	-0.1	0
21. Switzerland	3,940	0.7	1.8	11,043	0.7	2.2	0	+0.4
22. South Africa	3,200	0.6	1.5	10,257[9]	0.7	2.0	+0.1	+0.5
23. Argentina	5,722	1.0	2.6	9,905	0.7	2.0	-0.3	-0.6
24. Rumania	—	—	—	9,799[4]	0.6	2.0	—	—
25. Yugoslavia	2,343	0.4	1.1	8,151[4]	0.5	1.6	+0.1	+0.5
26. Turkey	2,452	0.5	1.1	8,011	0.5	1.6	0	+0.5
27. Pakistan	3,760	0.7	1.7	7,043	0.5	1.4	-0.2	-0.3
28. Indonesia	2,000	0.4	0.9	7,024	0.5	1.4	+0.1	+0.5
29. Denmark	2,908	0.5	1.3	6,945	0.5	1.4	0	+0.1
30. Austria	1,516	0.3	0.7	6,056	0.4	1.2	+0.1	+0.5
31. Hungary	2,315	0.4	1.1	5,890[4]	0.4	1.2	0	+0.1
32. Norway	1,898	0.4	0.9	5,852	0.4	1.2	0	+0.3
33. Venezuela	1,478	0.3	0.7	5,333*	0.4	1.1	+0.1	+0.4
34. New Zealand	1,610[10]	0.3	0.7	4,623	0.3	0.9	0	+0.2
35. United Arab Republic	1,989	0.4	0.9	4,150*	0.3	0.8	-0.1	-0.1

TABLE A VII.2 (Continued)

Rank No. 1962 GDP	1949 National Income[1] (In Million $ U.S.)	Per Cent of 1949 of World National Income[2]	Per Cent of 1949 of U.S. National Income	1962 Total GDP^p (In Million $ U.S.)	Per Cent of 1962 GDP of World	Per Cent of 1962 GDP of U.S.	Net Change In Per Cent of World GDP 1949–1962	Net Change In Per Cent of U.S. GDP 1949–1962
36. Colombia	1,456	0.3	0.7	4,112*	0.3	0.8	0	+0.1
37. Bulgaria	—	—	—	3,934[4]	0.3	0.8	—	—
38. Philippines	850	0.2	0.4	3,660	0.2	0.7	0	+0.3
39. Finland	1,399	0.3	0.7	3,471	0.2	0.7	−0.1	0
40. Chile	1,070	0.2	0.5	3,374	0.2	0.7	0	+0.2
41. Iran	1,450	0.3	0.7	3,164*	0.2	0.6	−0.1	−0.1
42. Greece	1,008	0.2	0.5	3,163	0.2	0.6	0	+0.1
43. Portugal	2,150	0.4	1.0	3,158	0.2	0.6	−0.2	−0.4
44. Nigeria	—	—	—	3,078*	0.2	0.6	—	—
45. Thailand	650	0.1	0.3	2,978	0.2	0.6	+0.1	+0.3
46. South Korea	700	0.1	0.3	2,874	0.2	0.6	+0.1	+0.3
47. Israel	395	0.07	0.2	2,824	0.2	0.6	+0.1	+0.4
48. Algeria	—	—	—	2,471*	0.2	0.5	—	—
49. Ireland	1,260	0.2	0.6	2,133	0.1	0.4	−0.1	−0.2
50. Puerto Rico	—	—	—	2,029	0.1	0.4	—	—
51. Cuba	1,550	0.3	0.7	1,975[11]	0.1	0.4	−0.2	−0.3
52. Morocco	—	—	—	1,960	0.1	0.4	—	—
53. Peru	820	0.2	0.4	1,931*	0.1	0.4	−0.1	0

TABLE A VII.2 (Continued)

Rank No. 1962 GDP	1949 National Income[1] (In Million $ U.S.)	Per Cent of 1949 National Income[2] of World	Per Cent of 1949 National Income of U.S.	1962 Total GDP[1] (In Million $ U.S.)	GDP of World Per Cent of 1962	GDP of U.S. Per Cent of 1962	Net Change In Per Cent of World GDP 1949–1962	Net Change In Per Cent of U.S. GDP 1949–1962
54. Federation of Rhodesia and Nyasaland	—	—	—	1,825	0.1	0.4	—	—
55. Saudi Arabia	240	0.04	0.1	1,530*	0.1	0.3	+0.06	+0.2
56. Federation of Malaya	—	—	—	1,474*	0.1	0.3	—	—
57. Congo (Leopoldville)	—	—	—	1,447*	0.1	0.3	—	—
58. Ceylon	487	0.09	0.2	1,431	0.09	0.3	0	+0.1
59. China (Taiwan)	[12]	—	—	1,376	0.09	0.3	—	—
60. Ghana	—	—	—	1,337	0.09	0.3	—	—
61. Burma	612[7]	0.1	0.3	1,329	0.09	0.3	−0.01	0
62. Uruguay	779	0.1	0.4	1,202[11]	0.08	0.2	−0.02	−0.2
63. Iraq	424	0.08	0.2	1,079*	0.07	0.2	−0.01	0
64. Ethiopia	570	0.1	0.3	1,050*	0.07	0.2	−0.03	−0.1
65. South Vietnam	—	—	—	980*	0.06	0.2	—	—
66. Sudan	—	—	—	874*	0.06	0.2	—	—
76. Afghanistan	600	0.1	0.3	870*	0.06	0.2	−0.04	−0.1
68. Ecuador	134	0.03	0.06	862	0.06	0.2	+0.03	+0.1
69. Kenya	—	—	—	728	0.05	0.1	—	—
70. Dominican Republic	170	0.03	0.08	689	0.05	0.1	+0.02	+0.02

TABLE A VII.2 (Continued)

Rank No. 1962 GDP	1949 National Income[1] (In Million $ U.S.)	Per Cent of 1949 National Income[2] of World	Per Cent of 1949 National Income of U.S.	1962 Total GDP[i] (In Million $ U.S.)	Per Cent of 1962 GDP of World	Per Cent of 1962 GDP of U.S.	Net Change In Per Cent of World GDP 1949–1962	Net Change In Per Cent of U.S. GDP 1949–1962
71. Tunisia	—	—	—	684[8]	0.05	0.1	—	—
72. Jamaica	—	—	—	683*	0.05	0.1	—	—
73. Guatemala	293	0.05	0.1	669	0.04	0.1	−0.01	0
74. Tanganyika	—	—	—	648	0.04	0.1	—	—
75. Syria	340	0.06	0.2	600*	0.04	0.1	−0.02	−0.1
76. Hong Kong	—	—	—	598*	0.04	0.1	—	—
77. Trinidad and Tobago	—	—	—	581	0.04	0.1	—	—
78. Singapore	—	—	—	567*	0.04	0.1	—	—
79. Senegal	—	—	—	491*	0.03	0.1	—	—
80. Luxembourg	162	0.03	0.07	489*	0.03	0.1	0	+0.03
81. Panama	140	0.03	0.07	489	0.03	0.1	0	+0.03
82. Ivory Coast	—	—	—	472*	0.03	0.09	—	—
83. Nepal	—	—	—	448*	0.03	0.09	—	—
84. Uganda	—	—	—	424	0.03	0.08	—	—
85. Lebanon	155	0.03	0.07	410*	0.03	0.08	0	+0.01
86. Haiti	150	0.03	0.07	395*	0.03	0.08	0	+0.01
87. Madagascar	—	—	—	391*	0.03	0.08	—	—

TABLE A VII.2 (Continued)

Rank No. 1962 GDP	1949 National Income[1] (In Million $ U.S.)	National Income[2] Per Cent of 1949 of World	National Income Per Cent of 1949 of U.S.	1962 Total GDP[1] (In Million $ U.S.)	GDP of World Per Cent of 1962	GDP of U.S. Per Cent of 1962	Net Change In Per Cent of World GDP 1949–1962	Net Change In Per Cent of U.S. GDP 1949–1962
88. Cameroon	—	—	—	387*	0.03	0.08	—	—
89. Jordan	—	—	—	380*	0.03	0.08	—	—
90. Honduras	110	0.02	0.05	379	0.03	0.08	+0.01	+0.03
91. Cambodia	—	—	—	365*	0.02	0.07	—	—
92. Borneo Territories[13]	—	—	—	356[11,14]	0.02	0.07	—	—
93. El Salvador	197	0.04	0.09	351	0.02	0.07	−0.02	−0.02
94. Mali	—	—	—	332*	0.02	0.07	—	—
95. Angola	—	—	—	332[15]	0.02	0.07	—	—
96. Costa Rica	105	0.02	0.05	331	0.02	0.07	0	+0.02
97. Mozambique	—	—	—	328[15]	0.02	0.07	—	—
98. Nicaragua	105	0.02	0.05	320[8]	0.02	0.06	0	+0.01
99. Bolivia	221	0.04	0.1	318[8]	0.02	0.06	−0.02	−0.04
100. Albania	—	—	—	252[4,16]	0.02	0.05	—	—
101. Cyprus	—	—	—	250[14]	0.02	0.05	—	—
102. Libya	—	—	—	231	0.02	0.05	—	—
103. Iceland	66	0.01	0.03	228[14]	0.01	0.05	+0.01	+0.02
104. Yemen	280	0.05	0.1	220[11,14]	0.01	0.04	−0.04	−0.06

TABLE A VII.2 (Continued)

Rank No. 1962 GDP	1949 National Income[1] (In Million $ U.S.)	Per Cent of 1949 National Income[2] of World	Per Cent of 1949 National Income of U.S.	1962 Total GDP[1] (In Million $ U.S.)	Per Cent of 1962 GDP of World	Per Cent of 1962 GDP of U.S.	Net Change In Per Cent of World GDP 1949–1962	Net Change In Per Cent of U.S. GDP 1949–1962
105. British Guiana	—	—	—	188[8]	0.01	0.04	—	—
106. Niger	—	—	—	167*	0.01	0.03	—	—
107. Dahomey	—	—	—	164*	0.01	0.03	—	—
108. Upper Volta	—	—	—	161*	0.01	0.03	—	—
109. Chad	—	—	—	160*	0.01	0.03	—	—
110. Paraguay	109	0.02	0.05	156*	0.01	0.03	-0.01	-0.02
111. Ryukyu Islands	—	—	—	152[11,14]	0.01	0.03	—	—
112. Guinea	—	—	—	150[11]	0.01	0.03	—	—
113. Mauritius	—	—	—	143	0.009	0.03	—	—
114. Sierra Leone	—	—	—	137[11,14]	0.009	0.03	—	—
115. Rwanda	—	—	—	133[11,14]	0.009	0.03	—	—
116. Laos	—	—	—	126*	0.008	0.03	—	—
117. Malta and Gozo	—	—	—	122[14]	0.008	0.02	—	—
118. Liberia	62	0.01	0.03	117[11,14]	0.008	0.02	-0.002	-0.01
119. Burundi	—	—	—	115[11,14]	0.008	0.02	—	—
120. Togo	—	—	—	108*	0.007	0.02	—	—
121. Central African Republic	—	—	—	96*	0.006	0.02	—	—
122. Somalia	—	—	—	95[11]	0.006	0.02	—	—

TABLE A VII.2 (Continued)

Rank No. 1962 GDP	1949 National Income[1] (In Million $ U.S.)	Per Cent of World National Income[2] 1949	Per Cent of U.S. National Income 1949	1962 Total GDP[1] (In Million $ U.S.)	Per Cent of 1962 GDP of World	Per Cent of 1962 GDP of U.S.	Net Change In Per Cent of World GDP 1949–1962	Net Change In Per Cent of U.S. GDP 1949–1962
123. Gabon	—	—	—	91*	0.006	0.02	—	—
124. Guadeloupe	—	—	—	87[11,14]	0.006	0.02	—	—
125. Martinique	—	—	—	87[11,14]	0.006	0.02	—	—
126. Congo (Brazzaville)	—	—	—	87*	0.006	0.02	—	—
127. Surinam	—	—	—	79[11,14]	0.005	0.02	—	—
128. Fiji Islands	—	—	—	78[11,14]	0.005	0.02	—	—
129. Barbados	—	—	—	75	0.005	0.02	—	—
130. Reunion	—	—	—	70[11,14]	0.005	0.01	—	—
131. New Guinea (Australian)	—	—	—	67[11,14]	0.004	0.01	—	—
132. Mauritania	—	—	—	57*	0.004	0.01	—	—
133. Aden[17]	—	—	—	51[11,14]	0.003	0.01	—	—
134. Western New Guinea	—	—	—	36[11,14]	0.002	0.007	—	—
135. Muscat and Oman	—	—	—	33[11,14]	0.002	0.007	—	—
136. Bhutan	—	—	—	33[11,14]	0.002	0.007	—	—
137. Zanzibar	—	—	—	31[14]	0.002	0.006	—	—

TABLE A VII.2 (Continued)

Rank No. 1962 GDP	1949 National Income[1] (In Million $ U.S.)	Per Cent of 1949 World National Income[2]	Per Cent of 1949 National Income of U.S.	1962 Total GDP[1] (In Million $ U.S.)	1962 GDP Per Cent of World	1962 GDP Per Cent of U.S.	Net Change In Per Cent of World GDP 1949-1962	Net Change In Per Cent of U.S. GDP 1949-1962
138. Papua	—	—	—	24[11,14]	0.002	0.005	—	—
139. Portuguese Timor	—	—	—	24[11,14]	0.002	0.005	—	—
140. Portuguese Guinea	—	—	—	24[11,14]	0.002	0.005	—	—
141. Gambia	—	—	—	20[11,14]	0.001	0.004	—	—

Note: For most of the underdeveloped countries of the world national accounts statistics do not exist with the same accuracy or in the same detail as those for the Western world. The statistics of this table can therefore be considered as less than completely accurate, and in some cases they may be subject to an error of up to 20 per cent. It will be seen, however, from the Lorenz curve of distribution of world income (Fig. 26) that even an error of as much as 20 per cent on the high or low side for per capita income in all countries with doubtful statistics does not make any major change in the inequality of distribution of incomes in the world.

Sources: All 1949 figures for national income (and in the following table for per capita national income) are from a U.N. study, "National and Per Capita Incomes, Seventy Countries – 1949." (United Nations, Statistical Office, Statistical Papers, Series E, No. 1, New York, October 1950).

Except where otherwise noted, all 1962 dollar figures for gross domestic product (or in the following table for gross domestic product per capita) are from the *United Nations Yearbook of National Accounts Statistics, 1963.* These figures are based on official GDP figures in national currency from the international tables of the *Yearbook* converted into U.S. dollars in the *Yearbook* by means of calculated parity rates. These parity rates were estimated by adjusting the official or free market exchange rates in 1938 for each country by the relative change in the level of prices from 1938 to the year in question, between the U.S. and the country concerned.

* 1961

1. National income is "the sum of the incomes accruing to factors of production supplied by normal residents of the given country before deduction of direct taxes." It is equal to "the value at factor cost of [the goods and services produced], after deduction of provisions for the consumption of fixed capital, attributable to the factors of production supplied by normal residents of the country".

GDP: Gross domestic product at factor cost. This is defined by the U.N. as follows: "the value at factor cost of the [total value of the goods and services of a country], before deduction of provisions for the consumption of fixed capital, attributable to factor services rendered to resident producers of the given country." It differs from GNP (gross national product at market prices) by "the exclusion of net factor incomes received from abroad" and by "the exclusion of the excess of indirect taxes over subsidies." (*U.N. Yearbook of National Accounts Statistics, 1963*, p. xi.)

The seventh column of figures in the table, entitled "Net change in per cent of world GDP, 1949–1962" is based on a comparison between 1949 national income figures and 1962 GDP figures. For most countries the difference between national income and GDP should be slight, but for particular countries deriving a high percentage of their income from abroad, this could understate their 1962 national income. The figures, even though inexact, however, do indicate an order of magnitude of considerable interest.

2. 1949 world national income is estimated at $540,298 million, 5.30 per cent above the national income of the 70 countries used in the U.N. study (U.N. Statistical Office, Statistical Papers, Series E, No. 1, "National and Per Capita Incomes, Seventy Countries – 1949," New York, October 1950). The 5.30 per cent figure is based on the ratio between GDP for these countries and for the rest of the world in 1962.

3. Source, 1962 figures for GNP (and for per capita GNP in the table below: U.S. Congress, Joint Economic Committee, "Annual Economic Indicators for the USSR," February 1964, Washington, U.S. Government Printing Office, 1964, p. 96.

4. Calculation of GDP was based on the assumption that the GNP figures were approximately 10 per cent above the GDP.

5. Excludes the Saar and West Berlin.

6. See footnote 1 in Table A VII.1 (Rank Order of 141 Countries According to Population).

7. 1948–1949.

8. GDP figures obtained by calculating the ratio between 1958 and 1962 figures in local currencies and applying this ratio to the 1958 figures in U.S. dollars given in the U.N. National Accounts Yearbook.

9. See footnote 5 in Table A VII.1 (Rank Order of 141 Countries According to Population).

10. 1949–1950.

11. 1958.

12. Presumably included in figures for China (mainland).

13. Brunei, Sarawak, and Sabah (formerly North Borneo).

14. These figures, from the *U.N. Yearbook of National Accounts Statistics, 1963*, were calculated by the U.N. by converting GDP figures in local currencies by the prevailing dollar exchange rates, rather than the parity rates used for the other GDP figures in the table (see paragraph on "Sources" above).

15. GDP figures were obtained by projecting the 1953–1958 growth rate for each country to 1962.

16. 1960.

17. See footnote 15 in Table A VII.1 (Rank Order of 141 Countries According to Population).

TABLE A VII.3

AN INDICATOR OF HUMAN WELFARE:

A RANK ORDER OF 141 COUNTRIES ACCORDING TO 1962 *PER CAPITA* GROSS DOMESTIC PRODUCT

Rank No. 1962 Per Capita GDP	1949 Per Capita National Income (In $ U.S.)[1]	Per Cent of 1949 U.S. Income	1962 Per Capita GDP (In $ U.S.)[1]	Per Cent of 1962 U.S. GDP Per Capita	1962 Per Capita GNP (In $ U.S.)[1]	Per Cent of 1962 U.S. GNP Per Capita	Net Change in 1962 GDP Per Capita Based on Income, 1949–1962	Net Change in 1962 GNP Based On 1962[1]
1. United States	1,453	100.0	2,691	100.0	2,980	100.0	0	0
2. Switzerland	849	58.4	1,951	72.5	2,101	70.5	+14.1	+12.1
3. Canada	870	59.9	1,887	70.1	2,119	71.1	+10.2	+11.2
4. New Zealand	856[2]	58.9	1,860	69.1	1,959	65.7	+10.2	+6.8
5. Sweden	780	53.7	1,833	68.1	2,071	69.5	+14.4	+15.8
6. Norway	587	40.4	1,608	59.8	1,776	59.6	+19.4	+19.2
7. Australia	679[3]	46.7	1,608	59.8	1,773	59.5	+13.1	+12.8
8. Luxembourg	553	38.1	1,543*	57.3	1,647*	55.3	+19.2	+17.2
9. Denmark	689	47.4	1,492	55.4	1,698	57.0	+8.0	+9.6
10. United Kingdom	773	53.2	1,454	54.0	1,668	56.0	+0.8	+2.8
11. West Germany	320	22.0	1,439[4]	53.5	1,654[4]	55.5	+31.5	+33.5
12. France	482	33.2	1,437	53.4	1,686	56.6	+20.2	+23.4
13. Netherlands	502	34.5	1,250	46.5	1,388	46.6	+12.0	+12.1
14. Iceland	476	32.8	1,250[5]	46.5	1,440[5]	48.3	+13.7	+15.5
15. Belgium	582	40.1	1,239	46.0	1,410	47.3	+5.9	+7.2
16. Israel	389	26.8	1,232	45.8	1,332	44.7	+19.0	+17.9
17. U.S.S.R.	308	21.2	1,052[6]	39.1	1,158	38.9	+17.9	+17.7
18. East Germany	—	—	971[6]	36.1	1,068	35.8	—	—

TABLE A VII.3 (Continued)

Rank No. 1962 Per Capita GDP	1949 Per Capita National Income (In $ U.S.)	Per Capita Income Per Cent of 1949 U.S.	1962 Per Capita GDP (In $ U.S.)	GDP Per Capita Per Cent of 1962 U.S.	1962 Per Capita GNP (In $ U.S.)	GNP Per Capita Per Cent of 1962 U.S.	Net Change in Per Capita Income, 1949–1962[1] Based On 1962 GDP Per Cent of U.S.	Net Change in Per Capita Income, 1949–1962[1] Based On 1962 GNP
19. Italy	235	16.2	917	34.1	1,048	35.2	+17.9	+19.0
20. Czechoslovakia	371	25.5	914$^{(6)}$	34.0	1,005	33.7	+8.5	+8.2
21. Austria	216	14.9	850	31.6	982	33.0	+16.7	+18.1
22. Puerto Rico	—	—	825	30.7	908	30.5	—	—
23. Finland	348	24.0	770	28.6	869	29.2	+4.6	+5.2
24. Ireland	420	28.9	755	28.1	890	29.9	−0.8	+1.0
25. Venezuela	322	22.2	701*	26.0	694*	23.3	+3.8	+1.1
26. Trinidad and Tobago	—	—	650	24.2	613	20.6	—	—
27. Poland	300	20.6	645$^{(6)}$	24.0	709	23.8	+3.4	+3.2
28. Hungary	269	18.5	585$^{(6)}$	21.7	644	21.6	+3.2	+3.1
29. South Africa	264$^{(3)}$	18.2	554$^{(7)}$	20.6	572$^{(7)}$	19.2	+2.4	+1.0
30. Japan	100	6.9	551	20.5	592	19.9	+13.6	+13.0
31. Rumania	—	—	525$^{(6)}$	19.5	577	19.4	—	—
32. Bulgaria	—	—	491$^{(6)}$	18.2	540	18.1	—	—
33. Argentina	346	23.8	462	17.2	500	16.8	−6.6	−7.0
34. Uruguay	331	22.8	435†	16.2	—	—	−6.6	—
35. Yugoslavia	146	10.0	433$^{(6)}$	16.1	476	16.0	+6.1	+6.0
36. Cyprus	—	—	432$^{(5)}$	16.1	455$^{(5)}$	15.3	—	—

TABLE A VII.3 (Continued)

Rank No. 1962 Per Capita GDP	1949 Per Capita National Income (In $ U.S.)	Per Cent of 1949 U.S. Per Capita Income	1962 Per Capita GDP (In $ U.S.)	Per Cent of 1962 U.S. GDP Per Capita	1962 Per Capita GNP (In $ U.S.)	Per Cent of 1962 U.S. GNP Per Capita	Net Change in Per Capita Income, 1949–1962 Based on 1962 GDP Per Cent of U.S.	GNP 1962¹ Based 1949–1962
37. Panama	183	12.6	429	15.9	446	15.0	+ 3.3	+ 2.4
38. Chile	188	12.9	422	15.7	456	15.3	+ 2.8	+ 2.4
39. Jamaica	—	—	418*	15.5	436*	14.6	—	—
40. Spain	—	—	406[8]	15.1	437[8]	14.7	—	—
41. Greece	128	8.8	374	13.9	441	14.8	+ 5.1	+ 6.0
42. Malta & Gozo	—	—	371[5]	13.8	450[5]	15.1	—	—
43. Mexico	121	8.3	361	13.4	—	—	+ 5.1	—
44. Portugal	250	17.2	352	13.1	383	12.9	– 4.1	– 4.3
45. Guadeloupe	—	—	340†[5]	12.6	—	—	—	—
46. Singapore	—	—	336*	12.5	—	—	—	—
47. Martinique	—	—	330†[5]	12.3	—	—	—	—
48. Barbados	—	—	323	12.0	371	12.4	—	—
49. British Guiana	—	—	314[8]	11.7	323[8]	10.8	—	—
50. Cuba	296	20.4	303†	11.3	—	—	– 9.1	—
51. Borneo Territories[10]	—	—	297†[5]	11.0	—	—	—	—
52. Surinam	—	—	290†[5]	10.8	—	—	—	—
53. Colombia	132	9.1	285*	10.6	298*	10.0	+ 1.5	+ 0.9
54. Turkey	125	—	272	10.1	296	9.9	—	—

TABLE A VII.3 (Continued)

Rank No. 1962 Per Capita GDP	1949 Per Capita National Income (In $ U.S.)	Income Per Capita Per Cent of 1949 U.S.	1962 Per Capita GDP (In $ U.S.)	GDP Per Capita Per Cent of 1962 U.S.	1962 Per Capita GNP (In $ U.S.)	GNP Per Capita Per Cent of 1962 U.S.	Net Change in Per Capita Income, 1949–1962[1] Based On 1962 GDP	Net Change Based On 1962 GNP
55. Costa Rica	125	9.1	260	9.7	285	9.6	+ 0.6	+ 0.5
56. Algeria	—	—	229*	8.5	269*	9.0	—	—
57. Lebanon	125	9.1	225*	8.4	—	—	− 0.7	—
58. Saudi Arabia	40	2.8	225*	8.4	244*	8.2	+ 5.6	—
59. Jordan	—	—	223*	8.3	—	—	—	—
60. Reunion	—	—	220†(5)	8.2	—	—	—	—
61. Dominican Republic	75	5.2	214	8.0	250	8.4	+ 2.8	+ 3.2
62. Fiji Islands	—	—	212†(5)	7.9	—	—	—	—
63. Mauritius	—	—	210	7.8	238	8.0	—	—
64. Federation of Malaya	—	—	207*	7.7	231*	7.8	—	—
65. Gabon	—	—	203*	7.5	—	—	—	—
66. Nicaragua	89	6.1	202(8)	7.5	230(8)	7.7	+ 1.4	+ 1.6
67. Honduras	83	5.7	194	7.2	207	6.9	+ 1.5	+ 1.2
68. Ecuador	40	2.8	188	7.0	196	6.6	+ 4.2	+ 3.8
69. Hong Kong	—	—	188*	7.0	—	—	—	—
70. Ghana	—	—	187	6.9	—	—	—	—
71. Libya	—	—	186	6.9	—	—	—	—

TABLE A VII.3 (Continued)

Rank No. 1962 Per Capita GDP	1949 Per Capita National Income (In $ U.S.)	Per Cent of 1949 U.S. Income Per Capita	1962 Per Capita GDP (In $ U.S.)	Per Cent of 1962 U.S. GDP Per Capita	1962 Per Capita GNP (In $ U.S.)	Per Cent of 1962 U.S. GNP Per Capita	Net Change in Per Cent of U.S. Per Capita Income, Based on 1949–1962 on GDP	Net Change in Per Cent of U.S. Per Capita Income, Based on 1949–1962 on GNP
72. Ryukyu Islands	—	—	180†(5)	6.7	—	—	—	—
73. Brazil	112	7.7	179*	6.7	204*	6.8	− 1.0	− 0.9
74. Federation of Rhodesia and Nyasaland	—	—	178	6.6	173	5.8	—	—
75. Peru	100	6.9	173*	6.4	178*	6.0	− 0.5	+ 0.9
76. Guatemala	77	5.3	166	6.2	178	6.0	+ 0.9	+ 0.7
77. Senegal	—	—	165*	6.1	—	—	—	—
78. Iraq	85	5.9	162*	6.0	—	—	+ 0.1	—
79. Tunisia	—	—	159(8)	5.9	—	—	—	—
80. Morocco	—	—	159	5.9	174	5.8	—	—
81. Albania	100	—	157‡	5.8	169‡	5.7	—	—
82. U.A.R.	85	6.9	156*	5.8	—	—	− 1.1	—
83. Iran	—	5.9	153*	5.7	152*	5.1	− 0.2	− 0.8
84. Ivory Coast	—	—	143*	5.3	—	—	—	—
85. Ceylon	67	4.6	137	5.1	145	4.9	+ 0.5	+ 0.3
86. El Salvador	92	6.3	134	5.0	143	4.8	− 1.3	− 1.5

TABLE A VII.3 (Continued)

Rank No. 1962 Per Capita GDP	1949 Per Capita National Income (In $ U.S.)	Per Cent of 1949 U.S. Per Capita Income	1962 Per Capita GDP (In $ U.S.)	Per Cent of 1962 U.S. GDP Per Capita	1962 Per Capita GNP (In $ U.S.)	Per Cent of 1962 U.S. GNP Per Capita	Net Change in Per Cent of U.S. Based on 1949–1962 Income, Per Capita GDP	GNP
87. Philippines	44	3.0	125	4.6	134	4.5	+ 1.6	+ 1.5
88. Liberia	38	2.6	122†(5)	4.5	—	—	+ 1.9	—
89. China (Taiwan)	(11)	—	121	4.5	139	4.7	—	—
90. Syria	100	6.9	119*	4.4	121	4.1	− 2.5	—
91. Republic of Korea	35	2.4	110	4.1	121	4.1	+ 1.7	+ 1.7
92. Congo (Brazzaville)	—	—	107*	4.0	—	—	—	—
93. Thailand	36	2.5	106	3.9	116	3.9	+ 1.4	+ 1.4
94. Congo (Leopoldville)	—	—	100*	3.7	102*	3.4	—	—
95. Zanzibar	—	—	99(5)	3.7	—	—	—	—
96. Haiti	40	2.8	93*	3.5	—	—	+ 0.7	—
97. Bolivia	55	3.8	90(8)	3.3	—	—	− 0.5	—
98. Nigeria	—	—	86*	3.2	—	—	—	—
99. Paraguay	84	5.8	86*	3.2	91*	3.1	− 2.6	− 2.7
100. Kenya	—	—	85	3.2	—	—	—	—
101. Dahomey	—	—	80*	3.0	—	—	—	—
102. Mali	—	—	79*	3.0	—	—	—	—
103. Central African Republic	—	—	78*	2.9	—	—	—	—

TABLE A VII.3 (Continued)

Rank No. 1962 Per Capita GDP	1949 Per Capita National Income (In $ U.S.)	Per Cent of 1949 U.S. Income	1962 Per Capita GDP (In $ U.S.)	GDP Per Capita Per Cent of 1962 U.S.	1962 Per Capita GNP (In $ U.S.)	GNP Per Capita Per Cent of 1962 U.S.	Net Change in Per Cent of U.S. Per Capita Income, Based 1949–1962 On 1962 GDP	Net Change, GNP Based 1949–1962 On 1962 GNP
104. China (mainland)	27	1.9	77[12]	2.9	85[12]	2.9	+ 1.0	+ 1.0
105. Mauritania	—	—	75*	2.8	—	—	—	—
106. Pakistan	51	3.5	74*	2.8	—	—	− 0.7	—
107. India	57[3]	3.9	73	2.7	—	—	− 1.2	—
108. Indonesia	25	1.7	73*	2.7	—	—	+ 1.0	—
109. Togo	—	—	73*	2.7	—	—	—	—
110. Sudan	—	—	72*	2.7	78*	2.6	—	—
111. Gambia	—	—	71†[5]	2.6	—	—	—	—
112. Madagascar	—	—	70*	2.6	—	—	—	—
113. Tanganyika	—	—	68	2.5	—	—	—	—
114. Laos	—	—	68*	2.5	—	—	—	—
115. Republic of Vietnam	—	—	68*	2.5	74*	2.5	—	—
116. Cambodia	—	—	68*	2.5	71*	2.4	—	—
117. Angola	—	—	67[13]	2.5	—	—	—	—
118. Sierra Leone	—	—	64†[5]	2.4	—	—	—	—
119. Aden[14]	—	—	64†[5]	2.4	—	—	—	—

TABLE A VII.3 (Continued)

Rank No. 1962 Per Capita GDP	1949 Per Capita National Income (In $ U.S.)	Per Cent of 1949 U.S. Per Capita Income	1962 Per Capita GDP (In $ U.S.)	Per Cent of 1962 U.S. Per Capita GDP	1962 Per Capita GNP (In $ U.S.)	Per Cent of 1962 U.S. Per Capita GNP	Net Change in Per Cent of U.S. Per Capita Income, 1949-1962 Based On GDP	Net Change Based On 1962 GNP
120. Cameroon	—	—	62*	2.3	—	—	—	—
121. Afghanistan	50	3.4	61*	2.3	—	—	− 1.1	—
122. Muscat and Oman	—	—	60†(5)	2.2	—	—	—	—
123. Chad	—	—	60*	2.2	—	—	—	—
124. Uganda	—	—	60	2.2	—	—	—	—
125. Niger	—	—	57*	2.1	—	—	—	—
126. Burma	36(3)	2.5	57	2.1	64	2.1	− 0.4	− 0.4
127. Rwanda	—	—	53†(5)	2.0	—	—	—	—
128. Burundi	—	—	53†(6)	2.0	—	—	—	—
129. Guinea	—	—	52†	1.9	—	—	—	—
130. Ethiopia	38	2.6	51*	1.9	—	—	− 0.7	—
131. Western New Guinea	—	—	50†(5)	1.9	—	—	—	—
132. New Guinea (Australian)	—	—	50†(5)	1.9	—	—	—	—
133. Papua	—	—	50†(5)	1.9	—	—	—	—
134. Portuguese Timor	—	—	50†(5)	1.9	—	—	—	—
135. Bhutan	—	—	50†(5)	1.9	—	—	—	—

TABLE A VII.3 (Continued)

Rank No. 1962 Per Capita GDP	1949 Per Capita National Income (In $ U.S.)	Income Per Cent of 1949 U.S. Per Capita	GDP 1962 Per Capita (In $ U.S.)	GDP Per Capita Per Cent of 1962 U.S.	GNP 1962 Per Capita (In $ U.S.)	GNP Per Capita Per Cent of 1962 U.S.	Net Change in GDP Per Capita, Based on 1962 Income, 1949-1962	GNP 1962 On 1961 Based Income, 1949-
136. Nepal	40	—	50†	1.9	—	—	—	—
137. Yemen	—	2.8	50†(5)	1.9	—	—	−0.9	—
138. Mozambique	—	—	49(13)	1.8	—	—	—	—
139. Somalia	—	—	48†	1.8	—	—	—	—
140. Upper Volta	—	—	43*	1.6	—	—	—	—
141. Portuguese Guinea	—	—	40†(5)	1.5	—	—	—	—

For general note on sources and possible statistical error, see note following Table A VII.2.

Sources: See note regarding sources at end of Table A VII.2 Population figures, used where per capita income figures were computed by us, were derived from the *United Nations Demographic Yearbook, 1963.*

* 1961.
† 1958.
‡ 1960.

1. For the definition of national income and of GDP (gross domestic product at factor cost) as used by the U.N., see footnote (1) to Table A VII.2. GNP (gross national product at market prices) is defined by the U.N. as follows: GNP is "the market value of [the total value of the goods and services produced] before deduction of provisions for the consumption of fixed capital, attributable to the factors of production supplied by normal residents of the given country. It is identically equal to the sum of consumption expenditure and gross domestic capital formation, private and public, and the net exports of goods and services plus the net factor incomes received from abroad." It differs from GDP (gross domestic product at factor cost) by the inclusion of net factor incomes received from abroad and the excess of indirect taxes over subsidies. (*U.N. Yearbook of National Accounts Statistics, 1963,* p. xi).

2. 1949–1950.
3. 1948–1949.
4. Excludes the Saar and West Berlin.
5. See footnote 14 in Table A VII.2.
6. See footnote 4 in Table A VII.2.
7. See footnote 5 in Table A VII.1.
8. See footnote 8 in Table A VII.2.
9. See footnote 3 in Table A VII.2.
10. See footnote 13 in Table A VII.2.
11. See footnote 12 in Table A VII.2.
12. See footnote 4 in Table A VII.2.
    See also footnote 1 in Table A VII.1.
13. See footnote 15 in Table A VII.2.
14. Includes the Protectorate of South Arabia.

Notes

1. For proposed definitions which differ from the conventional ones discussed in this section, see Chapter 4, pp. 96–106.

2. British, American, Canadian, Irish, Australian, and the people of New Zealand; in addition to Welshmen and Scotsmen, some of whom think of themselves at once as members of two peoples, the British and their own.

3. Spain, Argentina, Chile, Uruguay, Paraguay, Bolivia, Peru, Ecuador, Colombia, Venezuela, Panama, Costa Rica, San Salvador, Honduras, Nicaragua, Guatemala, Mexico, Cuba, the Dominican Republic, and Puerto Rico.

4. Germans, Swiss, Austrians, and Luxemburgers; and there is the problem of the Alsatians.

5. Some Arab speakers throughout this region consider themselves Arabs, but Egyptians speak Arabic and yet may think themselves Egyptian. Cf. H. A. R. Gibb, *The Arabs* (Oxford, Clarendon Press, 1941), p. 18.

6. Charles Maurras, *Mes idées politiques,* 1937, p. 252; cited in Alfred Cobban, *National Self-Determination* (London, Oxford University Press, 1945), p. 48.

7. John Stuart Mill, *Representative Government,* 1861, reprinted in part in Alfred Zimmern, *Modern Political Doctrines* (London, Oxford University Press, 1939), p. 206.

8. Ernest Renan, *What Is a Nation?,* 1862, in Zimmern, *op. cit.,* p. 203.

9. H. M. Chadwick, *The Nationalities of Europe* (Cambridge, Cambridge University Press, 1945), p. 1.

10. Otto Bauer, *Die Nationalitätenfrage und die Sozialdemokratie* (2nd Ed., Vienna, Brand, 1924), p. 135.

11. *Op. cit.,* pp. 124–125.

12. *Op. cit.,* pp. 114–115.

13. The same is true for the attempt of the philologist Karl Vossler to define "national character" as "the type of mind predominating in that particular language community." There is no necessity for the same "type of mind" to "predominate" among the "language community" of Englishmen and Irishmen; and the real process of community formation remains unexplained. Cf. *The Spirit of Language in Civilization* (London, Kegan Paul, 1932), p. 115.

14. St. Augustine, *The City of God,* Book 19, Chap. 21 and 24, in W. J. Oates, Ed., *Basic Writings of St. Augustine* (New York, Random House, 1948), pp. 497, 503.

15. ". . . which arise usually from the possession of a common religion . . . [To] demand a distinct and independent state, the national state . . . in my view . . . is not an essential element in the notion of nationality." K. C. Wheare, *Federal Government* (New York, Oxford University Press, 1947), p. 38, note 3. (Italics added.)

16. E. Burke, "Speech on the State of Representation of the Commons in Parliament" (1782), *Works* (World's Classics Ed., London, Oxford University Press, 1925–1930, Vol. III, p. 355). (Italics added.)

17. E. Burke, "An Appeal from the New to the Old Whigs" (1791), *Works* (Bohn Ed.), Vol. III, pp. 82–85. (Italics added.)

18. E. Burke, "Reflections on the Revolution in France" (1790), *Works* (World's Classics Ed.), Vol. IV, pp. 95, 106.

19. Lord Beaconsfield, *The Spirit of Whiggism,* 1836; in his *Whigs and Whiggism,* 1913, p. 343; cited in Frederick Hertz, *Nationality in History and Politics* (New York, Oxford University Press, 1944), p. 29. In a similar mood, defenders of established institutions have often insisted on seeing only "aliens" in those of their countrymen who challenged the existing order.

20. Sir Ernest Barker, *National Character and the Factors in its Formation* (New York and London, Harper, 1927), p. 17. (Italics mine.)

21. Bauer, *op. cit.* (Note 10), pp. 110–111.

22. J. V. Stalin, *Marxism and the National Question* (New York, International Publishers, 1942), pp. 16–17; with reference to J. Strasser, *Der Arbeiter und die Nation* (The Worker and the Nation) (Reichenberg, Runge, 1912), p. 33.

23. Graham Wallas, *Human Nature in Politics* (New York, Knopf, 1921), pp. 286–287. (Italics added.)

24. Quincy Wright, *A Study of War* (Chicago, University of Chicago Press, 1942), Vol. II, p. 999. Cf. also: ". . . the nation may be defined as a perfect community . . . including the entire population of an area. A perfect community is objectively one which manifests cultural uniformity, spiritual union, institutional unity, and material unification in the highest possible degree, and subjectively one with which the members consciously identify themselves. These . . . characteristics . . . are to some extent inconsistent with one another. . . . Clearly any realizable society must compromise among these desiderata." *Op. cit.,* p. 992.

25. C. Hayes, *The Historical Evolution of Modern Nationalism* (New York, R. Smith, 1931), pp. 57–68, 293–311; F. L. Schuman, *International Politics* (3rd Ed., New York, McGraw-Hill, 1941), pp. 300–365.

26. Even the extent of such success or failure might be hard to measure. There is some evidence that most men may be less moved by political symbols and more concerned with their immediate and personal affairs, no matter how often or how zealously the larger symbols are presented to them.

According to two recent investigators of the morale of German soldiers in World War II, "most men are members of the larger society by virtue of identifications which are mediated through the human beings with whom they are in personal relationships. Many are bound into the larger society only by primary group identifications. Only a small proportion possessing special training or rather particular kinds of personalities are capable of giving a preponderant share of their attention and concern to the symbols of the larger world." (E. A. Shils and Morris Janowitz, "Cohesion and Disintegration in the Wehrmacht in World War II," *Public Opinion Quarterly,* Vol. XII, 1948, p. 315.)

The most effective technique of durable mass indoctrination, according to these investigators, consists, then, in stiffening each small primary group of non-political persons by the addition of a "hard core" of one or more politically interested opinion leaders with such personal qualities and behavior that they acquire the personal trust and loyalty of others and thus become key members in each group (*op. cit.*, pp. 286–287).

27. "Nations are neither linguistic nor political nor biological, but spiritual ('seelische') unities." Quoted in R. M. MacIver, *The Modern State* (London, Oxford University Press, 1932), p. 123. For specific formulations, see Oswald Spengler, *Gedanken* (Munich, C. H. Beck, 1941), pp. 6, 58–59.

28. According to Alfred Cobban, for Lamprecht ". . . the nation is . . . a *Soziale Psyche*, created by habit and economic forces, 'a state and a national society which are no longer limited to the soil which . . . principally supports them today . . . [and] which aim to spread themselves through the entire world.'" A. Cobban, *National Self-Determination* (London, Oxford University Press, 1945), pp. 52–53, with reference to a quotation from Lamprecht in C. Andler, *Le pangermanisme philosophique, 1800–1914* (Paris, L. Conard, 1917), p. 139. Cf. Lamprecht, *Moderne Geschichtswissenschaft* (Freiburg, 1905), *passim.* Cf. also Lamprecht's chapter "Geschichte der Formen des Nationalbewusstseins," in his *Deutsche Geschichte* (6th Ed., Berlin, Weidmann, 1920), Vol. I, pp. 3–56.

29. F. Meinecke, *Weltbuergertum und Nationalstaat* (Leipzig, Koehler & Amelang, 1908), p. 2.

30. Don Luigi Sturzo, *Nationalism and Internationalism* (New York, Roy, 1946), pp. 13, 16–17; cf. also p. 24 and reference to Sturzo, *Inner Laws of Society* (New York, Kennedy, 1944). Cf. also G. B. O'Toole, *Race: Nation: Person* (New York, Barnes & Noble, 1944); and for the distinction between "individuality" and "personality," Jacques Maritain, *The Person and the Common Good* (New York, Scribners, 1947), pp. 21–79.

A highly simplified version of this philosophy has been applied to nationalistic politics by the President of Argentina, Juan D. Perón: "Each country has inborn manners, its own principles . . . a destiny providentially shaped that constitutes their inherent personality. The maintenance of this national personality, of this national individuality demands the subordination of the individual anxieties to, and veneration for, that *something* that constitutes the real tutelar genius of each people." "*Perón's Story;* Argentina Aims at New Deal in Realm of Culture," North American Newspaper Alliance, Inc., Release of June 11, 1948, p. 2, multigraphed. It should be noted that President Perón chose to identify "national individuality" and "national personality," as if they were one and the same. In M. Maritain's thinking, on the contrary, one of the most crucial distinctions is between "individuality" (which implies exclusiveness) and "personality" (which implies communication).

31. E.g., Meinecke, *op. cit.* (Note 29), p. 13; Cobban, *op. cit.* (Note 28), Charles E. Merriam, *Systematic Politics* (Chicago, University of Chicago Press, 1945), p. 263; Caroline Ware, "Ethnic Communities," *Encyclopaedia of the Social Sciences* (New York, 1937), Vol. 5, p. 607; George P. Murdock, "Ethnocentrism," *op. cit.*, p. 613; Karl Mannheim, *Freedom, Power and Democratic Planning* (New York, Oxford University Press, 1950), p. 56.

32. Reprinted from Ralph Linton, Ed., *The Science of Man in the World Crisis* (copyright 1945, by Columbia University Press), pp. 84–86.

33. Cf. Ruth Benedict, *Patterns of Culture* (New York, Pelican Mentor Books, 1947), pp. 1–51, 206–257.

34. R. M. MacIver, *The Modern State* (London, Oxford University Press, 1932), pp. 121–124.

35. N. Syrkin, "National Independence and International Unity" (1917), in *Essays on Socialist Zionism* (New York, Young Poale Zion Alliance of America, 1935), pp. 44–45.

36. H. Treitschke, *Zehn Jahre deutscher Kämpfe* (3rd Ed., Berlin, 1897, Vol. I), pp. 326 ff., translated in H. W. C. Davis, *Political Thought of H. von Treitschke* (London, Constable, 1914), pp. 110 ff.; cited in Hans Kohn, *The Idea of Nationalism* (New York, Macmillan, 1944), p. 583, note 13. (Italics mine.)

On Treitschke's anti-Semitism, see the excellent study in Hans Kohn, *Prophets and Peoples* (New York, Macmillan, 1946), particularly pp. 123–124.

37. "A true nationality is animated by consciousness of . . . kind. . . . The essence of nationality is we-feeling." Henry Pratt Fairchild, "Nationality," *Dictionary of Sociology* (New York, Philosophical Library, 1944), p. 201. By way of examples, Professor Fairchild describes the scattered members of the Jewish people as a nationality, because of their "desire to share a common life"; Switzerland he considers "a well-knit political unit [including] several nationalities"; and Canada and the United States he sees as mere political divisions of "what is practically a single nationality" (*ibid.*). Cf. also the articles on "People," p. 217, and "Ethnos," p. 109, *op. cit.*

Perhaps from a similar point of view, "British patriotism" has recently been described as the result of a "collective consciousness" which was "gradually evolved" by "the English, the Scots, and the Welsh." Sir Harold Butler, "Nationalism and the Western Tradition," in *The Western Tradition* (London, Vox Mundi, 1949), pp. 73–74. Such collective consciousness need not be linguistic: "When Europeans go to Asia or America they often feel themselves closer to other Europeans of different nationalities and languages than they do to Asiatics or Americans, who speak the same language" (*op. cit.*, p. 75).

38. "Thus the French nationality was born in 1789. A French nation, the population of the French kingdom, existed before. . . . But only the newly aroused consciousness and will made these elements active and effective. . . . Nationalities are created out of ethnographic and political elements when nationalism breathes life into the form built by preceding centuries." Hans Kohn, *The Idea of Nationalism* (New York, Macmillan, 1944), pp. 16–17.

Professor Kohn cites similar definitions of nationality in terms of "will" from Karl Hilty (1875), Henry Hauser (1916), and Robert Michels (1917). Related definitions in terms of "consciousness" or "sentiment" are cited from Pasquale Stanislao Mancini (1851), Max Weber (1913), A. J. Toynbee (1915), and Israel Zangwill (1917). Similar views have been expressed by W. Sulzbach, *National Consciousness* (Washington, D. C., American Council on Public Affairs, 1943), p. 66; Sir Alfred Zimmern, *Nationality and Government* (London, 1919), p. 55, cited in Sulzbach, *op. cit.*, p. 65; H. A. R. Gibb, *The Arabs* (Oxford, Clarendon Press, 1941), p. 28; and by R. M. MacIver, *op. cit.* (Note 34), pp. 121–124, and *The Web of Government* (New York, 1947), p. 159.

To some Pan-German writers in the pre-Hitler period it seemed that it might be sufficient for this "will" to be limited to the deliberate use of a language, and nationality would then follow as an automatic consequence: "The collective will to the common standard German written language [is] . . . the test of membership in the German people." H. Grothe, ed., *Grothe's kleines Handwoerterbuch des Grenz-und Auslandsdeutschtums* (Berlin, Oldenbourg, 1932), p. 97, Article, "Deutscher," with ref. to [K. C. v.] Loesch.

On the other hand, the whole concept of nationalism as making nations, or as breathing life into previously inert forms, has been sharply attacked by Don Sturzo: "The addition of 'ism' to 'national' gives evidence of some excess or deformation with reference to the original conception . . . Thanks to nationalism, the nation's character as the community of a people organized on the basis of its tradition . . . and culture, has come to be perverted; for nationalism is interpreted as being the principal efficient and final cause of the community." *Nationalism and Internationalism* (New York, Roy, 1944), p. 4.

39. *Nationalism, A Report*, etc. (London, Oxford University Press, 1939), p. xx.

40. Frederick Hertz, *Nationality in History and Politics* (New York, Oxford University Press, Inc., 1944), pp. 12–13. (Italics added.)

41. Cf. "Consciousness as such cannot be defined," H. P. Fairchild, *Dictionary of Sociology* (New York, Philosophical Library, 1944), pp. 61–62.

42. Cf. C. Kluckhohn and H. A. Murray, *Personality in Nature, Society and Culture* (New York, Knopf, 1949), pp. 7–11; R. Mueller-Freienfels, *History of Psychology* (New Haven, Yale University Press, 1935); etc.

43. Hertz, *op. cit.* (Note 40), pp. 13–14. (Italics added.)

44. Cf. Abraham Kardiner, "Basic Personality Structure," in Linton, *op. cit.* (Note 32), pp. 110–121. Cf. also A. Kardiner and L. Ovesey, *The Mark of Oppression: A Psychological Study of the American Negro* (New York, Norton, 1951).

45. Bertram Schaffner, *Father Land: A Study of Authoritarianism in the German Family* (New York, Columbia University Press, 1948); Ruth Benedict, *The Chrysanthemum and the Sword* (Boston, Houghton Mifflin, 1946); E. H. Erikson, "Hitler's Imagery and German Youth," in C. Kluckhohn and H. A. Murray, *Personality in Nature, Society and Culture* (New York, Knopf, 1949), pp. 485–510; and some of the work carried on by Margaret Mead at the American Museum of Natural History, New York. Cf. M. Mead, "People and Projects: Two Projects," *Human Organisation*, Vol. 8, No. 1, Winter 1949, pp. 28–30; Ruth Benedict, "The Study of Cultural Patterns in European Nations," *Transactions of the New York Academy of Sciences*, Ser. II, Vol. 8, No. 8, June 1946, pp. 274–279; "Child Rearing in Certain European Countries," *The American Journal of Orthopsychiatry*, Vol. 19, No. 2, April 1949, pp. 342–350. Cf. also Angus Campbell, *A Survey Research Approach to National Character* (Institute of Social Research, University of Michigan, Ann Arbor, 1949, multigraphed).

46. *Op. cit.* (Note 40), pp. 13–24. This definition seems to suggest that nations in the modern sense can only arise in those societies and cultures in which the concept of *interest* is meaningful. Generally, the notion of "interest"—whether it be economic interest, political interest, or interest paid on a sum of money—implies a situation in which individuals and groups are socially *mobile,* and in competition with each other, while depending for their external chances and fortunes on outside factors which can be manipulated at least in part by themselves. Under such conditions, every individual as well as each group, or organization, such as a corporation or a government, has a set of chances for achieving success in moving in the "desirable" social direction. His "interest" then consists in his chances of "getting ahead" of his fellows, or at least of preventing them from getting ahead of himself; it is the probability of his future economic or social advancement relative to his competitors, and it can often be measured by the amount of some scarce factor of production or power which he can control and which he can

deny to others. The individual can then pursue this "interest" at the expense of other members of a group, or jointly with these others, and he may subordinate some of his own "interests" to theirs or to those of the group; and thus he may possibly subordinate them to what may appear to him as the "interests" of the nation. Whether and to what extent such "national interests" are real has been hotly debated; and it may be well to remember how very limited in historic time have been the conditions under which problems of "interest" could be at all significant.

More generally put, "interest" expresses the probability that a player has to win in a competitive game; it represents his position in the game; and it depends therefore first of all on the question whether such a game has been set up at all, and to what extent he has come to participate in it. Cf. J. von Neumann and O. Morgenstern, *The Theory of Games and Economic Behavior* (Princeton, Princeton University Press, 1944); Benjamin Nelson, *The Idea of Usury* (Princeton, Princeton University Press, 1951); Charles A. Beard, *The Idea of the National Interest* (New York, Macmillan, 1934), esp. pp. 22–25; Werner Sulzbach, *Nationales Gemeinschaftsgefuehl und wirtschaftliches Interesse* (Leipzig, Hirschfeld, 1929); and "Der wirtschaftliche Begriff des 'Auslands,'" *Weltwirtschaftliches Archiv*, Jena, Vol. 32 (1930, II), pp. 55–80; Hermann Bente, "Die marktwirtschaftliche Bedentung der Kapitalanlage im Auslande," *op. cit.*, pp. 1–54.

I am indebted to Professor Hans Kohn for some helpful comments in putting this matter in historical perspective (oral communication, Cambridge, Mass., August 1951).

A more general concept of interest could be developed, and perhaps applied to the interests of nations, by assuming a "game" which is not competitive between human beings, but which is "played" against the limitations of nature which express themselves as poverty, sickness, and preventable death. It would then appear to the "interest" of individuals and nations to improve their chance of economic growth and physical survival for themselves, their descendants, and mankind. This would be a concept of "interest" in which the "interests" of individuals and groups might often be found to coincide—but it would be useless for defining nationalism, and it would differ considerably from the notions of "interest" which appear most widely held at present.

To unite the notion of the competitive "interest" of men in their struggle against men with that of the "interest" of men in their struggle against nature, it has been suggested that "nature" could be treated as a "fictitious player" in a competitive game in terms of von Neumann's and Morgenstern's theory, so that competition among human players could be assumed to continue but compromises at the expense of "nature" would become possible: if competing men impoverish each other, "nature" would be said to win; and if, on the contrary, all competitions follow strategies that leave them better off, "nature" would be said to lose. Cf. von Neumann and Morgenstern, *op. cit.*, pp. 505–510, 513, 540. This approach leaves unresolved the question whether "nature" can be reduced to the role of a fictitious player in a game limited by the restrictive assumptions of the games theory as it has been developed thus far by its authors. Cf. K. W. Deutsch, "Applications of Games Theory to International Politics: Some Opportunities and Limitations" (Princeton University, Center for International Studies, 1952, multigraphed), pp. 8–9.

47. E. H. Carr, *Nationalism and After* (New York, Macmillan, 1945, by permission of The Macmillan Company), p. 40. (Italics mine.) For a similar view of nationalism, with a hopeful reference to its eventual better understanding through the future progress of social psychology, see Crane Brinton, *Ideas and Men: The Story of Western Thought* (New York, Prentice-Hall, 1950), pp. 500–502, and *From Many One: The Process of Political Integration: The Problem of World Government* (Cambridge, Harvard University Press, 1948), pp. 73–78.

CHAPTER 2

1. Kluckhohn and Kelly, *op. cit.*, in R. Linton, *op. cit.* (Note 32, Chap. 1), p. 79.

2. Cf. B. M. Vlekke, *Evolution of the Dutch Nation* (New York, Roy, 1945), pp. 38–41.

3. A. Schulte, *Geschichte des mittelalterlichen Handels und Verkehrs zwischen Westdeutschland und Italien* (Leipzig, Duncker & Humblot, 1900, Vol. I, pp. 1–38, 169–230; cf. also G. Guggenbuehl, *Geschichte der Schweizerischen Eidgenossenschaft* (Zurich, Rentsch Verlag, 1947), Vol. I, pp. 80–92; Hans Nabholz *et al., Geschichte der Schweiz* (Zurich, Schulthess, 1932), pp. 104–125.

4. Karen Larsen, *A History of Norway* (Princeton, Princeton University Press, 1948), pp. 20–21, 24–25.

5. Preston E. James, *A Geography of Man* (Boston, Ginn, 1949), p. 42.

6. Cf. J. Nehru, *The Discovery of India* (New York, John Day, 1946), pp. 74–77, 242–243, 248–252.

7. Cf. G. Myrdal, *An American Dilemma: The Negro Problem and Modern Democracy* (New York, Harper, 1944), pp. 5–6, 13, 667–705, 812–815. The main Negro organizations have consistently accepted and expressed loyalty to the United States. *Op. cit.*, pp. 819–820, 830–842. For an emphasis on the desire of Negroes to share rather than change existing institutions in the United States, see Wilson Record, *The Negro and the Communist Party* (Chapel Hill, University of North Carolina Press, 1951), p. 118.

8. See S. F. Bloom, *The World of Nations* (New York, Columbia University Press, 1941), p. 59, and generally, pp. 57–73, with references.

9. E.g., "In the middle of the eighteenth century, perhaps less than three hundred families were seated on plantations in Tidewater Virginia. . . . This group formed a parochial aristocracy whose ranks were apparently even more difficult to enter than those of the English gentry. For over half a century 'gentlemen of the best families and fortunes' had been consciously coalescing into an exclusive ruling class based principally upon the possession of great tracts of land. In part they achieved their desire to perpetuate their families and their power by legal enactments requiring their estates to descend to their eldest sons, who in turn were forbidden to alienate any inherited lands. These were the famous laws of *primogeniture* and *entail* passed in 1705. The ranks of the gentry were further consolidated by carefully planned intermarriages among the great families, since in good eighteenth century fashion family plans always took precedence over dictates of the heart. The fruits of these arrangements forcibly struck all visitors:

'an aristocratic spirit and principle is very prevalent in the laws, policy and manners of this Colony,' observed Josiah Quincy, Jr., of Boston, while on a tour of the seaboard in 1773.

"Perennially writers emphasize the close resemblance of Tidewater Virginia to the country life of old England. . . . Actually these men were more American than they knew. In 1765 Virginians sincerely protested their loyalty to their king—*but it was a loyalty of their own defining.* Loyalty to their own class and tradition—to Virginia, as they would have put it—was their transcending loyalty. As early as 1759 an English parson named Andrew Burnaby had shrewdly taken the measure of the rulers of the Old Dominion. He noted that the public character of the Virginians corresponded with their private one: 'they are haughty and jealous of their liberties, impatient of restraint, and can scarcely bear the thought of being controlled by a superior power. *Many of them consider the colonies as independent states, unconnected with Great Britain,* otherwise than by having the same common king, and being bound to her with natural affection.' This is precisely the position taken by Thomas Jefferson in 1774 in his famous *Summary View.* . . . Here we have a native growth; there is nothing English in it." Carl Bridenbaugh, *Seat of Empire: The Political Role of Eighteenth-Century Williamsburg* (Williamsburg, Va., Colonial Williamsburg Inc., 1950), pp. 7, 9–10.

10. This statement, as well as the diagram in Fig. 1, was adapted by Dr. Lamb for the purpose of this chapter, and they are printed here with his permission. For a further discussion of this approach, see Robert K. Lamb, "The Entrepreneur and the Community" in William Miller, ed., *Men in Business* (Cambridge, Harvard University Press, 1952); and for a popular account, R. K. Lamb, "Suggestions for a Study of Your Hometown," *Human Organization,* Vol. 11, No. 2 (Summer 1952), pp. 29–32.

11. See, e.g., Henry Hamilton Fyfe, *The Illusion of National Character* (London, Watts & Co., 1940); Guy J. Pauker, "The Study of National Character Away from That Nation's Territory," *Studies in International Affairs,* Vol. 1, No. 1, June 1951 (Harvard University), pp. 81–103.

12. For a survey, see Margaret Mead, "The Study of National Character," in D. Lerner and H. D. Lasswell, eds., *The Policy Sciences: Recent Developments in Scope and Method* (Stanford, Stanford University Press, 1951), pp. 70–85, with references.

13. Howard Odum, *The Way of the South: Toward the Regional Balance of America* (New York, Macmillan, 1947), pp. 55–87; cf. also *Understanding Society: The Principles of Dynamic Sociology* (New York, Macmillan, 1947), *passim;* and *Southern Regions of the United States* (Chapel Hill, University of North Carolina Press, 1936), pp. 2, 87–89, 245–290, 535.

14. A. J. Toynbee, *A Study of History,* 2nd Ed. (London, Oxford University Press, 1935), Vol. I, pp. 22–46, 147–181.

15. Leo Frobenius, *Kulturgeschichte Afrikas* (Zurich, Phaidon-Verlag, 1933), pp. 29, 163, 166; Oswald Spengler, *The Decline of the West* (New York, Knopf, 1939), *passim.*

16. K. C. v. Loesch, "Eingedeutschte, Entdeutschte und Renegaten," in K. C. v. Loesch, Ed., *Volk unter Voelkern* (Breslau, Hirt, 1925), pp. 226–227; E. Rosenstock-Huessy, *Out of Revolution: Autobiography of Western Man* (New York, Morrow, 1938), pp. 167–216, 457, 473–479.

Similarly, the Hussite revolution of the fifteenth century has often been considered a crucial stage in the emergence of Czech nationalism and national character, or even as the process by which the Czech people were transformed into a nation; thus recently again by Eugen Lemberg, *Geschichte des Nationalismus in Europa* (Stuttgart, Curt E. Schwab, 1950), pp. 135–143.

Such critical periods in the development of particular nations have sometimes been interpreted as periods of voluntary decision, or, on the contrary, as periods of objective events changing the memories, will, and character of the populations influenced by them. Cf. the different views surveyed by J. Droz, "Concept français et concept allemand de l'idée de nationalité," in *Europa und der Nationalismus: Bericht über das III. internationale Historiker-Treffen in Speyer, 17. bis 20. Oktober 1949* (Baden Baden, Verlag für Kunst und Wissenschaft, 1950), pp. 111–127, and discussion, pp. 127–133.

17. C. Englert-Faye, *Vom Mythus zur Idee der Schweiz* (Zurich, Atlantic, 1940), pp. 235–272, 310–338, 485–512.

18. G. J. Renier, *The Dutch Nation: A Historical Study* (London, Allen & Unwin, 1944), pp. 14–16; *The Criterion of Dutch Nationhood* (London, Allen & Unwin, 1946), pp. 18–20.

19. Vlekke, *op. cit.* (Note 2, Chap. 2), pp. 1–70, esp. 68–70.

20. Preston E. James, *Latin America* (New York, Odyssey Press, 1942), pp. 4–8, with map on end paper; cf. also population cluster map of Japan in John F. Embree, *The Japanese Nation* (New York, Farrar and Rinehart, 1945), p. 48. Crude dot maps showing the distribution of the European population at various times are given in J. Haliczer, "The Population of Europe 1720, 1820, 1930," *Geography,* Vol. 19, No. 106, December 1934, pp. 261–273. An instructive map correlating "Transportation and the Urban Pattern" (i.e., urban population figures) in the United States for 1930 is given in the publication of the National Resources Committee, *Our Cities: Their Role in the National Economy* (Washington, D. C., U. S. Government Printing Office, June 1937), Fig. 44, opp. p. 38.

21. Derwent Whittlesey, *The Earth and the State* (New York, Holt, 1939), p. 10: "The term 'Ecumene' is Mark Jefferson's who defines it as the land within ten miles of a railroad; . . . To define the ecumene as it exists in all parts of the earth and in the long view of human history, every type of transportation route in being should be included. The zones in effective contact with the routes, be they wide or narrow, in conjunction with the areas of densest population, approximate the ecumene." *Op. cit.,* p. 21, note 1.

22. Cf. K. W. Deutsch, "Problems of Justice in International Territorial Disputes," in *Approaches to Group Understanding* (New York, Harper & Brothers, 1947, p. 251.

23. Thus in the case of Canada, according to a recent writer, "the St. Lawrence and its western extensions directed the course of Canadian national development and international competition. In a land where roads were useless for through traffic and in an age when railways were unknown, all plans for major travel hinged on the available waterways. The fur trade, which, with its subsidiary supply trades, was in early years the sole commercial pursuit of any importance, depended for its very existence on inland waterways from the Gulf of St. Lawrence to the Pacific coast. Goods imported from England had to be carried beyond Montreal, the furthest post accessible to ocean-going vessels, all the way to the

posts of the prairies; bringing back a return cargo of packs of furs to be shipped for sale in the English market. The system had to be efficient . . . because the Canadian traders were in active competition with rival concerns operating from New York State and Hudson Bay. For the Canadian traders the main route to the West began with the Ottawa River to Georgian Bay, and on through Lake Superior to Grand Portage on the far shore. There the cargoes of the large or "master" canoes were handed over to the crews of the small northern canoes, to be carried over river, lake, and portage to posts spread fan-wise over the West. . . . When trade rivalry gave way to war *in 1775 and 1812 the outline of a Canada, in terms of waterways and commerce, had already begun to appear:* so much so that the Montreal group of traders, in spite of discontent with the whole political regime in Canada, drew back after their first spontaneous gestures of sympathy with the revolutionaries, unwilling to break the commercial structure that stretched from London to the Rocky Mountains." G. P. de T. Glazebrook, "Nationalism and Internationalism on Canadian Waterways," in *Essays in Transportation,* H. A. Innis, ed. (Toronto, University of Toronto Press, 1941), p. 2–3. (Italics added.)

24. "No accurate world-map superimposing transportation zones on population density has been constructed. Figure 1 is a crude version of it." Whittlesey, *op. cit.* (Note 18, Chap. 2), p. 21, note 1. Transportation between particular areas may, of course, drop off sharply for social or political reasons, despite unchanged geographical and technological conditions. This happened in the shifts of trade routes during the Mohammedan, and later the Mongolian, Conquests; still later in the closing of Japan to foreign commerce in the Tokugawa period; and it might happen in the years to come in the "cold war" which might destroy the world ecumene for some time, much as the ecumene of the Mediterranean was destroyed for a time by the split between Moslems and Christians. Any major shift of this nature might in turn promote some shifts in the areas of greatest density of population.

25. Leonard Bloomfield, *Language* (New York, Holt, 1933), p. 52.

26. H. Paul, *Principles of the History of Language* (New York, 1889), pp. 30–31, 34–35; Gustav Grober, *Grundriss der romanischen Philologie* (Strassburg, 1904–1906), pp. 536–541; G. G. Kloeke, *De Hollandsche Expansie in de 16de en 17de eeuw en haar weerspiegeling in de hedendagsche Nederlandsche dialecten* (The Hague, 1927), pp. 38–39; and "Dutch Language," in *Encyclopaedia Britannica,* 14th Ed., 1937, Vol. 7, p. 771; J. Vendryes, *Language: A Linguistic Introduction to History* (New York, 1925), p. 265.

27. Cf. Percy M. Roxby, "China as an Entity," *Geography,* March 1934, pp. 1–20.

28. Stanley Rundle, *Language as a Social and Political Factor in Europe* (London, Faber and Faber, 1946), pp. 42–44, with map and table.

29. Cf. E. H. Chamberlin, *The Theory of Monopolistic Competition,* 3rd Ed. (Cambridge, Harvard University Press, 1938), p. 10.

30. Joan Robinson, *The Economics of Imperfect Competition* (London, Macmillan, 1936), p. 17. Miss Robinson's definition goes farther, in requiring the commodity to be "consumable." *Ibid.*

31. Cf. Karl Polanyi, *The Great Transformation* (New York, Farrar, 1944), *passim;* Sanford A. Mosk, "Pathology of Democracy in Latin America: An Econ-

omist's Point of View," *The American Political Science Review*, Vol. 44, No. 1, March 1950, pp. 129–142.

32. Cf. Bertil Ohlin, *Interregional and International Trade* (Cambridge, Harvard University Press, 1933), *passim;* Jacob Viner, *The Customs Union Issue* (New York, Carnegie, 1950), pp. 43–55.

33. Robinson, *op. cit.* (Note 26, Chap. 2), pp. 179–180, 185–186.

34. Cf. G. P. Murdock, "Ethnocentrism," *Encyclopaedia of the Social Sciences* (New York, 1937), Vol. 5, p. 613.

35. Robinson, *op. cit.* (Note. 26, Chap. 2), p. 187.

36. Cf. Seymour Harris, Ed., *Economic Problems of Latin America* (New York, McGraw-Hill, 1944), pp. 7–11, 104–105.

37. F. W. Taussig, *Principles of Economics* (New York, Macmillan, 1912), p. 223.

38. C. McWilliams, *Factories in the Field* (Boston, Little, Brown, 1939), p. 118, and generally Chap. VIII, "Our Oriental Agriculture," pp. 103–133. For a study of discrimination in an urban setting, cf. K. M. Landis, *Segregation in Washington*, A Report of the National Committee on Segregation in the Nation's Capital, 1948.

39. This contradicts Professor Taussig's view that "ordinarily . . . there is . . . likely to be an increase in . . . supply" of the temporarily privileged factor. Taussig, *op. cit.* (Note 33, Chap. 2), pp. 223–224.

40. G. v. Haberler, *The Theory of International Trade* (New York, Macmillan, 1937), pp. 190–195.

41. Robinson, *op. cit.* (Note 26, Chap. 2), pp. 225, 302–304; K. W. Deutsch, "Some Economic Aspects of Nationalistic and Racial Pressure Groups," *Canadian Journal of Economics and Political Science* (February 1942), pp. 109–115; and "The Economic Factor in Intolerance," in *Approaches to National Unity*, Lyman Bryson, et al., eds. (New York, Harper, 1945), pp. 368–374, 381–384.

42. "Wealth" in this sense is not necessarily identical with "welfare." A poorer population might conceivably use its more meager resources more wisely, and arrives at a higher level of general satisfaction than might be found among their richer neighbors who might spend much of their time and treasure on competitive advertising, long journeys to work, smoke-producing chimney stacks, and expensive anti-smoke devices. In the words of one national income analyst: "The egg on the peasants' table will not have been subjected to grading, packing, refrigeration, etc., but when consumed is certainly no less gratifying than if these costs had been incurred." W. I. Abraham, "The Distribution of World Income," *The American Statistician*, April-May 1951. In contrast to "welfare," however, national income figures and other measures of wealth might indicate the extent of resources or incomes that *could* be allocated to various purposes, at least within limits, if the populations concerned so choose. High income figures per capita thus indicate a larger range of opportunities, including opportunities for more adequate income distribution or other welfare policies.

43. Cf. the well-known real income figures by Colin Clark, *The Conditions of Economic Progress* (London, Macmillan, 1940), pp. 39–42, 53–58; and the more recent United Nations Surveys of Nutrition, summarized in the *New York Times*, December 4, 1949, Sec. 2, p. 7, and of Per Capita Incomes, *New York Times*, November 30, 1950, p. 35:3, and December 4, 1950, p. 1:6, and Statistical Office

of the United Nations, *National and Per Capita Incomes of Seventy Countries in 1949* (St/Stat/Ser. E/1), New York, October 1950, with additional data in *United Nations Monthly Bulletin of Statistics*, Vol. 6, June 1952, pp. vii–xii.

CHAPTER 3

1. For a more extended discussion, cf. K. W. Deutsch, "The Crisis of Peace and Power in the Atom Age," in *Conflicts of Power in Modern Culture*, L. Bryson, et al., eds. (New York, Harper, 1947), pp. 608–611; and for a different view on this particular point, Franz Neumann, "Approaches to the Study of Political Power," *Political Science Quarterly*, Vol. 65, No. 2, June 1950, p. 161.

2. Cf. Dr. Warren Weaver's concluding paragraph in C. E. Shannon and W. Weaver, *The Mathematical Theory of Communication* (Urbana, University of Illinois Press, 1949). For a notion of "will," related to this approach, cf. K. W. Deutsch, "Higher Education and the Unity of Knowledge," in *Goals for American Education* (New York, Harper, 1950), pp. 123–126.

3. For the notion of the future as a "program," i.e., as a physical disposition of present elements, I am indebted to Professor P. W. Bridgman of Harvard University, and to Professor Giorgio de Santillana for the suggestion that this view "extends to the physical world, curiously enough, the idea of man's existence as a 'project' which goes perforce beyond his life-span."

4. George Orwell, *Nineteen Eighty-Four* (New York, Harcourt Brace, 1949), p. 270. Cf. also "Power is power over human beings. Over the body—but, above all, over the mind. Power over matter, external reality . . . is not important." *Op. cit.*, p. 267.

5. They express, in a phrase of Giorgio de Santillana's, "the newly discovered staleness and futility of mere power over matter, for which even a production engineer is competent enough. They express . . . the emptiness of power in terms of bigger and better, which has become now not an affirmation of decision or of personality, but a vacuous total social trend. That is for the men, who want more. . . ." Unpublished communication, Massachusetts Institute of Technology, June 1951.

6. Bertrand de Jouvenel, *On Power* (New York, Viking, 1949), p. 25.

7. Jacques Maritain, "The Concept of Sovereignty," *The American Political Science Review*, Vol. 44, No. 2, June 1950, pp. 343–357.

8. *Op. cit.*, p. 351.

9. As distinct from its legal and philosophical exaggerations, so effectively exposed by Jacques Maritain (*ibid.*). Professor Maritain, however, considers these exaggerations as unavoidably implied in the connotations given to the concept of sovereignty by the sixteenth-century jurists.

10. "The important element in . . . integrative behavior is that the person who acts in its spirit is not only unwilling to superimpose his own view and will upon the other fellow—the essence of the domineering attitude—but he is tolerant of disagreement . . . *in the expectation of enlarging his own personality by absorbing some features of a human being essentially different from himself. . . .* [The] democratic personality welcomes disagreement because it has the courage

to expose itself to change. . . . [Such] openness to change is only within reach of the person who really feels secure, and therefore is unafraid of losing either status or individuality by . . . [being] exposed to the . . . exchange of ideas." Karl Mannheim, *Freedom, Power and Democratic Planning* (New York, Oxford University Press, 1950), p. 201 (italics added); cf. also the whole passage, pp. 199–206, and references on p. 355 to psychological studies by H. H. Anderson, J. Piaget, Herbert Read, and D. W. Harding.

CHAPTER 4

1. In President James B. Conant's usage this might be a "conceptual scheme"; cf. *On Understanding Science* (New Haven, Yale University Press, 1947), *passim*.

2. By "reasoning" I mean any sequence of socially standardized and retraceable mental operations in which every step is clearly marked, and all steps are defined by fixed rules and follow upon each other according to such rules, so that anybody can repeat the whole sequence with identical results. This accurate repeatability is sometimes called the "cogency" of reason. Reasoning is a retraceable trail, like the pebbles in the story of Hansel and Gretel, or the thread of Ariadne. It consists of so marking every step in an argument that it can be retraced and checked for its formal accuracy in an impersonal manner.

Rational behavior in this formal sense need not lead to scientific truth or practical success. It is found in any culture where some kinds of mental behavior have become so highly standardized that they form a calculus, i.e., that they can be retraced impersonally. Science is a special kind of rational behavior which attempts to predict events in nature.

Some sociologists, like Karl Mannheim, use the word "rationality" in the sense of behavior adequate to reach a particular goal. This view of rationality involves difficulties, for it requires prophecy before the goal has been reached and hindsight afterwards.

Irrational behavior cannot be retraced in the manner described above, but it may prove successful, and it may be learned.

Cf., for a somewhat different approach, K. Mannheim, *Man and Society in the Age of Reconstruction* (New York, Harcourt, Brace & Co., 1949), pp. 52–60.

3. Cf. N. Wiener, *The Human Use of Human Beings* (Boston, Houghton Mifflin, 1950), pp. 77–84, 103–111; C. Kluckhohn and H. A. Murray, *Personality in Nature, Society and Culture* (New York, Knopf, 1948), pp. 7–32; D. O. Hebb, *The Organization of Behavior* (New York, Wiley, 1950), *passim;* Jacques Maritain, *The Person and the Common Good* (New York, Scribners, 1947), pp. 28–32.

4. Linton, Ralph, ed., *op. cit.* (Note 32, Chap. 1), p. 79.

5. See Linton, Ralph, ed., *loc. cit.;* Ruth Benedict, *Patterns of Culture* (New York, Mentor Books, 1948), pp. 19–22, 42–51, 206–257. Dr. Benedict stressed the configurational aspect of culture, but did not distinguish sharply between "culture" and "society," or between "community" and "society," as proposed here.

6. Kluckhohn and Kelly, *loc. cit.* (the passage is cited at greater length in Chapter 1, p. 10). In the words of L. K. Frank, "Culture approached operationally is the sum total of the way people pattern their functions and behavior into conduct and transmit those patterns to their children. Culture, then, is a

process, an activity, not an entity or a thing." Cited in C. Kluckhohn and H. A. Murray, *Personality in Nature, Society and Culture* (New York, Knopf, 1948), p. 115.

7. Unfortunately, major writers have differed widely in their choice of terms. The usage given in the text is perhaps closest to that of anthropologists like Clyde Kluckhohn and Margaret Mead. Some distinguished writers, on the other hand, have accepted almost exactly the opposite usage; starting perhaps from the sociologists' study of urban settlements which are often called "communities," they have used the term "community" for "the physical, spatial, and symbiotic aspects of human group life," i.e., for those aspects which have least to do with communication. There seems no way of settling the difference in usage; this writer reluctantly has made his choice, but he remains well aware of other men's right to their own terms, as well as of his tentative impression that both schools differ perhaps less in what they are saying than in the terms they use in saying it. Cf. on this subject the discussions in *The World Community*, Quincy Wright, ed. (Chicago, University of Chicago Press, 1948), p. 21, and generally, pp. 1–66, particularly the statements by Quincy Wright, Louis Wirth, and Margaret Mead.

8. Perhaps it would be possible to say that culture, like a flame or a traffic pattern, is both a process and an entity. It consists of a changing collection of events, distributed in a specific manner, determined by their own past states and in part by other things or events which function as their channels, as updrafts do in a flame, or streets and intersections in a traffic pattern. For a discussion of different elements of culture, see also Ralph Linton, *The Cultural Background of Personality* (New York, Appleton-Century, 1945), pp. 32–46. Cf. J. Ruesch and G. Bateson on "Structure and Process in Social Relations," *Psychiatry*, May 1949, pp. 120–121.

9. The complementarity of two parts of a physical or social system can be measured by the extent to which an operation performed on one of them is transmitted to the other, and by the range of different operations so transmitted. Tests for complementarity of parts of a channel of communication, or of a team of human beings, are discussed on pp. 107–115, below.

10. Louis Wirth, in Wright, *op. cit.* (Note 7, Chap. 4), pp. 11–17.

11. *Op. cit.*, pp. 16–17.

12. J. S. Huxley, *Man in the Modern World* (New York, Pelican-Mentor, 1947), "The Uniqueness of Man," pp. 1–33.

13. Edmund Burke, "Reflections on the Revolution in France" (1790), *Works* (World's Classics Ed.; full reference, Notes 16 and 18, Chap. 1), Vol. IV, p. 106.

14. Somewhat differently phrased, a communications *network* is "a system of physical objects interacting with each other in such a manner that a change in the state of some elements is followed by a determinate pattern of changes in other related elements, in such a manner that the changes remain more or less localized and independent of other changes in the system from other sources" (Walter Pitts); a communications *channel* is "a physical system within which a pattern of change can be transmitted so that the properties of that pattern (*or message*) are more or less isolated from other changes in the system" (Norbert Wiener). "A state *description* is a specification of which of its possible states each element of the network is in. A *message* is any change in the *state description* of a network or part of it" (Pitts); or again, somewhat differently stated, "A message is a reproducible pattern regularly followed by determinate processes de-

pending on that pattern" (Wiener). Oral Communications, Massachusetts Institute of Technology, Spring 1949.

15. For a discussion of this entire subject, see N. Wiener, *Cybernetics: Communication and Control in the Animal, the Machine and Society* (Cambridge, M.I.T. Technology Press and New York, Wiley, 1948), and *The Human Use of Human Beings* (Boston, Houghton Mifflin, 1950); C. Shannon and W. Weaver, *The Mathematical Theory of Communication* (Urbana, University of Illinois Press, 1949); K. W. Deutsch, "Some Notes on . . . Models in the Natural and Social Sciences," *Synthese*, Amsterdam-Bussum, Netherlands, 1948–1949, Vol. 7, No. 6-B, pp. 506–533.

16. General distinctions between society and community, without, however, the concept of information, were drawn by F. Toennies, Max Weber, O. Bauer, and others. A survey of such terms in current usage has been given in Quincy Wright, *A Study of War* (Chicago, University of Chicago Press, 1942), pp. 1433. According to S. F. Bloom, Marx considered that nations were societies, and that groups of Germans in Hungary or Poland should regard themselves as Hungarians or Poles. *The World of Nations* (New York, Columbia University Press, 1941), pp. 16–27, with references.

17. H. M. Chadwick, *The Nationalities of Europe* (Cambridge, Cambridge University Press, 1945), p. 1; see the discussion in our first chapter, p. 19.

18. Cf. Max Huber, "Swiss Nationality," in *Modern Political Doctrines*, Sir Alfred Zimmern, ed. (London, Oxford University Press, 1939), pp. 216–217.

19. Ernst Schuerch, *Sprachpolitische Erinnerungen* (Bern, Paul Haupt Verlag, 1943), pp. 36–37.

20. This fundamental connection between a people and a community of mutual understanding seems to be reflected in some languages in the etymology of the terms involved. According to Karl Lamprecht, "the word *Deutsch* is found already in the second half of the eighth century derived from the West-Aryan word root *diot*, 'people,' and its derivations *diutin*, 'to adapt to the people' (*volksgemaess machen*) and *githiuti*, 'intelligibility'; and this word *Deutsch* is developed in the meaning of 'intelligible to the people' and applied to the language" (Karl Lamprecht, *Deutsche Geschichte*, 6th Ed. (Berlin, Weidmann, 1920), Vol. I, pp. 18–19). This development occurred first in border areas, where Germanic speech appeared as something common to different Germanic tribes, and in contrast to the Romance dialects of their neighbors (*ibid.*, p. 18). Even in modern German the similarity between *Deutsch* and *deuten* (to point, to explain, to interpret), *deutlich* (clear, distinct), and *Deutung* (interpretation), seems suggestive. It seems to hint that there is an element of communication in the very concept of a people, and an element of social community in the very concepts of understanding and interpretation. For examples of extreme overstatements of this view by Richard Wagner and others see Louis L. Snyder, *German Nationalism: The Tragedy of a People* (Harrisburg, Pa., Stackpole, 1952), pp. 162–163, 171, with references.

21. Cf. J. K. Roberts and E. L. Gordy, "Development," in *Research in Industry, Its Organization and Management*, C. C. Furnas, ed. (New York, Van Nostrand, 1948, pp. 32–34.

22. Insufficient appreciation of this relationship often led to trouble. If attempts were made to suppress a nationality group, it would live on in the communicative characteristics of its individual members. If these individuals gained

recognition for their rights, as in the Minorities Treaties after World War I, they would tend to act again as groups. "It was individuals—nationals of a state who differed from the majority in 'race, language or religion'—who were guaranteed against discrimination in linguistic and cultural as well as in their religious and civil rights. But the rights of language, education and culture are really *group* rights, requiring social institutions for their implementation and realization. Such institutions became the bulwark of a minority in the struggle to preserve its nationality and culture. Yet the minority *as a group was legally non-existent,* and could therefore exercise no effective control over its cultural agencies. The state, required by the Minorities Treaties to provide adequate educational facilities for the children of minorities, retained full control of the public schools. And the state, as the embodiment of the national-cultural aspirations of the majority, would naturally favor the dominant culture. In east-central Europe, with its heritage of forced assimilation, of which we must never lose sight, such a relationship was bound to result in strife." Oscar I. Janowsky, *Nationalities and National Minorities* (New York, Macmillan, 1945), pp. 132–133, with reference to the opinion rendered by a majority of the Permanent Court of International Justice in the Albanian Minority Schools case, *Judgment, Orders and Advisory Opinions,* Series A-B, Fascicule No. 64.

23. "'Yes,' resumed the young stranger after a moment's interval. 'Two nations; between whom there is no intercourse and no sympathy; who are as ignorant of each other's habits, thoughts, and feelings, as if they were dwellers in different zones, or inhabitants of different planets; who are formed by a different breeding, are fed by a different food, are ordered by different manners, are not governed by the same laws.'

"'You speak of . . .' said Egremont, hesitatingly.

"'The rich and the poor.'"

Earl of Beaconsfield (Benjamin Disraeli), *Sybil, or Two Nations* (London, Longmans, Green and Co., 1913), pp. 76–77.

24. Erich Eyck, *Bismarck* (Zurich, Eugen Rentsch Verlag, 1943), Vol. II, p. 36 (the reference is to a speech of Bismarck's in the Prussian Chamber of Deputies in 1865, long before his well-known social insurance legislation of the 1880's).

25. V. I. Lenin, *Imperialism, The Highest State of Capitalism* (New York, International Publishers, 1939), New, Revised Translation, pp. 105–108.

While Lenin, writing in 1917, insisted in this passage that only a section of "the British proletariat" was merging with the middle class or accepting its leadership, he cited in this context two letters from Frederick Engels, written in 1858 and 1882, respectively, which spoke of "a bourgeois proletariat" and "the workers" as sharing the fruits of England's monopoly of the colonies, without distinction of sections (*ibid.*). For the future, Lenin predicted ever-increasing rivalries among "a few imperialist powers" and concluded that "opportunism, therefore, cannot now triumph in the working class movement of any country for decades as it did in England in the second half of the nineteenth century" (*ibid.,* p. 108).

26. Otto Bauer, *Die Nationalitaetenfrage und die Sozialdemokratie,* 2nd Ed. (Vienna, Brand, 1923), p. 135. "Modern capitalism slowly demarcates more sharply the lower classes of the various nations from each other, for they, too, gain a share in national education, national cultural life, and the national standard language. . . . [The] socialist society . . . , through the differences in national

education, . . . will mark off the entire peoples so sharply from each other, as today only the educated strata of the different nations are separated from each other" (*ibid.*).

27. Alexander H. Leighton, *The Governing of Men: General Principles and Recommendations Based on Experience at a Japanese Relocation Camp* (Princeton, Princeton University Press, 1946), p. 258.

28. Arthur Young, *Travels During the Years 1787, 1788, and 1789* (London, 1792), pp. 146–147; cited in H. A. Innis, *Empire and Communication* (Oxford, Clarendon Press, 1950), p. 198.   The rapid spread of the Revolution through much of France suggests that by 1789 there may already have been more effective "circulation of intelligence" among the French people than Arthur Young surmised; but the principle of his test—which he had no means of carrying through with any thoroughness—seems to have been sound enough.

In contrast to this situation in France in the 1780's, a senior educational specialist of the United Nations gave this description of conditions preceding the partition of India in 1947: "The national movement . . . has been like a twin clock with springs that work in opposing directions.   As the Hindus were being wound up in one direction against the British, the Muslims wound themselves in the opposite direction. . . . [The] vast majority of Muslims in India and Pakistan are converts from Hinduism and racially in the same stock as the latter. . . . Despite the common racial origins . . . *intermarriage between the two communities was very rare.* . . . I am convinced that there have been more intermarriages between Hindus and Westerners on the one hand, and between Muslims and Westerners on the other, than between Hindus and Muslims. . . . Ordinarily every city has its separate Hindu and Muslim restaurants.   Water served to the passengers in the trains of the country is labeled 'Hindu water' and 'Muslim water.' . . . While Islam does not prohibit dining with other groups, the caste Hindu social attitude towards Muslims has, especially in recent years, developed a negative counterreaction. *Now, the Muslims frown upon dining with other groups.* . . . On the doctrinal side, the aggression and intolerance of the Muslim . . . has brought about counter-aggression in the Hindu. . . . [The] Muslim is socially tolerant but doctrinally intolerant, while the Hindu is doctrinally tolerant but socially intolerant.   These fundamental differences, among many others, have . . . continued to generate intense fear and hostility."   K. T. Behanan, "Cultural Diversity and World Peace," in *Current Trends in Social Psychology,* Wayne Dennis, ed. (Pittsburgh, University of Pittsburgh Press, 1948), pp. 50–70; citations from pp. 57, 61–63.   (Italics supplied.)   For similar data, see also Pars Ram and Gardner Murphy, "Recent Investigations of Hindu-Muslim Relations in India," *Human Organisation,* Vol. 1, No. 4, Spring 1952, pp. 13–16.

29. See citations and Notes 17 and 19, Chap. 1.

30. Herman Finer, in *Goals for American Education,* L. Bryson et al., eds. (New York, Harper, 1950), p. 108.

31. Benjamin Franklin, "Observations Concerning the Increase of Mankind" (1751), par. 23; in L. M. Hacker, *The Shaping of the American Tradition* (New York, Columbia University Press, 1947), p. 113.

32. Or a somewhat lesser improbability of such a rise.   In either case, the difference in vertical social mobility may become as important as the basic difference in the effectiveness of social communication.

33. For an elaboration of "social processes" and organizations promoting face-to-face contacts and possible substitutions between members of different social classes, see W. Lloyd Warner and Paul S. Lunt, *The Status System of a Modern Community* (New Haven, Yale University Press, 1942), pp. 5–66, and particularly p. 20ff. and the chart on p. 17. It is striking that the only organization on this chart which offers vertical contacts throughout the authors' six social classes is a nationalistic organization, The American Legion.

34. J. Ortega y Gasset, *Invertebrate Spain* (New York, Norton, 1937), p. 39.

35. Léon Blum, *For All Mankind* (New York, Viking Press, 1946), pp. 92–93.

36. On Karl Marx's conception of having the industrial workers assume the function of the "leading class" in a particular country, see S. F. Bloom, *The World of Nations* (New York, Columbia University Press, 1941), pp. 56–64. On the other hand, leading groups may also change in regional terms, as with the growth of Prussian influence in nineteenth-century Germany; or in terms of ethnic groups, as in the case of the growing political influence of Americans of Irish descent in certain parts of the United States since 1910, and perhaps particularly in nationalistic veterans' organizations.

37. Cf., e.g., Pitirim Sorokin, *Social Mobility* (New York, Harper, 1927).

38. See H. A. R. Gibb, *The Arabs, passim.*

39. On Japan's dynamic change beneath a conservative surface, see H. Norman, *The Emergence of Japan as a Modern State* (New York, Institute of Pacific Relations, 1940); Edwin O. Reischauer, *Japan, Past and Present* (New York, Knopf, 1946), pp. 116–134. For a convenient summary of Sir George Sansom's view, somewhat different in emphasis, see *The Western World and Japan: A Study in the Interaction of European and Asiatic Cultures* (New York, Knopf, 1949), pp. 334–339. Cf. also Nobutaka Ike, "Taxation and Landownership in the Westernization of Japan," *Journal of Economic History*, Vol. 7, No. 2, November 1947, pp. 160–182.

40. "Although patriotism and nationalism tend to coalesce, they are apparently of different origins. Both doubtless are natural and primary feelings; but the former seems to spring from love of home and the desire to preserve and protect it, while the latter is inspired by opposition or aversion to persons and things which are strange or unintelligible." H. M. Chadwick, *op. cit.* (Note 17, Chap. 4), p. 3.

Strictly speaking, patriotism is an effort or readiness to promote the interests of all those persons born or living within the same *patria*, i.e., country, whereas nationalism aims at promoting the interests of all those of the same *natio*, i.e., literally a group of common descent and upbringing, or rather, as we have seen, of common culture, that is to say, of complementary habits of communication. Patriotism appeals to all residents of a country, regardless of their ethnic background. Nationalism appeals to all members of an ethnic group, regardless of their country of residence. Patriotism, based on residence, often appears at an earlier stage of economic and political mobilization, such as was found in Europe during the later Mercantilist era, and up to the middle of the nineteenth century. As mobilization progresses and comes to involve larger masses of the population in more intense competition and greater political insecurity, patriotism is replaced by nationalism which is based on far more intimate and slow-changing personal characteristics and communications habits of each individual.

CHAPTER 5

1. If we test the concept of a "wood" by measuring the average distance of the trees from each other, or by the amount of shadow on the ground, or by the shriveling of lower branches, we are apt to get the same verdict, "This is a wood," from each of these three testing operations in the middle of the forest. However, as we come to the edge of the wood, each of these three tests may give a slightly different result, and in speaking of the edge of the woods we may have to specify whether we are interested in cool shadow or tall timber.

2. G. W. Allport and L. J. Postman, "The Basic Psychology of Rumor," *Transactions of the New York Academy of Science*, Ser. II, VIII, 1945, pp. 61–81, reprinted in *Readings in Social Psychology*, T. M. Newcomb and E. L. Hartley, eds. (New York, Holt, 1947), pp. 547–558, with graph of percentage of details lost at each stage, p. 551, Fig. 2. Cf. also F. C. Bartlett, "Social Factors in Recall," in Newcomb and Hartley, *op. cit.*, pp. 69–76, especially on "The Method of Serial Reproduction," *ibid.*, p. 72.

Anthropologists have used mainly tests for individuals rather than for group performance but have found group characteristics in their results. Experiences with the following eight tests are discussed by Laura Thompson and Alice Joseph in *The Hopi Way* (University of Chicago Press, Chicago, 1944), pp. 89–98, 100–101, 108–112: Grace Arthur Point Performance Test, Goodenough Draw-a-Man Test, Stewart's Emotional Response Test, Bavelas' Test of Moral Ideology, The Story of the Stolen Melon and the Axe, Free Drawings, Murray's Thematic Apperception Test (revised), Rorschach's Psychodiagnostic (Inkblot) Test. For particular tests, see also Mary G. Arthur, *A Point Scale of Performance Tests*, 2 vols. (New York, Commonwealth Fund, 2nd ed. 1943); A. Bavelas, "A Method of Investigating Individual and Group Ideology," *Sociometry*, vol. 5, 1942, pp. 371–377; B. Klopfer and D. M. Kelley, The *Rorschach Technique* (Yonkers, N. Y., World Book Co., 1942); H. A. Murray, *Thematic Apperception Test Manual* (Cambridge, Harvard University Press, 1943) and *The Use of the Thematic Apperception Technique in the Study of Personality-Culture Relations*, Thesis, University of Chicago, 1944; Florence L. Goodenough, *Measurements of Intelligence by Drawing* (Yonkers, N. Y., World Book Co., 1926); R. W. Russell and W. Dennis, "Studies in Animism," *Journal of Genetic Psychology*, Vol. 55, 1939, pp. 382–400; and further references in *The Hopi Way*, pp. 142–144. See also John Elderkin Bell, *Projective Techniques* (New York, Longmans, Green, 1948).

Professor Bell's survey pays very limited attention to the national implications of cultures in the tests. A number of the tests consists in noting the frequencies of the subject's deviation from the responses of a limited number of subjects who are believed to be normal, presumably in terms of their national culture. In the so-called "world tests," for instance, subjects who put fences around the world they construct are considered to have unusual anxieties (p. 470), but there are marked differences with which peoples put actual fences around the actual gardens in their culture. Similarly, word association tests are based on the frequency of particular associations, and these may easily vary in different cultures. The index to the book contains seven references to culture, two to race, and one to Navajo Indians; nationalism and nationality are not mentioned. For a recent survey of psychological research methods which at least touch upon the problem of nationalism, see Marie Jahoda, Morton Deutsch, and Stuart W. Cook, *Research Methods in Social Relations with Especial Reference to Prejudice*, Part I (New York, Dryden Press, 1951), with a good discussion of problems of measurement, pp. 92–127.

For the entire subject matter of this chapter, see also the excellent surveys by Otto Klineberg, *Tensions Affecting International Understanding: A Survey of Research* (New York, Social Science Research Council, 1950); and George A. Miller, *Language and Communication*, New York, McGraw-Hill, 1951, esp. pp. 174–274.

3. Cf. Anna J. Aucamp, *Bilingual Education and Nationalism with Special Reference to South Africa* (Pretoria, J. L. Von Schaik, Ltd., 1926), *passim*.

4. Cf. "Tests of Perception and Memory," in Marie Jahoda et al., *op. cit.* (Note 2, Chap. 5), pp. 223–225.

5. Allport and Postman, *op. cit.* (Note 2, Chap. 5), p. 556; cf. also p. 555. Cf. also J. M. Levine and G. Murphy, "The Learning and Forgetting of Controversial Material," Newcomb and Hartley, *op. cit.* (Note 2, Chap. 5), pp.108–114.

6. Hans Kohn, *The Idea of Nationalism* (New York, Macmillan, 1944), p. 5.

7. Chapter 1, above, and Abraham Kardiner, *The Individual and His Society* (New York, Columbia University Press, 1939), pp. 12, 126f, 467f.

8. Quincy Wright in *Perspectives on a Troubled Decade: 1940–1950*, L. Bryson, L. Finkelstein, and R. M. MacIver, eds. (New York, Harper, 1950), p. 364.

9. A. Leighton, *op. cit.* (Note 27, Chap. 4), p. 365.

10. "Revolution implies . . . the speaking of a previously unheard of language, . . . the emergence of another kind of logic, operations with other proofs. . . . Each major revolution has used another style of argument, a way of thinking which prerevolutionary men simply could not conceive nor understand. Men might hear with their ears, but there could be no meeting of minds between Poincaré and Lenin, Burke and Robespierre, Charles V and Luther. Once men begin to talk according to the new syntax of a major revolution, a rupture of meaning has occurred; and the old and the new type of man appear insane to each other.

"This is why, in such epochs, times are truly out of joint. Brothers, friends, colleagues, who shared a common education, suddenly rise up against each other and understand each other no more. They can no longer deal as man to man: the old are for the new corpses, ripe to rot; and to the old, the new appear as madmen. Both are indignant. The old Adam is inwardly beside himself with rage about this new madness. The revolutionist lifts his sword because he lives outside this old dead world and considers it a good riddance.

". . . The result is a revaluation of all values. Those men who have not been revolutionized, and those who have, live in opposite universes of values, and, therefore, do not seem human to each other. The Russians call their emigres 'former people.' Guelfs and Ghibellines, Legitimists and Jacobins have hated each other with equal fervor. . . ." Eugene Rosenstock-Huessy, *Die Europaeischen Revolutionen* (Jena, Diederichs, 1931), pp. 23–24.

It should be noted that this analysis is intended by its author to apply only to one stage of the process: "No epoch of revolution ends with a complete erasure of the old type of man, but rather with a new reunion . . . a symbiosis of the old natural ethnic traditions with the spiritualized carriers of the revolution. Instead of the mutual war of annihilation there follows . . . the labor of education . . . the test of everyday life." *Op. cit.,* p. 25.)

11. Robert Luther Duffus, "Clues to an Understanding of John Bull," *New York Times Magazine,* August 20, 1950, p. 41.

12. Geoffrey Gorer, "Some Aspects of the Psychology of the People of Great Russia," *The American Slavonic and East European Review,* Vol. 8, October 1949, p. 164. Gorer claims that this relationship does not prevail among the Great Russians, for whom, he says, "it is impossible by intuition or introspection to know what the wishes of authority will be," and thus, "the emotional division between ruler and ruled appears very marked. There would seem to be a connection between this fact and the fact that the earliest constraint—the swaddling [of Great Russian babies]—is not part of the self, and not personified" (*ibid.*). There is no evidence given in the article sufficient to permit judgment on the accuracy of the asserted fact, or on the validity of the suggested explanation. There are formidable difficulties in obtaining a representative sample of the population remaining in a country by interviewing mainly those who have fled it, particularly if that country has gone through a long series of social upheavals.

That emigrees were a highly unrepresentative sample of the French people as a whole, geographically and sociologically as well as in matters of political ideology, appears from the data given by David Greer, *The Incidence of Emigration During the French Revolution* (Cambridge, Harvard University Press, 1951), pp. 62, 70–72, 79–80, tables on pp. 109–138, and map opposite p. 38. The proportionate composition of emigrations, according to these data, differed strikingly from the sociological and geographical proportions of the French population as a whole; its description by Greer as "a comprehensive representation of social France" (p. 91) cannot be accepted in any quantitative sense. Conditions were somewhat more favorable for a "long-distance analysis" of Japanese culture by American anthropologists, since the persons who emigrated from Japan after 1917 and the Japanese immigrants to the United States represented many shades of Japanese opinion, and included many, particularly among the Japan born *Issei,* who accepted completely the social and political institutions of their native country.

Whatever the difficulties of representative sampling in some particular countries or revolutionary regimes, the point remains significant that governments are closer to the ruled if their actions are predictable from introspection. For Gorer's approach, see Geoffrey Gorer and John Rickman, *The People of Great Russia: A Psychological Study* (New York, Chanticleer Press, 1950), *passim.* Cf. also, Geoffrey Gorer, *The American People—A Study in National Character* (New York, Norton, 1948), *passim.* For a sharp criticism of this whole approach, see John F. Embree, "Standardized Error and Japanese Character: A Note on Political Interpretation," *World Politics,* Vol. 2, No. 3, April 1950, pp. 439–443.

13. "[This] notion of the rule of law . . . is fundamental; *the* foundation of foundations. Where you have the rule of law, the individual knows where he is . . . today, and where he will be tomorrow; he lives a life . . . of expectability. . . . [An] expectable life in the political community is something parallel, in its value, to the expectable order of events, and the chain of ordered causation, which the development of science discovers in the goings of the universe." Sir Ernest Barker, "The Nature and Origins of the Western Political Tradition," in *The Western Tradition: A Series of Talks Given on the B.B.C. European Programme*

(London, Vox Mundi, Ltd., 1949), p. 30. Cf. also, "If we want an expectable life—and the more adult we are, the more we want that sort of life—we must ourselves have some share in its making. The life that is made for me, over my head, can never satisfy my demand for expectability." *Op. cit.*, pp. 31–32.

14. Peter Drucker, *The End of Economic Man* (New York, John Day, 1939), pp. 13–14.

15. Even where a man does not use introspection and identification in order to predict how other people will act, his own attention will be powerfully guided to those elements of information with which he can connect or identify himself. In an attempt to investigate "this quality of 'me-ness,' this self-identification with the news," W. Schramm found that one potential reader in two actually read news items dealing with his own community, but only one reader in six read items dealing with persons or places which he did not know well. Similarly, almost every reader read to the end stories with which he could vividly identify himself or his family and friends, but abandoned merely half-read all stories which did not produce such identification. "The Nature of News," in W. Schramm, *Mass Communication* (Urbana, University of Illinois Press, 1949), pp. 299–300.

16. Christ Anastasoff, *The Tragic Peninsula* (St. Louis, Blackwell Wielandy Co., 1938), p. 245. "The Greeks, in common speech, call their Slav Macedonian minority 'Bulgarians,' but in official language, 'Slavophone Greeks.'" Elizabeth Barker, *Macedonia: Its Place in Balkan Power Politics* (London & New York, Royal Institute of International Affairs, 1950), p. 11.

17. Cf. in this connection the survey of types of fictional heroes in certain mass circulation magazines, in P. Johns-Heine and H. H. Gerth, "Values in Mass Periodical Fiction, 1921–1940," in *Mass Communication*, W. Schramm, Ed., pp. 379–380; and the discussion of models of speech in Otto Jespersen, *Mankind, Nation and Individual from a Linguistic Point of View* (London, Allen & Unwin, 1946), pp. 69, 71–73, 105–108.

The social group whose behavior is being imitated may feel this as an embarrassing infraction of their separateness or their privileged position. "The fishwife's children say 'Mother,' Mevrouw's children say 'Mom'; the fishwife's children say 'Mom,' Mevrouw's children say 'Ma'; the fishwife's children say 'Ma,' and Mevrouw's children say again 'Mother.'" Carry van Bruggen, *Hedendagsch Fetischisme* (Amsterdam, Querido, 1948), p. 84 (in Dutch). "The people like to call their children Paulus, Johannes, Theodores, Gerardus. Just because this is so, Paul, Johan, Gerard and Theo 'sound' much 'better' (*beschaafder*)." *Op. cit.*, p. 145.

18. See, for instance, Charles A. Beard's "Control of Immigration in the Interest of Nationality," in the United States, in his book, *The Idea of National Interest* (New York, Macmillan, 1934), pp. 352–357, and his chapter, "American Nationality," in his *The Open Door at Home, A Trial Philosophy of National Interest* (New York, Macmillan, 1934), pp. 179–209. The summary of Beard's own views suggests the line of his approach, which shows him opposed to racial theories and yet markedly hesitant to believe that immigrants from different stocks could learn to become equally effective members of the American nation: "The American nation is republican, secular, and essentially economic in character. . . . The American nation is not and cannot be racial, as race is conceived in Nordic fantasies, although composed largely of Northern European stocks. . . . It has distinct political and economic ways of life due to its natural endowment and

the process of settlement and expansion; and these ways of life give it peculiar characteristics, objective and subjective. . . . Social cohesiveness and capacity to cooperate on a large scale are indispensable to political and economic management on a large scale. . . . *Current immigration policy is based on a fixation of racial composition* as disclosed by the "national origins" principle. . . . *An extension of that principle in some form to all areas not yet covered by it is desirable.* . . . Policy will lend no countenance to racial fanatics who speak with pontifical assurance about the "superiority" of this race and the "inferiority" of that race. It will reject the alleged findings of intelligence testers and eugenicists respecting the "innate capacities" of races, as ignoring fundamental economic and cultural considerations, as not proved, and as not susceptible of scientific verification. . . . The principle for the guidance of policy in matter of immigration is the necessity *for maintaining social cohesiveness and cooperative capacity,* which are indispensable to political and economic management on a national scale." (*Ibid.,* pp. 208–209; italics added.)

In point of fact, no fixed "racial composition" in terms of "Northern European stocks" seems to have been necessary for the considerable "social cohesiveness and cooperative capacity" displayed by members of such diverse American organizations as the United States Marine Corps, the theoretical physics section of the Manhattan Project, or the football team of Notre Dame.

The American ability to organize effective cooperation among persons from a wide variety of cultural or ethnic backgrounds has even been pointed out as a peculiarly American character trait by Margaret Mead, *And Keep Your Powder Dry: An Anthropologist Looks at America* (New York, Morrow, 1942), pp. 221–237.

19. The cases in which assimilation was reversed have been discussed by Dorothy Swaine Thomas and Richard B. Nishimoto in *Japanese American Evacuation and Re-Settlement: The Spoilage* (Berkeley and Los Angeles, University of California Press, 1946). Of the emotional background of the original evacuation, they say: "Nationally known writers 'uncovered' dangers and presented 'solutions' in their syndicated columns. Henry McLemore in the *San Francisco Examiner* and other papers of January 29, 1942, argued for the removal of every Japanese American on the West Coast 'to a point deep in the interior.' He didn't mean, he pointed out, a 'nice part of the interior either. . . . Herd 'em up, pack 'em off and give 'em the inside road in the badlands. Let 'em be pinched, hurt, hungry and dead up against it. . . . Let us have no patience with the enemy or with anyone whose veins carry his blood. . . . Personally, I hate the Japanese. And that goes for all of them,' while Westbrook Pegler urged that 'the Japanese in California should be under armed guard to the last man and woman right now and to hell with habeas corpus until the danger is over.' (*Fair Enough,* February 16, 1942. In *Los Angeles Times* and other papers.) . . .

"To many of the Japanese Americans, the apparent general public hostility and the widely reported activities of anti-Japanese pressure groups were taken as convincing evidence that the evacuation orders were motivated more by racial prejudice than by the Army's stated regard for military necessity. Much later this belief was confirmed in the minds of the evacuees when General De Witt was reported in the public press as saying: 'A Jap's a Jap. . . . It makes no difference whether he is an American citizen or not. . . . I don't want any of them. . . . They are a dangerous element. . . . There is no way to determine their loyalty.' (*Los Angeles Times,* April 14, 1943, and various other West Coast newspapers.)

"In the months that followed, this statement was quoted by many Japanese Americans as incontrovertible evidence of the prejudice that had motived the evacuation. (The official transcript of the hearings, thus quoted in the newspaper, records the General as saying, less colloquially: 'I don't want any of them here. They are a dangerous element. There is no way to determine their loyalty. . . . It makes no difference whether he is an American citizen, he is still a Japanese. American citizenship does not necessarily determine loyalty.' [U. S. Congress, House Committee on Naval Affairs. *Investigation of Congested Areas.* Hearings before a Subcommittee. 78th Congress, 1st Session, Washington, Government Printing Office, 1943, pp. 739–740.]

"There are many similar statements by General De Witt on record, e.g., 'The Japanese race is an enemy race and while many second and third generation Japanese born on United States soil, possessed of United States citizenship, have become "Americanized," the racial strains are undiluted.' [U. S. Army, Western Defense Command and Fourth Army, *Final Report, Japanese Evacuation from the West Coast, 1942.* Washington, Government Printing Office, 1943, p. 34.]) Thomas and Nishimoto, *op. cit.,* pp. 18–20, and notes 58 and 60.

The results of the process by the end of the war are summarized by the authors as follows: "With mass renunciation of citizenship by the Nisei and Kibei, the cycle which began with evacuation was complete. Their parents had lost their hard-won foothold in the economic structure of America. They, themselves, had been deprived of rights which indoctrination in American schools had led them to believe inviolable. Charged with no offense, but victims of a military misconception, they had suffered confinement behind barbed wire. They had been stigmatized as disloyal on grounds often far removed from any criterion of political allegiance. They had been at the mercy of administrative agencies working at cross-purposes. They had yielded to parental compulsion in order to hold the family intact. They had been intimidated by the ruthless tactics of pressure groups in camp. They had become terrified by reports of the continuing hostility of the American public, and they had finally renounced their irreparably depreciated American citizenship.

"Many of them have since left the country, voluntarily, to take up life in defeated Japan. Others will remain in America, in the unprecedented and ambiguous status of citizens who became aliens ineligible for citizenship in the land of their birth. . . . The total number of these 'citizens with alien status' remaining in America will probably exceed 3,000." (Thomas and Nishimoto, *op. cit.,* p. 361 and footnote 108.)

20. "The basic categories of 'thinking' are implicit. . . . [They] are . . . transmitted . . . mainly, probably, through the language. Especially the morphology of a language preserves the unformulated philosophy of the group. . . . Every language is also a device for categorizing experience." Kluckhohn and Kelly, *op. cit.* (Note 32, Chap. 1), p. 100.

21. Cf. the seven hundred year history of certain German settlements in Eastern Europe; and the cases cited by Caroline F. Ware, "Ethnic Communities," *Encyclopaedia of the Social Sciences* (New York, Columbia University Press, 1931), Vol. V, pp. 607–613.

22. Cf. the view of Carlton J. H. Hayes, *France: A Nation of Patriots* (New York, Columbia University Press, 1930), pp. 5–16; and the citations in the next note, below.

23. *"The Republique une et indivisible* was the first to demand acceptance of the French language [in Alsace], though in vain. But it succeeded in something else: the change of social strata, the destruction of the dominant German social stratum, the nobility of the old patriciate of the German Imperial cities. These were replaced by a new *bourgeoisie* composed of newly rich and immigrants—the stratum of the notables. . . . Ninety per cent of its members, to be sure, were of German blood . . . but in their hearts they had completely turned away from the development of the German tradition. The large landowners, but above all, the factory owners, who were also tied by their economic interests to the French unitary state (although they were mostly Calvinists from German Switzerland, and often from Old Germany beyond the Rhine), became bearers of the French idea. The people . . . were dazzled by the victories of Napoleon, economically tied to the social changes brought by the French Revolution, inspired by the great and simple political idea of France, and by the widely publicized opportunities for careers in army and administration." [Karl C. v. Loesch Ed., *Volk unter Voelkern* (Breslau, Ferd. Hirt, 1925), pp. 226–227.]

This power of the French Revolution was not limited to the Alsace. "The city [of Fribourg] was in 1481 mostly French. Now (after joining the Swiss Confederation in the 16th century) the German language became dominant, and leading families . . . took German names, such as the Von der Weid, formerly Du Pasquier. . . . This continued until the French Revolution. Since that time the Von der Weid are speaking French again." [Ernst Schuerch, *op. cit.* (Note 19, Chap. 4), p. 9.]

24. Cf. Max Weber, *General Economic History* (New York, Greenberg, 1927), pp. 195–196.

25. Otto Bauer, *op. cit.* (Note 26, Chap. 4), pp. 133–135.

26. Gottfried Feder, *Hitler's Official Programme and its Fundamental Ideas* (London, Allen & Unwin, 1934), p. 76. (The publisher's note contains the words, "The present book is a full and faithful translation of the fifth German edition of this book.")

In the 1934 edition the passage continued, "We should explain, however, that we have not any thought of wishing to effect the forcible absorption of Germans living outside Germany under Danish, Polish, Czech, Italian or French rule. We do, however, expect that our German brothers living under foreign governments shall be accorded equal rights with the rest of the citizens in those countries."

Within six years after the publication of this edition the Germans living in all those five territories had been reabsorbed into the Reich, in four cases by military conquest, and in the fifth, the return of German minorities in the Italian regions of the Tyrol, by a wholesale population transfer arranged between the two dictators, with scant regard for the wishes of the individuals concerned.

The underlying nationalistic image of an "indelible character," irrevocable by the will of individuals, seems to have been originally a religious conception. According to Hebrew law, birth from a Jewish mother indelibly confers membership of the chosen people; and, according to Catholic Canon Law, the sacrament of ordination confers the indelible character of priesthood which forever after marks off the ordained priest from the layman regardless of whatever he may do. The transfer of this religious notion into the field of nationalist politics should perhaps be seen in the context of the general tendency of modern nationalism to appropriate for its own secular purposes the ancient patterns and symbols of religion.

27. "[Where] the nationalities live in their close settlements far away from the Magyar culture, all school Magyarization is impossible *because the school with its four hours of instruction is quite impotent against the twenty hours of real life.* If, in every village of the great Rumanian settlement in Transylvania, every elementary school were to consist of children blessed with the linguistic talent of Count Albert Apponyi [in those times the chief exponent of this policy of artificial Magyarization] and if every elementary school were a model institution and not a single crowded room with one or two poorly paid and poorly qualified teachers, even then the Magyar language of instruction, forcibly imposed, could only have the result that the children would learn some phrases in Magyar which life would soon erase from their memory. . . ." The passage is cited in English from Oscar Jaszi, *The Evolution of the Nation States and the Nationality Problem* (in Hungarian), Budapest, 1912, in his later book, *The Dissolution of The Hapsburg Monarchy* (Chicago, University of Chicago Press, 1929), p. 330. (Italics added.)

CHAPTER 6

1. Cf. Julius Isaac, *The Economics of Migration* (London, Kegan Paul, French, Trubner, 1947); Karl Polanyi, *The Great Transformation* (New York, Farrar & Rinehart, 1944); Hope Tisdale, "The Process of Urbanization," *Social Forces,* Vol. 20, No. 3, March 1942, pp. 311–316.

2. What becomes more intensive, i.e., more frequent over time, under the conditions envisaged is communication between persons in *different* families, villages, or small districts. Such mobilization for more intensive communication over somewhat greater distances may quite possibly sometimes go hand in hand with a diminished intensity (i.e., frequency and range) of communications at the local level. In this manner, e.g., small-town communities may be reduced to mere "dormitory areas" on the outskirts of big cities. For these local communities, this result would be the opposite of the "parochialization" or "self-reference effect," according to which individuals and groups tend to respond to wider or more unfamiliar experiences first of all by an increased preoccupation with themselves and their own familiar affairs, as seen by Harold D. Lasswell (*The World Revolution of Our Time: A Framework for Basic Policy Research,* Stanford, Calif., Stanford University Press, 1951, pp. 30–32); but it might correspond in the long view to the "enlargement of the self," which Lasswell sees as a subsequent stage (*ibid.,* pp. 31–32).

The essential point of the present approach is that communication is seen as a function of *social learning,* and more indirectly, of economic and social development. It is not, therefore, to any major extent, a function of biology, heredity, or genetics. Our view differs therefore very much, and in its basic assumptions, from the interesting mathematical approach of Professor Nicholas Rashevsky to the changing levels of activity in social groups and the "interaction of nations." Professor Rashevsky assumes that members of the "active population" differ from the "passive population" by hereditary constitution, and that the relative proportions of "active" and "passive" population then develop according to certain patterns of genetics and natural selection, depending largely on the numbers and density of total population. To what extent some of Professor Rashevsky's mathematical techniques could be applied to more realistic social and economic assumptions, and particularly to processes of social learning in contrast to mere heredity, only the future can show. Cf. N. Rashevsky, *Mathematical Theory of Human Relations: An Approach to a Mathematical Biology of Social Phenomena* (Bloomington, Ind., Principia Press, 1947), pp. 127–148, and especially the statements about nations, pp. 145–148.

3. Statistical Office of the United Nations, Dept. of Social Affairs, Population Division, *Data on Urban and Rural Populations in Recent Censuses* (U. N. Publications Sales No. 1950, XIII, 4, Lake Success, N. Y., 1950), Table I, pp. 14–15. See also note 17, Chap. 6.

4. See note 18, Chap. 6.

5. *Annuaire Statistique de Finlande*, Année 1949 (Helsinki, Statsrådets tryckeri 1950), pp. 5–6, 29; U. Toivola, ed., *The Finland Yearbook 1947* (Helsinki, Mercatorin Kirjapaino Ja Kustannus, 1947), pp. 17–18, 20–22.

6. Cf. John H. Wuorinen, "Scandinavia and National Consciousness," in *Nationalism and Internationalism: Essays Inscribed to Carlton J. H. Hayes*, Edward Mead Earle, ed. (New York, Columbia University Press, 1950), p. 474 and note 14. Also E. N. Setälä, *La lutte des langues en Finlande* (Paris, Champion, 1920), pp. 12–13.

7. See references in Appendix II.

8. Cf. Suniti Kumar Chatterji, *Languages and the Linguistic Problem*, 2nd Ed. (Oxford Pamphlets on Indian Affairs No. 11, London, Oxford University Press, 1944), pp. 22, 24. A. Z. Ahmad, ed., *National Language for India: A Symposium* (Allahabad, Kitabistan, 1941), and Appendix.

9. "The Highlanders in the towns . . . still spoke Gaelic, and churches in which this language was used were erected in Glasgow, Greenock, Paisley and Dundee." D. F. MacDonald, *Scotland's Shifting Population 1770–1850* (Glasgow, Jackson, 1937), p. 72, with references. Cf. also the data in I. F. Grant, *The Economic History of Scotland* (London, Longmans Green, 1934), pp. 212–215, 267; and Appendix IV.

10. Numerical data could perhaps be obtained by sampling and the communications tests suggested in Chapter 3, bearing in mind the problems of measurement scales discussed by S. S. Stevens and summarized in Marie Jahoda et al., *op. cit.* (Note 2, Chap. 5), pp. 119–127.

11. It might be worth exploring whether the shortest distance between any two dots—which will often be a diagonal—might not correspond, loosely, and in the absence of deliberate reinforcements of national or class barriers, to what sociologists call "social distance." Cf. E. S. Bogardus, "The Measurement of Social Distance," in Newcomb and Hartley, *op. cit.* (Note 2, Chap. 5), pp. 503–507.

12. So that the distance between I and III is in fact not much smaller than the sum of the distances between I and II, and II and III. Whether this is in fact the case can be tested by some of the means indicated in Chapter 3. If it is not the case, only pairs of two languages or cultures can be represented by this method.

13. As stated before, the principle of this illustration could be extended to any number of languages whose differences were such that they could be represented as additive, that is to say, that they could be represented in such a way that the sum of the distance between languages I and II and between languages II and III would give at least approximately the distance between I and III. (By distance would be meant transfer losses, i.e., loss of semantic meaning of a printed or spoken text in language I to the reader or listener in language II. Such transfer losses or linguistic distances in a diagram would be smaller between such languages as Swedish and Norwegian, somewhat larger between German and Dutch, and very large indeed between English and Chinese.) If the distances between languages are not additive, so that languages I and III were less distant from each other in terms of communication than the sum of the distance between I and II and II and III, then separate diagrams would have to be drawn for each group of languages among whom the differences could be represented as additive without serious distortion. Finally, if a group of speakers of similar languages live side by side with a population speaking a radically different language, such as Frenchmen and Italians in North Africa living side by side with an Arab-speaking population, or Greeks, Macedonians, and Bulgars meeting Turks near Adrianople, then the differences between the similar languages might all be small as compared to their common distance from the last language from which they are all so radically different. In this case, a jagged vertical line down the diagram could be used to indicate that the true communicative distance between the last language and the group of the others has been underrepresented in order to keep the entire diagram within the limits of a page.

It should be noted that the radical nature of the difference depends not merely on the grammatical structure of the languages but also on the difference in the vocabularies. If there is continued contact under favorable social conditions between the speakers of the different languages, a mixed vocabulary or a mixed language may arise even from two extremely incongruous "linguistic parents." Thus, the Rumanian vocabulary contains Slavic and Turkish as well as Rumanian words; pidgin English has long proved a workable mixture of English and Chinese, and another workable combination between Chinese and Malayan called Baba Malay has been observed at Singapore. Cf. Victor Purcell, *The Chinese in Malaya* (London, Oxford University Press, 1948), pp. 293–295, with references to the *Journal of the Royal Asiatic Society, Straits Branch*, December 1913, Vol. lxv, pp. 49–63. Although such mixed languages may never develop significant literatures of their own, they may nevertheless be an effective means of national assimilation of some of the persons who speak them and who may use them as a bridge before learning one or the other of the full-fledged "major languages."

14. Figures from Czechoslovak Republic, *Statistical Yearbook* and *Statistical Handbook*, 1921–1938. For details, see Appendix II.

15. Colin Clark, *The Conditions of Economic Progress* (London, Macmillan, 1940), pp. 337–339.

16. Heinrich Rauchberg, *Der national Besitzstand in Boehmen* (Leipzig, Duncker & Humblot, 1905), Vol. I, pp. 331–335, and especially pp. 420–421; cf. also pp. 643–644, 664, 682, 686–701.

17. Since the communication tests for it have been suggested, and much of the data are already in existence in the census files of the various countries, it

seems a question of time and manpower when this information will be brought together. As was pointed out before, this section of our study can only suggest what data it would be desirable to bring together, and why; if the information thus obtainable is wanted, then sooner or later it will be obtained. We cannot at this stage carry out such a compilation of statistics; all we can do is try to show what its usefulness could be. Thirteen countries, who have published in one or more of their censuses some form of cross tabulation of language or ethnic nationality with their data on rural and urban populations, are listed in *Data on Urban and Rural Populations in Recent Censuses* (United Nations Population Studies, No. 8, Sales No. 1950, XIII, 4, Lake Success, N. Y., 1950), Table 1, pp. 14–15. The countries and census years listed are Canada (1941), Mexico (1940), United States (1940), Turkey (1935), Union of South Africa (1936), Belgium (1930), Bulgaria (1934), Czechoslovakia (1930), Finland (1940), Hungary (1930), Roumania (1930), Switzerland (1941), and U.S.S.R. (1926).

18. The rates of assimilation can be calculated where data are available for the numbers and natural rates of increase of an ethnic or language group. In the absence of this last type of information, the rate of assimilation can still be estimated, if the numbers of such a group are known over a period of years; if they differ significantly from the trend disclosed by the numbers of population as a whole; if there is no reason to impute a significantly different rate of natural increase to the group compared to the rest of the population; or if that natural rate of increase can be estimated in some way. Thus it should be possible to estimate the rate of assimilation between Swedes and Finns in Finland; between Czechs and Germans in Bohemia; and in many other cases. For data on the spread of several languages, see A. C. Woolner, *Languages in History and Politics* (London, Oxford University Press, 1938).

Ready-made figures for the rate of assimilation, on the other hand, have rarely, if ever, been published. In an age of nationalism, governments risk being accused of practicing oppression or tolerating privilege if they admit that appreciable numbers of their subjects find it expedient to change their linguistic, cultural, or ethnic group affiliations. Persons who assimilate, and sometimes even groups who receive them, may not be anxious to advertise the fact. In other cases, however, data on the "Americanization," "Australianization," or "Peruanization," of immigrants, or on the assimilation of Indians in Latin American states, might be available.

An extreme case of estimating a rate of assimilation in the teeth of considerable difficulty has been that of estimating the numbers of light-colored Negroes passing for Whites in the United States. "The possible methods for estimating the extent of passing are: (1) getting at genealogies by direct questioning or other means; (2) noting discrepancies between the observed numbers of Negroes in the census and those which may be expected on the basis of the previous census and birth and death figures for the intercensal years; (3) noting deviations from normal in the sex ratio of Negroes. All these methods have been employed, but—for one reason or another—have not permitted us to state the extent of passing." Gunnar Myrdal, *An American Dilemma: The Negro Problem and American Democracy* (New York, Harper, 1944), pp. 129 and 1207, note 49. The first method was used by Caroline Bond Day (*A Study of Some Negro-White Families in the United States* [Cambridge, Peabody Museum of Harvard University, 1932], but the estimated rate of 15 out of every 1000 Negroes as passing was derived from an unrepresentative sample). The second method was used by Hornell Hart (*Selective Migration as a Factor in Child Welfare in the United States with Special Reference to Iowa* [Iowa City, University of Iowa, 1921], but the estimated rates of 25,000 Negroes passing each year between 1900 and 1910, and of 4–6 per cent of all those with some Negro blood as having passed, all depended on insufficiently accurate census data and vital statistics of the pre-1921 period. "The third method of estimating the extent of passing—that of noting discrepancies in sex ratio—was used by Charles S. Johnson ('The Vanishing Mulatto,' *Opportunity*, October 1925, p. 291) and by Everett V. Stonequist (*The Marginal Man: A Study in Personality and Culture Conflict*, New York, Scribners, 1937, pp. 190–191). The application of this technique has not only all the weaknesses of all the original census data, but it also could only reveal the extent to which men pass more than women and not the total amount of passing." Myrdal, *op. cit.*, p. 1208. The techniques—and perhaps some of the pitfalls—of estimating the extent of passing should apply at least to some degree in different settings to problems of estimating the extent of linguistic or cultural assimilation.

19. In computing the rates of mobilization or assimilation, care should be taken, of course, to allow for the distinction between the adult population and the total population which includes children. For many statistics about literacy, the population over ten years of age is used as a base. See *United Nations Statistical Yearbook*, 1948, pp. 429–437.

20. For a discussion of the chances for accelerated mobilization in backward countries, see Warren Wilhelm, "Soviet Central Asia: Development of a Backward Area," *Foreign Policy Reports*, Vol. 25, No. 18, Feb. 1, 1950, pp. 218–220. Cf. also the wealth of data in Kingsley Davis, *The Population of India and Pakistan* (Princeton, Princeton University Press, 1951).

21. Cf. Percy M. Roxby, "China as an Entity: The Comparison with Europe," *Geography*, Vol. 19, Part 1, No. 103, March 1934, pp. 1–20; and John de Francis, *Nationalism and Language Reform in China* (Princeton, Princeton University Press, 1950), especially Chap. 11: "Dialects or Languages," pp. 192–198.

22. "Unidad Del Idioma," in Ramón Menéndez Pidal, *Castilla: La Tradición: El Idioma* (Argentina, Espasa Calpe, 1945), pp. 208–212.

23. In this approach *n* would be the average rate of excess of birth over death per capita of the mobilized and assimilated population *N*, the main carrier of the predominant nationality or language; *n'* would be the number of newly mobilized and assimilated people who came to join it; and so forth.

CHAPTER 7

1. Cf., e.g., the compilation of "maximum rates of absolute decline of population occupied in agriculture" in Colin Clark's *The Economics of 1960* (London, Macmillan, 1942), p. 39. These data are drawn from eight countries—U.S.A., Germany, Britain, Switzerland, Sweden, Italy, France, and Czechoslovakia—over various periods between 1890 and 1938. The rates of decline of agricultural population range from 0.2 per cent per year in U.S.A., 1922–1929, and Germany, 1925–1933, to 1.4 per cent per year in Switzerland, 1920–1930. The average of the 20 rates listed is somewhat below 0.7 per cent, both with and without weight-

ing, according to periods covered. Figures on changes in the numbers of the agricultural population in a number of countries in the 1930's and 1940's are given by the Food and Agriculture Organization of the United Nations (FAO) in its *Yearbook of Food and Agricultural Statistics*, 1950, Vol. I, "Production," pp. 18–20.

2. These rates may differ considerably for different kinds of labor and may cause, e.g., skilled and unskilled to move in opposite directions. "In fact 'labour' as a factor of production consists of numerous not directly competing groups and sub-groups of unskilled, skilled and technical labour. Each of these groups has a different demand and supply schedule. A skilled worker, therefore, who intends to migrate, is interested not only in the general real income level in the new country; but also in the margin between the average income and the income prevalent in his group or sub-group. This margin is, broadly speaking, wider in countries with a low than in those on a higher standard of living. Skill is at a premium, as Prof. A. G. B. Fisher has pointed out, (1) in countries at an early stage of economic development. The income differences between qualified and unqualified labour tend, however, to narrow in countries with a high standard of living where technical training and apprenticeship is comparatively easy to obtain. For a skilled worker in a country with a comparatively low standard of living the advantages of a favourable ratio between the wages of skilled and unskilled labour may outweigh the advantages offered by the high standard of living in economically more developed countries. The standard deviation of the wage rates for skilled workers in the various professions expressed as a percentage of the average wage, computed for different countries, lends support to this suggestion. Colin Clark gives the figures for nine countries as follows (2):

Sweden	13.7	Australia	14.7	Canada	24.5
France	14.0	Great Britain	17.7	Jugoslavia	40.0
Switzerland	14.5	Spain	24.3	Japan	42.0

It is therefore not astonishing that skilled and unskilled labour often move in opposite directions.

"Switzerland, which has a surplus of skilled labour, until lately sent many workers abroad, but employed many thousands of foreign workers in manual work. (3) Bank clerks and technicians emigrated in large numbers from Austria and Germany to the Balkans in spite of the lower standard of living there. (4) Movements of similar character, from highly capitalized to less developed countries, occur also in the course of industrial expansion; they are often accompanied by wage discrimination between foreign and native workers in favour of the foreigners." J. Isaac, *Economics of Migration* (New York, Oxford University Press, 1947), pp. 30–32, with references as follows. (1) *International Labour Review*, Vol. 25, p. 758 ff. (2) Colin Clark, *The Conditions of Economic Progress* (London, Macmillan, 1940), p. 251. ("The exception provided by Canada's wide margin is explained by the comparative weakness of Trade Unions in Canada." Isaac.) (3) P. Sorokin, *Social Mobility* (New York, Harper, 1927), p. 234. (4) John W. Brown, *World Migration and Labour* (Amsterdam, International Federation of Trade Unions, 1926), p. 194.

3. Cf. the papers in "Economic Growth, A Symposium," *The Journal of Economic History*, Supplement VII, 1947, especially Simon Kuznets, "Measurement," pp. 10–34.

4. Cf. W. L. Langer, *The Diplomacy of Imperialism*, Vol. I (New York, Knopf, 1935), pp. 213–223, with references; W. M. Macmillan, *Africa Emergent*, Rev. Ed. (Harmondsworth, Eng., Penguin Books, 1949), pp. 304–305.

5. In practice some of the higher level jobs specifically requiring assimilation would be filled by members of the mobilized but differentiated group H, who might continue their previous change of habits from rural to urban by now completing their national assimilation. If, however, as we assumed, the total demand for members of M—the total mobilized population—has not fallen, then every person leaving H for N must be replaced in H by another entrant, most usually from R, so that the net demand for entrants from R would not be changed.

6. The importance of the rate at which an underlying differentiated population is mobilized for political and economic competition emerges clearly in a British observer's account of the rise of South African nationalism after World War I: "This last generation has seen a large and very desirable increase both of schools and of colleges. Being chiefly in Afrikaans-speaking districts, which were formerly distant and poorly served, they too are staffed with men of the new age. But the young men they have produced, especially those trained at the predominantly Afrikaans-speaking university colleges, have not yet quite found their level. Having no flair for commerce or industry, and perhaps neither the will nor the means to go back to the land, these have caused rather a glut in the Civil Service, in Education and in Law, the three callings to which they flock. Here is more 'frustration.' Many of these are unfruitfully placed, constituting something dangerously like a black-coated proletariat, which, as elsewhere, proved fertile soil for Fascist doctrine. In the burst of emotionalism that marked the celebration of the Voortrekker centenary in 1938 there began to develop an Action Front, the notorious Ossewabrandwag or 'O.B.,' i.e., literally, 'ox-waggon fire-guard.' The ox-waggon is, of course, the symbol of the Voortrekker. . . . In recent times the Nationalists have striven for an exclusively Afrikaner government, disdaining even to make the effort to convert non-Afrikaners to the Republican way of thinking. Their appeal has consistently been to Afrikaner national sentiment; hardly at all to political reason." W. M. Macmillan, *op. cit.* (Note 4, Chap. 7), pp. 324–325, 327.

More schools for Afrikaners, of course, were only part of a broader process. "In 1926, 61% of the Afrikaner male population was rural, while 73% of the English-speaking South African male population was urban. Since then the younger Afrikaners have drifted steadily to the towns. . . . This movement is reflected in the 1946 census figures which show that two-thirds of the increase in the European population took place in the Transvaal, where the rate of increase was almost 30%, while that in the Orange Free State, the traditional Afrikaner-Nationalist stronghold, was only one-half per cent. With the development of the new gold fields in the Orange Free State the tendency towards urbanization will most certainly be accentuated there as well." Nicholas Mansergh, *The Commonwealth and the Nations: Studies in British Commonwealth Relations* (London, Royal Institute of International Affairs, 1948), pp. 88–89.

7. An example of this process might be the dual effect of the growth of Vienna between 1890 and 1914 on the growth of "white-collar" strata of Germans and a simultaneous influx of Czechs, with the rise of nationalistic organization among each group. These organizations, schools, etc., then generated a specific demand for additional personnel to staff them. See also note 17 to this chapter, below.

8. For Mr. Shaw's amusing and perceptive views of English-Irish differences see his "Preface for Politicians" to "John Bull's Other Island," in *John Bull's Other Island and Major Barbara* (New York, Brentano's, 1928), pp. v to xl; particularly pp. vi to xvii.

9. The significance of the frequency and kind of contacts seems indicated by the investigations of the numbers of Japanese-Americans who registered themselves as "disloyal" to the United States at the Tule Lake Relocation Center in 1943, or were transferred there from other centers:

"Within a given location in the project, the 'loyalty' issue was . . . closely dependent upon preevacuation background, economic status, and social distance from the majority group. Statistical analysis of variations in proportions 'disloyal' indicates significant and systematic 'net' relationships (when all possible factors are held constant) with a number of exogenous factors. The most striking relationships are in factors manifesting variations in acculturation or assimilation; religious preference for the Occidental patterns of Christianity or agnosticism versus the Oriental pattern of Buddhism; biculturalism in training and education, the extremes being the 'pure' Nisei, educated only in America, and the Kibei returning recently after years of education in Japan; origin in certain areas of California, where economic and social segregation from the majority group was pronounced, as against origin in the more tolerant Pacific Northwest; occupation in nonagricultural pursuits, where, on the whole, contact with and accommodation to the majority group occurred to a greater degree than was true with the farming element. In brief, Buddhists were proportionately more 'disloyal' than Christians or agnostics; the order of 'disloyalty' proportions descended from Kibei to Issei to Nisei; Californians were more 'disloyal' than Northwesterners. Less consistent on a 'net' basis, but suggestive, were the differentials in occupation, the farming groups tending to be more 'disloyal' than the nonagriculturists." Thomas and Nishimoto, *The Spoilage*, pp. 105–106, and Note 49, with reference to statistical data in a manuscript by George M. Kuznets, "The Ecology of Disloyalty," publication forthcoming.

10. Cf. Phillip K. Hitti, *The Arabs: A Short History* (Princeton, Princeton University Press, 1943), pp. 80–81, for a case of social subordination following upon religious conversion.

11. Stoyan Christowe, *This is My Country* (New York, Carrick & Evans, Inc., 1938), p. 4.

12. Gurkin, the old immigrant, returned from America in western dress but kept his mustache.

13. For the latter example, see A. J. Toynbee, *A Study of History* (London, Oxford University Press, 1935), Vol. III, pp. 50–111.

14. On the background of this attitude, see F. Neumann, *Behemoth* (New York, Oxford University Press, 1942), pp. 98–129.

15. Jean Simon, "L'aire et la durèe des dialectes coptes," *Actes du quatrième Congrès International de Linguistes* (Copenhagen, Munksgaard, 1938), pp. 182–185.

16. Otto Zarek, *A Short History of Hungary* (London, Selwyn & Blount, 1939), p. 98.

17. Cf. N. Wiener, *Cybernetics* (New York, Wiley and Technology Press, 1948), *passim;* and K. W. Deutsch, "Mechanism, Teleology and Mind," *Philosophy and Phenomenological Research,* Vol. 12, No. 2, December 1951, pp. 185–223.

18. O. I. Janowsky, *Nationalities and National Minorities* (New York, Macmillan, 1945), pp. 139–143, with reference to S. P. Ladas, *The Exchange of Minorities: Bulgaria, Greece and Turkey* (New York, Macmillan, 1932), pp. 122–123, 441–442, 465, 720 ff.

19. By 1949, about 40,000,000 Muslims remained in India, forming about 11 per cent of her population, and more than 13,000,000 non-Muslims had remained in Pakistan, forming almost 17 per cent of the population of the latter country. K. Davis, *The Population of India and Pakistan* (Princeton, Princeton University Press, 1951), pp. 197–198. "Not all of the Muslims could live in Pakistan, any more than all of the Jews could live in Israel." *Ibid.*, p. 198.

20. For the balance of material rewards, cf., e.g., the following statement: "The enthusiasm for Pakistan among the Muslims of Bengal came less from their political leaders than from the working and lower middle classes. Dacca contains more mosques than any other city in the subcontinent. East Bengal had been the most receptive soil for the puritan Islamic revival of the Wahabis in the previous century. The illiterate and uneducated Bengal Muslim never forgot that his ancestors *had become converts to Islam because they came from a class oppressed by Hinduism.* He remembered, too, that Muslims had ruled the province until the counterpoise of Hindu influence had been created by the British. To the labourers, cultivators, boatmen and artisans the religious appeal of an Islamic state was simple and effective. The middle classes, all who aspired to positions under the Government, all who wanted licenses to trade in controlled goods, all who hoped to win scholarships, to teach, or practice at the Bar, *saw Pakistan as a state in which the way to advancement would no longer be blocked by the wealthier and better educated Hindu.*" Richard Symonds, *The Making of Pakistan* (London, Faber & Faber, 1950), pp. 144–145. (Italics added.)

CHAPTER 8

1. On the concepts of awakening and consciousness in the *logos* of Heraclitus, see W. Jaeger, *Paidea* (New York, Oxford University Press, 1945), Vol. I, p. 180, and p. 460, note 162; cf. also *The Theology of the Early Greek Philosophers* (Oxford, Clarendon, 1947), pp. 113–114.

2. "Areopagitica," in *Areopagitica and Other Prose Writings*, W. Haller, ed. (New York, Book League of America and Macmillan, 1929), p. 56.

3. Chapter 1, pp. 25–26.

4. On the whole subject of feedback and control, see Norbert Wiener, *Cybernetics,* and *The Human Use of Human Beings* (full references, Note 15, Chap. 4); K. W. Deutsch, *op. cit.* (Note 17, Chap. 7); and, by the same writer, "Mechanism, Organism, and Society," *Philosophy of Science,* Vol. 18, No. 3, July 1951, pp. 230–252, and "Communication Models in the Social Sciences," *Public Opinion Quarterly,* Vol. 16, No. 3, Fall 1952, pp. 356–380.

5. See Chap. 4.

6. An outline for specific research on this topic has been given by the writer in a paper on "Innovation, Entrepreneurship and the Learning Process," in *Change and the Entrepreneur, Postulates and Patterns for Entrepreneurial History,* A. H. Cole, ed. (Cambridge, Harvard University Press, 1949), pp. 24–29.

7. Cf. Petrarca, Eclogue VIII: ". . . the lands on this [French] side of the mountain begin to seem despicable to me, the western sky misty and stormy, and the stars themselves melancholy. . . . On the farther [Italian] side of the mountain the violets . . . are of a paler tint of yellow; the roses emit a sweeter scent . . . and grow to a deeper red; . . . the stream of my fathers . . . flows through the meadows; and the crops of Ausonia have for me now a sweeter taste." Cited in M. E. Cosenza, *Francesco Petrarca and the Revolution of Cola di Rienzo* (Chicago, University of Chicago Press, 1913), p. 170; and in Hans Kohn, *The Idea of Nationalism* (New York, Macmillan, 1944), p. 601.

8. The limited effectiveness of secondary symbols has been commented on by students of mass communications in a different context: "Prevailing beliefs in the enormous power of mass communications appear to stem from successful cases of monopolistic propaganda or from advertising. But the leap from the efficacy of advertising to the assumed efficacy of propaganda aimed at deep-rooted attitudes and ego involved behavior is as unwarranted as it is dangerous. Advertising is typically directed toward *the canalizing of preexisting behavior patterns* or attitudes. It seldom seeks to instil new attitudes or to create significantly new behavior patterns. 'Advertising pays' because it generally deals with a simple psychological situation. For Americans who have been socialized in the use of a toothbrush, it makes relatively little difference which brand of toothbrush they use. Once the gross pattern of behavior or the generic attitude has been established, it can be canalized in one direction or another. Resistance is slight. But mass propaganda typically meets a more complex situation. It may seek objectives which are at odds with deep-lying attitudes. It may seek to reshape rather than to canalize current systems of values. And the successes of advertising may only highlight the failures of propaganda. Much of the current propaganda which is aimed at abolishing deepseated ethnic and racial prejudices, for example, seems to have had little effectiveness. Media of mass communication, then, have been effectively used to canalize basic attitudes but there is little evidence of their having served to change these attitudes." Paul F. Lazarsfeld and Robert K. Merton, "Popular Taste and Organized Social Action," in *Mass Communication*, Wilbur Schramm, ed., p. 477.

9. Cf. A. M. Reder, "Inter-Temporal Relations of Demand and Supply within the Firm," *Canadian Journal of Economics and Political Science*, Vol. 7, February 1941, pp. 26–30; K. W. Deutsch, "Some Economic Aspects of the Rise of Nationalistic and Racial Pressure Groups," *ibid.*, Vol. 8, February 1942, pp. 109–115.

10. Just as secondary symbols are added to information or behavior shared by the national group, similar symbols may be appended to things or actions that are to be restricted or eliminated. Thus, much as one would bell a cat, Catalan nationalists in the early 1920's exhorted their followers to "hang a bell around Castilian," i.e., to speak it with a Catalan accent. Karl Vossler, *The Spirit of Language in Civilization* (London, Kegan Paul, 1932), p. 159.

11. Cf. K. Polanyi, *The Great Transformation* (New York, Farrar and Rinehart, 1944). For a critical view, see also A. M. Sievers, *Has Market Capitalism Collapsed? A Critique of Karl Polanyi's New Economics* (New York, Columbia University Press, 1949), especially pp. 46–97.

12. Ernst H. Kantorowicz, *"Pro Patria Mori* in Medieval Political Thought," *The American Historical Review*, Vol. 56, No. 3, April 1951, pp. 472–492. I am

indebted to Professor Kantorowicz for letting me see a pre-publication copy of his manuscript.

13. For another aspect of this process, cf. "The most important effect of machine production on the imaginative picture of the world is an immense increase in the sense of human power. This is only an acceleration of a process which began before the dawn of history; [but] the acceleration has been so great as to produce a radically new outlook. . . ." Bertrand Russell, *A History of Western Philosophy* (New York, Simon and Schuster, 1945), p. 728.

14. *Macbeth*, Act I, Scene 5.

15. *Preussentum und Sozialismus* (Munich, Beck, 1922), p. 98. "We need . . . a class of socialist lords and masters [*eine Klasse sozialistischer Herrennaturen*]. Once again: socialism is power, power, and always again power." *Ibid.*

16. Hans Kohn, *Force or Reason: Issues of the Twentieth Century* (Cambridge, Harvard University Press, 1937, p. 26.

17. "The Defenders of this Realm [Britain] . . . think that they have pacified Ireland. They think that they have purchased half of us and intimidated the other half. They think that they have foreseen everything, think that they have provided against everything; but the fools, the fools, the fools—they have left us our Fenian dead, and while Ireland holds these graves, Ireland unfree shall never be at peace." Patrick Pearse's Speech at the grave of O'Donovan Rossa, Glasnevin, July 1915, cited in Nicholas Mansergh, *op. cit.* (Note 6, Chap. 7), p. 166, with reference to Miss Macardle, *The Irish Republic* (London, Gollancz, 1937), pp. 139–142.

18. "Easter, 1916," *The Collected Poems of W. B. Yeats* (New York, Macmillan, 1949), pp. 207–209. Cf. also "Sixteen Dead Men" and "The Rose Tree," *op. cit.*, pp. 209–211.

19. *Liederbuch der deutschen Nationalsozialistischen Arbeiterpartei* (Ed. Hans Buchner, 20th Ed., Munich, Eher Verlag, 1933). Cf. also "Heldische Feier," in *Wir aber sind das Korn*, Gerhart Schuman (Munich, Langen-Mueller, 1936); and Ruth Deutsch, *Der Glaube an die Toten: Ein Motiv in anderthalb Jahrhunderten deutscher politischer Dichtung* (unpublished).

20. N. Mansergh, *op. cit.* (Note 6, Chap. 7), pp. 164–192.

21. W. M. Macmillan, *Africa Emergent* (Note 4, Chap. 7), p. 327.

22. *Op. cit.*, p. 328.

Bibliography

SOME BIBLIOGRAPHIES AND MAJOR SURVEYS

All works except Pinson are listed in alphabetical order. Titles listed in Pinson are marked P in the rest of my bibliography.

Pinson, Koppel S., *A Bibliographical Introduction to Nationalism*. New York, Columbia University Press, 1935. A selected and critically annotated bibliography.

Epstein, F. T., "A Short Bibliography on the Slavs," *The Slavonic and East European Review*, Vol. 22, No. 60, October 1944, pp. 110–119.

Jahoda, Marie, Morton Deutsch, and Stuart W. Cook, *Research Methods in Social Relations with Especial Reference to Prejudice*. New York, Dryden Press, 1951. 2 vols.

Klineberg, Otto, *Tensions Affecting International Understanding: A Survey of Research*. New York, Social Science Research Council, 1950.

Kohn, Hans, *The Idea of Nationalism: A Study in Its Origins and Background*. New York, Macmillan, 1944.

Lasswell, Harold D., Ralph D. Casey, and Bruce Lannes Smith, *Propaganda, Communication and Public Opinion: A Comprehensive Reference Guide*. Princeton, Princeton University Press, 1946.

———, *Propaganda and Promotional Activities: An Annotated Bibliography*, Minneapolis, University of Minnesota Press, 1935.

Mead, Margaret, "The Study of National Character," in *The Policy Sciences: Recent Developments in Scope and Method*, D. Lerner and H. D. Lasswell, Stanford, Calif., Stanford University Press, 1951, pp. 70–85.

Nationalism: A Report by a Study Group of Members of the Royal Institute of International Affairs (Chairman: E. H. Carr). London, Oxford University Press, 1939.

Notestein, F. W., et al., *The Future Population of Europe and the Soviet Union: Population Projections 1940–1970*. Geneva, League of Nations, 1944; Publ. No. 1944. II. A. 2. "Selected Bibliography on Population Projections," pp. 219–234.

Rose, Arnold M., *Studies in Reduction of Prejudice*, Revised Ed. Chicago, American Council on Race Relations, 1948.

Williams, Robin M., Jr., *The Reduction of Intergroup Tensions: A Survey of Research on Problems of Ethnic, Racial, and Religious Group Relations*. Social Science Research Council Bulletin 57, 1947.

Wright, Quincy, *A Study of War*. Chicago, University of Chicago Press, 1942. 2 vols.

United Nations Commission on Human Rights, *The Main Types and Causes of Discrimination* (Memorandum Submitted by the Secretary-General). (Lake

Success, N. Y., 1949; U.N. Publications, Sales No.: 1949. XIV. 3.) "Selected Bibliography on Discrimination and Related Subjects," pp. 58–88.

——, *Definition and Classification of Minorities* (Memorandum Submitted by the Secretary-General) (Lake Success, N. Y., 1950; U.N. Publications, Sales No.: 1950. XIV. 3). "Selected Bibliography," pp. 26–51.

Statistical Office of the United Nations, *Data on Urban and Rural Populations in Recent Censuses.* New York, 1950; U.N. Publications, Sales No. 1950. XIII. 4.

——, *National and Per Capita Incomes of Seventy Countries in 1949.* U.N. St/ Stat/Ser. E/1, New York, October 1950.

GENERAL WORKS ON NATIONALISM

Akzin, B., M. Ancel, B. Mirkine-Guetzevitch, J. Ray: *La nationalité dans la science sociale et le droit contemporain,* Recueil Sirey, Paris, 1933.

Barker, Sir Ernest, *National Character and the Factors in Its Formation.* London, Harper, 1927. P.

Baron, Salo W., *Modern Nationalism and Religion.* New York, Harper, 1947.

Bauer, Otto, *Die Nationalitaetenfrage und die Sozialdemokratie,* 2nd Ed. Vienna, Volksbuchhandlung, 1924. P.

Beard, Charles A., *The Idea of National Interest: An Analytical Study of American Foreign Policy.* New York, Macmillan, 1934. P.

——, *The Open Door at Home: A Trial Philosophy of National Interest.* New York, Columbia University Press, 1934. P.

Bloom, Solomon F., *The World of Nations: A Study of the National Implications in the Work of Karl Marx.* New York, Columbia University Press, 1941.

Braunthal, Julius, *The Paradox of Nationalism.* London, St. Botolph Publishing Co., 1946.

Butler, Sir Harold, "Nationalism and The Western Tradition," in *The Western Tradition.* London, Vox Mundi, 1949, pp. 73–77.

Carr, Edward H., *Nationalism and After.* New York, Macmillan, 1945.

Chadwick, Hector M., *The Nationalities of Europe and the Growth of National Ideologies.* Cambridge, Cambridge University Press, 1945.

Cobban, Alfred, *National Self-Determination.* London, Oxford University Press, 1945.

Delos, Joseph T., *La nation.* Montreal, Editions de l'Arbre, 1944.

Deutsch, Karl W., "The Growth of Nations: Some Recurrent Patterns of Political and Social Integration," *World Politics,* Vol. 5, No. 2, January 1953, pp. 168–195.

Earle, Edward Mead, ed., *Nationalism and Internationalism: Essays Inscribed to Carlton J. H. Hayes.* New York, Columbia University Press, 1950.

Emerson, Rupert, *Government and Nationalism in Southeast Asia.* New York, International Secretariat, Institute of Pacific Relations, 1942.

Europa und der Nationalismus: Bericht über das III. internationale Historiker-Treffen in Speyer, 17. bis 20 Oktober 1949 (H. Gregoire Introduction), Baden Baden, Verlag für Kunst und Wissenschaft, 1950.

Finot, Jean: *Les prejuges des races,* 2nd Ed. Paris, Alcan, 1905.

Friedmann, W., *The Crisis of the National State,* London, Macmillan, 1943.

Hancock, William K., *Politics in Pitcairn, and Other Essays*. London, Macmillan, 1947.

Hayes, Carlton J. H., *Essays on Nationalism*. New York, Macmillan, 1926. P.

———, *The Historical Evolution of Modern Nationalism*. New York, Macmillan, 1948. P.

Hertz, Friedrich O., *Nationalgeist und Politik*. Zurich, Europa Verlag, 1937.

———, *Nationality in History and Politics: A Study of the Psychology and Sociology of National Sentiment and Character*. London, Kegan Paul, 1944.

Hula, E., "National Self-Determination Reconsidered," *Social Research*, Vol. X, 1943.

Janowsky, Oscar I., *Nationalities and National Minorities* (With Special Reference to East-Central Europe). New York, Macmillan, 1945. "Selected Bibliography," pp. 193–207.

Keller, Hans K. E. L., *Der Kampf um die Völkerordnung*. Forschungs und Werbebericht der Akademie für die Rechte der Völker und der Internationalen. Arbeitsgeneinschaft der Nationalisten. Berlin, F. Vahlen, 1939.

———, *Das rechtliche Weltbild*. Berlin, Batschari Verlag, 1935.

Kautsky, Karl, *Nationalitaet und Internationalitaet, Ergaenzungshefte zur neuen Zeit*, No. i, 1907–1908 (Jan. 18, 1908), Stuttgart, P. Singer, 1908. P.

King, James C., *Some Elements of National Solidarity*. Chicago, University of Chicago Press, 1935.

Kohn, Hans, *Prophets and Peoples: Studies in Nineteenth Century Nationalism*. New York, Macmillan, 1946.

———, *World Order in Historical Perspective*. Cambridge, Harvard University Press, 1941.

———, *Revolutions and Dictatorships: Essays in Contemporary History*. Cambridge, Harvard University Press, 1941.

———, "Nationalism," in *Before America Decides*, ed. by Frank P. Davidson, Harvard University Press, 1938, pp. 13–26.

———, "The Roots of Modern Nationalism," in *Bulletin of the International Committee of the Historical Sciences*, Paris: Les Presses Universitaires, 1938, pp. 388–391.

———, "Nationalism and the Open Society," in Hans Kohn's *The Twentieth Century*, Macmillan, 1949, pp. 19–31.

Lemberg, Eugen, *Geschichte des Nationalismus in Europa*, Stuttgart, C. E. Schwab Verlag, 1950.

Macartney, C. A., *National States and National Minorities*. London, Oxford University Press, 1934. P.

Meinecke, Friedrich, *Weltbuergertum und Nationalstaat*, 7th Ed. Munich and Berlin, Oldenbourg Verlag, 1928. P.

Mitscherlich, Waldemar, *Nationalismus: Die Geschichte einer Idee*. Leipzig, L. C. Hirschfeld, 1929. P.

O'Toole, G. B., *Race: Nation: Person*. New York, Barnes and Noble, 1944.

Pouthas, Charles H., *Le Mouvement des Nationalités en Europe dans la Premiére Moitié du XIX Siècle*. Paris, Centre de Documentation Universitaire, 1945.

Richards, Ivor A., *Nations and Peace*. New York, Simon and Schuster, 1947.

Rocker, Rudolf, *Nacionalismo y cultura*. Buenos Aires, Ediciones Imán, 1942.

Simonds, Frank H., *The Great Powers in World Politics: International Relations and Economic Nationalism*. New York, American Book Co., 1937.

Stalin, Iosif V., *Joseph Stalin: Marxism and the National Question.* New York, International Publishers, 1942.

Stavenhagen, Kurt, *Das Wesen der Nation,* Berlin, Engelmann, 1934 (Heft 1, Rigaer Volkstheoretische Abhandlungen).

Stengel von Rutkowski, Lothar, *Was ist ein Volk? Der biologische Volksbegriff.* Erfurt, Verlag Kurt Stenger, 1943.

Strasser, Josef, *Der Arbeiter und die Nation,* 2nd Ed., Reichenberg, Runge, 1912.

Sturzo, Luigi, *Nationalism and Internationalism.* New York, Roy Publishers, 1946.

Sulzbach, Walter, *National Consciousness.* Washington, D. C., American Council on Public Affairs, 1943.

Vossler, Otto, *Der Nationalgedanke von Rousseau bis Ranke.* Munchen und Berlin, Verlag von R. Oldenbourg, 1937.

Weill, Georges: *Race et nation.* Collection Descartes: Pour la verité. Albin Michel, 1939.

Winternitz, J., *Marxism and Nationality.* London, Lawrence and Wishart, 1944.

Wright, Quincy, Ed., *The World Community.* Chicago, University of Chicago Press, 1948.

Zimmern, Sir Alfred E., *Modern Political Doctrines.* London, New York, Oxford University Press, 1939.

Zipf, George K., *National Unity and Disunity: the Nation as a Bio-Social Organism.* Bloomington, Ind., The Principia Press, 1941.

Znaniecki, Florian, *Modern Nationalities: A Sociological Study.* Urbana, Ill., University of Illinois Press, 1952.

POLITICAL SCIENCE

Boggs, S. Whittemore, "Geographic and Other Scientific Techniques for Political Science," *American Political Science Review,* Vol. 42, No. 2, April 1948, pp. 223–238; especially list of proposed studies, pp. 235–237.

Brinton, Crane, *From Many One: The Process of Political Integration: The Problem of World Government.* Cambridge, Harvard University Press, 1943.

Brodie, Bernhard, Ed., *The Absolute Weapon: Atomic Power and World Order.* New York, Harcourt, Brace, 1946.

Carr, Edward Hallett, *Conditions of Peace.* London, Macmillan, 1942.

Ebenstein, William, *Man and the State: Modern Political Ideas.* New York, Rinehart, 1948. "From Nationalism to World Order," pp. 551–748, "Bibliographical Notes" (on this topic), pp. 771–776.

Elliott, William Yandell, et al., *The British Commonwealth at War,* New York, Knopf, 1943.

——, *International Control in the Non-Ferrous Metals.* New York, Macmillan, 1937.

——, *The Pragmatic Revolt in Politics: Syndicalism, Fascism, and the Constitutional Republic.* New York, Macmillan, 1928.

——, "The Pragmatic Revolt in Politics: Twenty Years in Retrospect," *Review of Politics,* Vol. 2, No. 1, January 1940, pp. 1–11.

Elliott, William Yandell, et al., "Prospects for 'Personal Freedom and Happiness for All Mankind,'" *Annals of the American Academy of Political and Social Sciences*, Vol. 268, March 1950, pp. 173–182.

———, and Neil A. McDonald, *Western Political Heritage*. New York, Prentice-Hall, 1949.

Emerson, Rupert, "Point Four and Dependent Areas," *Annals of the American Academy of Political and Social Science*, Vol. 268, March 1950, pp. 112–121.

Fainsod, Merle, *International Socialism and the World War*. Cambridge, Harvard University Press, 1935.

Fox, William T. R., *The Super-Powers*. New York, Harcourt, Brace, 1944.

Friedrich, Carl J., *Constitutional Government and Politics*, 2nd Ed. Boston, Ginn, 1950.

———, "The Agricultural Basis of Emotional Nationalism," *Public Opinoin Quarterly*, Vol. 1, No. 2, April 1937, pp. 50–61.

———, *The New Belief in the Common Man*. Boston, Little, Brown, 1942. Enlarged Ed., Beacon Press, 1950.

Holcombe, Arthur N., *The Middle Class in American Politics*. Cambridge, Harvard University Press, 1940.

———, *Our More Perfect Union*. Cambridge, Harvard University Press, 1950.

Jouvenel, Bertrand de, *Power: Its Nature and the History of Its Growth*. New York, Viking, 1949.

Kohn, Hans, "The Permanent Mission: An Essay on Russia," *Review of Politics*, Vol. X, No. 3, July 1948, pp. 267–289.

———, "The Heritage of Masaryk," *The Annals of the American Association of Political and Social Sciences*, Vol. 258, July 1948, pp. 70–74.

Lasswell, Harold D., *The Analysis of Political Behavior: An Empirical Approach*. New York, Oxford University Press, 1949.

———, *National Security and Individual Freedom*. New York, McGraw-Hill, 1950.

———, *Politics: Who Gets What, When, How*. New York, McGraw-Hill, 1936.

———, *Power and Personality*. New York, Norton, 1948.

———, *Psychopathology and Politics*. Chicago, University of Chicago Press, 1934.

———, *World Politics and Personal Insecurity*. New York, Whittlesey House, McGraw-Hill, 1935.

———, and Dorothy Blumenstock, *World Revolutionary Propaganda: A Chicago Study*. New York, Knopf, 1939.

———, and H. Kaplan, *Power and Society: A Framework for Political Inquiry*. New Haven, Yale University Press, 1950.

———, et al., *Language of Politics: Studies in Quantitative Semantics*. New York, G. W. Stewart, 1949.

Leighton, Alexander H., *The Governing of Men: General Principles and Recommendations Based on Experience at a Japanese Relocation Camp*. Princeton, Princeton University Press, 1946.

———, *Human Relations in a Changing World: Observations on the Use of the Social Sciences*. New York, Dutton, 1949.

Maritain, Jacques, "The Concept of Sovereignty," *American Political Science Review*, Vol. 44, No. 2, June 1950, pp. 343–357.

———, *Man and the State*. Chicago, University of Chicago Press, 1951.

———, *The Person and the Common Good*. New York, Scribners, 1947.

Maritain, Jacques, "The End of Machiavellianism," *Review of Politics*, Vol. 4, No. 1, January 1942, pp. 1–33.

Merriam, Charles E., *The Making of Citizens: A Comparative Study of the Methods of Civic Training*. Chicago, University of Chicago Press, 1931. P.

Morgenthau, Hans, *Politics Among Nations*. New York, Knopf, 1948.

――, "Conduct of American Foreign Policy," *Parliamentary Affairs*, Vol. 3, 1949, pp. 1–16.

――, "The Conquest of the United States by Germany," *Bulletin of the Atomic Scientists*, Vol. 6, 1950, pp. 21–26.

――, *Scientific Man vs. Power Politics*. Chicago, University of Chicago Press, 1946.

――, and Kenneth W. Thompson, *Principles and Problems of International Politics: Selected Readings*. New York, Knopf, 1950.

Neumann, Franz, *Behemoth: The Structure and Practice of National Socialism*. New York, Oxford University Press, 1942.

――, "Approaches to the Study of Political Power," *Political Science Quarterly*, Vol. 65, No. 2, June 1950.

Neumann, Siegmund, *Permanent Revolution: The Total State in a World at War*. New York, Harper, 1942.

Padelford, Norman J., *International Relations: Fundamentals and Problems*. Cambridge, Massachusetts Institute of Technology Press, 1950 (especially Chaps. V–VI).

――, *Contemporary International Relations: Readings*. 1950–1951. Cambridge, Harvard University Press, 1951 (especially Chap. III).

Reves, Emery, *The Anatomy of Peace*. New York, Harper, 1946.

Russell, Bertrand, *Power: A New Social Analysis*. New York, Norton, 1938.

――, *Authority and the Individual*. New York, Simon and Schuster, 1948.

Schmidt, C. T., *The Corporate State in Action*. New York, Oxford University Press, 1939.

――, *The Plough and the Sword: Labor, Land, and Property in Fascist Italy*. New York, Columbia University Press, 1938.

Schuman, F. L., *International Politics: The Western State System in Transition*, 3rd Ed. New York, McGraw-Hill, 1941.

――, *The Nazi Dictatorship: Social Pathology and the Politics of Fascism*, 2nd Rev. Ed. New York, Knopf, 1936.

Spengler, Oswald, *Gedanken*. Munich, H. C. Beck, 1941.

――, *The Decline of the West*. New York, Knopf, 1939.

――, *Preussentum und Sozialismus*. Munich, H. C. Beck, 1922.

United Nations, Department of Social Affairs, *A Study of Statelessness*. Lake Success, New York, 1949, E/1112, 1 February 1949, 3/1112/Add. 1, 19 May 1949; Sales No.: 1949, XIV, 2.

Wheare, K. C., *Federal Government*, 2nd Ed. New York, Oxford University Press, 1951.

THEORY OF COMMUNICATION

A *Bibliography of Cybernetics*, compiled by the Group Networks Laboratory and by the Industrial Relations Laboratory, Massachusetts Institute of Technology, 1951. Multigraphed.

Deutsch, Karl W., "Innovation, Entrepreneurship, and the Learning Process," in *Change and the Entrepreneur*, Arthur H. Cole and R. Richard Wohl, eds. Cambridge, Harvard University Press, 1949.

———, "Mechanism, Organism, and Society," *Philosophy of Science*, Vol. 18, No. 3, July 1951, pp. 230–252.

———, "Mechanism, Teleology and Mind: The Theory of Communications and Some Problems in Philosophy and Social Science," *Philosophy and Phenomenological Research*, Vol. 12, No. 2, December 1951, pp. 185–223.

———, "Communication Theory and Social Science," *The American Journal of Orthopsychiatry*, Vol. 22, No. 3, July 1952, pp. 469–483.

———, "On Communication Models in the Social Sciences," *Public Opinion Quarterly*, Vol. 16, No. 3, Fall 1952, pp. 356–380.

Hebb, D. O.: *The Organization of Behavior*. New York, Wiley, 1949.

Innis, Harold A., *The Bias of Communication*. Toronto, University of Toronto Press, 1951.

Miller, George A., *Language and Communication*. New York, McGraw-Hill, 1951.

Morris, C. W., *Signs, Language, and Behavior*. New York, Prentice-Hall, 1946.

Ruesch, J., and G. Bateson, "Structure and Process in Social Relations," *Psychiatry*, Vol. 12, No. 2, May 1949, pp. 105–124.

———, *Communication: The Social Matrix of Psychiatry*. New York, Norton, 1951.

Shannon, C. E., and W. Weaver, *The Mathematical Theory of Communication*. Urbana, University of Illinois Press, 1949.

Stevens, S. S., ed., *Handbook of Experimental Psychology*. New York, Wiley, 1951.

Wiener, N., *Cybernetics*. New York, Wiley and Massachusetts Institute of Technology Press, 1948.

———, *Extrapolation, Interpolation, and Smoothing of Stationary Time Series*. Cambridge, Massachusetts Institute of Technology Press, 1949.

———, *The Human Use of Human Beings: Cybernetics and Society*. Boston, Houghton Mifflin, 1950.

———, "Speech, Language, and Learning," *Journal of the Acoustical Society of America*, November 1950.

CULTURAL ANTHROPOLOGY, SOCIOLOGY, AND SOCIAL PSYCHOLOGY

Adorno, T. W., E. Frenkl-Brunswik, D. J. Levinson, and R. N. Sanford, *The Authoritarian Personality*. New York, Harper, 1950.

Allport, G. W., "Prejudice: A Problem of Psychological and Social Causation," *Social Issues*, Supplement Series No. 4, 1950.

Bateson, Gregory, "Atoms, Nations, and Culture," *The International House Quarterly*, Vol. II, No. 2, Spring 1947, pp. 47–50.

———, "Morale and National Character," in *Civilian Morale: Second Yearbook of the Society for the Psychological Study of Social Issues*, Goodwin Watson, ed. New York, Houghton Mifflin, 1942, pp. 71–91.

———, "The Patterning of an Armaments Race." Part I, "An Anthropological Approach"; Part II, "An Analysis of Nationalism." *Bulletin of Atomic Scientists*, Vol. 2, No. 5 and 6, 1946, pp. 10–11; No. 7 and 8, pp. 26–28.

Cantril, Hadley, ed., *Tensions that Cause Wars: Common Statement and Individual Papers by a Group of Social Scientists Brought Together by UNESCO.* Urbana, University of Illinois Press, 1950.

Embree, John F., "Standardized Error and Japanese Character: A Note on Political Interpretation," *World Politics,* Vol. 2, No. 3, April 1950, pp. 439–443.

Fromm, Erich, *Man for Himself: An Inquiry into the Psychology of Ethics.* New York, Rinehart, 1947, especially "The Marketing Orientation," pp. 67–82.

Kluckhohn, Clyde, *Mirror for Man: The Relation of Anthropology to Modern Life.* New York, McGraw-Hill, 1949.

——, and H. A. Murray, eds., *Personality in Nature, Society, and Culture.* New York, Knopf, 1948.

Lazarsfeld, Paul F., "Communication Research and the Social Psychologist," in *Current Trends in Social Psychology,* Dennis Wayne, ed. Pittsburgh, University of Pittsburgh Press, 1948.

——, and F. N. Stanton, eds., *Communications Research.* New York, Harper, 1949.

Linton, Ralph, *The Cultural Background of Personality.* New York, Appleton-Century, 1945.

——, ed., *The Science of Man in the World Crisis.* New York, Columbia University Press, 1945.

Locke, Alain LeRoy, and Bernhard J. Stern, *When Peoples Meet: A Study in Race and Culture Contacts,* Rev. Ed. New York, Hinds, Hayden, & Eldredge, 1946.

McGranahan, Donald G., and Ivor Wayne, "German and American Traits Reflected in Popular Drama," *Human Relations,* Vol. 1, 1948, pp. 429–455.

MacIver, Robert M., *Discrimination and National Welfare.* New York, Harper, 1949.

——, *The More Perfect Union: A Program for the Control of Inter-Group Discrimination in the United States.* New York, Macmillan, 1948.

Mead, Margaret, ed., *Cooperation and Competition among Primitive Peoples.* New York, McGraw-Hill, 1937.

Parsons, Talcott, "Racial and Religious Differences as Factors in Group Tensions," in *Approaches to National Unity,* L. Bryson et al., eds. New York, Harper, 1945.

Recasens-Siches, Luís, *Lecciones de Sociología.* Mexico, Editorial Porrua, 1948.

——, *Vida humana, sociedad y derecho: fundamentos de la filosofía del derecho,* 2nd Ed. Mexico, Fondo de Cultura Economica, 1945.

Riesman, David, and N. Glazer, *The Lonely Crowd.* Yale University Press, 1950.

Rose, Arnold M., Ed., *Race Prejudice and Discrimination.* New York, Knopf, 1950.

Thompson, Laura, *Culture in Crisis: A Study of the Hopi Indians.* New York, Harper, 1950.

Tisdale, Hope, "The Process of Urbanization," *Social Forces,* Vol. 20, No. 3, March 1942, pp. 311–316.

Warner, William Lloyd, et al., *Social Class in America: A Manual of Procedure for the Measurement of Social Status.* Chicago, Science Research Associates, 1949.

——, and Leo Srole, *The Social Systems of American Ethnic Groups.* New Haven, Yale University Press, 1946.

Wilson, George and Monica, *Social Change*. Cambridge, Cambridge University Press, 1945.

LINGUISTICS

Ahmad, A. Z., Ed., *National Language for India: A Symposium*. Allahabad, Kitabistan, 1941.

Bodmer, Frederick, *The Loom of Language*. New York, Norton, 1944.

Chatterji, Suniti Kumar, *Languages and the Linguistic Problem*. Oxford Pamphlets on Indian Affairs, No. 11, 2nd Ed. London, Oxford University Press, 1944.

De Francis, John, *Nationalism and Language Reform in China*. Princeton, Princeton University Press, 1950.

Deutsch, Karl W., "The Trend of European Nationalism—The Language Aspect," *American Political Science Review*, Vol. 36, No. 3, June 1942, p. 533–541.

Jakobson, Roman, "Sur la theorie des affinités phonologiques des langues," *Actes du quatrième Congrès International de Linguistes* (*1936*), Copenhagen, E. Munksgaard, 1938, pp. 48–58.

———, "The Beginnings of National Self-Determination in Europe," *The Review of Politics*, Vol. 7, No. 1, January 1945, pp. 29–42.

———, "Franz Boas' Approach to Language," *International Journal of American Linguistics*, Vol. 10, No. 4, October 1944, pp. 188–195.

Laubach, Frank C., *Teaching the World to Read: A Handbook for Literacy Campaigns*. New York, Friendship Press, 1947.

Mencken, H. L., *The American Language*, 4th Ed. New York, Knopf, 1937.

Menéndez Pidal, Ramón, *Castilla, la tradición, el idioma*. Buenos Aires, Espasa-Calpe Argentina, S. A., 1945.

North, E. M., *The Book of a Thousand Tongues*. New York, Harper, 1938.

Pei, Mario A., *The World's Chief Languages*, 3rd Ed. London, Allen & Unwin, 1949.

Stalin, Joseph V., "On Marxism in Linguistics," *Pravda*, June 20, 1950, translated in *The Current Digest of the Soviet Press*, Vol. 2, No. 21, July 8, 1950, pp. 3–9.

Woolner, A. C., *Languages in History and Politics*. London, Oxford University Press, 1938.

HISTORY, GENERAL

Brinton, Crane, *Ideas and Men: The Story of Western Thought*. New York, Prentice-Hall, 1950.

Brockelmann, Carl, *History of the Islamic Peoples*. New York, Putnam, 1947.

Carr, Edward Hallett, *A History of Soviet Russia*. Vol. 1, *The Bolshevik Revolution, 1917–1923*. London, MacMillan, 1950.

Curti, Merle, *The Roots of American Loyalty*. New York, Columbia University Press, 1946.

Fay, Sidney B., *Origins of the World War*, 2 vols. New York, Macmillan, 1934.

——, *The Rise of Brandenburg-Prussia to 1786*. New York, Holt, 1937.

Hayes, Carlton, *A Generation of Materialism, 1871–1900*. New York, Harper, 1941.

——, "The Church and Nationalism—A Plea for Further Study of a Major Issue," *The Catholic Historical Review*, Vol. 28, No. 1, April 1942, Washington, D. C., pp. 1–12.

Hitti, Phillip K., *The Arabs: A Short History*, Princeton, Princeton University Press, 1943.

Kantorowicz, Ernst, "*Pro Patria Mori* in Medieval Political Thought," *The American Historical Review*, Vol. 56, No. 3, April 1951, pp. 472–492.

Kohn, Hans, *The Twentieth Century*. New York, Macmillan, 1949.

Koht, Halvdan, "The Dawn of Nationalism in Europe," *American Historical Review*, January 1947, Vol. 52, No. 2, pp. 265–280.

Langer, William L., *European Alliances and Alignments, 1871–1890*. New York, Knopf, 1950.

——, *The Diplomacy of Imperialism, 1890–1902*, 2 vols. New York, Knopf, 1951.

Rosenstock-Huessy, Eugen, *Out of Revolution: Autobiography of Western Man*. New York, Morrow, 1938.

Toynbee, Arnold J., *A Study of History*, 6 vols. London, Oxford University Press, 1945–1946.

——, *The World and the West*. New York, Oxford University Press, 1953. Especially Chap. 5.

ECONOMIC HISTORY

Bonn, Moritz J., *The Crumbling of Empire: The Disintegration of World Economy*. London, Allen & Unwin, 1938.

——, *Die englische Kolonisation in Irland*. Stuttgart-Berlin, Cotta, 1906.

Brady, Robert A., *Business as a System of Power*. New York, Columbia University Press, 1943.

Burns, Arthur R., *The Decline of Competition: A Study of the Evolution of American Industry*. New York, McGraw-Hill, 1936.

Clark, Grover, *The Balance Sheets of Imperialism: Facts and Figures on Colonies*. New York, Columbia University Press, 1936.

Davis, Kingsley, *The Population of India and Pakistan*. Princeton, Princeton University Press, 1951.

Dodd, William E., *The Cotton Kingdom: A Chronicle of the Old South*. New Haven, Yale University Press, 1919.

Heckscher, Eli F., *The Continental System: An Economic Interpretation*. Oxford, Clarendon Press, 1922.

——, *Mercantilism*, 2 vols. London, Allen & Unwin, 1935.

——, "A Plea for Theory in Economic History," *Economic History*, Vol. 1, January 1929, pp. 525–534.

Innis, Harold A., *Empire and Communication*. Oxford, Clarendon Press, 1950.

Jenks, Leland H., *Migration of British Capital to 1875*. New York, Knopf, 1938.

Mosk, Sanford, *The Industrial Revolution in Mexico*. Berkeley, University of California Press, 1950.

Mosk, Sanford, "Pathology of Democracy in Latin America: An Economist's Point of View," *American Political Science Review*, Vol. 44, No. 1, March 1950, pp. 129–142.

Norman, Herbert E., *Japan's Emergence as a Modern State: Political and Economic Problems of the Meiji Period*. New York, Institute of Pacific Relations, 1940.

Polanyi, Karl, *The Great Transformation*. New York, Farrar & Rinehart, 1944.

Rippy, J. Fred, *Latin America and the Industrial Age*, 2nd Ed. New York, Putnam, 1947.

Rostow, W. W., *The British Economy of the Nineteenth Century*. Oxford, Clarendon Press, 1948.

Usher, Abbott Payson, "The Application of Quantitative Methods to Economic History," *Journal of Political Economy*, Vol. 40, No. 2, April 1932, pp. 186–209.

——, "Population and Settlement in Eurasia," *Geographic Review*, New York, Vol. 20, 1930, pp. 110–132.

Wilhelm, Warren, "Soviet Central Asia: Development of a Backward Area," *Foreign Policy Reports*, Vol. 25, No. 18, February 1, 1950.

Weber, Max, *General Economic History*. New York, Greenberg, 1927.

Wright, Chester W., *Economic History of the United States*. New York, McGraw-Hill, 1941.

Wythe, George, *Industry in Latin America*, 2nd Ed. New York, Columbia University Press, 1949.

ECONOMICS

Abraham, W. I., "The Distribution of World Income," *The American Statistician*, April–May 1951, p. 39.

Bente, Hermann, "Die marktwirtschaftliche Bedeutung der Kapitalanlage im Auslande," *Weltwirtschaftliches Archiv*, Jena, Vol. 32, 1930, II, pp. 1–54.

Clark, Colin, *The Conditions of Economic Progress*. London, Macmillan, 1940.

——, *The Economics of 1960*. London, Macmillan, 1942.

——, "Economic Life in the Twentieth Century," *Measure*, Vol. 1, No. 4, Fall 1950, pp. 329–347.

Condliffe, J. B., *The Commerce of Nations*. New York, Norton, 1950.

Deutsch, Karl W., "The Economic Factor in Intolerance," in *Approaches to National Unity*, L. Bryson et al., eds. New York, Harper, 1945, pp. 368–386.

——, "Medieval Unity and the Economic Conditions for an International Civilization," *Canadian Journal of Economics and Political Science*, Vol. 10, No. 1, February 1944, pp. 18–35.

——, "Some Economic Aspects of the Rise of Nationalistic and Social Pressure Groups," *Canadian Journal of Economics and Political Science*, Vol. 8, No. 1, February 1942, pp. 109–115.

"Economic Growth: A Symposium," *Journal of Economic History*, Supplement 7, 1947.

Engliš, Karel, *Regulierte Wirtschaft*. Prague, Orbis, 1936.

Haberler, G. v., *The Theory of International Trade, with Its Application to Commercial Policy*. New York, Macmillan, 1937.

Harris, Seymour R., *Economic Planning; the Plans of Fourteen Countries with Analyses of the Plans.* New York, Knopf, 1949.

———, ed., *Economic Problems of Latin America.* New York, McGraw-Hill, 1944.

Hawtrey, E. G., *Economic Aspects of Sovereignty.* London, Longmans, Green, 1930.

Hilferding, Rudolf, *Das Finanzkapital.* Vienna, Wiener Volksbuchhandlung, 1923.

Isaacs, Julius, *Economics of Migration.* London, Kegan Paul, 1947.

Keynes, John Maynard, *The End of Laissez-Faire.* London, Hogarth, 1926.

———, *Essays in Persuasion.* New York, Harcourt, Brace, 1932.

———, *The General Theory of Employment, Interest, and Money.* New York, Harcourt, Brace, 1936.

Kindleberger, Charles Poor, *The Dollar Shortage.* New York, Wiley and Massachusetts Institute of Technology Press, 1950.

———, "Group Behavior and International Trade," *Journal of Political Economy,* Vol. 59, No. 1, February 1951, pp. 30–46.

Kuznets, Simon Smith, *National Income: A Summary of Findings.* New York, National Bureau of Economic Research, 1946.

Lenin, V. I., *Imperialism, the Highest Stage of Capitalism: "New Data,"* E. Varga and L. Mendelsohn, eds. New York, International Publishers (1936–1937?).

National Bureau of Economic Research, *Problems in the Study of Economic Growth.* New York, 1949 (multigraphed).

Ohlin, Bertil, *International and Interregional Trade.* Cambridge, Harvard University Press, 1933.

Robbins, Lionel, *Economic Aspects of Federation.* London, Macmillan, 1941.

———, *The Economic Causes of War.* London, Cape, 1939.

Robinson, Joan, *The Economics of Imperfect Competition.* London, Macmillan, 1933.

Rostow, Walt Whitman, *The Process of Economic Growth.* New York, Norton, 1952.

———, "Some Notes on Mr. Hicks and History," *American Economic Review,* Vol. 41, No. 3, June 1951, pp. 316–324.

———, "The Terms of Trade in Theory and Practice," *Economic History Review,* 2nd Ser., Vol. 3, No. 1, 1950, pp. 1–20.

———, "The Historical Analysis of the Terms of Trade," *Economic History Review,* 2nd Ser., Vol. 4, No. 1, 1951, pp. 53–76.

Salin, Edgar, "Von den Wandlungen der Weltwirtschaft in der Nachkriegszeit," *Weltwirtschaftliches Archiv,* Jena, Vol. 35, 1932, pp. 1–33.

Samuelson, Paul Anthony, *Economics: An Introductory Analysis.* New York, McGraw-Hill, 1948.

———, *Foundations of Economic Analysis.* Cambridge, Mass., Harvard University Press, 1947.

———, "Welfare, Economics and International Trade," *American Economics Review,* Vol. 23, No. 2, June 1938, pp. 261–266.

Schumpeter, Joseph, *Capitalism, Socialism and Democracy.* New York, Harper, 1942.

———, *Imperialism and Social Classes.* New York, A. M. Kelley, 1951.

———, *The Theory of Economic Development,* Cambridge, Harvard University Press, 1936.

Sulzbach, Walter, *Nationales Gemeinschaftsgefuehl und Wirtschaftliches Interesse,* Leipzig, L. L. Hirschfeld, 1929.

——, "Der wirtschaftliche Begriff des 'Auslands,'" *Weltwirtschaftliches Archiv,* Jena, Vol. 32, 1930, II, pp. 55–80.

Sweezy, Paul M., *The Theory of Capitalist Development: Principles of Marxian Political Economy.* New York, Oxford University Press, 1942.

Viner, Jacob, *The Customs Union Issue.* New York, Carnegie Endowment for International Peace, 1950; "Bibliography," pp. 171–211.

GEOGRAPHY, GEOPOLITICS, AND REGIONAL PLANNING

De Castro, J., *The Geography of Hunger.* Boston, Little, Brown, 1952.

Dickinson, Robert E., *City Region and Regionalism: A Geographical Contribution to Human Ecology.* New York, Oxford University Press, 1947.

East, Gordon, *An Historical Geography of Europe.* New York, Dutton, 1935.

Haushofer, Albrecht, *Zur Problematik des Raumbegriffes.* Berlin, Grunewald, K. Vowinckel, 1932.

Haushofer, Karl, Ed., *Weltwirtschaftsdaemmerung. Festschrift zum zehnjaehrigen Bestehen des Weltwirtschaftsinstitutes der Handelshochschule Leipzig.* Stuttgart, W. Kohlhammer, 1933.

James, Preston E., *A Geography of Man.* Boston, Ginn, 1949; with bibliographical references, pp. 574–580.

——, *Latin America.* New York, Odyssey Press, 1942.

MacKinder, Sir Halford J., *Britain and the British Seas.* New York, Appleton, 1902.

——, *Democratic Ideals and Reality: A Study in the Politics of Reconstruction.* New York, Holt, 1942.

Strausz-Hupé, Robert, *Geopolitics:* The Struggle for Space and Power. New York, Putnam, 1942.

Taylor, Griffith, *Environment and Nation.* Chicago, University of Chicago Press, 1936.

——, Ed., *Geography in the Twentieth Century.* New York, Philosophical Library, 1951.

Whittlesey, Derwent, *The Earth and the State: A Study of Political Geography.* New York, Holt, 1939.

BIOLOGY, GENETICS, RACE

Benedict, Ruth, *Race: Science and Politics.* New York, Modern Age Books, 1940.

Boas, Franz, *Race, Language and Culture.* New York, Macmillan, 1940.

Coon, Carleton Stevens, *The Races of Europe.* New York, Macmillan, 1939.

Haldane, J. B. S., *Heredity and Politics.* New York, Norton, 1938.

Huxley, Julian Sorell, *Evolution: The Modern Synthesis.* New York, Harper, 1943.

——, and A. C. Haddon, *We Europeans: A Survey of "Racial" Problems.* New York, Harper, 1936.

Klineberg, Otto, Ed., *Characteristics of the American Negro*. New York, Harper, 1944.

———, *Race Differences*. New York, Harper, 1935.

Montagu, M. F. Ashley, *An Introduction to Physical Anthropology*, 2nd Ed. Springfield, Ill., C. C. Thomas, 1951.

———, *Statement on Race*. New York, Schuman, 1951. "A Select Annotated List of Books and Pamphlets on Race," pp. 159–165.

Voegelin, Eric, "The Growth of the Race Idea," *Review of Politics*, Vol. 2, No. 3, July 1940, pp. 283–317.

SPECIFIC PEOPLES, AREAS, OR PROBLEMS

Adamic, Louis, *My Native Land*. New York, Harper, 1943.

———, *A Nation of Nations*. New York, Harper, 1945.

Antonius, George, *The Arab Awakening: The Story of the Arab National Movement*. Philadelphia, Lippincott, 1939.

Benedict, Ruth, *The Chrysanthemum and the Sword: Patterns of Japanese Culture*. Boston, Houghton Mifflin, 1946.

Beneš, Edvard, *Bohemia's Case for Independence*. London, Allen & Unwin, 1917.

———, *Future of the Small Nations and the Idea of Federation*. New York, Czechoslovakia Information Service, 1942.

Bonne, Alfred, *The Economic Development of the Middle East: An Outline of Planned Reconstruction after the War*. New York, Oxford University Press, 1945.

Ebenstein, William, *The German Record: A Political Portrait*. New York, Farrar and Rinehart, 1945.

Embree, John F., *The Japanese*, Washington, The Smithsonian Institution, 1943.

Englert-Faye, *Vom Mythus zur Idee der Schweiz*. Zurich, Atlantic-Verlag, 1940.

Erikson, Erik H., "Hitler's Imagery and German Youth," *Psychiatry, Journal of Biology and Pathology of Interpersonal Relations*, Vol. 5, No. 4, 1942, pp. 475–493. (Reprinted in *Personality in Nature, Society, and Culture*, Clyde Kluckhohn and H. A. Murray, Eds., pp. 485–510).

Gibb, H. A. R., *The Arabs*. Oxford, Clarendon Press, 1940.

Hayes, Carlton, *France: A Nation of Patriots*. New York, Columbia University Press, 1930.

Ike, Nobutaka, *The Beginning of Political Democracy in Japan*. Baltimore, Johns Hopkins Press, 1950.

Kohn, Hans, *A History of Nationalism in the East*. New York, Harcourt, Brace, 1929.

———, *Nationalism and Imperialism in the Hither East*. New York, Harcourt, Brace, 1932.

———, *Nationalism in the Soviet Union*. New York, Columbia University Press, 1933.

———, *Pan-Slavism*, South Bend, Ind., University of Notre Dame Press, 1953.

———, *Western Civilization in the Near East*. New York, Columbia University Press, 1936.

———, "Napoleon and the Age of Nationalism," *Journal of Modern History*, Vol. 22, No. 1, March 1950, pp. 21–37.

Kohn, Hans, "The Eve of German Nationalism," *Journal of the History of Ideas*, Vol. 12, No. 2, April 1951, pp. 256–284.

——, "Arndt and the Character of German Nationalism," *American Historical Review*, Vol. 54, No. 4, July 1949, pp. 787–803.

——, "Father Jahn's Nationalism," *Review of Politics*, Vol. 11, No. 4, October 1949, pp. 419–432.

——, "The Paradox of Fichte's Nationalism," *Journal of the History of Ideas*, Vol. 10, No. 3, June 1949, pp. 319–343.

——, "Romanticism and the Rise of German Nationalism," *Review of Politics*, Vol. 12, No. 4, October 1950, pp. 443–472.

——, "Zionism," in *Revolutions and Dictatorships*, Harvard University Press, 3rd Printing, 1943, pp. 229–330.

——, "Ahad Ha' am: Nationalist with a Difference," *Commentary*, Vol. 11, No. 5, June 1951, pp. 558–566.

Lamprecht, Karl, *Deutsche Geschichte*, Vol. 1. Berlin, Weidmann, 1920. ("Geschichte der Formen des Nationalbewusstseins," pp. 3–56.)

Lattimore, Owen D., *The Situation in Asia*. Boston, Little, Brown, 1949.

——, *Pivot of Asia: Sinkiang and the Inner Asian Frontiers of China and Russia*. Boston, Little, Brown, 1950.

Macartney, C. A., *Hungary and Her Successors: The Treaty of Trianon and its Consequences, 1919–1937*. London, Oxford University Press, 1937.

Macmillan, W. M., *Africa Emergent*, Revised Ed. Harmondsworth, England, Penguin Books, 1949.

Mansergh, Nicholas, *The Commonwealth and the Nations: Studies in British Commonwealth Relations*. London, Royal Institute of International Affairs, 1948.

Masaryk, T. G., *The Making of a State*. New York, Stokes, 1927.

——, *The New Europe*. London, Eyre & Spottiswoode, 1918.

Mitrany, David, *The Effect of the War in South-Eastern Europe*. New Haven, Yale University Press, 1936.

Myrdal, Gunnar, *An American Dilemma: The Negro Problem and Modern Democracy*. New York, Harper, 1919.

Nehru, Jawaharlal, *The Discovery of India*. London, Meridian Books, 1947; New York, John Day, 1946.

——, *Nehru on Gandhi*. New York, John Day, 1948.

——, *Toward Freedom: The Autobiography of J. Nehru*. New York, John Day, 1941.

Ortega y Gasset, José, *Invertebrate Spain*. New York, Norton, 1937.

Padelford, Norman Judson, *The Panama Canal in Peace and War*. New York, Macmillan, 1942.

Purcell, Victor, *The Chinese in Southeast Asia*. London, Oxford University Press, 1950.

Rašín, Alois, *Financial Policy of Czechoslovakia during the First Year of its History*. London, New York, H. Milford, 1923.

Reischauer, E. O., *Japan, Past and Present*. New York, Knopf, 1946.

Renier, G. J., *The Dutch Nation: An Historical Study*. London, Allen & Unwin, 1944.

——, *The Criterion of Dutch Nationhood*. London, Allen & Unwin, 1946.

Rennie, Ysabel F., *The Argentine Republic*. New York, Macmillan, 1945.

Schlesinger, Rudolf, *Federalism in Central and Eastern Europe.* London, Kegan Paul, 1945.

United States, Department of State, *Blue Book on Argentina: Consultation among the American Republics with Respect to the Argentine Situation. Memorandum of the United States Government,* Washington, D. C., February 1946. New York, Greenberg, 1946.

Vlekke, Bernhard, H. M., *Evolution of the Dutch Nation.* New York, Roy, 1945.

Wiskemann, Elizabeth, *Czechs and Germans.* London, Oxford University Press, 1938.

INDEX